Net Worth

Using the Internet for Personal Financial Planning

Second Edition

Carrie Mauriello

Routledge
Taylor & Francis Group

LONDON AND NEW YORK

First published 2001 by Butterworth-Heinemann

Published 2021 by Routledge
2 Park Square, Milton Park, Abingdon, Oxon OX14 4RN
605 Third Avenue, New York, NY 10017

Routledge is an imprint of the Taylor & Francis Group, an informa business

ISBN 13: 978-1-884133-83-1 (pbk)

Library of Congress Cataloging-in-Publication Data

Mauiellollo, Carrie
   Net Worth : using the Internet for personal financial planning / Carrie Mauriello.--2nd ed.
      p. cm.
   Includes index.
   ISBN 1-884133-83-5 (pbk. : alk. paper)
   1. Finance, Personal--Computer network resources--Directories. 2.
   Investments--Computer network resources--Directories. 3. Securities--Computer
   network resources--Directories. 4. Insurance--Computer network resources--Directories.
   5. Consumer credit--Computer network resources--Directories. 6. Income tax--Computers
   network resources--Directories. 7. Web sites--Directories.

HG179 .R3934 2001
025.06,33202401--dc21

                                                                              2001037756

British Library Cataloguing-in-Publication Data
A catalogue record for this book is available from the British Library.

The publisher offers special discounts on bulk orders of this book.
For information, please contact:
Manager of Special Sales
Butterworth–Heinemann
225 Wildwood Avenue
Woburn, MA 01801-2041
Tel: 781-904-2500
Fax: 781-904-2620

CONTENTS

CHAPTER 1

INTRODUCTION

Wealth is not without its advantages and the case to the contrary, although it has often been made, has never been proved widely persuasive. — **John Kenneth Galbraith, The Affluent Society**

THE SHREWD INVESTOR'S MOST IMPORTANT PARTNER: THE INTERNET

Along with delivering everything from real-time weather to video-clips of your favorite band, the Internet provides a heretofore unheard-of degree of information on investment and financial planning. In fact, some of the richest resources on the Internet and World Wide Web address the information needs of those interested in stock and bond investment, estate planning, life insurance, debt management, and real estate. Thus, for the shrewd investor or financial planner, the Internet can be a robust, powerful, and *profitable* resource.

Net Worth is designed to help you navigate, use, and get the most out of the rich financial resource that is the Internet. To that end, *Net Worth* comprises both a primer on personal financial management and an exhaustive cyber-guide indentifying a collection of finance-related tools, pointers, and resources on the Internet. In sum, *Net Worth* has been designed to help you take maximum advantage of the Internet's many financial resources and, thus, make the electronic superhighway your personal partner in wealth-building.

FOR INVESTORS IN STOCKS, BONDS, OPTIONS, FUTURES, AND MUTUAL FUNDS...

Net Worth provides tools and techniques with which you can view real-time quotes and even buy and sell securities via the Internet. The book also shows you how to dig into authoritative on-line research databases (such as those maintained by Morningstar Mutual Funds and Value Line), and how to view real-time Internet charts and graphs that track stocks and mutual funds right on-line. Figure 1.1 shows the Morningstar Web site where you can get information about mutual funds.

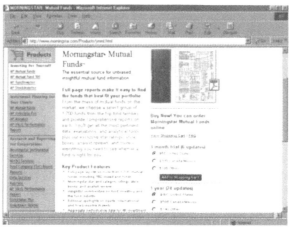

Figure 1.1 Mutual fund information available from Morningstar on the World Wide Web.

FOR PURCHASERS OF LIFE, HEALTH, AUTO, AND HOME INSURANCE...

Net Worth is your guide to Internet tools and resources to help you insure yourself, your life, your health, your possessions, and your family—and do so without paying a dime more in premiums than you have to! Figure 1.2 shows the MetLife Web site where you can get information on life insurance.

Figure 1.2 Life insurance information available at MetLife on the World Wide Web.

FOR THOSE SHOPPING FOR MORTGAGES AND OTHER TYPES OF LOANS...

Net Worth gives you complete, exhaustive, information on how to use the Internet to comparatively shop for loans from a range of lenders and even make applications for credit right over the Internet!

And there's more. *Net Worth* is crammed with information on how to use the Internet to help with **estate planning, income tax planning,** and **retirement planning**. It also features a host of Internet tools and information resources that are essential for those involved in **real estate investment**. Figure 1.3 shows the IRS Web site where income tax information is available.

Figure 1.3 Income tax information available from the IRS on the World Wide Web.

Whether you want to find and read corporate annual reports on-line or download terrific investment software from a score of excellent finance-related archives, *Net Worth* will make it all easy to do. In the process, *Net Worth* will turn you into the ultimate cyber-finance guru capable of using the Internet to leverage your own personal net worth!

YOUR CORNUCOPIA OF OPTIONS

Most people, over the years, use a number of different financial instruments to achieve their various financial objectives. In these complex economic times, the average middle-class or upper-middle-class individual is usually involved at one level or another with an amalgam of financial tools including common stocks, bonds, mutual funds, insurance, fixed and variable annuities, IRAs, home real estate, and cash savings. Planning for the interplay of these various instruments, at the right times and in the right amounts, is what financial planning is all about.

It is also what this book is all about. *There is no better tool than the Internet to help you gather information on the cornucopia of financial instruments and options made available to you. There is no better resource than the Internet to help you construct the series of coordinated plans that will work in unison for the achievement of your overall, long-term, financial objectives.* Figure 1.4 shows The Street Web site produced by an A list of financial journalists offering financial information.

Figure 1.4 Wall Street savvy financial information from The Street on the World Wide Web.

THE SEARCH FOR WEALTH

Pirates of yore, searching for treasure, most often had a map to guide them. Olympic athletes, working diligently through long years of childhood and adolescence in their quest for another form of gold, have precise training plans without which their quest would be in vain. Like these seekers of different forms of gold, we must all be careful to plot well-planned strategies in order to ensure our own fortunes. And then, we must conduct ourselves according to these strategies. The treasure map that guides you to wealth and financial security is your personal *financial plan.*

What I have in mind when I speak of financial planning for the maximization of wealth is not a *get-rich-quick* scheme, or a method of ferreting out "fast plays" on the stock market that are "sure-bets" for vast returns with minimal risk. Not at all. What I have in mind when I speak of financial planning is as follows. (Get out your highlighter for this one!)

Personal financial planning is the construction of a series of coordinated plans that will work in unison for the achievement of one's overall, long-term, financial objectives.

Planning and careful, strategic investment are your keys to safe-and-secure old age, the ability to fund your children's college education, and so on. Your financial planning also provides the keys to the luxuries of life: a ski lodge, a sailboat, or whatever other "perks" your instincts steer you towards.

Over the years, investors have used a number of different financial instruments to achieve their various financial objectives. Your use of these various instruments, at the right times, and in the right amounts, in a way that assures both short- and long-term solvency for yourself and your dependents, is what financial planning is all about. It is also what this book is all about. Figure 1.5 shows the Web site for the New York Stock Exchange where you can find valuable information.

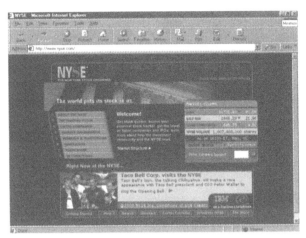

Figure 1.5 Information about the New York Stock Exchange on the World Wide Web.

WHO SHOULD PLAN?

Everybody. And most especially, *you.*

The notion still lingers that if one's name is not Vanderbilt or Morgan, then one need not spend much time worrying over financial matters: that one's pot is so small as to not matter very much, and that one's options are so limited as not to count for much. One should simply put whatever one can afford away, possibly in an IRA (individual retirement account), and hope for the best.

But the fact is that even this lazy approach to financial planning forces one to make critical choices. Should the IRA be invested in the money market or in stock mutual funds? If you decide on a stock mutual fund, should the fund be aggressive growth, income, or balanced fund?

If you are like many people, you may not fully understand what a mutual fund is, how such a fund operates, or how to use a mutual fund as an investment vehicle, let alone terms such as aggressive growth or balanced fund. Don't worry. That's what this book is for. And, as you read through these chapters, you will find there are thousands of other financial and investment resources on the Internet and the World Wide Web.

Of course, the most sophisticated tools of investment and planning (T-bills, zero-sum bonds, and tax-free municipal bonds) tend to be used by those with high incomes, large properties, and extended business interests. But the majority of investment and planning tools are of as much value to the average investor as they are to a Dupont or a Rockefeller.

In fact, the rise of the middle class over the past half-century has dramatically increased both the need for and the complexity of financial planning. Never before in the history of the planet have the "non-rich" been so in need of planning to balance and maintain the stability of their income, assets, gifts, inheritances, and investments. In short, what we most need to manage is the fabled affluence of the common man—the affluence of John Kenneth Galbraith's "affluent society."

START PLANNING AND MAXIMIZING YOUR WEALTH RIGHT NOW

The time to start planning for your financial future is now at this very moment. Remember the old cliché: *Today is the first day of the rest of your life.* Well, today is truly the first day of the rest of your financial life.

Within this book, you will find tools and directions to help you not only navigate, but to create and cultivate the terrain of your financial landscape. You have a great stake in caring for, protecting, and nurturing this landscape because it is where you are going to live for the rest of your life. Like other neighborhoods, your financial surroundings will inevitably change over the years. Your actions will decide how your financial surroundings evolve.

THE PLANNING PROCESS AS PRESENTED IN NET WORTH

Your first steps in personal financial planning include identifying your objectives, analyzing your present position, considering your alternatives, and developing and implementing your plan. Then, over time, you must periodically review and revise your plan based on your investment results and changes in your personal circumstances. For now, however, you simply need to get started.

What are your objectives? Do you want to try to pay off your 30-year mortgage in 15 years, thus, getting out of hock in time to finance your child's tuition for college? Do you want to create a retirement-investment plan that will leave you with at least a million dollars cash when you turn 70? Or do you want to establish an even more aggressive savings program that will let you afford to retire early at age 60, so you can go to the French Riviera and write a novel?

These are the types of ambitions we all have, in various shapes, sizes, and forms. Only you know your unique agenda. No book can do much to help you define your personal financial goals. You know best where you want to end up; no two of us want to end up in exactly the same place. But this book will provide you with the know-how and resources you will come to find invaluable in fulfilling your long-term objectives, whatever they may be. Figure 1.6 shows one place to look for discussions on financial planning.

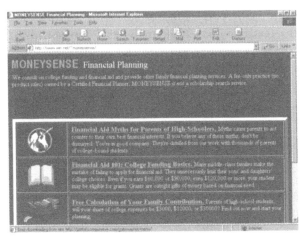

Figure 1.6 Discussions about financial planning that you will find on the World Wide Web.

ONE MAN'S CEILING IS ANOTHER MAN'S FLOOR

Not everyone has the same financial needs or the same financial goals. Is life insurance something that makes sense for you? If so, then what type? What percentage of your non-IRA capital can you (or should you) invest in stocks and bonds, as opposed to cash set aside for day-to-day living and emergencies? If stock market investment is part of your picture, should you invest in a mutual fund or buy individual stocks via a broker? If mutual funds make the most sense for you, should you go with Load or No-Load Funds? And what is the difference between such funds anyway? A good investment for one person may be a bad investment for another. Stocks are good investment vehicles for some of us and lousy for the rest of us. Mutual funds (funds managed by a professional manager who combines your investment dollars with those of other investors to purchase and range of stocks or bonds) make sense for many of us but not others. Term life insurance is an excellent approach for some but just awful for others. The same applies to bonds. Thus, this book includes very few broad pronouncements of investment rules. You will rarely find this book explicitly saying, "Do this" or "Do that." Instead, what you will find is "Consider this and then consider that and this and that. And by the way, here are a few check points and analytical tools to help you decide which of these possible approaches might be right for you." Of course, I will make a few, loud obvious interjections related to financial discipline. I will absolutely condemn utterly stupid practices such as building up large amounts of non-deductible credit-card debt that comes with outrageous interest rates. Such personal exclamations will be few and far between but will always smack of truth. In tandem with providing information and analysis tools that will help you make financial plans, this book will provide information to help you implement the financial decisions you make. For example, you will learn the mechanics of choosing a broker and setting up a brokerage account. You will learn the "gimmicks" you should watch out for as you choose among the many perplexing life insurance options. Always, throughout this book, the thrust of the text remains: What is the best for you? That will be the constant question in real estate, in stock and bond investment, in IRAs, and in all other aspects of your financial life. What is the best for you?

WHY PLANNING IS OFTEN NEGLECTED

Your Need to Plan

Gee, I meant to do some of that financial planning and strategic investing. I have just been so busy with other things. Retirement always seemed so far away. Looking back, I regret not taking financial planning more seriously, but I thought my retirement and social security benefits would cover most of my bills. I'm not sure what I was smoking when I thought that, but there's no use complaining now. Why be miserable? Fact is, my trailer is so small that it is pretty easy to keep clean. And the view of the sewage treatment plant isn't so bad unless the wind blows this way. I don't mind working a few days a week at WalMart. Scary yet?

Many people fail to plan their finances because they feel they do not have sufficient assets to warrant coming up with a plan, or they think their affairs are already in good working order. In most cases, however, the reason people fail to plan is simply: *procrastination.* Some people procrastinate because they are genuinely busy. Others procrastinate because they fear financial planning in that it involves taking a long, clear look at, sometimes, harsh financial realities. Still, more procrastinate and do not engage in financial planning because they assume the costs of the financial advice they will require are prohibitive. This is not the case.

GETTING ONTO THE INTERNET

The first step to using the Internet is to get onto the Internet. You do this by using your modem, connected to a standard phone line and dialing into an Internet provider or an online service.

Internet providers are companies that will let you access the Internet through their host computer, which is connected to the Internet. There are many providers out there, and the monthly fees are usually reasonable, although it does pay to do some comparison shopping before you sign up. In addition to base pricing, look into whether or not the provider offers a dial-up number that is a local call from where you will work. Otherwise, your phone bills can add up.

USING AN ON-LINE SERVICE

Another attractive option for connecting to the Internet is to use an on-line service, such as CompuServe, Prodigy, or America Online. An on-line service is often your least expensive way to get "on-line." Additionally, if you are a casual (and perhaps technophobic) computer user, on-line services offer user-friendly interfaces that make the Internet easier to navigate than an Internet provider. Figure 1.7 shows what you would encounter when looking for financial information on the Internet provider, America Online.

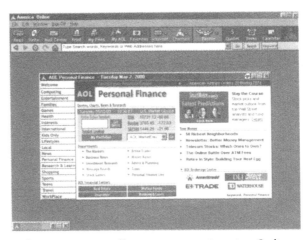

Figure 1.7 Financial information you will encounter on America Online.

The real price you pay for the economically and technically "safe" connection to the Internet offered by an on-line service is speed. This is not a big issue when you are dealing with text-based Internet services such as newsgroups and mailing lists, but it can become annoying when you are accessing graphics-intensive Web resources, such as hypertext documents, on the World Wide Web. Figure 1.8 also shows financial information that can be found on the Microsoft Network.

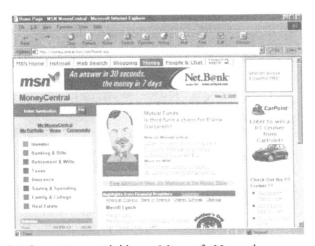

Figure 1.8 Financial information available on Microsoft Network.

If your Internet connection via an on-line service is not fast enough (for example, if you are logged into an on-line service at a rate of 2,400 baud, as opposed to the minimum 14,400 baud that is recommended for all Web usage), you are going to be in for some extremely slow surfing of the World Wide Web. Depending on the speed of your connection (say 28,800 baud) may be able to download in less than 30 seconds. Figure 1.9 shows financial information from an on-line service provider, CompuServe.

Figure 1.9 *Financial information available from CompuServe.*

ON-LINE INVESTING

Across the Internet, you will find extensive information on all aspects of personal finance. You can also find sites from which you can download historical data for specific stocks or even get stock quotes (in delayed or even real time). If you are in touch with financial news, you will find there is a rapidly growing amount of companies that offer on-line stock trading. In most cases, you can trade directly on-line or through an on-line broker. You can use a discounted company such as E*Trade, Datek, Ameritrade, Suretrade, Charles Schwab, Fidelity, and Waterhouse Securities with per-trade fees from $8 to $170. Although you can trade through the likes of Merrill Lynch and Co. and Prudential Securities Inc., they do not intend to compete with the discounters. Some will even require that traders have assets of $100,000 or more. Opportunities for on-line trading with instruction and research are readily available. You can even check account balances and holdings on-line.

UNDERSTANDING CHAT SESSIONS

This book is filled with sites across the World Wide Web that examine all aspects of investing. In addition to these Web sites, many investors exchange information using on-line chat sessions. In general, you can think of an on-line chat as a conference call with an unlimited number of participants. In short, using the keyboard, users "chat." You will find chat sessions that discuss topics at all levels. For example, in one chat session you may learn how to connect to an on-line broker. In another session you will learn how to download historical data for mutual funds. While in a third chat session, you may learn how the "cold spell" in the South may impact orange futures. If you are interested in participating in an on-line chat, contact your on-line service or Internet provider, and ask them how you get started. You might even ask then where to locate the financial chat sessions. In the future, you will find that many financial sites will offer chat sessions hosted by experts in various fields (stocks, bonds, options, and so on). Within such a chat session, you can get answers to your questions from people "in the know."

This Just in: Investment Clubs Thrive on the Internet

You may or may not remember investment clubs. Maybe your grandma was in one. She and a few of her old-lady friends pooled their pennies and bought a few shares of this and a few shares of that, dabbling in the market with their pin money. They did it for fun. They did not involve themselves with a lot of research. They bought safe, conservative stocks with names they recognized: household names like Nabisco and Sears and Gerber. Nevertheless, despite their conservatism, they often made money to spring for an expensive lunch in Manhattan around the holidays and tickets to the Christmas Show at the Radio City Music Hall. Sometimes, she even had enough to take you along, and you loved it!

That was then. This is now. Granny's gone, and you're all grown up. And now, investment clubs are serious business. Like other serious businesses, when they are done well, can leverage technology to the max. The most lucrative investment clubs are now complex networks of cyberspace lurkers who pounce on the latest investment and/or business gossip, share it with fellow club members (who may be located thousands of miles away), and, based on that news, make strategic buy and sell decisions which are often executed right on-line.

The typical member of the traditional, non-digital investment club, as identified as in research conducted by the National Association of Investors Corporation, is female, over the age of 50, and inclined to invest cautiously in blue chips. According to research conducted by Find/SVP, the new-style Internet investment club member is typically a 36-year old male who wants to make a lot of money fast. In order to do so, he is willing to speculate in highly combustible, high-technology start-ups.

Today's investment club member is using his or her computer to pick up investment leads ranging from breaking news on business wires (like Reuters and Bloomberg) to rumors posted to newsgroups and listserv mailing lists. These investment club members are swapping information on-line via e-mail, tapping into Web sites that offer free financial information, downloading business reports, and doing everything possible to become as informed as possible about stocks and stock market conditions.

Investment clubs have traditionally been composed of tightly knit groups of friends and family members. Memberships have traditionally been limited in number, small in scope. But the Internet is changing even this aspect of investment clubs.

Consider the FCS Investment Club, based in Calgary, Alberta, Canada. FCS boasts more than 300 members who live in Canada, the United States, Britain, and Germany. Members who can't attend the club's monthly meeting in a conference room at a Calgary office building can catch up on the discussion via minutes available through electronic mail or downloadable files from the club's Web site.

There are innumerable investment clubs on-line: far, far too many for us to list in this book. And there are dozens of new Internet investment clubs starting up every day. To find them, perform a keyboard search for "investment club" using Alta Vista, Web Crawler, Lycos, or some other popular Web search engine. Figure 1.10 shows information about on-line investment clubs.

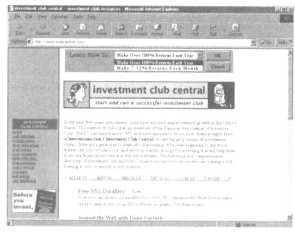

Figure 1.10 All about investment clubs at Investment Club Central on the World Wide Web.

ADVICE FROM EMERSON

Ralph Waldo Emerson once wrote that:

> *Shallow men believe in luck. Wise and strong men believe in cause and effect.*

Please keep this bit of wisdom in mind as you digest the details of your various investment options described in *Net Worth*, and chart your course for financial security. Gambling takes place at casinos here in Las Vegas. Shrewd, thoughtful, pragmatic investment is for those who ultimately win at everything. The gap between gambling and strategic investment is wide. Always be sure to place yourself on the correct, profitable side of the canyon.

Finally, keep in mind that "Past performance dos not represent future results. Investment returns and principal value vary, and you may have a gain or a loss when you invest." If you encounter recommendations, whether on the Internet or from your "good friend," keep in mind that no investment is a "sure thing." Your best chance is to be an informed investor.

CHAPTER 2
WHERE ARE YOU STARTING?
CALCULATING YOUR NET WORTH

Money and goods are certainly the best of references. — Charles Dickens, *Our Mutual Friend*

PLEASED TO MEET YOU

Please let me introduce myself. I am a 28-year old freelance copy editor, write, and photographer. I have a Bachelor's degree in English and a minor in political science. I am a wife, a mother of a three-year old daughter, and have two more children from my husband's previous marriage. Personally, I invested in my first mutual fund two years ago, and I recently invested a chunk of my savings in a friend's dot com company that is scheduled to go IPO in December of 2001. We have other small investments, and my husband started a retirement fund some time ago.

Having said all that, I can tell you, on someone else's good authority, one very important truth: *Before you can set a course for where you want to go, you must have a precise and perfect knowledge of exactly where you are starting from.*

Knowing where you want to go is a wonderful thing. It is essential to have that vision. Without a goal, the future or any other voyage is a pointless quest. But without a clearly defined place of departure, there is no beginning and, consequently, no journey. To start the journey toward wealth and financial security, it is as vital to have a clear idea of where you are *right now* as it is to know the places you want to end up.

WHO ARE YOU?

You, like me, are inevitably many things. You have many guises. If you are not a writer, then you are a graphic designer or a housekeeper or a plumber or a basketball coach, and so on. You may or may not be a parent. (And the extent to which the presence or absence of children will impact your financial planning cannot be overemphasized.) You may have your hands in many things, or perhaps, you are set in a particular career path that maintains your general focus. Hopefully, you have other interests you are passionate about that have nothing to do with the simple-interest yield that shows up on a spreadsheet. Whoever you may be, you cannot set a course for where you are going without knowing where you are starting from.

In addition to these varied things, you (like me) define your present location in life by a *precise dollar amount*. You, like me, are worth *x, y,* or *z*. This is my net worth. This is your net worth. This is an aspect of where our life is moored at the moment.

CALCULATING MY (AND YOUR) NET WORTH

Calculating one's net worth involves finding out *where* one is, not *who* one is. It is worth remembering what the old mogul Joseph P. Kennedy always told his children: money was a *means* and not an *end*. Consider the fact that in calculating one's net worth, we discount our most valuable possessions. My daughter is excluded from the equation, as is my family, my friends, my health, my faith, my life's experiences, and whatever small amount of wisdom I've been lucky enough to accumulate through it all.

For the purposes of calculating net worth, I must ignore my *real* wealth and instead focus on such incidentals as liquid cash-on-hand, real estate equity, brokerage account balances, and the current value of stocks, bonds, and other securities I hold, as well as, computers, automobiles, and so on.

Having said that, the math involved in calculating net worth could not be simpler. To calculate your net worth, just do the following.

Add up your cash-on-hand, your equity in insurance policies you own, the *market-value* (the value at which you can realistically sell) of any real estate you own, the accumulated market-value of such items as automobiles, computers, furniture, or stamp collections, and the value of any stocks, bonds, or other securities you hold within or outside of a 401 (k) or other retirement plan.

Now subtract any or all debt: mortgage debt, credit card "revolving-credit" debt, home-improvement debt, auto-loan debt, and so on.

The result is your net worth. It is the point from which you begin the chart the rest of your journey.

Calculating Gino's Net Worth

Gino wants to figure out what he is worth, so he starts doing some math.

On the plus *side, he's got $10,000 in the bank. He's got a house that's worth $200,000. He's got an IRA that's worth $70,000. Then there are his various computers (one can never have enough) worth $7,000, his sailboat ($8,000), his car ($12,000), his stamp collection ($5,000), whole life insurance policy ($50,000), and his miscellaneous stocks and bonds outside his IRA ($6,000). Wow, that's a total of $358,000!*

But wait. There is a minus side to this equation, as well. The house has a mortgage lien to the tune of $160,000. He owes $3,000 on the computers, $4,000 on the sailboat, and $10,000 on the car. That's a total of $177,000 of debt.

So $338,000 minus $177,000 gives us (and Gino) his real net worth of $181,000.

Kiplinger's Personal Finance Magazine and Free Guides

Kiplinger's Finance Magazine examines all aspects of personal investing. Providing you with explanations you can understand on taxes, funds, stocks, retirement and more. You can call 800-544-0155 for a year subscription for $23.95. You can ask to be billed, and if for any reason, you are not completely satisfied with the magazine, simply write "CANCEL" on the invoice and return it. In addition to your subscription, Kiplinger's will send you three money guides: *How to Invest For Retirement, How to Pick Winning Stocks,* and *How to Pick Winning Mutual Funds.*

Merrill Lynch Offers a Free Financial Handbook for Women

Whether you are male or female, your need for financial literacy is great. Unfortunately, Merrill Lynch research has shown that gender has influenced behaviors in the past. More women than men had not identified clear financial goals. To provide women with a good financial tool with which they can begin their financial planning, Merrill Lynch offers a free handbook for women titled *Women's Guidebook* that you can obtain by calling 800-MERRILL ext. 1285 or send email to *askml@ml.com.* You can also visit the Merrill Lynch website at *http://www.ml.com* shown just below in Figure 2.1. If you are running or thinking about running a business, ask Merrill Lynch to send you a free copies of their excellent handbooks titled *Are you Ready to Do Business in the YEAR 2000?* and *Solutions for Women Business Owners.*

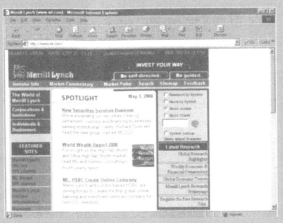

Figure 2.1 The Merrill Lynch Web site.

WHERE WOULD YOU LIKE TO GO THIS DECADE?

Windows 95 users are familiar with the Microsoft greeting: *Where would you like to go today?*

From a financial point of view, it is more appropriate to ask: *Where would you like to go this decade? And the next? And the next?*

Consider. You are 30 years old, with an income of $65,000 a year. You have 20% equity in a $250,000 house. The balance is mortgaged at a fixed 8.5% annually with 25 years left on a 30-year note. You have $10,000 in an IRA growing at a rate of approximately 9% a year. And you have a seven-year old daughter who speaks of one day becoming a surgeon. It is pretty clear where you want to go this decade. You want to arrive at a place where you will have the cash to send that daughter to a good college (and quite possibly, unless her plans change, to graduate school after that) while at the same time being able to cover your anticipated commitments.

And what of the decade after that? Perhaps you would like to try to retire sooner rather than later, at age 50 rather than 70. Perhaps, with your daughter grown and practicing surgery or some other worthy profession, you would hope to realize other dreams for yourself. Not only will you not want to be in hock for your daughter's education, you will want to be in a position to cut your professional ties to possibly sail around the world.

Will a rigorous program of stock investment get you there? If so, what percentage of your income should you dedicate? Will doing without a slightly larger – but still adequate – boat right now give you the boat of your dreams when you are 50?

Financial Help for Parents with Kids

If kids are part of your financial future, you may have tons of questions, not only about the best ways to plan for their financial future, but also ways to help teach your kids about budgeting and investing. Luckily, there are several good books to which you can turn for sound advice. To start, you might try Kiplinger's book (and audio tape) titled *Money Smart Kids* (ISBN: 0-938721-27-5). The book discusses ways parents can teach their kids the value of money, budgeting and managing their allowance. You can visit Kiplinger at their Web site shown below in Figure 2.2 at *http://www.kiplinger.com*.

In addition, Stein Roe & Farnham offer investment-related activities and games for kids at their Web site at *http://www.younginvestor.com*. If you decide to invest through Stein Roe & Farnham and become a member of the Young Investor's Fund, you will receive a Welcome Kit and Activity Booklet for your kids. You will also receive a newsletter every quarter called the *Dollar Digest*. For more information on Stein Roe & Farnham, call 800-403-KIDS or visit their Web Site shown in Figure 2.3 below at *http://www.steinroe.com/*.

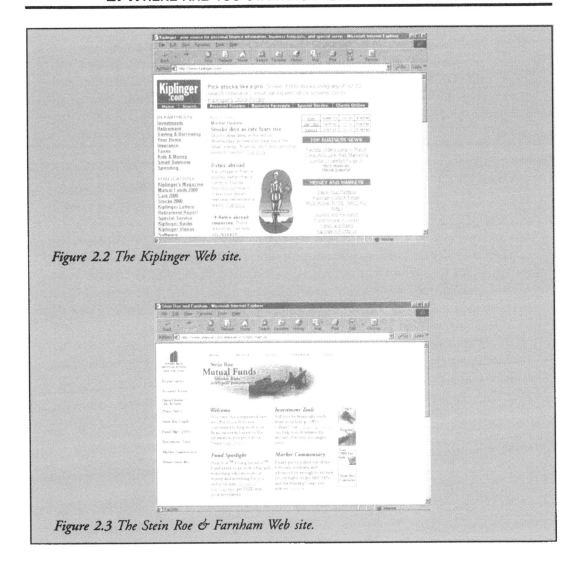

Figure 2.2 The Kiplinger Web site.

Figure 2.3 The Stein Roe & Farnham Web site.

PREPARE TO NAVIGATE

Once again, let me ask you the question in order that you might ask it of yourself. Where would you like to go this decade? And the next? Your choice of destinations is entirely up to you. This book is full of navigational aids to help you get just about anywhere across the financial globe. But you must ascertain your own starting point, and you must define your own destinations.

Thinking of Staring a Business? A Free Copy of Inc. Magazine

If you have your own business or are thinking about becoming a business owner, you should check out *Inc. Magazine*. Visit their Web site at *http://www.inc.com/*

incmagazine. Each month, *Inc.* provides a wealth of articles that discuss all aspects of owning and running a business: health care issues, compensation, cost reduction and much more. Get a free trial issue, and if you like the magazine do nothing. You will receive issues for the rest of the year for only $14. If, for any reason, you are not completely satisfied, simply write "CANCEL" on your invoice and pay nothing. *Inc.* will even let you keep your free gift copy of the *Guide to Small Business Success.*

Helping You Plan Your Financial Future

If you are just getting started thinking about your financial future, you might want the help of The Investment Planner from American Century. Visit their Web site shown below in Figure 2.4 at *http://www.americancentury.com*. They have online advisors who will give you advice on investments and mutual funds. You will have to go through a one time set-up that will take anywhere from 45 minutes to 2 hours. Have all your account information ready including checking accounts, mutual funds, CDs, stocks, bonds and so on. The program will help you set and track goals, as well as, allow you to manipulate the system to make it perform "what if" scenarios. It will allow you to assign different investments to different goals and then tell you whether your investment is on track to meet that goal or what more you might need to reach it. If you have any more questions, you can call 800-690-3913.

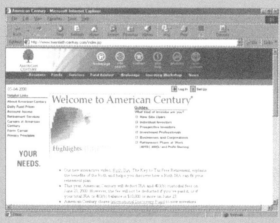

Figure 2.4 The American Century Web site.

BRITISH PERSONAL FINANCE AND INVESTMENTS

http://www.moneyworld.co.uk

FINANCECENTER

http://www.financenter.com/

NAIC
(NATIONAL ASSOCIATION OF INVESTMENT CLUBS)

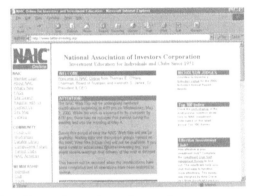

http://www.better-investing.org/

LIFENET – PERSONAL FINANCE WEB SITE

http://www.lifenet.com

PR NEWSWIRE (FINANCIAL COLUMNS)

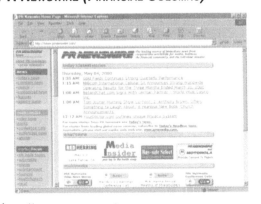

http://www.prnewswire.com

A GUIDE TO PERSONAL FINANCE

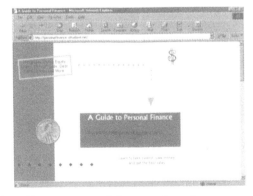

http://www.personal-finance.virtualave.net

FINANCE AND FOLLY

http://www.fool.com

PERSONAL FINANCE 101

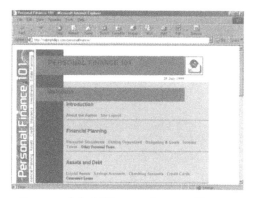

http://www.ralphphillips.com/personalfinance

STUART THE MANIAC'S PERSONAL FINANCE PAGE

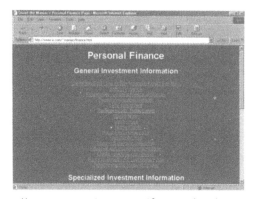

http://www.io.com/~maniac/finance.html

THE MONEY PAGES – PERSONAL FINANCE MADE EASY

http://www.wildcomputer.com/money

INVESTOR GUIDE CLASSIC: PERSONAL FINANCE

http://www.investorguide.com/PersonalFinance.htm

GE FINANCIAL NETWORK: PERSONAL FINANCE AND INVESTING SOLUTIONS

http://www.ge.com/financial

CHAPTER 3

THE BASICS OF CAPITAL ACCUMULATION

A feast is made for laughter, and wine maketh merry: but money answereth all things. —
Ecclesiates, 10:19.

A TRUE STORY

Coco Chanel once wrote, "There are people who have money and people who are rich." And
F. Scott Fitzgerald shrewdly observed that, "the rich are not like us." At the root of Chanel's
and Fitzgerald's suggestion is in fact that there is a fundamental gulf between the two species
of humankind, the rich and the not rich. On one side of the gulf stand people who have to
accumulate capital before they can accumulate wealth, and on the other side *sit* those who
have the capital and wealth handed to them and, through financial inertia, inevitably accumulate even more.

Now, here is a true story. Jay Gould is a legendary, Gilded-Age robber-baron who made an
enormous fortune on Wall Street during the late 19th century. When he died in 1892, he left
an estate of $97 million. That's $97 million in *pre-inflation 1892 dollars*. The value-equiva-
lent today would be more than a billion dollars.

The Gould estate took a small hit during the stock market crash of 1929 but nothing
catastrophic. Large portions of the estate were invested in relatively cheap real estate on
the then underdeveloped French Riviera and not in stocks and bonds. We all know what
has happened there.

Thus, his great grandson lives a happy vagabond life, flying or being driven from one house to
the next, fishing for trout when the mood strikes, just as his great grandfather did. When
being pinned down to pick a time for an appointment, he said, "I come and go like the tide.
I couldn't *begin* to guess what I'll be doing or where I'll be next week."

He knows little about savings programs and investment. He has people to manage that kind
of thing for him. And those people have a very easy job because it is not hard to use wealth to
accumulate even more wealth. The trick is accumulating *some* wealth where there is little or
no wealth to begin with.

CAPITAL: THE SEED OF WEALTH

Assuming that you do not count Jay Gould or John D. Rockefeller among your forebears, then the first, most fundamental aspect of your personal financial plan must be the accumulation of investment capital: the seed of wealth.

To put it quite simply, capital is accumulated and wealth is grown when you create a situation whereby your inflow of cash is greater than your outflow of cash *over time,* and you regularly put the excess cash into sound investments, whether those investments be stocks or other securities, real estate, or cash equivalents.

AN INSIDE PEEK OF HOW THE OTHER HALF LIVED

http://www.georgian.edu/

George Jay Gould (the son of railroad magnate/Wall Street financier Jay Gould) never worked a day in his life. Nevertheless, he built this little place called Georgian Court in 1896. George commissioned New York society architect Bruce Price to transform a dense wilderness outside Lakewood, New Jersey into a lavish country estate. What George Jay Gould had in mind was nothing less than a copy of the great landed estates of England and Scotland and the fine Georgian mansions that so often defined them. Of course, George Jay Gould could well afford to get what he had in mind. Despite all its splendor, however, none of his children appeared to want Georgian Court after George Jay Gould's death. So they gave it away, furniture and all, to an order of nuns, the Sisters of Mercy. And the Sisters founded a college there: Georgian Court College. The home the family held onto is George Jay Gould's rustic cabin retreat in the Catskill Mountains made of hand hewn native logs.

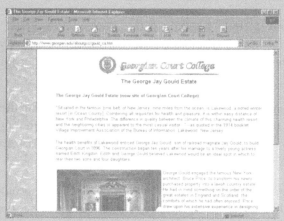

Figure 3.1 The Gould's Georgian Court.

WEIGHING RISK VERSUS RETURN IN CHOOSING AN INVESTMENT

Your charter for excess cash is straightforward: you want your excess cash to earn the highest possible total return *within the boundaries of risk with which you are personally comfortable.*

In other words, your projected rate of return (your projected *yield*) of an investment is far from the only thing to consider when you choose where to put your money. There are many other issues. For example, if you are likely to need the capital you are investing any time soon, then a very pertinent question is how certain your promised return is *in the short-term.* In such a situation of limited liquidity (where you may need fast access to your cash), a comparatively low-yielding (but insured and guaranteed) certificate-of-deposit (CD) might be a "better" investment than a speculative stock issue that will probably do extremely well over time but may swing wildly up and down in the immediate future.

THE VARIOUS FORMS OF INVESTMENT

Rejoice. You have multitudes of investment options. As you set out to examine your investment options, you will find investment opportunities that balance yield, risk, security, growth, and liquidity. In short, you will find investment opportunities that will fit your personal investment goals.

In the following chapters we will survey the advantages, disadvantages, and idiosyncracies of a host of *variable-dollar* investments, including common stock, mutual funds, closed-end investment companies, options, and other derivatives. We will also examine the details of *fixed-dollar* investments such as corporate bonds and preferred stock, U.S. government securities, municipal bonds, and more. Later in the book, we will discuss how you can use real estate and real estate limited-partnerships as investment vehicles.

Your Money *Magazine*

Your Money is a bi-monthly magazine that will provide you with information on mutual funds, retirement plans, life insurance, and more. You can call 800-777-0025 and asked to be billed. You will receive your first issue free. If, for any reason, you are not completely satisfied, simply return your invoice marked "CANCEL" and pay nothing. If you like the issue, do nothing, and you will receive your remaining issues for $15.97 a year.

DIVERSIFY AND CONQUER

Not *a single* one of investment options we will discuss in *Net Worth* is right for most investors. For the majority of investors, a combination of different investment vehicles (a diversification of investments) is the ticket to success.

Diversification is your invaluable tool for managing risk. If you have your entire $100,000 nest egg in the stock of a single company, and that stock loses 20% of its value, then you are out $20,000. But, if you own many different stocks and bonds, and also have other investments under the umbrella of your $100,000 investment capital, the value of your portfolio may hardly notice the 20% decline in any single given stock which may represent just 2% of your capital.

In short, diversify your portfolio by simply using a mix of different investments such as some stocks, some bonds, a mutual fund, some real estate, and so on. In this way, you spread your risks across several diverse investments.

Mutual funds, which we will discuss later, offer a form of automatic diversification among specific classes of stocks and bonds. Also, diversification is inherent in the percentage of your savings you allocate through life insurance, your investment in your home, and so on.

> ### U.S. Coin Exchange, Inc.
>
> As you will learn throughout the pages of this book, there are many ways you can invest your money: stocks, bonds, options, commodities, real estate and more. In addition to these "common" investment techniques, investors turn to works of art and even rare coins. To help you learn more about investing in rare coins, the U.S. Coin Exchange, Inc. has put together a great, free information kit that even included a video. If you saved coins as a kid and are thinking about doing so again, this is a great place to start. To get your free information kit, call 800-741-4246.

BUT THE MAIN POINT IS...

If you spend everything you make – *regardless of how much you make* – you will never be wealthy. You must set aside the investment capital that is the seed of wealth. You must *save*. You must *invest*. You must establish a regular program of socking away a portion of your monthly income in tune with a structured, sound, long-term investment strategy. Only then will you be on the road to true financial independence.

You shall see as you read this book, investment can and *should* take many forms. It may take the form of paying off your mortgage on a faster schedule than necessary, putting the maximum annual contribution into your 401K, making regular payments into a mutual fund, and so on. Ideally, your investment program should be a combination of all these things in proportions you design to match your risk-comfort level and financial goals.

> ### Your Financial Health
>
> Look at this section as an exercise in health. Look at debt as cholesterol clogging the veins of your financial body. Look at egregious spending on luxuries like sugars that will give momentary pleasure but in the end will leave you obese, unhappy, and unfulfilled.

> Look at regular investment as a discipline akin to that of a regular workout. Look at diversification of investments as you would look at diversification of your diet: a little of everything is generally healthy, and a lot of one thing is never really a good idea.
>
> In short, look at sound personal financial planning and regular investment as I hope you look at regular exercise and a healthful diet. These are *all* things you can do to help insure a long, robust, and healthy future.

SOME THOUGHTS ON MONEY FROM A MAN WHO HAD IT

Not long ago, writing in one of his newspaper columns, William F. Buckley, Jr. spoke of new technology developed by the TeleRead Corporation for storing and displaying texts of hundreds of books on laptop computers becoming "everyone's personal library." Buckley writes, "Andrew Carnegie, if he were alive, would probably buy TeleRead from Mr. Rothman for $1, develop the whole idea at his own expense, and then make a gift of it to the American people."

Buckley could not be more correct. Carnegie was probably the greatest philanthropist in the history of the planet.

"Man does not live by bread alone," Carnegie writes. "I have known millionaires starving for lack of nutrient which alone can sustain all that is human in man, and I know workmen, and many so-called poor men, who revel in luxuries beyond the power of those millionaires to reach. It is the mind that makes the body rich. There is no class so pitiably wretched as that which possesses money and nothing else. Money can only be the useful drudge of things immeasurably higher than itself. Exalted beyond this, as it sometimes is, it remains Caliban still and still plays the beast. My aspirations take a higher flight. Mine be it to have contributed to the enlightenment and the joys of the mind, to things of the spirit, to all that tends to bring into the lives of the toilers…sweetness and light. I hold this the noblest possible use of wealth."

Carnegie built hundreds of libraries across the United States. Over the doors of the Carnegie Library of Pittsburgh, carved in stone to stand forever, are the words "Free to the People." And then there is Carnegie Hall, Carnegie-Mellon University, and other such small enterprises. During his life, Carnegie – who did not believe in the concept of inherited wealth – gave away virtually all of his fortune from the steel industry he pioneered - $350,695,653, to be precise. And upon his death, the remaining $30,000,000 in his estate was likewise given away to foundations and charities. The Carnegie Corporation remains to this day one of the great philanthropic organizations of the world.

"This, then, is held to be the duty of the man of wealth," he wrote elsewhere. "First, to set an example of modest unostentatious living, shunning display; to provide moderately for the legitimate wants of those dependents upon him; and, after doing so, to consider all surplus revenues which come to him simply as trust funds which he is strictly bound as a matter of duty to administer in the manner which, in his judgment, is best calculated to produce the mot beneficial results for the community."

There are, of course, all sorts of things that can be done with great wealth. Unfortunately, Henry Ford published anti-Semitic newspapers. Thankfully, Carnegie built libraries. Bill Gates, take note.

For more information on Andrew Carnegie, his philosophy of life and finance, and his writings, check out the Web site *http://www.pbs.org/wgbh/amex/carnegie* shown below in Figure 3.2.

Figure 3.2 Information about Andrew Carnegie.

CHECK OUT AN ON-LINE FINANCIAL NEWSLETTER

John Bollinger, CFA, CMT, is a financial analyst who has served as the Chief Market Analyst for the Financial News Network (FNN) and has provided financial commentary for CNBC. To obtain a free copy of his weekly, *Capital Growth Letter,* contact Bollinger Capital Management at 310-798-8855 or get it directly from his Web site at *http://www.BollingerBands.com* shown below in Figure 3.3. The Web site also offers a free tutorial. Bollinger is the originator of Bollinger Bands, an analytical technique that provides traders with buy and sell signals.

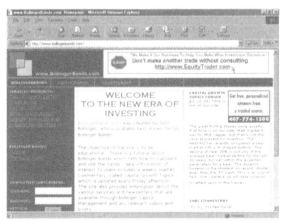

Figure 3.3 The Bollinger Web site.

Try Out a Free Issue of Individual Investor

Individual Investor is a monthly magazine that covers all aspects of personal finance from mutual funds, to bonds, to stocks, and even IPOs. You will find information well suited for the individual investor. To receive a free issue of *Individual Investor*, call 800-383-5901. If you enjoy your sample copy, you will continue to receive the next 11 issues for $34.95. If, for any reason, you are not completely satisfied, write "CANCEL" on your invoice and return it.

You can also get a full year's subscription to the *Special Situations Report*, the newsletter for Undiscovered Stocks, for $195.00. You can call 800-446-9118 and/or check out the *Special Situations Report* on the Web at *http://www.individualinvestor.com* shown below in Figure 3.4.

Figure 3.4 The Individual Investor *Web site.*

WHAT IS YOUR RISK TOLERANCE LEVEL?

The more you risk, the more your potential return. That is an important rule to remember.

Another important rule to remember is that unless you are investing in highly speculative financial investments, such as junk bonds (more on these later in the book), just about any investment you make is probably going to do pretty well *over time*. The wider your investment horizon, the longer your timeline, the less risk you have to contend with. The bulk of all investment risk is *short-term risk*.

If you are like me, with at least 30 or more years to go until you retire, you can afford (for the moment) to be invested in speculative financial instruments and/or mutual funds leveraging future contracts, stock options, foreign investments, and even the occasional junk bond. Long-term, these will, as a group of investments, go up in value more dramatically than many safer, more conservative investments.

If you have fifteen years or so to go before retirement, you may want to modify your holdings somewhat to incorporate more table stock and bond growth, mortgage-backed securities, corporate bonds, blue chip stocks, life insurance contracts, and perhaps some rental estate. The rate of your return will generally slow somewhat at this point, but your investments should still outperform what you'd get in a savings account or even with a Treasury Bill.

Finally, if you are very near to retirement, you won't want to gamble with your nestegg. You will want to look seriously at T-bills, Treasury Bonds, Annuities, utility stocks, short-term bond mutual funds, and zero-coupon books, as well as, plain-vanilla bank CDs, and money market mutual funds. Your return will be modest, but your capital risk will be virtually non-existent.

THE ONE THING YOU CAN'T GET ENOUGH OF: INFORMATION

One of the most useful sites on the Web today is Consumer World's collection of money and credit links, which are addressed *http://www.consumerworld.org/* as shown in Figure 3.5 below. It literally contains hundreds of links, broken down alphabetically, covering every aspect of finance and investment from annuities to zero-coupon bonds. At this site, you will find links to mutual funds, on-line stock brokerages, international currency exchanges, banks across the Web, insurance writers, and much, much more. I mention Consumer World here, in this chapter on basics, because it really is the most basic, most important, most fundamental resource for anyone interested in using the Internet help plan to implement their financial future. This Web site, offering what amounts to "one stop" shopping for financial information on the Internet, is an item for your Web-browser's hot-list if there ever was one.

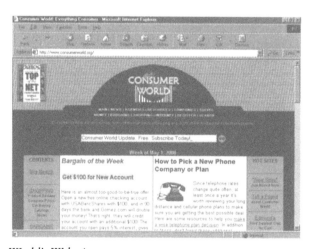

Figure 3.5 Consumer World's Web site.

The National Post – Canada's Business Voice

If you live in Canada or if you have interests in the Canadian business market, you can turn to *The National Post*, Canada's business voice. In Canada, you will receive a

Monday-Saturday delivery for $12.84 per month (Canadian dollars). In the U.S., you will receive a Saturday issue only for $15.17 per month. For specifics on the offer that will best suit your needs, contact *The National Post* at 800-668-7678.

BASIC FINANCIAL PLANNING RESOURCES ON THE INTERNET

As you surf the World Wide Web, you may encounter sites that discuss various aspects of financial planning, budgeting, and more. The following site list should help you locate the resources you need.

BRUCE R. GLICKMAN'S FINANCIAL PLANNING TIPS

http://www.brucerglickman.com

Bruce R. Glickman, an accountant and financial consultant in New York's Westchester County, provides an impressive collection of links and information on financial planning that includes a very useful (and downloadable) budget and cash-flow worksheet for Excel. Figure 3.6 shows Glickman's Web page on financial planning.

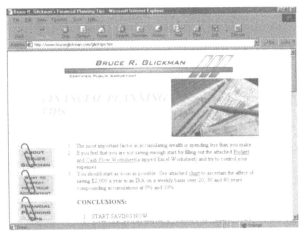

Figure 3.6 Bruce R. Glickman's Financial Planning Tips.

THE FINANCIAL PLANNING PROCESS: A TUTORIAL

http://www.leggmason.com/

This informative Web site takes you step-by-step through the process of identifying your goals and objectives, gathering data, analyzing your present situation, and implementing and monitoring your long-term financial plan. The tutorial and reference information includes handy on-line calculators for figuring investment return, mortgage payments, life insurance vesting, and more. Figure 3.7 shows the Financial Planning page.

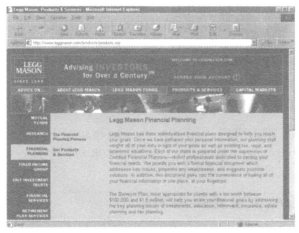

Figure 3.7 The Financial Planning Process.

DELOITTE AND TOUCHE'S CENTER OF EXCELLENCE FOR FINANCIAL COUNSELING SERVICES

http://www.dtonline.com

This Web site gives you news and information on personal finance, taxes and business. The Financial Planning page includes guides to tax planning, estate planning, and principles of retirement planning shown in Figure 3.8 below. It also maps out a four-step goal process and contains featured articles.

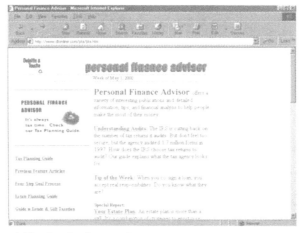

Figure 3.8 Deloitte and Touche On-line Web site.

WOMEN'S FINANCIAL PLANNING SERVICES

http://www.women.com/services/financialplanning

This Web site provides help for asset allocation, budgeting, managing personal debt, education funding, taxes, and 401(k) planning. They will assist you in deciding what kind of financial help best suits your needs by using on-line access, personalized plans, and even telephone support. Figure 3.9 shows this particular page from *women.com*.

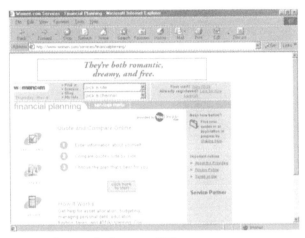

Figure 3.9 *The women.com financial planning Web page.*

CHAPTER 4
THE JOY OF STOCKS

Money and goods are certainly the best of references. — *Ralph Waldo Emerson, Nominalist and Realist*

LONG-TERM JOY

For the man or woman who wants his or her capital to grow as fast as possible, there is no better investment than stocks. This is the most important statement in the book. Do I need to repeat it? *If you want your capital to grow as fast as possible, there is no better investment than stocks.*

Since 1925, the stock market has returned about 11% per year, compared to about 6% for bonds and 4% for things like money market funds and T-bills.

The long-term spiral of Wall Street spins constantly in the direction of stock prices. However, this trend has historically always been interrupted by "corrections" and "bear markets" which have caused the market as a whole to "lose value" in the short term. Thus, those mostly likely to get burned in the stock market are speculators who shun investing for the long-term and, instead, bet big on wild, short-term swings of one stock or one group of stocks. Those with the wisdom to ferret out fairly-priced stocks of strongly-positioned companies, and the patience to hold those securities over time and weather short-term shifts in Wall Street's mood, will find "the Street" a happy and prosperous place to be.

In Brief: Why Companies Issue Stock

Emerging companies who wish to grow either through expansion or acquisition often encounter difficulties finding the cash to implement their strategy. There is, after all, a limit to the amount of corporate bonds a firm can issue before the firm's debt becomes so great that further bond offerings become unaffordable.

One solution—one sure-fire way to raise large amounts of cash without incurring large amounts of debt—is for the firm to "go public." To do so, the company issues and sells shares of stock in the corporation, and the firm takes the cash promising, of course, to pay a due portion (share) of future revenues to the new *part-owners* of the corporation who are the shareholders.

In Brief: Why People Buy Stocks

Quite simply, over time stocks have historically, on average, gone up in value faster than any other investment available to mortal man. There's no arguing with history. In short, investors hope to make money on their stock investment in one of two ways. First, the company may choose to offer a dividend, in which it pays a shareholder a small amount (a piece of the company profit) for each share of the stock the stockholder owns. Second, as the company's profits increase, so too will the company's stock price (as discussed next). When the shareholder feels the stock has reached a high value, the shareholder can sell his/her shares to another investor. The difference between the price the original shareholder bought and sold the stock for becomes the shareholder's profit (or loss).

In Brief: What Makes Stocks Go Up and Down in Value

Like any other commodity, stocks go up and down in price with the ebb and flow of demand. And demand for a given stock, or group of stocks, is driven by multitudinous factors: the interest-rate outlook, the Price to Earnings (P/E) ratio of any given stock, forecasted industry trends, and so on. Learn to keep track of all the variables and accurately forecast the ups and downs of many different stocks, and you are set for a six-figure mutual-fund manager's job.

WHAT IS COMMON STOCK?

Common stock represents residual ownership in a corporation with rights to a percentage "share" in the net operating profits of a corporation after taxes. Ownerships in shares in a corporation usually also entitles the shareholder to voting rights at annual meetings. In other words, common stock is fundamental ownership equity and comes with all the potential risks and rewards of such ownership. There is no guarantee that a stock's price will not go down; there is no guarantee that a corporation will be in a position to declare a dividend for shareholders in any given year. It's important to note, however, that although your investment is at risk (meaning the company can perform poorly and you can lose the money you invested in your stock) you do not have other "ownership liabilities." For example, a disgruntled ex-employee cannot sue you personally as a shareholder for the actions of the company.

Successful investment in stock requires homework. It requires research and attention to detail. And it requires skill at ascertaining actual, long- and short-term values for stocks. This is homework that can be mastered by any investor ready to put in the effort. But there are ways around the homework, such as finding a broker whose recommendations you can trust, or investing in stock mutual funds with track records—and therefore, investment managers—you respect. (See Chapter 7 for detailed information on the mechanics of mutual fund stocks.)

How Does Common Stock Differ from Preferred Stock?

Common stock, as we have said, is a full share in the ownership, risk, and potential profits of a firm. *Preferred stock,* on the other hand, is considerably different. Those who own preferred stock get—you guessed it!—*preferential* treatment over owners of common stock. When there are not enough profits to go around, owners of preferred stock may well be the only investors in the firm to receive a dividend. And if the firm goes bust and must sell off its assets, owners of preferred stock are entitled to receive the money they've invested before the owners of common stock receive a dime. On the down side, dividends on preferred stock are fixed and do not increase, even if corporate profits go through the roof. Thus, overall, preferred stock is not unlike a bond (see Chapter 6 for information on bonds) save for the fact that it has no fixed maturity date. Most average investors deal with common stock as opposed to preferred stock, and all the basic math of stocks considers common stock rather than preferred stock.

Dun & Bradstreet Information Services

Dun & Bradstreet is one of the world's foremost leaders in business information. They publish many different directory and software programs that may provide you with key investment information. In fact, Dun & Bradstreet employs over 3,000 people whose task is to update their databases each day—making over 650,000 changes a day! For more information on Dun & Bradstreet services or to obtain a free catalog, call Chuck Bell at 800-526-0651 ext. 6744.

The Basic Math of Common Stock

There are five basic numbers that go into the subtle (and sometimes not-so-subtle) appraisal of the value of common stock. These basic numbers are a stock's *Earnings-Per-Share, Cash-Flow-Per-Share, Price-Earnings (P/E) Ratio, Net Asset Value (Book Value),* and *Yield.* These figures, combined with knowledge of the particular company's position within the industry and the industry trends, are fundamental tools for evaluating whether or not a stock is a good long- or short-term investment.

Earnings-Per-Share for any stock is calculated by taking net corporate profits after taxes, subtracting any preferred dividends, and dividing the remainder by the number of common shares outstanding. An example: Claire's Software (an imaginary company) had a net-profit of $1,000,000 for the past year after subtracting expenses (not including non-recurring capital expenses), interest, and taxes. Of this amount, $100,000 has gone to meet preferred dividend requirements attached to preferred stock. The remaining balance of $900,000 amounts to $3 per share of the 300,000 units of common stock outstanding. This is the Earnings-Per-Share calculation for the year for Claire's Software.

Whenever data is available, Earnings-Per-Share calculations are computed annually, quarterly, and semi-annually.

Note that Earnings-Per-Share in a given amount does not ensure a dividend in that same amount. Many companies plow some or all earnings back into the growth of the firm at the discretion of the firm's management and Board of Directors. Nevertheless, the Earnings-Per-Share calculation has obvious importance in estimating a stock's value.

The example I just gave is based on what analysts call "trail earnings." In other words, these are past actual earnings of the corporation that leave nothing to the imagination. The numbers are a matter of historical record. On some occasions, analysts will *estimate* future Earnings-Per-Share and base other calculations, including the Price-Earnings Ratio (see below), on this estimate. When analysts provide Earnings-Per-Share or Price-Earnings information, they will invariably follow the number quoted with a phrase indicating whether the quoted figure is based on past earnings or estimated future earnings. Most future earnings estimates are pretty much on the mark, but you should keep in mind that estimates based on past earnings are obviously less ephemeral.

Cash-Flow-Per-Share is similar to Earnings-Per-Share, but is calculated by adding non-cash back-depreciation expense to net profit less preferred dividends, and then dividing by the number of common shares outstanding. The idea here is to be better able to compare the real profits of different firms by discounting depreciation policies, which vary from firm to firm.

Neither Earnings-Per-Share nor Cash-Flow-Per-Share is routinely provided in newspaper listings of stock values and performance. But any good broker should be able to provide these figures, and many do so via Web databases that are available on-line. If you are motivated, you may also derive a stock's true historical ("trailing") Earnings-Per-Share information from a stock's P/E Ratio and market price quoted in daily newspapers. How? Read on.

The *Price-Earnings (P/E) Ratio* is a very straightforward calculation that can always be found in the newspaper listing for any stock you are interested in. How is the P/E Ratio derived? As its label implies, the P/E Ratio is nothing more than a stock's market price divided by Earnings-Per-Share. Thus, the P/E Ratio for Claire's Software, if we assume a market price per share of $30, would be 10 to 1 ($30 divided by $3). Conversely, you can take the P/E Ratio and market price of the stock quoted in the newspaper to derive historical Earnings-Per-Share ($30 / 10= $3 Earnings-Per-Share).

The P/E Ratio is the most highly regarded and commonly used tool for ascertaining a stock's value and comparing it to the value of other stocks because it gives a good capsule picture of the stock price as compared to earning power.

Generally speaking, the lower a P/E Ratio for any given stock, the better value the stock is likely to be. If Claire's Software's earnings had been $4 per share, rather than $3, the P/E Ratio would have been 7.5 to 1 instead of 10 to 1 (although 10 to 1 is not all that bad either). When you get down into the mid-single digits, you are starting to talk about strong P/E Ratios. From 1935 to 1990, the P/E Ratio for the Dow Jones industrial average was about 15 to 1.

But it is important to remember that P/E Ratios, though significant, are only *part* of the story for any stock. There may well be a very good reason for a stock to hold what seems to be a high P/E Ratio. The price of the stock may have been run up by "the street" in anticipation that the firm's future earnings will be significantly higher than current earnings. In such a situation, the stock may well be worth buying despite the high P/E. However, in the absence of such an *educated* anticipation as this, a high P/E is your signal that a stock is overpriced.

The *Net-Asset-Value (or Book-Value)* per share measures the assets the corporation has working per each share of common stock outstanding. To derive this figure, analysts take the net balance sheet value of the corporation's assets, then subtract the face-value of claims by creditors and preferred shareholders, and divide this by the number of shares of common stock outstanding.

Let's go back to Claire's Software for an example. At the end of the latest fiscal year, Claire's Software closed its books with assets of $30 million and debts and preferred stock obligations totaling $10 million. The balance of $20 million boiled down to a per-share Net-Asset-Value (Book Value) of $66.66 ($20 million divided by 300,000 shares).

But because of the nature of the business engaged in by Claire's Software, the book value may not mean much. Here's why.

For businesses whose assets are a good measure of earning power, such as timber companies, Book-Value can be a significant figure. However, keep in mind that the Book-Value of assets are based *on cost*, not earning power. Intangible assets—such as superb market positioning, staff excellence, and first-rate R&D processes—may be more to the point in judging the value of most stocks. And these items do not figure into the Book-Value equation.

The dynamic new technology stocks, such as Claire's Software, are a case in point. High-tech growth companies such as Microsoft, Netscape, and Claire's Software routinely have stock prices that are dramatically higher than Book-Value. Why? Because the sum of such companies is considerably more than the combined cost of their warehouses, office buildings, parking lots, and patents. In Microsoft's case, for example, the projected earnings value of its software programs and operating systems is many, many times greater than what it costs Microsoft to develop them. And Book-Value, I repeat, is based on the *cost* of assets, *not* their earnings potential.

There is, of course, another side of the coin. When it comes to stagnant and mismanaged firms, or firms in declining industries, the Book-Value will sometimes be a better indicator of real worth than are recent histories of poor earnings. Why? Because the earnings, or lack of earnings, suggest that whatever intangibles are in play do not count for much. And the real worth of the firm may well be in its *liquidating value*: the value of the firm's land, buildings, and patents. When the wreck of the firm is written off, it is usually done in the same way you write-off the wreck of your car—at Book-Value. Another measure that is sometimes used on these wrecks of firms is called *Liquidating-Value-per-Share*. This is calculated very much in the same way as Book-Value but uses the liquidating values of assets (what they can be sold for) rather than balance sheet values (which are based on historical cost). Corporate raiders—*a la* Michael Douglas in the film *Wall Street*—are most often interested in the Liquidating-Value-per-Share.

Yield—sometimes called the *Yield Percentage* or *Current Yield*—indicates the percentage relationship between the annual cash dividend of a stock and that stock's current market price. With a $3 dividend and a $30 stock price, Claire's Software has an astonishingly excellent yield of 10%. If only the firm actually existed.

The Yield figure is often, *but not always,* an excellent indication of the reasonableness of a stock's current price. Generally, the higher the yield, the better. But there are exceptions to this rule. If a stock has low dividends compared to a high asking price there may be, and often is, no reason (other than stupidity) as to why the market has "overvalued" the security in question.

Consider a firm that has declared low or no dividends over recent years. This can be, of course, because the firm is poorly run, poorly positioned within its industry, or part of an industry that is declining overall. In this case, the low- or no-yield figure is a red flag telling you, the investor, to stay clear. But what if the firm is actually well managed and on the rise within a thriving industry? What if the firm's management skipped dividends because they are plowing capital into R&D that will most assuredly enable them to dominate a lucrative, high-demand market two or three years from now? In this case, the unattractive yield percentage does not mean much and neither does a high P/E Ratio.

In short, there is much more to the homework of the "street" than just a quick survey of P/E Ratios and Current Yields over your morning cup of coffee. You've got to do your homework.

Watch How Insiders Trade

One way some investors get a "sense" about a specific company is to watch the buy and sell trades made by corporate insiders. If, for example, a corporate insider is buying a large number of the company's shares, another investor might construe the insider's action as an indication that the insider feels comfortable with the company's future earnings. One way you can get information on such insider trades is through Vicker's Weekly Insider Report. To examine a free copy of this newsletter, contact Vicker's Research Corp. at 800-645-5043. Visit their Web site at *www.argusgroup.com*.

Consider the Source of On-Line Stock Gossip

The NASD (National Association of Securities Dealers) has a word of caution for you about the Internet. Specifically, it is a word of caution about some of the stock gossip you may pick up stock-related newsgroups on-line.

As NASD's Mary L. Schapiro said to the *New York Times,* the Internet also poses some serious threats. "My real worry about the Internet right now," says Schapiro, "is that the nature of the medium is such that people who are intent on perpetrating a fraud can do it very quickly and very cheaply and to a vastly broader audience than they can utilizing the telephone or the mail."

An example? Schapiro says that the NASD is tracking price and volume changes in some very low-priced stocks and seems able to correlate these against Internet messages related to those stocks. "We're looking into the chat rooms and looking at what stocks people are talking about and who they are representing themselves to be when they talk about these stocks," says Schapiro.

Schapiro says the NASD has seen a definite correlation between the number of Internet messages about various stocks and dramatic increases in the prices and volumes of these stocks. "Maybe it's all legitimate, honest-to-goodness investors just sharing ideas about new companies," says Schapiro. "But maybe there are insiders who are, anonymously or using aliases, promoting stocks that are eventually going to dump on the public. Or maybe there is a brokerage firm, with a large inventory of stock that it wants to get rid of, hyping that stock on the Internet for the same reason."

And that would be profoundly illegal.

As Schapiro makes clear, it is important to educate the public to the fact that people might often have all sorts of ulterior motives in hyping a stock on the Internet. "And it may not just be to share with you their idea of a great new company. They may have lots of self-serving reasons for doing it, and people need to understand that because they see it on the screen, it should have no greater credibility to them than a phone call from a cold caller."

Pinnacle Data Corp. Databases

Pinnacle Data Corp. provides three different databases for PC-compatible systems. The IDX package, for example, contains financial data (such as CPI, money rates, DOW averages, and so on) dating back from 1901! The CLC package contains data on commodities futures since 1969. Also, the COT package contains the Commitment of Traders Reports dating back to 1983. They have recently added another product called the Complete Historical Collection which includes 8,000 commodity contracts. For more information on these databases, contact Pinnacle at 800-724-4903 or by email at *pinnacle@servtech.com*. You can also check out their Web site at *www.pinnacledata.com*.

THE VARIOUS MARKET INDEXES

Part of your homework involves the various market indexes. A good way to measure the performance of your portfolio is to match it against the performance of some or all of the standard stock market indexes. We've all heard of the Dow Jones Industrial Average, the S&P 500, and so on. But what are they, and what do they mean?

The *Dow Jones Industrial Average* is the grandpa of all major stock indexes. The Dow, as it is popularly called, is a composite of stock prices of 30 major industrial companies. These are all mature, long-established firms who are consumer-oriented. In short, they are all household names: American Express, IBM, Sears Roebuck, Coca-Cola, and so on. Since the Dow does not include any new, small, or medium-sized companies, it is no longer as directly indicative of the market's overall behavior as it once was. Dow-Jones maintains three other averages in addition to the Industrials. These are the *Dow-Jones Transposition Average,* the *Dow-Jones Utilities Average,* and the *Dow-Jones Composite Average* (of 65 representative stocks). But *the* Dow-Jones Average constantly quoted by the media everyday is the Dow-Jones Industrial Average, the Dow.

Since the Dow Industrials are no longer representative of the broad market, many savvy investors and professional money managers choose to measure the performance of their investments against other, more representative indexes such as *Standard and Poor's 500 Composite Stock Price Index* (the S&P 500). The S&P tracks 500 large companies traded on the New York and American stock exchanges, as well as over-the-counter. The stocks in the S&P 500 represent a broad cross-section of 70% of the total market and are weighted by market value. In other words, each individual stock influences the index in proportion to its importance in the market. This leads to subtler shifts than what one finds in the unweighted Dow. Generally speaking, the popular wisdom is that the S&P 500 will move 1 point for every 7-point move in the Dow.

Additional indexes include the *Russell 2000*, the *Wilshire Small Cap Index*, the *Ibbotson Small Company Index*, the *Wilshire 4500*, and the *NASDAQ Composite Index*. The *Russell 2000* includes 2,000 small-capitalization stocks. The *Wilshire Small Cap Index* includes about 250 such securities. The *Ibbotson Small Company Index* incorporates approximately 2,700 firms: the bottom 20% (from a capitalization point of view) of stocks traded on the New York Stock Exchange. The *Wilshire 4500* incorporates all U.S. exchange-traded stocks, minus those included in the S&P 500. Finally, the *NASDAQ Composite Index* includes approximately 4,000 small- and medium-cap companies, all of them traded in the Over-The-Counter (OTC) market. (See the section below entitled *The Various Stock Exchanges* for an explanation of the various exchanges, including the New York Stock Exchange and the OTC market.)

INVESTMENT CATEGORIES OF COMMON STOCKS

Various stock categories have been promulgated over the years: growth stocks, defensive stocks, cyclical stocks, and so on. It is important to know and understand these terms. But it is also important to understand that these labels—like most other labels in business or in life—are not mutually exclusive. Just as my physician can be both a physician and a tennis player, just as my home can be both a fortress and refuge, just as a bit of landscape can be both a pristine wilderness and a battleground, so can a stock be a growth and a speculative stock, and an income and a Blue Chip stock.

Growth stocks are shares in firms that are growing in sales *and earnings* faster than the general economy. These firms tend to be ones that take an aggressive, pragmatic, pro-active approach to their future. They tend to be innovation-oriented and technology-driven. And they tend to have undesirable Yields and horrible P/E Ratios. Why? Because they often invest the majority of their earnings into future expansion. Over time, however, as their businesses build, so do the values of shares in these firms.

This being said, it should be obvious that Growth Stocks are for the long-term investor. This is even more clearly the case when we take a moment to understand the short-term combustibility of these issues.

Because of their nature, Growth Stocks tend to go up in value faster than do other stocks. However, at the first sign that a firm's earnings might slow or not be quite up to expectations, the stock is likely to plummet. Recovery is usually in the wings. But one must have the patience and leisure to wait out the depressed stock price. In other words, short-term money that you will have to call on at some point to meet day-to-day expenses does not belong in the stock market generally, and most especially, does not belong in either Growth or Speculative issues.

One of the best ways to find Growth Stocks is to browse Standard & Poor's regularly updated list of "200 Rapid Growth Stocks." This list routinely highlights the "cream" of some 6,000 issues.

Unlike Growth Stocks, *Income Stocks* tend to have attractive P/Es and high yields. Though they have a track record of reliable and generous dividend income they, in turn, don't go up in value as quickly as Growth Stocks.

As always, the truth is not all in the numbers. Just because a stock has an attractive P/E and a high yield at the moment does not mean it automatically qualifies as a good, long-term Income Stock. It might be that the price of the stock is low because of long-term concerns about the strength of the firm despite balance-sheet results that are attractive in the short-term. Does the firm have a "lock" on a market that will disappear with the demise of a patent scheduled to expire one year from now? If so, then you are not looking at an Income Stock when you look at the high dividend-return as compared to a low asking price for the stock. You are looking at something quite different. You are looking at a long-term albatross. You know, the dead kind you tie around your neck.

But genuine Income Stocks are just the thing for some investors.

The classic Income Stocks are those of utility companies. With established franchises and regulated prices, these predictable stocks are perhaps the most reliable dividend-delivery systems Wall Street has to offer. And with their stable share prices, the utility stocks fall into yet another broad category: *Defensive Stocks.* These are stocks that tend to hold their value even in periods of declining markets. Just as utility stocks and other Defensive Stocks do not regularly shoot up in value, neither do they dive down.

Another category of stock is, at first glance, a seemingly conflicted and cross-purposed hybrid. This is the category of *Growth and Income Stocks*. Growth *and* Income? Sounds like a contradiction in terms. But, in fact, there is no contradiction here because the growth we are talking about is moderate as opposed to robust, and the same goes for the income. The growth is somewhat less than you will see in pure Growth issues; the dividend yield is somewhat less than what you will see in pure Income issues. In the best of all possible worlds, the dividend yield and increasing asking-price on Growth and Income Stocks combine to deliver a profitable investment over time.

The antithesis of the Defensive Stock is the *Cyclical Stock*. This is a stock for a company with earnings that fluctuate sharply with the overall business cycle of a country, a region, or industry. Generally, the firm is one that does splendidly in a robust economy, and terribly is a distressed economy. Defensive stocks, such as income-generating utilities, can remain strong in recessionary times of high inflation and high interest. In such dire economic times as was represented by the "Carter" economy of double-digit inflation and interest, people still needed to buy electricity and natural gas to light and heat their homes. But they did *not* need to buy automobiles. Thus, the stock of Ford and other car companies suffered, as did the stock of all other such cyclical firms. As Wall Street legend Peter Lynch always says when the topic of cyclicals comes up, "What goes round comes round."

Blue Chip Stocks are high-grade issues of major, well-established companies with extensive track records of earnings growth and dividend payment *regardless of shifts in economic climate*. Here we are talking IBM, DuPont, General Electric, Proctor & Gamble, and so on. All of the stocks in the Dow-Jones Industrials Average are Blue Chip. Firms are not necessarily considered Blue Chip forever. There is no tenure in the financial markets. Stocks of firms of troubled industries, such as railroading and US domestic steelmaking, once considered Blue Chip are no more.

International Stocks are the Ameri-centric (to coin a phrase) term that Americans apply to stock in all "offshore" firms whether they are based in Tokyo, London, or Paris. While these shares may be traded directly on many European and Asian exchanges, US investors need to buy *American Depository Receipts (ADRs)* in order to trade international or foreign stocks. These ADRs are issued by US banks, which act as trustees and hold the underlying foreign shares represented by the ADR. Generally, ADRs are only available for the very largest "foreign" companies such as Sanyo (Japan), Toyota (Japan), Glaxo Holdings (Great Britain), and British Petroleum. ADRs are denominated in US dollars. They are traded on the New York Stock Exchange and over-the-counter and can be purchased through any broker. Note that in addition to being subject to the usual uncertainties of the marketplace, ADRs have an additional risk. They are greatly impacted by currency fluctuations, especially fluctuations in the relationship of the dollar to the Japanese yen and the British pound.

BLUE CHIP VERSUS TECHNOLOGY STOCKS

Something has to be said here about the historic rise in the "new-economy stocks" making people rich. The NASDAQ has grown at an inspiring rate for the last couple of years. People are buying like crazy hoping to be the next Yahoo or America Online shareholder of escalating price per shares. But the consensus regarding technology stocks seems to be that investors need to find companies that trade at reasonable prices while finding success in their niche. And in comparison to Blue Chip stocks, technology stocks can have a harder time bouncing back after a downturn if they fall behind technologically. Blue Chip stocks continue to live up to their reputation of standing the test of time. Does that mean you should dump your tech stocks? Of course not! Continuing globalization and technological advancements will continue to propel both types. Just *diversify* your stock portfolio. Risks are involved in any investment. Do your research.

Money *Magazine*

Money magazine is on of the best-known personal-finance magazines. Each month, *Money* brings you insight on stocks, funds, bonds, retirement plans, mortgages, and more. To try out a free issue of *Money* magazine, visit the Money Web at *http:// www.moneymag.com*, as shown below in Figure 4.1, or send your request to Money, Box 61790, Tampa, Florida 33661-1790. If you enjoy the magazine, do nothing, and you will receive the next 10 issues for $26.96. If, for any reason, you are not completely satisfied with the magazine, simply write "CANCEL" on your invoice and pay nothing.

Figure 4.1 The Money *magazine Web site.*

THE VARIOUS STOCK EXCHANGES

The stocks of virtually all major companies of the world are traded on two primary exchanges, both of which are located in New York City (by Wall Street, of course.) The oldest of these two exchanges, the **New York Stock Exchange**, is also sometimes called the *NYSE* or the *Big Board*. The NYSE lists approximately 2,000 of the largest, oldest, and most well-known companies in the world. The other major exchange, the **American Stock Exchange (the Amex)**, lists the stock issues of a thousand or so younger and smaller firms.

Despite the large shadows of the NYSE and the Amex, the fact is that these days a great deal of the real action of Wall Street actually happens in the **Over-the-Counter Market (OTC)**. Here you will find the stocks for 20,000 or so of the very newest, fastest-growing companies on the planet.

A great many of these firms are technology-oriented. Thus, it is somewhat appropriate that the OTC market is not an actual physical marketplace as are the floors of the NYSE and the Amex, but rather a virtual marketplace (or a cyber marketplace, if you will). The OTC market is maintained on a national computer network. The trading results for OTC stocks—many of them the issues of small-cap firms—appear in newspapers under the name of the *National Association of Securities Dealers Automated Quotations (NASDAQ)*. (Note that the *Wall Street Journal* and a few other papers with heavy financial orientations list the NASDAQ results under a different heading: *National Market Issues*.)

Around the world there are numerous other stock exchanges where NYSE, Amex, and NASDAQ issues are actively traded. Many of these stock exchanges have their own Web sites, all of them listed in the Internet Resources section of this chapter.

CHOOSING A BROKER

Although it is *possible* to trade stocks without a broker (see the section below entitled Doing It Without a Broker), as a practical matter the typical investor will find it hard to live without one. The question usually is not whether or not you need a broker, but rather whether you need a *full service* or a *discount* broker. The differences between these two animals are significant, and extend far beyond mere price.

A *full-service broker* is the type you will find within the offices of Merrill Lynch, Dean Witter, and other such large firms. These brokers do more than just execute trades of stocks and bonds. They offer investment advice. And they have their firm's impressive research to back up their trade recommendations. But you pay for this research and expertise in the form of per-trade commissions that can be as much as 4.5 times that of commissions charged by discount brokers. On the other hand, if you don't feel like doing your own homework and you need the advice of the full-service broker, the high commissions are generally worth it.

Note, however, that it is *always a mistake* to blindly follow the recommendations of a full-service broker without at least doing *some* independent investigating of a stock and its prospects. Why? Because this is an imperfect world, and the law of the economic jungle says only the fittest survive. And part of being unfit is not being alert. No one—I repeat, *no one*—cares as much or will *ever* care as much about the safety of your investment capital as you do.

Most full-service brokers are completely honest and eminently intelligent people who will always do their best to make sure a client maximizes his or her return in the market. The majority of full-service brokers realize, quite smartly, that the only way for the brokerage to make the most money possible in the long-term is for the client to make the most money possible in the long-term.

However, you should nevertheless at least double-check the basic numbers, information, and logic behind a broker's stock recommendations before diving in with precious capital. And you should also be on the alert for a broker who might be "churning" your account. This is a broker who recommends numerous buy and sell orders that result in limited or no return to you while generating terrific commission income for the broker. At the first sign of this you should cry foul in letters to the Federal Securities and Exchange Commission and your local, state-level securities regulators. (See the section below entitled *The Broker's Better Business Bureau and Other Resources*.)

Beyond full-service brokers, the other type of broker is the type you will find in the offices of Charles Schwab or Fidelity or any one of a number of other firms that loudly and proudly declare themselves as *discount brokerages*. A discount broker has no backup infrastructure of extensive financial research behind him or her. And thus, he or she will not be offering you any advice whatsoever. The discount broker is there for one purpose only: to execute buy and sell orders issued by you once *you* have done your research and arrived at your investment decisions. *You* are the research department. And since you are doing so much of the work, you will pay considerably less per trade to a discount broker than you would to a full-service broker.

Fortune *Magazine*

Fortune magazine is a monthly magazine whose articles detail all aspects of business and finance. Within *Fortune*, you will find insights on what makes the world's largest companies (the Fortune 500) tick, what companies are the "up and comers," and specifics on all financial markets. Visit their Web site shown below in Figure 4.2 at *http://www.fortune.com*.

Figure 4.2 The Fortune *magazine Web site.*

THE BROKER'S BETTER BUSINESS BUREAU AND OTHER RESOURCES

To check out a broker's reputation before you entrust him or her with your money, contact the outfit that I call the "Broker's Better Business Bureau." Actually, the organization's name is the National Association of Securities Dealers (NASD), and they have a toll-free number: 800-289-9999. The good people at the NASD can tell you if there has every been any disciplinary action taken by the NASD against a specific broker or the broker's firm, whether federal or state regulators have ever filed charges against the broker or the broker's firm, and whether any criminal convictions have ever been handed down. Note that though you may phone-in your inquiry to the NASD using the "800" number above, they will invariably respond to your inquiry by letter. And their response will not include reference to any *pending complaints* against a broker or his or her firm.

If you have a bad experience with a broker yourself, if you suspect you are being cheated or "churned," or if orders are executed which you did not request or approve, you should contact your state securities and exchange regulators and also the *Federal Securities and Exchange Commission (SEC),* Consumer Affairs Branch, 450 Fifth Street, NW, Washington, DC 20549. Note that all complaints must be in writing *on paper.* We are talking snail-mail. As of yet, e-mail to the SEC simply does not cut it. Neither does a telephone call. They do, however, have a Web site where you will find some information of interest: *http://www.sec.gov.*

BUYING AND SELLING WITH A BROKER: LEARNING THE LINGO

After you have chosen and established an account with a broker, the process of issuing "buy" and "sell" orders is fairly simple, assuming you have first mastered the lingo of Wall Street. I am talking about not just *market orders* but also *GTC orders*, and *stop-loss orders*.

A *Market Order* is the most basic form of communication you will ever have with your broker. This is your message to your broker to buy or sell securities at the best price possible given present market conditions. Your market order instructs your broker to buy or sell "at the market." In other words, you are assigning your broker authority to buy or sell at whatever price the market will bear: at the best price he or she believes can possibly be gotten.

You will often have occasions when you will want to convey more explicit instructions than a simple market order. You will want to set some parameters for the terms of the buying or selling that will be going on in your name and with your cash. You will want to give your broker less discretion. Thus the other elements of Wall Street lingo come into play.

You will sometimes want to use a *Limit Order*. This comforting breed of order is one to consider using in an uncertain market where prices are fluctuating dramatically and quickly. Using a limit order, you can indicate the upward limit of the price you are willing to pay for a given security, when buying. When selling, you can indicate a downward limit: the least you are willing to take in exchange of the securities you are offering for sale.

There are also time constraints that you can impose upon an order to buy or sell. Unless otherwise specified, a buy or sell order is considered an *Open Order*, or a *Good Till Canceled (GTC)* order. You may, however, designate your buy or sell order as a *Day Order*. This type of order would stipulate that it is good only for the day on which it is issued.

Another safety-oriented type of order is called the *Stop Loss Order*. This type of order is designed, obviously, to minimize your risk of loss. It instructs your broker to dump all or a number of your shares of a given security should the market price fall below a specific defined dollar amount. Inherent in the Stop Loss Order is the fact that your purpose is to stop or slow your losses in a particular equity given a particular market situation.

Selling Short

You never want to sell yourself short, as they say, but you may sometimes want to sell a stock short. It depends upon how inherently pessimistic you are, and how risky you like your stock-trading to be. Because selling short is very risky business.

Selling short involves selling stocks you do not currently own in the hope that the stock will soon drop in value. With selling short, the classic buy low/sell high formula for stock investment is simply reversed: sell high and *then* buy low. When investors buy a security with the hope that it will go up in value, they have assumed what, in the parlance of Wall Street, is called a *long* position. When they do the reverse, they've assumed a *short* position.

With most brokerage accounts, settlement for trades is generally expected by the end of the third day of business after the trade. If the investor has purchased shares, then he or she is expected to pay the broker for them within three business days after the trade. Likewise, if the broker has sold shares on behalf of the investor, the broker is expected to deposit the proceeds of the sale into that investor's account within three business days after the trade. And the investor must deliver the sold shares within the same time frame.

Thus, within the three-day window, the short-seller will often *borrow* shares of stock with which to make delivery on shares sold short. Usually these shares may be borrowed from the short-seller's broker. Short-sellers are in turn responsible for making good on any dividends or splits that are declared on stock that they have borrowed.

So long as the price of a given stock actually declines, the short-seller is in good shape. However, if the stock goes up, the short-seller is in proverbial hot water. In fact, he or she will be taking a bath. Clearly, this aggressive and risky investment policy is for people who have both the knowledge and the cash-flow to support it and for no-one else.

Free (Delayed) Quotes, Free Charts, Free Indices, and More On-Line!

MarketWatch is a real-time quote service where you can find historical data, breaking headline news, delayed quotes, information on Canadian and international stocks, and more. For more information, visit the Data Broadcasting Corporation (DBC) Web site, shown below in Figure 4.3, at *http://www.dbc.com*.

Figure 4.3 The DBC Web site.

MARGIN ACCOUNTS

The vast majority of investors open what are called *cash accounts* with their brokers. This, obviously, means that cash settlement is called for within five days of all trades.

Some investors, however, maintain *margin accounts* with their brokers (or with a commercial bank). What this means, basically, is that you don't play with your own money. You borrow money with which to buy stocks, putting up only a portion of your own cash for each trade. Interest is due on the principal of every margin loan, and should the stocks you purchase on margin decline (or not grow in value at a rate higher than the interest you must pay on your margin debt), you will take a loss. And it can often be a substantial loss.

If your name is Louis Rukeyser or Speed Vogel and you really, really, really know what you are doing, then feel free to play fast-and-loose with a margin account. Otherwise stick to cash. It is a great "reality check."

THE GOOD NEWS THAT IS BAD NEWS

There is an old saying that Wall Street hates good news. With tidings of a booming economy, low unemployment, and robust new home sales inevitably comes the very real possibility that the Federal Reserve, anxious to slow growth and cut inflation, will raise interest rates. Wall Street hates this kind of good economic news precisely because of what it does to interest rates.

Higher interest rates hurt Wall Street two ways. First of all, higher interest rates, of course, increase the cost of money for businesses, and thereby impact the bottom-line of virtually every corporation in the NYSE, Amex, and OTC markets. Second, higher interest rates conspire to offer investors attractive options other than stocks. When interest rates on bonds and money market funds reach a certain level, large amounts of money can sometimes flow out of the stock market. And why not? Why risk money in the stock market when one can get a high return in the relatively safe bond- or money-markets? And that, kids, is why Wall Street hates good economic news.

> ### End of Day Historical Stock Market Quotes
>
> Primate Software, Inc. provides end of day and historical stock market quotes. They have over 130,000 symbols on stocks, indices, bonds, funds, futures, and options. By subscribing to Primate Software, Inc.'s on-line service, you can access data using a toll-free number and download unlimited quotes per month. You will also receive a

FREE Window Charting Program (CHART MONKEY!) with over 12 technical studies including Bollinger Bands, Stochastics, MACD, RSI, Moving Averages, and Candlesticks, etc. Visit the Web site, shown below in Figure 4.5, and try it for FREE. Download the software and see how easy it is to use. For more information on Primate Software, Inc., call 714-879-8023 or go to *http://www.primate.com*.

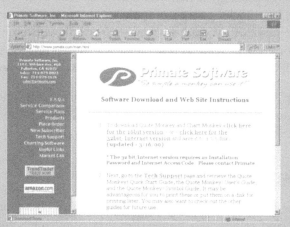

Figure 4.5 The Primate Software, Inc. Web site.

The Spear Report

The *Spear Report* is a consensus system that provides a collection of seven top-ranked (by *Hulbert Financial Digest*) newsletters considered the backbone to maintaining an Internet portfolio. Visit their Web site at *http://www.spearreport.com*, shown below in Figure 4.6, and get four free special reports and 13 weekly issues for $39. For more information on these newsletters, call 800-491-7119.

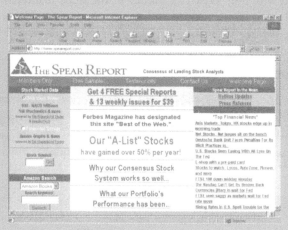

Figure 4.6 The Spear Report Web site.

DOING IT WITHOUT A BROKER: DIRECT-PURCHASE AND DIVIDEND REINVESTMENT PLANS

You don't need a broker to buy stock. Let me repeat that. *You don't need a broker to buy stock.* At least you don't need a broker to buy *some* stock.

A number of companies—more than a thousand of them, in fact—accept direct investment in their stock and also offer dividend reinvestment schemes that can be quite appealing. Under such plans, you are allowed to purchase a certain amount of stock annually, direct from a firm, without using a broker, or having to pay a broker's commission. You may also be allowed to reinvest your quarterly dividends directly back into stock equity. Some firms will even provide you with a small discount on shares purchased from dividend reinvestment. So not only do you save on the broker's commission, but you compound your savings with a discount from "street" price.

Your broker won't tell you about direct-stock-purchase options and dividend-reinvestment plans because your broker can't make any money on them. He or she is superfluous to the deal. He or she is as unnecessary as a raincoat in the Mojave Desert.

To enroll in a firm's direct-purchase or dividend-reinvestment plan, you must first own at least one share of the firm's stock as purchased through a traditional broker channel. And the stock must be in your name. (In other words, if your broker is holding the stock in the brokerage firm name, you must file the paperwork and have the registration changed to list yourself as owner.) Once that is done, talk to the firm's investor-relations office about enrollment for direct-purchase and dividend reinvestment. A *few* firms (including Exxon and W.R. Grace & Co.) will agree to sell you your initial shares directly. But most expect you to already be an investor when you knock on their door.

Note that many corporate Web sites contain information relating to direct-purchase and dividend reinvestment plans.

An Excellent Guide to Dividend Reinvestment Plans

If you are interested in learning more about the companies that offer dividend reinvestment plans, you should get a copy of *The MoneyPaper Guide to Dividend Reinvestment Plans* from Temper of the Times Communications, Inc. The guide specifies the requirements for more than 900 companies that offer DRP's. For more information on the guide, call 800-388-9993.

MetaStock for Windows

MetaStock for Windows provides Windows-based software you can use to download stock and investment information for charting and analysis using very powerful built-in software. Using its built-in powerful software, *MetaStock for Windows* lets you chart trends, apply investment indicators that range from Absolute Breadth Index, to the Candlestick, to the Zig Zag indicator. Using the downloader software, you can get your stock data from Reuters Datalink. If you have no idea how to use *MetaStock for Windows*, you can get Martin Pring's MetaStock Tutorial that teaches you how to use *MetaStock for Windows*. To learn more about this software, contact equis at 800-882-3040 or visit their Web site, shown below in Figure 4.7, at *http://www.equis.com*.

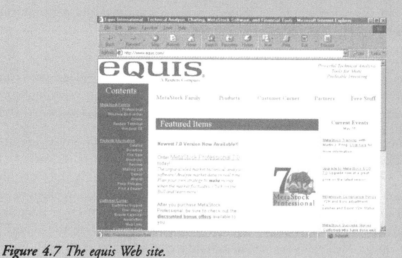

Figure 4.7 The equis Web site.

TRADING STOCKS ON THE INTERNET

Virtually every large and small brokerage company now has a presence on the World Wide Web, with more and more such establishments coming on-line daily. A few years ago, online trading made its debut and has since captured over 30% of all NASDAQ trading. Online trading is the most efficient way to trade if you want low commissions and daily account information with access to free services. Several discount brokerages have emerged to the forefront including Ameritrade, Charles Schwab, DATEK, DLJdirect, E*Trade, Merrill Lynch and Suretrade.

Just to give you an idea, DATEK is one of the pioneers in Internet trading. They pride themselves on offering some of the fastest executions, as well as, real-time account information including updating your portfolio in real-time. You have free access to charts, news, stock or fund reports, and trades commissions for all types of orders (market, limit and stop) are $9.99 up to 5,000 shares. They offer extended hours trading, account demos, and you can reach Customer Support 24-hours a day, seven days a week.

If you are trading a 100 shares or a 100,000 shares, Ameritrade offers market orders for only $8.00, and limit orders are $5.00 more. They offer investment tools, including free real-time quotes, customizable charts, market summaries, research tools, customer profiles, and earnings estimates. After opening an account, you can trade online, by Interactive Voice Response (IVR) telephone system, through a broker, or on a wireless phone. Like most others, their customer service representatives can be reached all day, every day, and if you visit the Web site, you can participate in an online trading demo. Suretrade offers much of the same services, but charges $7.95 for market orders.

There are a few drawbacks to online trading. Brokerages require a minimum of $1,000 to $20,000 to open an account depending on your needs, and although you get discount trade commissions, it can be quite time-consuming. With discount brokerages, you have to do your homework—that means research by yourself. If you are willing to make the effort, you can be quite successful.

(You can find more detailed information on Charles Schwab, E*Trade, and Merrill Lynch towards the end of this chapter among the Internet resources.)

On-Line Trading from Siebert

Muriel Siebert & Co. Inc. has been a member of the New York Stock Exchange since 1967, longer than any other discount brokerage firm. Using Siebert Online, you can get real-time stock quotes and account information, trade stocks, options, and mutual funds. They charge $14.95 per trade for market or limit orders. For more information, call 800-USA-0711 or visit their Web site at *http://www,siebertnet.com.*

On-Line Trading from The Net Investor

The Net Investor is a discount brokerage firm developed specifically to service investors via the Internet. Using *The Net Investor*, you can obtain on-line quotes, news, stock charts, and company financial information. In addition, you can place orders on-line. *The Net Investor* is a small company who answers their phones within three rings. You will always talk directly to a human being, and since they are only at one location, any issue you have question with, can be handled and resolved right then and there. If you are just getting used to trading on-line and still have concerns or apprehension, you can call in your order. They have no minimum for setting up an account, and trades start at $19.95 plus a penny per share or 4% of the total cost, whichever is lower. For more information about setting up an account, call 800-880-4693 or visit their Web site, shown below in Figure 4.8, at *http://www.netinvestor.com*.

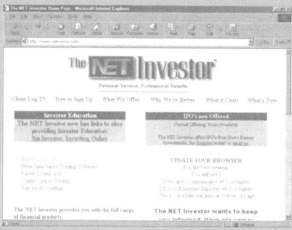

Figure 4.8 The Net Investor Web site.

On-Line Trading Using Trader's Access

Trader's Access is a Windows-based program from T.B.S.P. Inc., with which you can download quotes, chart trends, and trade stocks, options, futures, funds, and indices on-line. Using the software you can download daily, weekly, and monthly trading information for over 120,000 symbols. To get started, you pay a one-time membership fee of $24.95. In return, you will get the software you need to connect to and download information from T.B.S.P. databases. Then, for a monthly charge, you can download data as you need. For more information on Trader's Access, call 714-721-8603 or check out their Web site at *http://www.tbspinc.com*, as shown below in Figure 4.9.

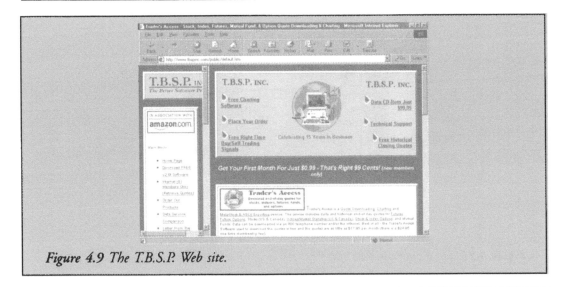

Figure 4.9 The T.B.S.P. Web site.

On-Line Trading Using PC Financial Network

PC Financial Network (founded in 1988) is a service of Donaldson, Lufkin, & Jenrette Securities Corporation, the firm that handles 10% of the daily volume at the New York Stock Exchange. Using *PC Financial Network*, users can buy and sell stocks, bonds, options, CDs, precious metals, and more. Over 500,000 *PC Financial Network* customers trade on-line with an individual account and no broker. You can download great software right from their Web site that will help you run your portfolio. They do not charge a minimum to open an account, and the standard commission is $20 per trade up to 1,000 shares, plus $.02 per share thereafter. For more information call 800-825-5723 or visit their Web site at *http://www.dljdirect.com.*

On-Line Trading Using Accutrade

Accutrade is a Windows-based (although there are DOS and Mac versions) service with which you can make trades, get quotes, manage your accounts, view positions, and more. Booklets are available for free on topics such as Tax Planning, Retirement Planning, and Estate Planning. Call 800-228-3011 to request the booklet of your choice. For more information about *Accutrade*, visit their Web site, shown in Figure 4.10, at *http://www.accutrade.com.*

Figure 4.10 The Accutrade Web site.

Use Analyst Watch on the Internet to Learn What Experts Think

Analyst Watch is an on-line service with which you can access the daily analysis performed by the Chicago-based Zacks Investment Research gatherers. You will find company profiles, buy/hold/sell recommendations from over 2,700 analysts. Using the on-line reports, you can quickly list growth companies whose growth exceed 30% a year, low-priced stocks priced under $10 but with attractive P/E ratios, and more. You can select from 16 individual research models. For more information, call 800-399-6659 or visit their Web site at *http://www.zacks.com*, shown below in Figure 4.11.

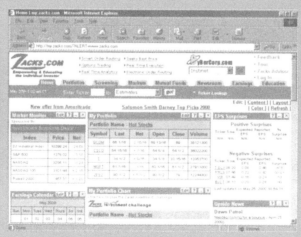

Figure 4.11 The Analyst Watch Web site.

Using Telescan to Assist Your Investment Decisions

Telescan Investors Platform (TIP) consists of software programs that utilize the power of Windows and the Internet to create charting capabilities and portfolio management. In addition to the Telescan Investors Platform, they offer ProSearch, a software program that lets you search through stocks to filter out key performers. For more information on Telescan, visit their Web site, shown below in Figure 4.12, at *http://www.telescan.com* or call 800-748-8990.

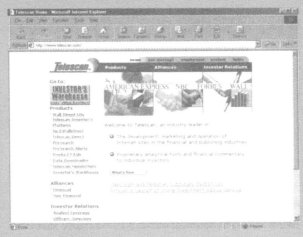

Figure 4.12 The Telescan Web site.

ONE LAST TIP: WATCH YOUR MOUTH

That's right. Just watch your mouth. *Yes you! I mean you! Mind your manners!* And remember what you learned at your grandma's knee: If you don't have anything nice to say about a company, its staff, or its stock, then just don't say anything at all. Or at least make sure what you are saying is true.

This is the motto you should have in mind when engaging in on-line chat. Otherwise you might find yourself sued for libel.

That's right. It has happened before, and it'll happen again. Don't let it happen to you.

Recently a brokerage firm successfully sued *Prodigy* over damning but false statements about that brokerage that were posted to *Prodigy's* "Money Talks" bulletin board. A *Prodigy* "chatter" posted a message to the bulletin board falsely claiming that the brokerage in question, and its president, were involved in "major criminal fraud."

This was not the case. There is, in fact, absolutely no history of criminal charges being filed against the brokerage.

Prodigy wound up apologizing in order to avoid continuation of the lawsuit. The person who posted the message got away with it, simply because he or she was anonymous and had swiped someone else's log-on. But the libeled brokerage tried very hard to find the source of the message and would definitely have filed a lawsuit against the person who posted the message had they been able to find him or her.

So be careful out there!

Interested in Stocks Priced Under $3 a Share?

If you are interested in low-priced stocks, specifically stocks that are priced under $3 a share, you might want to check out the Bowser Report, a newsletter that examines stocks priced for $3 a share or less. To obtain a free copy of the newsletter, call 757-877-5979.

Also, you may want to consider the *Savvy Investor* newsletter that features stocks priced under $10 a share. To obtain a free copy of this newsletter, call 409-291-8004 or visit their Web site, shown below in Figure 4.13, at *http://www.savvyinvestor.com*.

Figure 4.13 The Savvy Investor Web site.

In addition to the newsletters discussed above, you may want to check out *Market Central*. It features free investment newsletters, stock quotes, news, mutual fund information, on-line stock brokers, world markets, IPO reports, investment guides, and an investment bookstore. *Market Central* provides the Stock of the Day and Insider Trading Reports. Visit their Web site, shown below in Figure 4.14, at *http://www.marketcentral.com*.

Figure 4.14 Market Central's Web site.

Company Profiles

Avenue Technologies publishes comprehensive company profiles on 25,000 leading U.S. public and private and international companies. Their company profiles include recent news on new products, key executives, financial summaries, and industry comparisons. For more information, call 800-989-4636 or check out the Avenue Technologies Web site at *http://www.avetech.com*, shown below in Figure 4.15.

Figure 4.15 The Avenue Technologies Web site.

Understanding the Dates by Which Companies Pay Dividends

If you own a stock or plan to purchase a stock of a company that issues dividends, there are three dates that will be important to you.

The *pay date* is the date on which the company will issue (pay) the dividend. In other words, it is the day you will get the money (or the date that the company puts your dividend check in the mail).

The *record date* is a date that precedes the pay date, normally by two weeks, by which you must own the stock in order to receive the dividend. You must own the stock on or before the record date.

The *ex-dividend date* is a date such that your purchase of the stock will not include the dividend (such as the day following the record date). In other words, your purchase of the stock would be without (ex-) the dividend.

INTERNET RESOURCES FOR STOCK INVESTORS

As you surf the World Wide Web, you may encounter sites that discuss stocks, the international markets, on-line trading, and more. The following site list should help you locate the resources you need.

THE AMERICAN STOCK EXCHANGE

http://www.amex.com

The home page for the AMEX comprises a great place to get information on action at the exchange as well as details on virtually all of the 800 companies listed. The site includes details on the AMEX average as well as reports on activity related to the day's most active stocks, the day's largest percentage gainers, and the day's largest percentage decliners. With regard to options, the site includes details on the day's unit volume, the day's dollar volume, advancers and decliners, most active series, and most active classes.

As a bonus, the site includes a complete hypertext library of AMEX press releases going back more than a year, links to the Web sites of all listed companies, as well as a quick-lookup tool for ticker symbols. View their Web site below in Figure 4.16.

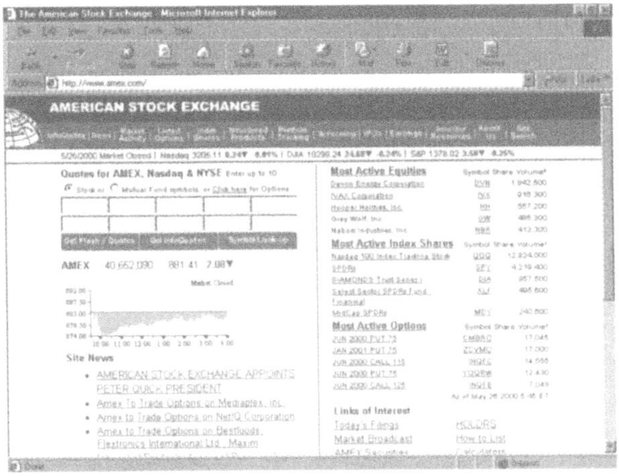

Figure 4.16 The American Stock Exchange Web site.

ASIA FINANCIAL NEWS

http://www.asia-inc.com

Come here for the latest Asia-related financial news supplied by the Knight-Ridder Financial News Service, as well as end-of-the-day Asia Stock Market Closings supplied by Lippo Securities, and a Daily Technical Commentary providing technical analysis of three major currency markets (US dollar versus yen, US dollar versus Deutschmark, and US dollar versus sterling), provided by Trendsetter/Reuters. The *Asia Financial News* also provides access to the Hong Kong Daily (Business) News Summary, an invaluable information service for investor interested in Hong Kong and related business. As this is being written, they are in the process of rebuilding their Web site, shown below in Figure 4.17. But you can still check out their award-winning magazine and get a complimentary copy on-line.

Figure 4.17 Asia Financial News Web site.

BRIEFING: CONCISE MARKET ANALYSIS AND REAL-TIME QUOTES

http://www.briefing.com

Charter Media's *Briefing* provides valuable market information to help you make informed investment and trading decisions. Updates are posted throughout the day as developments occur. Economic and market forecasts are included in the mix, along with real time stock quotes, averages, and futures and options information. *Briefing* is of similar design and content to real time information products used by top Wall Street traders. Such services are delivered over quote terminals by suppliers that include Reuters, Quotron, Telerate, Knight-Ridder, and Bloomberg for subscription costs of $200 to $325 per year. *Briefing* brings these same services to the Internet at a fraction of that cost. Visit their Web site, shown below in Figure 4.18, for a free trial.

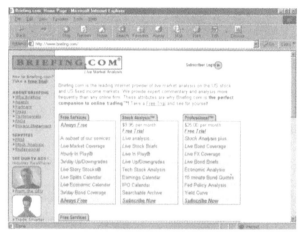

Figure 4.18 Briefing: Concise Market Analysis and Real-Time Quotes Web site.

CANADA NET FINANCIAL PAGES

http://www.mortgagemag.com/guide/c005/c005707

The *CanadaNet Financial Pages* provide an extensive information resource for investors in Canadian stocks and mutual funds. With regard to stocks, the site provides end-of-the-day stock quotes from the Toronto, Vancouver, Alberta, and Montreal Stock Exchanges. The stock quotes are archived daily and historical data is available going back more than a year. The databases can be searched by symbol, price change or volume traded. For many of the companies, you may access corporate profiles and annual reports that the database links to the company's ticker symbol and stock pricing in the database. With regard to mutual funds, you use a name-search tool to find the fund you want and then may get one month, three month, six month, or one to ten year results data for the fund for any period of dates you specify. Check out their Web site below in Figure 4.19.

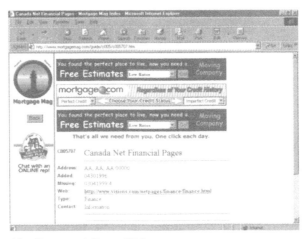

Figure 4.19 Canada Net Financial Pages Web site.

THE CHICAGO BOARD OPTIONS EXCHANGE

http://www.cboe.com

The Web site of the Chicago Board Options Exchange provides easy access to market statistics, news releases, new option listings, and research bulletins as well as background information about the exchange and employment opportunities there.

Don't know much about options? Then read Chapter 5. Feel like you need to know more about options after reading Chapter 5? Then check out the excellent hypertext tutorial located on this Web site entitled *Education*, which provides a basic introduction to options, a handy FAQ, a recommended reading list, and a glossary of options-related terms.

The site also gives details on CBOE options products, copies of literature, information available through the CBOE, and instructions for ordering additional documents. Come here also for information on LEAPS (Long-Term Equity Anticipation Securities), the educational extension of the exchange called The Options Institute, and more.

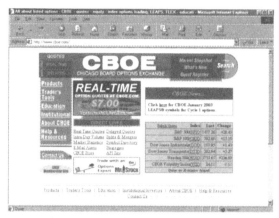

Figure 4.20 The Chicago Board Options Exchange Web site.

Take Advantage of Web-based Search Engines

To help you find information that is stored across the Web, you can visit special sites that provide *search engines* with which you can search for specific topics. Many users may have heard of Yahoo, the best-known search engine (much because of its explosive initial public offering). As it turns out, however, there are actually several excellent sites that offer search engines on the Web. To search information, start at one of the sites listed here:

http://www.yahoo.com

http://guide.infoseek.com

http://altavista.digital.com

http://www.mckinley.com

http://www.lycos.com

CNNFN FINANCIAL NEWS AND STOCK QUOTES

http://www.cnnfn.com

Now there's a new way to look at business from the company that changed the way you look at the world. This is CNNfn. It is more than a cable channel. It is a fantastic Web site.

At this Web site, as well as on cable "air", CNNfn brings the fast-moving CNN mission for timely and accurate reporting to business, presenting stories as they break with the accuracy and expert analysis that has become CNN's trademark.

CNNfn's news stories come from the same news engine that drives CNN, including reports from CNN's highly-regarded television business news anchors and correspondents.

In addition, for the Web site, they've assembled a dedicated CNNfn team of "multimedia business journalists" to bring you the latest information in new and exciting ways.

With regard to the stock, bond, and options markets, CNNfn has the numbers you don't want to wait for. As soon as they're available, CNNfn provides the major stock indices from around the world plus a place to search for stock quotes. CNNfn also provides currency rates along with commodities and interest information. In the daily hypertext *Small Business* column, CNNfn experts address such questions as how to grow your business, how to keep a big business strong, how to stay sane in the process, and other key points. Through case studies and interviews with the chieftains of industry, CNNfn reveals the techniques and personalities behind successful management.

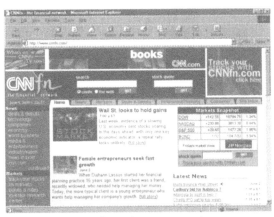

Figure 4.21 CNNfn Financial News and Stock Quotes Web site.

E*TRADE

http://www.etrade.com

Superior technology equals low commissions for on-line Internet trading with E*TRADE.

E*TRADE's founders were among the first to introduce electronic brokerage services to the individual investor. E*TRADE's focus on on-line trading has enabled them to create one of the most streamlined, efficient, and economical on-line brokerage systems available.

E*TRADE rewards you for taking control of your investments by offering one of the lowest commission structures in the industry. E*TRADE's electronic trading system uses leading-edge technology to connect you directly to the markets. Using your personal computer or touch-tone phone, you can place stock or option orders, get quotes, and track your portfolio 24-hours a day, seven days a week.

E*TRADE offers fast execution, comprehensive trading capabilities, and on-line portfolio management. Uninvested cash earns daily interest in one of E*TRADE's money market funds. And checking is free.

With an E*TRADE account you can buy and sell OTC and listed stocks and options directly from your personal computer or touch-tone phone. E*TRADE supports a wide range of order types, including market orders, limit (good-till canceled or day) orders, stop orders, and short sales. And you can review, change, or cancel your open orders at any time.

E*TRADE provides a time-stamped audit trail for all trades, orders, changes, cancellations and expirations while at the same time updating your on-line portfolio, tax records, broker-age transaction records, and trading records. You also receive printed trade confirmations and detailed statements summarizing your brokerage activity.

Interested in buying securities on margin? Assuming a $2,000 minimum account balance, E*TRADE allows you to borrow up to 50% of the current value of your marginable securities (those trading above $5.00). (All accounts, save for retirement, custodial and options ac-counts, can be opened as margin accounts). Options, of course, are not marginable.

E*TRADE will also handle options trading for you *if* you meet certain minimum net worth and income guidelines.

Want to get a feel for what it would be like to trade on-line via E*TRADE? Then stop off at the Web site and experience the Trading Demo that you'll find there. While you are at it, check out E*TRADE's extremely competitive pricing, and by all means treat yourself to a round of E*TRADE's great on-line Stock Market Game. View their Web site in Figure 4.22 below.

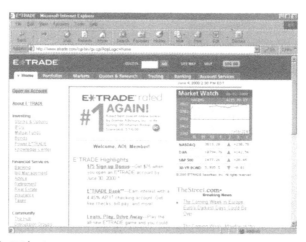

*Figure 4.22 E*Trade Web site.*

INSIDE WALL STREET

http://www.insidewallstreet.com

"*Inside Wall Street* is a free service for investors seeking information and ideas not readily available from most brokerages or research services on some of today's hottest growth stocks.

By presenting insights on undiscovered growth companies, *Inside Wall Street* strives to provide investors access to opportunities often overlooked."

So says the Sysop and he does not tell a lie. But also be advised that *Inside Wall Street* is provided by Continental Capital & Equity Corporation, "a full-service, investor relations firm." In short, the folks at Continental are on salary from the firms whose stocks they hype here.

This does not mean that the information you'll find here is suspect. As a matter of fact, it would be a federal offense for either Continental Capital or their clients to misrepresent the appeal-of or figures-related-to the stocks represented here. But nevertheless, you should be advised of Continental's special relationship with the companies whose stock you'll find discussed here.

That being said, you can learn a lot reviewing the various sections of this Web site which include:

- *Featured Companies* – New and emerging-growth companies. If you see something interesting, request a free corporate profile or else hotlink to the company's Web pages, press releases, or current stock quotation.

- *Hot Stock of the Week* – Provides a new pick every week, what it's trading at, and its set target.

- *IPO Information* – The latest IPO news including pricing data, recent filings, company summaries, and research.

- *Word on the Street* – Great articles on stocks and market forecasts from top financial editors and analysts.

- *Inside Wall Street's E-News* – Register for a free subscription to the Web's newest small-cap list server, exclusively from *Inside Wall Street*.

- *Special Situations* – Fact sheets and articles on special situation equity plays.

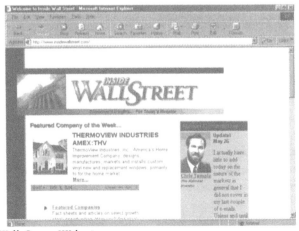

Figure 4.23 Inside Wall Street Web site.

INVEST-O-RAMA!

http://www.investorama.com

According to the Webmaster, *Invest-O-Rama!* is "the hippest directory of the best sites on the net for individual investors." And who are we to disagree? Check out:

- **Financial Guides** – includes the stock market, investing on-line, mutual funds, retirement, and DRIPS, just to name a few.

- **Invest-O-Rama! Essentials** – includes various research tools, free software, financial glossary and $1 Million Portfolio Tool.

- you will always get featured articles, but in 1999, *Invest-O-Rama!* added message boards, community tools, live chats, and more personalized features.

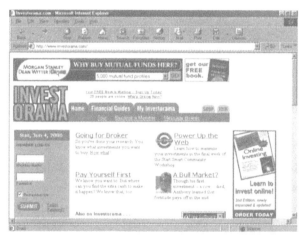

Figure 4.24 Invest-O-Rama! Web site.

JADCO STOCK CHARTS—FREE SAMPLES

http://www.jadco.com

Spend your time analyzing data, not gathering it. Jadco can supply you with real-time charts of price, earnings, and revenue data for more than 2,000 companies. FREE sample charts that you can access include Apple Computer, American Online, Compaq, Dell, Disney, Hewlett-Packard, GE, Intel, Lucent Technologies, McDonald's, Motorola, Microsoft, AT&T, and Microsoft. Plus, there is a chart for the Dow Jones Industrial Average. These charts include plots for historic price, earnings and revenue data. Some (including those for Microsoft and the other high-tech stocks) also include earnings and revenues projections.

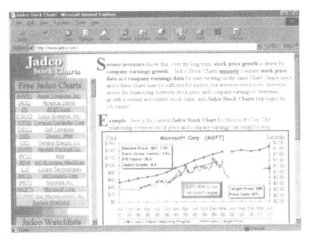

Figure 4.25 Jadco Web site.

MORGAN STANLEY DEAN WITTER ON-LINE

http://www.online.msdw.com

This Web site offers "the self-directed investor investment products, including stocks, bonds, options, and thousands of mutual funds, and access to quality information and superior customer service are additional benefits." Trade stocks bonds and mutual funds via the Internet with Morgan Stanley Dean Witter On-line. They offer a variety of account types to meet your needs, in addition to, innovative products, services, and industry leading financial information. They also have demos for placing stock orders and trading.

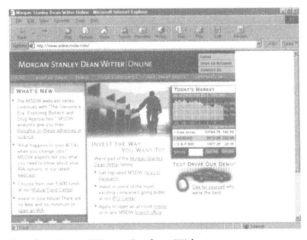

Figure 4.26 Morgan Stanley Dean Witter On-line Web site.

MERRILL LYNCH

http://www.merrill-lynch.ml.com

Merrill Lynch will soon offer on-line trading to their customers while trying to avoid the discount brokerage persona. You can register for a 30-day free research trial, and check out *Investor News*, which provides featured articles regarding business and government news stories.

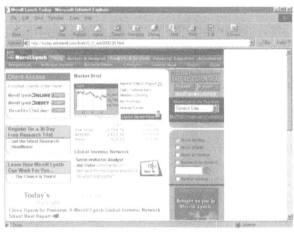

Figure 4.27 The Merrill Lynch Web site.

NASDAQ INFO

http://www.nasdaq.com

Say, what happened on the NASDAQ today? If you ask yourself that question any time after 5PM eastern time, just log onto this great Web site for the answer. You get reports and graphs giving you not only the closing NASDAQ composite index, but also total share volume, the NASDAQ-100 Index market data, and more. You'll find out how many stocks advanced, how many declined, how many remained unchanged, and how many hit new lows. And you'll get to review a fantastic graph tracking NASDAQ composite index value and volume for the last 12 months.

Special tools allow you to see which stocks are most active. If you are interested in a particular stock, use the Company Look-Up tool to find the company's stock symbol, and then get a closing quote as well as a market-value history. How much does all this great information cost? Nothing. Not a thing. Go for it.

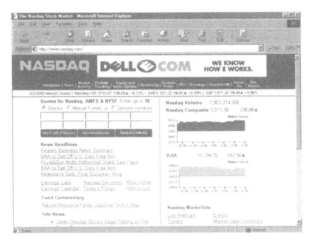

Figure 4.28 NASDAQ Web site.

THE MOTLEY FOOL: THE ON-LINE FINANCIAL FORUM FOR THE INDIVIDUAL INVESTOR

http://www.fool.com

Brothers Tom and Dave Gardner, who used to run the *Motley Fool* Web site on America Online but now have their own site on the World Wide Web, prescribe a moderate, value-oriented mode of investing that balances risk with caution. This not-so-foolish philosophy has earned the Gardners approximately 350,000 devotees (*Fools*) who log onto their Web site regularly to benefit from their highly-profitable wisdom.

The brothers Gardner urge investors to cast aside mutual funds, which seldom beat market averages. They similarly urge investors to fire their full-service brokers (who also seldom beat market average performance), and to take an extremely skeptical view of prognostications voiced by financial journalists and other high-priced Wall Street pundits. Instead, the brothers urge their followers to use the Internet to search out esoteric, but valuable, information on start-ups and other small-cap stocks. Most of all, they urge investors to GET IN EARLY. Smells speculative? NOT. The brothers recommend homework and patience in the spirit of Warren Buffet: Buy shares in companies you know well, and hold on to them.

Moreover, the Gardners preach that it is holy to stay away from derivatives (see Chapter 5). And they urge their devotees not to give more than one-third of their portfolio to any one particular stock.

One huge benefit of Fooldom is the Web site's bulletin boards. Here Fools from around the world exchange information on countless stocks too small to be tracked in a big way by the big time Wall Street "professionals."

Do yourself a favor and make a visit to the *Motley Fool*.

Figure 4.29 *The Motley Fool Web site.*

THE NEW YORK STOCK EXCHANGE

http://www.nyse.com

Come to the home page for the New York Stock Exchange (NYSE) for a detailed database of listed companies, a daily market summary, and late-breaking news from the Exchange. All the biggies are here of course on this grandpa of Exchanges: Dow Chemical, AT&T, American Express, Boeing, Eastman Kodak, and so on.

On-line daily market summaries include share volume, number of trades, and total daily value of trading (which is routinely above $16 billion for this $6.2 trillion Exchange). You also get year-to-date totals for average daily share volume, average daily trades, and average daily value of trading.

The on-line archives include a fully searchable NYSE company symbol guide. This is updated daily and contains the stock symbol, company name, specialist name, trading post, and trading panel of each issue. The guide can be searched by symbol, company name, or partial name. And results are hot-linked to appropriate corporate Web pages. A comma delimited text copy of the current file (containing stock symbol, company name, and issue description) is always available for free downloading.

Historically inclined? Then you might be interested in the extensive database file summarizing NYSE statistics related to trading activity for 1879 through 1966. These include data on daily reported volumes and daily closing values for NYSE indices. If you want the file you can download it here for free.

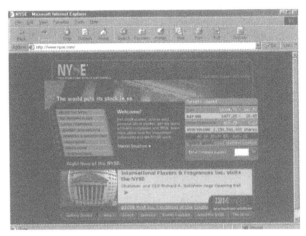

Figure 4.30 The New York Stock Exchange Web site.

Understanding Margin Accounts

When you open an account with a brokerage firm, you can, in general, establish two types of accounts: a cash account and a margin account. A *cash account* is one for which you must pay for each of your investments, in full, by the specified settlement date. With a *margin account*, on the other hand, you can borrow funds from your brokerage firm to cover a percentage of the total cost of your investment. Regulation T of the Federal Reserve currently limits the margin amount to 50% of your investment. When you borrow such funds from your brokerage firm, you then pay interest on your loan at a specified rate. Also, brokerage firms will apply additional borrowing limits (called maintenance requirements), often at 30% of your initial investment. Should the value of your securities drop below this 30% threshold, your brokerage firm will require you make a maintenance payment to bring your equity above the 30% amount.

THE NEWS PAGE: DAILY BUSINESS NEWS BY INDUSTRY

http://www.newspage.com

With thousands of categorized stories updated daily, *NewPage* is the Web's leading source of daily business news. Simply select from any number of industry categories and then select the news most relevant to you as arranged under 1,000 topic headings and received from over 40 information sources.

Topic categories include computer hardware and peripherals, computer software, computer professional services, data communications, interactive media and multimedia, semiconductors, telecommunications, aerospace and defense, automotive, banking and finance, real-estate, business management, consumer electronics, energy, environmental services, healthcare, insurance, media and communications, transportation and distribution, travel, hospitality, and gaming. With over 1,000,000 users, this Web site is designed to give you an edge since it is designed for you, the individual investor.

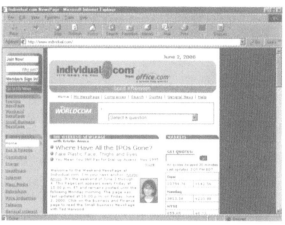

Figure 4.31 The News Page Web site.

Where You Can Turn for Help

If, whether you invest on-line or through a traditional relationship with a broker, you become concerned that the broker or your investment firm has acted (intentionally and unethically) in a manner that has harmed or damaged your finances, you have organizations to which you can turn. Understand, however, that investments have risks. Should you lose money on the basis of your broker's recommendations, your broker has probably done nothing (intentionally or unethically) wrong—in other words, you must take your broker's good recommendations right along with the bad (or less profitable) ones. However, if you feel the broker's actions were intentional (such as "churning your account" where sells and buys stocks aggressively with the primary motivation of racking up commissions), contact the brokerage firm, and then call the Securities and Exchange Commission at 212-748-8055. In addition, you can contact the National Association of Securities Dealers (the NASD of the NASDAQ) at 212-858-4400. Finally, if you still fail to get resolution, you can file suit within the courts.

QUOTE.COM STOCK INFORMATION

http://www.quote.com

Quote.Com is a service dedicated to providing quality financial market data to Internet users. This includes current quotes on stocks, options, commodity futures, mutual funds, and bonds. It also includes portfolio services via Web and e-mail, real-time business news, market analysis and commentary, fundamental (balance sheet) data, company profiles, annual reports, and stock price alarms via e-mail.

Quote.Com's industry-leading sources include Reuter's PR Newswire, BusinessWire, Standard & Poor's, Zack's, and Trendvest, to name just a few, and numerous domestic and international security exchanges.

Some of this stuff is free, some is moderately priced, and some is a little expensive.

For free, you can get unlimited (delayed) security quotes for securities traded on US and Canadian exchanges, retrieval of limited balance sheet data with each quote, ticker symbol and company name searches as well as unlimited updates for one portfolio of up to seven securities, standardized daily/weekly/monthly stock price charts, market index charts daily for market movers, daily data for major industry groups, and foreign exchange rate data.

For a $9.95 basic monthly subscription you can get all of the above plus updates for up to two portfolios tracking 100 securities with end-of-day portfolio updates, access to the *Newsbytes News Network*, your choice of ten customized charts per month, your choice of 10 historical data files per month, and annual reports ordering service (for printed copies delivered via the US mail).

Prices escalate from there, but some services which can also be purchased piece-meal (for example, a stand-alone *S&P News* subscription is just $12.95 per month). Visit the Web site for more details on content and pricing.

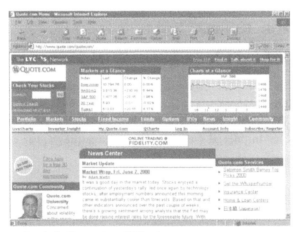

Figure 4.32 Quote.Com Stock Information Web site.

PRUDENTIAL SECURITIES

http://www.prusec.com

As of yet, Prudential Securities won't let you trade on-line, but they will let you play on-line and learn on-line about investing and financial planning. And they will also let you view your Prudential accounts on-line should you already be trading with Prudential.

Come to this Web page to take the *Investment Personality Quiz*, designed to help you discover exactly what kind of investor you are. Then, access a tutorial on retirement planning that includes playing with a great on-line wealth accumulation calculator. Finally, read Prudential's

Daily Market Commentary, featuring insights and forecasts from some of the most highly respected analysts on Wall Street.

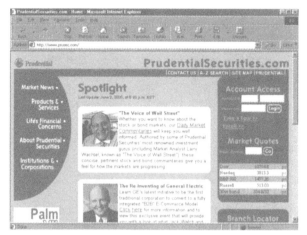

Figure 4.33 Prudential Securities Web site.

NEW LEADERS FOR BETTER BUSINESS

http://www.net-impact.org

You want to make money on Wall Street, but you don't want to be a pirate and make profits off of polluting industries, armaments manufacturers, or exploiters of child labor. Am I right? Then check out this Web forum, where you can learn how to make a profit while still clinging to your conscience. Net Impact is committed to using the power of business to "create a better world."

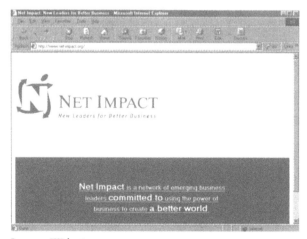

Figure 4.34 The Net Impact Web site.

CHARLES SCHWAB DISCOUNT BROKERAGE ON-LINE: E.SCHWAB

http://www.schwab.com

Charles Schwab Discount Brokerage is currently the largest of on-line brokers. The minimum amount to open an account can range from $1,000 to $20,000 with quarterly account fees. On-line stock trades are $29.95 per trade up to a 1,000 shares plus $.03 per share commission after the first 1,000.

The site also offers research resources, planning tools that are convenient and easy to use, and representatives are always on hand to answer your questions.

e.Schwab tracks your investment activity automatically. You just download updated information whenever you need it, and then see exactly where you stand via sophisticated graphics and reporting functions. What's more, you get 24-hour access to all kinds of invaluable investment information including real-time quotes and other market indicators, as well as price alerts and market indicator alerts.

You also get access to a variety of on-line news and research, including company research reports, Reuters, Standard & Poor's, Morningstar, and more.

Want to get a feel for what it would be like to trade through *e.Schwab*? Then access the Web site and tap into the *e.Schwab* demo that is among the many goodies you'll find there.

Figure 4.35 eSchwab Web site.

SILICON INVESTOR: FREE RESOURCES FOR TECH STOCK INVESTORS

http://www.siliconinvestor.com

Launched in August 1995, *Silicon Investor* was created to meet the needs of everyone and anyone interested in technology stocks. By providing quotes, charts, discussion forums, and links to other Web sites, *Silicon Investor's* sysops Brad and Jeff Dryer have managed to create a unique, large, and growing on-line environment where one can locate information quickly, discover new ideas, and exchange facts and opinions with other like-minded investors. You can get top news provided by Reuters, Hot Stock Talk articles regarding market insight research including quotes, charts, stock screener and IPOs. Register absolutely free!

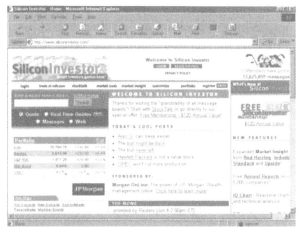

Figure 4.36 The Silicon Investor Web site.

SMALL CAP CENTER

http://www.smallcapcenter.com

What stocks are hot this week? What's the latest market buzz? What's going to happen next week? Next year? A large group of subscribers, thousands of them, have reason to believe that the analysts at the Small Cap Center have a successful line in to just this sort of prognostication. The Small Cap Center focuses on small and micro cap investors offering more original content, in-depth search capabilities, investment tools, newsletters and portfolio management. Many areas are free of charge, but a membership is where you get the goods. Try out a premium membership free for two weeks.

Figure 4.37 The Small Cap Center Web site.

STOCKMASTER.COM

http://www.stockmaster.com

This was for free for a long time from MIT. But now the party is over and the proprietor has, I guess, graduated and, of course, gone commercial. Who can condemn him for that? Certainly not me. Not in a book about how to create and maximize wealth with the Internet.

Stockmaster.Com is a great resource for recent stock market information, including previous day's closing prices and one-year graphs of historical prices. The site includes stock charts of price and volume movement updated daily, mutual fund charts of price movement, top stocks (the most frequently traded stocks of late), ticker symbols sorted by company and by symbol, a directory of historical data files extracted and used to draw the graphs at the site, information about how the stock graphs were drawn, and more.

Figure 4.38 The StockMaster Web site.

WALL STREET RESEARCH NET

http://www.wsrn.com

Wall Street Research Network consists of over 110,000 links to help professional and private investors perform fundamental research on actively traded companies and mutual funds and locate important economic data that moves markets.

This site includes, among other things, a database (that you may view using a downloadable Java applet, if you'd like) of detailed financial information on more than 20,000 individual companies from around the world, a mutual fund database comprising 5,000 listings, and much, much more.

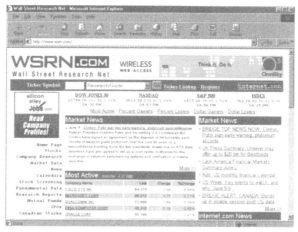

Figure 4.39 *The Wall Street Research Net Web site.*

WESTERGAARD ONLINE

http://www.westergaard.com

This is a leading provider of micro-cap investment research (with micro-cap being defined as firms under $300 million in market capitalization). *Westergaard Online* is a division of Westergaard Publishing Corporation, founded in 1960. Founder/Editorial Director John Westergaard is known on Wall Street as *the* guru of small stock investment research. Research on over 200 companies is available at this site at no cost to visitors.

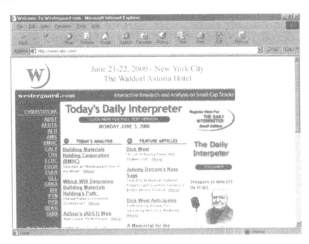

Figure 4.40 The Westergaard OnLine Web site.

ARIZONA STOCK EXCHANGE

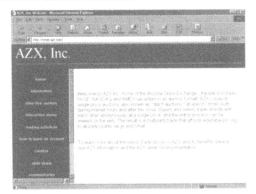

http://www.azx.com

BEIRUT STOCK EXCHANGE

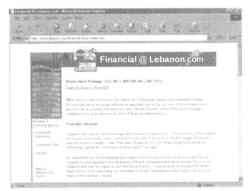

http://www.lebanon.com/financial/stocks/ index.htm

(AUSTRIA) VIENNA STOCK EXCHANGE

http://apollo.wu-wien.ac.at/cgi-bin/boerse1.pl

CANADIAN MARKETS

http://www.eucanect.com/investments

INTERACCESS

http://www.interaccess.com

(FRANCE) BOURSE DE PARIS

http://www.bourse-de-paris.fr

HOLT'S DAILY MARKET REPORT

http://turnpike.net/metro/holt/index.html

INTERNET SECURITIES, INC.

http://www.securities.com

DBC ONLINE STOCK QUOTES

http://www.dbc.com

LONDON INTERNATIONAL FINANCIAL FEATURES AND OPTIONS EXCHANGE

http://www.liffe.com

STOCK POINT

http://www.irnet.com

INVESTOR'S GALLERY

http://centrex.com

(ITALY) MILAN'S STOCK EXCHANGE

http://www.robot1.texnet.it/finanza

(INDONESIA) JAKARTA STOCK EXCHANGE

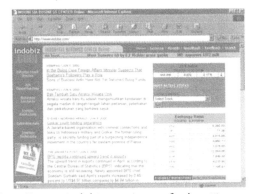

http://www.indobiz.com/news_fin.htm#jse

ISRAEL'S STOCK EXCHANGE INFORMATION

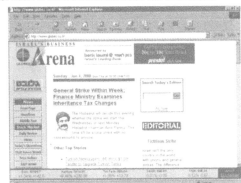

http://www.globes.co.il

MONEY MAGAZINE STOCK QUOTES

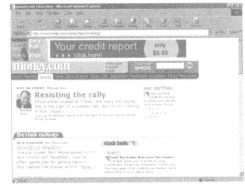

http://www.money.com/depts/investing

DLJ DIRECT

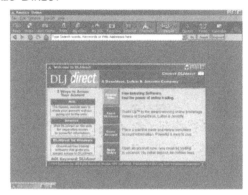

Available on *America Online* and *Prodigy*

PCQUOTE STOCK QUOTE SERVER

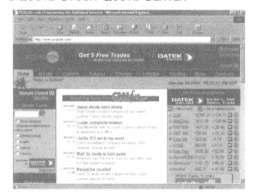

http://www.pcquote.com

(PORTUGAL) LISBON STOCK EXCHANGE

http://www.bvl.pt

NEW ZEALAND INVESTMENT CENTER

http://www.nzinvest.com

NORWAY FINANCIAL

http://nettvik.no

WALL STREET JOURNAL DAILY MONEY AND INVESTING UPDATE

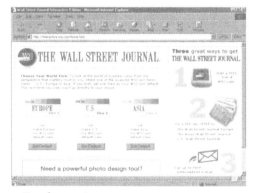

http://update.wsj.com

SECURITY *APL* STOCK QUOTE SERVER

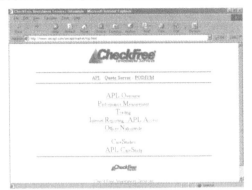

http://www.secapl.com/cgi-bin/qs

THE SECURITIES AND EXCHANGE COMMISSION (U.S. FEDERAL)

http://www.sec.gov

(SPAIN) BOLSA DE MADRID

http://www.bolsamadrid.es

SINGAPORE STOCK EXCHANGE

http://www.asia1.com.sg/btstocks

(SRI LANKA) COLOMBO STOCK EXCHANGE

http://www.lanka.net/stocks

FIDELITY INVESTMENTS

http://www100.fidelity.com

STANDARD & POOR'S 500 INDEX

http://www.secapl.com/secapl/quoteserver/
sp500.html

THE STOCKCENTER END-OF-DAY QUOTES

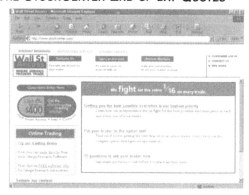

http://www.stockcenter.com

STOCK EXCHANGES WORLDWIDE

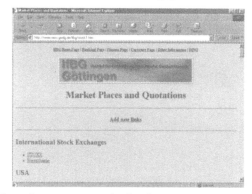

http://www.wiso.gwdg.de/ifbg/stock1.htm

(SWITZERLAND) GENEVA STOCK EXCHANGE

http://www.bourse.ch

USA TODAY END-OF-DAY QUOTES AND MARKET ANALYSIS

http://www.usatoday.com/money/mfront.htm

THE RED CHIP REVIEW

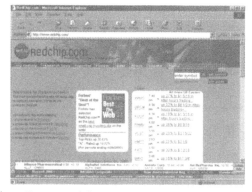

http://www.redchip.com

RAGING BULL

http://www.ragingbull.com

YAMBO QUOTES

http://www.yambo.com

THE STOCK CONSULTANT

http://www.stockconsultant.com

BLUE CHIP SUCCESS

http://www.bluechipsuccess.com

EZ RESEARCH – STOCKS

http://www.ezresearch.com

THE STOCK WIZARD

http://www.stock-wizard.com

ALL STOCKS

http://www.allstocks.com

AMERITRADE

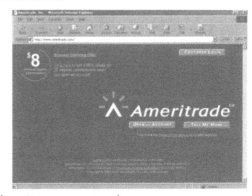

http://www.ameritrade.com

DATEK

http://www.datek.com

SURETRADE

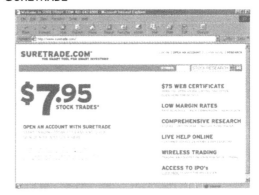

http://www.suretrade.com

CHAPTER 5

FOR THE RICH AND/OR BRAVE:
STOCK OPTIONS, IPOS, AND
COMMODITIES FUTURES

A fool and his money are soon parted. — **English Proverb**

YOU CAN NEVER SEPARATE RISK FROM REWARD

If investment in standard issues of common stock contains neither enough risk nor enough potential return for your taste, you may engage in other investment techniques and strategies that will provide an experience that more closely approximates a roller-coaster ride and will do more to keep your adrenaline going. The roller-coaster includes investments in *put and call options*, *new issues* or *initial public offerings (IPOs)*, and *commodity futures*.

None of these investments is for the faint of heart. *And none of them are for people who cannot afford to lose the money they invest.*

Only a fool bets the farm in options trading, or on an IPO, or in the futures market. My advice to you is not to be that fool. On the other hand, if you are lucky enough to have a lot of cash that you could live without while, at the same time not downgrading your lifestyle, then perhaps the high risk and high rewards of these investment vehicles will be appealing.

WHAT IS A PUT AND WHAT IS A CALL?

In Chapter 4, you learned that investors (normally, unless they are shorting a stock) buy shares of a stock hoping the stock's price will rise in value so they can sell their shares for a profit. If investors only bought and sold shares of stocks, the stock market would be pretty easy to understand. If one investor wants to sell shares of stock for a price another investor is willing to pay, the sale of the stock (the transaction or stock trade occurs). As discussed, a large demand of investors who want to buy a specific stock will increase the stock's price while a large supply of sellers will reduce the price.

But, as you will learn in this chapter, there's more to the stock market than simple buy and sell transactions. These additional transactions are often called "puts and calls" or "options." Using puts and calls, investors can leverage their investment dollars when they feel strongly that a stock's price is going to rise or fall within a specific window of time. As you will learn, just as investors buy and sell stocks, they also trade (buy and sell) put and call options.

A *put* is an option to sell someone a certain stock at a set price (the *exercise* or *striking price*) at any moment one cares to within a certain window of time. In other words, prior to the option's expiration date, I can *put* shares of a stock to you at an agreed price. If the stock's current price is below our agreed price, I win, and well, you don't. I would buy a *put* option if I think the stock's price is going to drop during the specified window of time.

A *call* is an option to purchase a specific stock at a specific price at any moment within a certain window of time. In other words, before the option's expiration date, I can *call* the shares of a stock that you own from you at an agreed price. If the stock's current price is above our agreed price, I win, and well, you know. I would buy a *call* option if I think the stock's price is going to go up during the specified window of time.

Each individual option is usually for (controls) what is called a *round lot* of common stock, which equals 100 shares. So when I put shares to you or call shares from you, we do so 100 shares at a time.

Options listed on the leading exchanges have standardized quarterly expiration dates. These dates are most often the Saturdays following the third Friday of January, April, July, and October each year.

When an investor purchases an option, the investor pays a *premium* to the individual to whom the investor would later put the stock or from whom the investor would call the stock. The option premium is one of the other investor's motivations for letting you put or call stock.

THE MATH OF CALL OPTIONS

With put and call options one can make money, *big* money. One can also lose money, *big* money. In short, options are a speculative exercise, a gamble—based on whether you think the price of a particular stock is either going to go up or down. The best way to see the logic behind options is with an example.

Meet Frederick Astor Vanderbilt Whitney VI. He wears silk shirts, buys his shoes at Armani, and always makes a point of showing up for the Groton School homecoming every October. His family fortune is today invested in a safe, conservative portfolio just as it has been for generations. But Freddie (as his friends call him) has a little slush fund of a few thousand dollars with which he amuses himself by dabbling in the options market.

Right now Freddie's eye is on the stock for Claire's Software. He thinks that at $30 the stock is priced way *under market*. He believes the street price for the security is too low and that it will soon go up. To buy a hundred shares of the stock would cost Freddie $3,000. But he can buy a call option for 100 shares of Claire's Software for only $3.50 per share: $350 (the premium). If Freddie guesses right and the stock price goes up significantly, Freddie will profit. If, however, Freddie is wrong and the price goes down or simply stays the same, Freddie will only lose the $350 premium he invested in the option. In other words, his call option would be worthless.

It is January when Freddie is doing all this research. The option he is considering buying is listed in the trade journals as a "Claire'sCommon October 30 call option." This means the *exercise price* for a 100-share block of Claire's Software (the *underlying stock* of the option) is $30 per share, and that the expiration date is the Saturday following the third Friday in October.

Freddie prefers options to actual shares of stock because by playing with options he maximizes his potential return, getting the greatest *swing* possible out of every dollar he invests. By playing the options game with his cash, Freddie even gets a wider swing than he would by buying common stock on margin. But he also, of course, runs the extreme risk that the swing will go *against* him and that he will lose every dime he puts into the premium for an option. But he doesn't care. He is using what is to him pin-money. He can afford to lose it.

As it turns out, you don't have to exercise your option, meaning you don't have to put the stocks to the other investor or call stocks from the investor. Instead, just as you can trade stocks, you can also trade options. Freddie, for example, will probably never exercise his option on Claire's stock, even if the market price of the stock goes up in value just as he believes it will. Instead he will simply speculate with the option on the stock, buying and selling it as he would any other negotiable security.

Let's say that Freddie's assumption about Claire's Software proves correct. The stock goes up in value and by August it is selling for $40 per share. Of course, this fact will have a dramatic impact on the premium (the price Freddie can now get for selling the option) associated with Freddie's $30 per-share option expiring in October. It will cause the premium to grow significantly in value.

Consider: If Claire's Software is selling for $40 in August or September, then the premium for $30-per-share options could easily go up to, say, $7 and still be a very good value reflecting, as it would, a total per-share price for Claire's Software of only $37 while the current market price is $40. It is at this point that Freddie would most likely sell his call option. He bought it at a premium of $350. He will sell at $700.

Thus, while the actual stock for Claire's Software went up in value only 25%, Freddie enjoyed a 100% return on his cash investment in the *option* on the stock.

However, had Freddie been wrong in his forecast of increased prices for Claire's Software, and if the stock had remained at its $30 price or actually gone down, Freddie would have suffered a 100% *loss* of the $350 premium he paid for the option.

The Brief History of Put and Call Options

To some degree, trading in options to sell and buy common stocks has been going on for generations over-the-counter. However, the market for *puts* and *calls* really blossomed only after 1973. This was the year that the Chicago Board Options Exchange (the CBOE) first started trading listed options with standardized exercise prices and expiration dates. Since 1973, many other exchanges have followed suit, among them the Amex along with the Philadelphia, Pacific, and Midwest Stock Exchanges.

Free Options Video and Free Options Seminars

The Options Industry Council (OIC) consists of five participant exchanges (the American Stock Exchange, the Chicago Board Options Exchange, the New York Stock Exchange, the Pacific Stock Exchange, and the Philadelphia Stock Exchange) and the Options Clearing Corporation. Their charter is to enhance the acceptance of equity options by brokers and individual investors. To help you understand the benefits of options as an investment tool, the OIC offers two videos *The Options Tool* and *How to Optimize Your Stock Portfolio with Options.* In addition, the OIC offers free options seminars! To get your free copy of these videos and a schedule of upcoming (free) seminars, call 800-444-4360. In addition, you should check out their Web site at *http://www.optionscentral.com* shown below in Figure 5.1.

Figure 5.1 The Options Industry Council (OIC) Web site.

THE MATH OF PUT OPTIONS

Once again we have the swing principle at work. Once again we have an option at the center of the deal. And once again we have Freddie in his Armani shoes. But the speculative logic of Freddie's option transaction is now reversed.

Freddie sees another stock, for a firm called Idiots Are Us, that he believes (perhaps because of the firm's name and what it infers about the firm's management) is likely to go down in value. Freddie buys a put option that gives him an option to sell a block of shares of Idiots Are Us at the current market price for a set period of time.

If Freddie is correct in his forecast, and the share price for Idiots Are Us goes into a free fall, the premium for Freddie's put option will increase dramatically above the relatively small amount he paid for it. However, if the stock remains at its current price over time, or goes up in market value, then the value of Freddie's option will be *zero!*

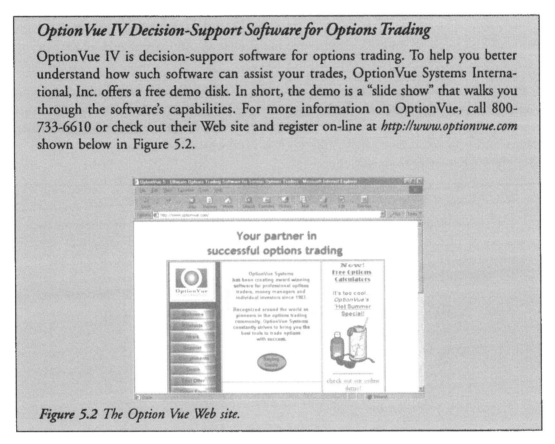

OptionVue IV Decision-Support Software for Options Trading

OptionVue IV is decision-support software for options trading. To help you better understand how such software can assist your trades, OptionVue Systems International, Inc. offers a free demo disk. In short, the demo is a "slide show" that walks you through the software's capabilities. For more information on OptionVue, call 800-733-6610 or check out their Web site and register on-line at *http://www.optionvue.com* shown below in Figure 5.2.

Figure 5.2 The Option Vue Web site.

THE SCOOP ON NEW ISSUES, BETTER KNOWN AS INITIAL PUBLIC OFFERINGS (IPOS)

New Issues (better known these days as *Initial Public Offerings*, or *IPOs*) are stocks being offered by corporations for the very first time.

By their nature, the majority of IPOs are associated with small, often unknown and newly formed corporations. There is no history to them—no extensive track record of market performance or corporate earnings.

Many of these companies will ultimately plummet and crash. A few will endure and turn into robust financial animals. Don't forget that such unknown outfits as IBM and Microsoft once launched what in retrospect appear to have been extremely low-priced IPOs into a skeptical marketplace. But keep in mind also that countless other IPOs have proved to be little more than incinerators for investors' cash. For every Microsoft there are 50 bankruptcies.

The shares of many New Issues—especially those of technology-oriented firms—tend to soar immediately after the initial offering. As many will recall, this is what happened in 1995 with the much ballyhooed IPO of NetScape. In this case, of course, you had an IPO from a firm which was already establishing itself as a dominant player in the field of Internet Web-browser technology. But even the stock of many companies less-well-positioned than NetScape has tended to shoot up immediately after the initial offering. And you should be wary of this because what goes up fast often comes down fast.

It is your job as the investor to make sure there is some *substance* to the new offering. Luckily, there are several highly-useful on-line resources (provided by Dun & Bradstreet and other reporting firms) which let you check a company's financial disclosures and other information designed to help you decide whether the stock is worthwhile. These resources are detailed in the Internet Resources section of this chapter.

IPO Monitor Service Keeps You Informed on New IPO Filings

The IPO Monitor provides investors with e-mail or fax notification of initial public offerings filed with the Securities and Exchange Commission. Subscribers to this service receive timely reports (each morning) on companies who file for initial public offerings. IPO Monitor is providing readers of Net Worth a 30-day free trial offer. For more information, call 213-612-6091 and mention Net Worth. Also, you can send e-mail to *ipoinfo@ipomonitor.com*. Lastly, check out their Web site at *http://www.ipomonitor.com/ipo/* shown below in Figure 5.3.

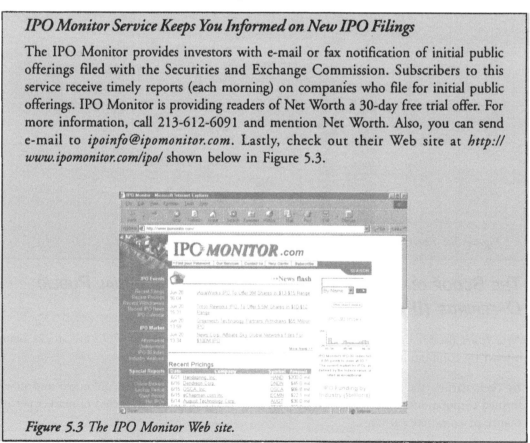

Figure 5.3 The IPO Monitor Web site.

Everycontractor.com

Everycontractor.com is an example of an up and coming company with the eventual goal of an initial public offering. The company has created a vertical portal for the building and construction industry. The Web site acts as a directory for the building and construction industry, hosting Web pages from tile layers to architects. The site includes 50 state pages for easy and organized access to the voluminous subscribers. The basic rate for a company to subscribe is $299.00 a year. Banners may be purchased, as well. The site has a host of other benefits. Keep on the lookout for their scheduled IPO in December of 2001. Check out their Web site at *http:// www.everycontractor.com* shown below in Figure 5.4.

Figure 5.4 Everycontractor.com Web site.

ECONOMIC BUNGEE JUMPING: THE HIGH-FLYING RISK OF COMMODITIES FUTURES

What's more risky than betting money—big money—on a horse race? What's more risky than betting on a roulette wheel? How about betting money—big money—on something as unpredictable as the weather? And I don't mean next week's weather. I mean the weather long-term, over time. And I don't mean the weather in one specific corner of the country or the world, I mean the weather across continents. If this kind of thing sounds appealing to you, then get out your *Farmer's Almanac* and some cash and strap yourself in for a wild ride through the unpredictable world of Commodities Futures Trading, where you may well go broke, but you will never get bored.

WHAT ARE COMMODITIES FUTURES?

Commodities Futures are actually *futures contracts.* These contracts represent agreements to either buy or sell a specific commodity in a specific quantity at a specific price on a specific *future* date. The commodities in question might be any number of things wheat, corn, oats, soybeans, potatoes, platinum, copper, silver, cocoa, eggs, lumber, or even the fabled "pork bellies," which in popular culture have come to epitomize the typical commodities investment. (If you don't know what a pork belly is, then you should go to the entertaining Web site addressed as *http://www.shkfoods.com/shk/FunBaconFacts* to find out.)

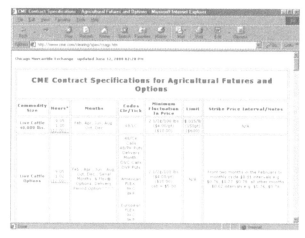

Figure 5.5 Information on pork bellies and more.

This futures stuff is, of course, risky business. To count on success in the futures market, no small amount of clairvoyance is called for. Either that or be a very good long-term weather forecaster. A drought in Idaho can drive up the price of potatoes. A remarkably temperate summer in Iowa can drive down the price of corn. *Round and round and round it goes. Where it stops, nobody knows.*

Videos from the Chicago Mercantile Exchange

To help you better understand futures, options, and commodities, the Chicago Mercantile Exchange has put together a video titled "Power. Performance. Possibilities" which looks at how various investors view the challenges of trading agricultural futures and options, particularly livestock and meat. For more information on this video, call 800-336-3332. In addition, they offer a second video titled "The Currency Opportunity" which is a humorous "talk show" look at how world currency is priced. For more information on these videos, call 800-273-8383. In addition, you should check out their Web site at *http://www.cme.com* shown below in Figure 5.6.

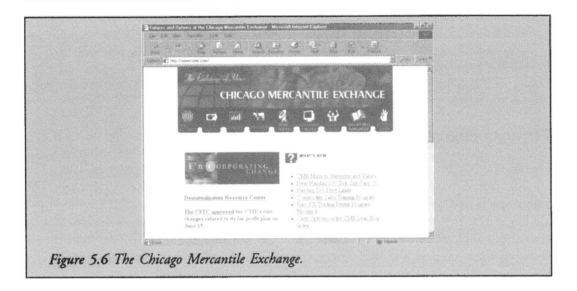

Figure 5.6 The Chicago Mercantile Exchange.

FUTURES VERSUS SPOT COMMODITIES: WHAT IS THE DIFFERENCE?

A futures contract does, of course, have an expiration date when the goods in question are to be delivered at the price specified. However, the speculator in commodities futures practically never stays "in" the investment long enough to see the expiration of the contract. The speculator nearly always "closes out" his position prior to the expiration of a futures contract. And the actually commodity itself never changes hands between speculators. In this way, should you speculate in the pork bellies market, you will normally be "out of your futures position" before you need to hand over the bacon.

Contracts to buy and sell physical commodities (rather than futures) are made in the cash market (commonly called the *spot market*). Note that commodities futures prices and spot commodity prices are listed in major daily newspapers and virtually all financial newspapers.

But it is futures contracts, rather than actual commodities, which are bought and sold by speculating investors. Let me mention here, before you or I go any further, that leading experts in the field estimate that speculators in commodities futures *lose money* 75% to 80% of the time. Got it? That is 75% to 80% of the time.

Free Commodities Starter Kits

The Great Pacific Trading Company is a full service commodity brokerage services to traders who are just beginning or are experienced in commodities trading. To help you get started, they will provide readers of *Net Worth* a free starter kit that is filled instructions and terms you will need to know. Call 800-479-7920, mention *Net Worth*, and request the starter kit.

The Iowa Grain Company provides institutional and individual investors with products and information for all markets. To help you get started, they offer the free booklet *Speculating in Futures* and the *Speculating Workbook*. To obtain their free starter kit, call 800-545-6426 and mention *Net Worth*.

FUTURES BROKER: COMMODITIES TRADING ADVISORS

The Futures Market has its own exchanges, separate from the standard stock exchanges. So too does it have its own set of brokers, separate from the standard run of stockbrokers. The highly specialized set of brokers dealing in commodities futures are called Commodities Trading Advisors (CTAs). Many CTAs are now on-line with their own Web sites, not so much for trading but more often for quick and easy distribution of the cumbersome disclosure statements—packed with performance statistics, rankings, and graphs—which each CTA is required by law to provide to potential customers. You will find the listings for dozens of CTA Web sites in the Internet Resources section of this chapter. You will also find great sets of data resources from such firms as Stark Research and TradeScan that will give you a good idea of any individual CTA's track-record of investment success.

Free Futures and Options Trading Kit Is a Great Way to Start

The futures and options market can be an expensive place to "learn" investing. A far better way to understand this market is to get the free *Futures and Options Trading Kit* from Fox Investments. The kit is packed with helpful booklets that examine futures contracts, currencies, options, and more. To get your free starter kit, call 800-554-6290. It's a great kit.

Free Futures Booklets

Infinity Brokerage Services is a full-service and discount futures and options dealer. To help you get started with and better understand futures and options, call 800-322-8559 and ask Infinity to provide you with a copy of *Rules of the Rich*, which specifies 25 key trading rules. The company also offers an excellent booklet titled *Trading in Futures* and a home study course.

GOING LONG IN COMMODITIES FUTURES: THE RETURN OF FREDDIE

In addition to playing around with options, Frederick Astor Vanderbilt Whitney VI likes to entertain himself with the occasional play in commodities futures.

In August, Freddie decides he thinks the price of oats is going to go up in the coming months. So, he calls his CTA and arranges to enter into a futures contract (in this case, a

5,000-bushel *full contract*) to *buy* December oats at a price of $5 per bushel. Five dollars, you see, is the market price for December oats in August, when Freddie is entering into the contract. But keep in mind, Freddie anticipates that the price of December oats is likely to go *up*.

With the futures contract executed, Freddie is now *long* in December oats. They don't exist yet. They haven't been harvested. But he owns them. And he has put $25,000 at risk (5,000 bushels x $5) in the process.

Suppose Freddie's prognosis for the price of December oats was correct. A flood hits several major oat-growing regions, and in September alone the price of December oats rises from $5.00 per bushel to $6.00. Freddie may, of course, hold on to the futures contract in the hope that the price for December oats will go even further. Or he may decide to *close out* of the future by selling the 5,000 bushels of December oats immediately at $6.00, or $30,000 total. Thus, he would make a profit of $5,000 (20%) on the $25,000 he originally put at risk. Freddie may have made his return even more appealing by buying his commodities contract on margin, thereby, maximizing the swing of his investment capital. (See Chapter 4 for a detailed description of trading on margin.) Margin requirements in commodities trading are often quite low and *can be as little as 5%* of the value of the commodity being traded. If, for example, Freddie had purchased the futures contract discussed above on 5% margin, his actual cash investment would have been only $1,250 (5% of $25,000) while his return remained $5,000. This would be the equivalent of a 400% return on actual cash invested in the scope of about a month. But keep in mind that though Freddie only threw down $1,250, he was at all times responsible for, and would eventually have to make good on, the *full amount* of the contract: $25,000. Which brings us to our next scenario.

Suppose Freddie was wrong. Suppose there were no floods in the oat-growing regions, and the crop was looking strong and plentiful in September. Suppose this in turn brought the price of December oats down from $5 to $4 per bushel. Freddie can hold on to the futures contract, chew his nails for a while, and hope for something to happen to affect the price of December oats in a way that would work to his advantage. Or he can cut his losses and close out of the contract: taking a loss of $5,000, or 20% of his investment capital. It may, of course, be something more like a loss of 400% if he was speculating on margin. And the loss could grow even larger if he holds on to the contract and the December price for oats deteriorates further. Where are those earthquakes and swarms of locusts when you need them?

GOING SHORT IN COMMODITIES FUTURES

If Freddie had thought the price of December oats was going to go down, he probably would have played the commodities futures market in a different way. He would have gone short, rather than long, in December oats.

He would have written a contract in August to *sell* 5000 bushels of oats for delivery in December at $5 per bushel. In this case, Freddie would have hoped to close out the transaction by covering his short position after the price of December oats fell below (hopefully well-below) $5 per bushel.

Suppose Freddie was right. Let's say, for example, that the price of December oats had, by September, deteriorated to $4 per bushel. Freddie might wait and hope for the price of December oats to go down even further. Or he might close out the transaction by purchasing 5000 bushels of December oats at $4 and then immediately selling them for $5, thus making a profit of $5,000.

Suppose Freddie was wrong. It is impossible to say what percentage of the cash Freddie had at risk would be represented by the $5,000 return elucidated in the previous paragraph, simply because when one short sells commodities the cash-at-risk can fluctuate widely and wildly. One really does not know how much cash one is risking, because one cannot forecast where prices are going to go. You see, by the terms of the contract by which he went short on oats, Freddie is committed to deliver 5000 bushels of December oats at $5 per bushel. As we have seen, if the December price comes down he is in good shape. But if the December price goes up he is in terrible shape: and in worse shape the higher it goes. At $6 per bushel he takes a hit of $5,000. At $7 per bushel he takes a hit of $10,000. At $10 per bushel he takes a hit of $25,000! In theory, there is no limit to your potential exposure when going short on commodities futures. The downside risk is *enormous* and, worse, *open-ended*.

Futures Pro and Option Pro – Software to Help Your Trading Discipline and Strategies

To help you better understand options and futures trading and to provide you with strategies you can apply to improve your trading discipline, Essex Trading Company, Ltd. offers two software packages *Futures Pro* and *Options Pro*. Each program helps users develop a trading plan, improve their trading discipline, and quantify and control risk. To help you get started, they offer free demo disks for both programs. For more information on these products, call 800-726-2140 or check out their Web site at *http://www.essextrading.com* shown below in Figure 5.7.

Figure 5.7 The Essex Trading Company Web site.

WHAT IS A DERIVATIVE?

You will occasionally hear the term *derivative*. What is the financial meaning here? The answer is quite straightforward. Any negotiable security that piggybacks on an item of real value for its worth is a *derivative*. An option is a derivative; it ultimately *derives* its value from the equity in the stock with which it is related. And a future is a derivative. It ultimately *derives* its value from the commodity with which it is associated. For more on derivatives see the great collection of articles on this topic by Don M. Chance, Professor of Finance in the Center for the Study of Futures and Options Markets at Virginia Tech. This great collection of easy-to-understand essays is now being published in paperback form. You can visit his personal Web site at *http://www.cob.vt.edu/finance/faculty/dmc/index.ht*m shown below in Figure 5.8.

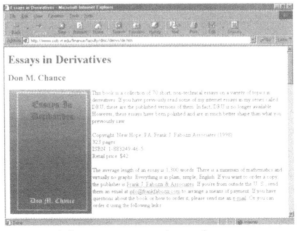

Figure 5.8 Making options and futures easy to understand.

ONE LAST WORD TO THE WISE

All of the high-risk, highly speculative investment options outlined in this chapter are, at best, for very small, limited percentages of your investment portfolio. No dollar you cannot afford to lose should ever be invested in options trading, IPOs, or commodities futures. While these vehicles offer the prospect of larger than normal returns, they also offer the *very likely* prospect of larger than normal losses. When Frederick Astor Vanderbilt Whitney VI makes a bad move, it does not impact his standard-of-living. He barely notices that the money is gone. He still has plenty of cash with which to pay for the groceries, not to mention uniforms for the staff. Make sure any cash *you* put into options, IPOs, or commodities is cash you won't notice the absence of should it suddenly evaporate from out of your hands.

> ### First American Discount Corp. Offers Free Booklet and Other Great Stuff
>
> To help you better understand the futures markets, First American Discount Corp. offers a free booklet titled *Trading Tactics of the Pros.* The booklet examines the psychology and behavior or trading and helps the reader to identify trading patterns. Check out their Web site for a complete list of free offers including other books entitled, *The Steps to Success, Getting Started with Stochastics, The Relative Strength Index, Tax Trips for Traders,* and the ever-popular *12 Cardinal Mistakes in Futures Trading* by Walter Bressert. You can also view a futures trading calendar current for the month or entire year, get discounted news subscriptions and so much more. Visit their Web site at *http://www.fadc.com* shown below in Figure 5.9 or call 800-824-8532.
>
>
>
> *Figure 5.9 The First American Discount Corp. Web site.*

> ### Understanding Triple Witching Friday
>
> If you listen to the business news, you may periodically hear the term "triple witching hour." As discussed, all options have expiration dates. If you study options, you

will learn that you can trade equity options as well as stock index options. Once each quarter, it happens that the equity options, stock index options, and futures all expire on the same day. Normally, the market experiences very heavy trading on this day and can be quite volatile (either rising or falling dramatically).

Free Demo Disk Presents Futures Charting Software

To help you better spot and analyze trends in the futures market, Ira Epstein & Company Futures offers downloading and charting software. Their Windows-based software is easy to use, allowing you to spend less time trying to understand your software and more time studying futures. Check out their Web site at *http://www.iepstein.com* shown below in Figure 5.10, and you can get a 20-day trial offer of the company's charting software. You can also get a free futures calculator, free cash seasonal charts, and free access to trading pit commentaries.

Figure 5.10 The Ira Epstein & Company Futures Web site.

Understanding the Federal Reserve's Role in Interest Rates

The Federal Reserve Board (often simply called the "Fed") is a government agency that regulates the U.S. banking industry. The primary vehicle by which the Fed controls interest rates in the discount rate, which specifies the rate at which the Federal Reserve Board will lend money to its member banks overnight. The member banks, in turn, loan money to its customers at a premium to the discount rate. By controlling the discount rate, the Fed controls the interest rates across the country (and many will argue around the world).

In addition to controlling the discount rate, the Fed can control the money supply, which in turn controls how much money is available for lenders to lend. The Federal

Open Market Committee (FOMC) consists of five (of the twelve) Regional Federal Reserve Bank Presidents, as well as, seven members of the Fed's Board of Governors. The FOMC can require the Federal Reserve member banks to sell or buy U.S. government securities (to or from the Fed), which in turn, controls the money supply.

INTERNET RESOURCES FOR OPTIONS, IPO AND FUTURES INVESTORS

As you surf the World Wide Web, you may encounter sites that discuss commodities, options, currency markets, derivatives, and more. The following site list should help you locate the resources you need.

@GRICULTURE ON-LINE AGRICULTURAL MARKET REPORTS

http://www.agriculture.com/markets/

This page not only gives you quotes for commodity futures but also "market moving weather maps," and more. Be sure to check out the Grassroots Advisory Service, featuring weekly commentaries by a host of noted futures pundits:

- Roy Smith, a Nebraska corn and soybean farmer

- Scott Stewart, a nationally-known analyst adept at both predicting markets and making them understandable to readers

- Craig Coberly, a former Kansas farm boy bent on bringing futures chart analysis to the Web

- Ron and Susan Mortensen of Fort Dodge, Iowa, who are commodity brokers with a farm clientele and have a penchant for writing newsy, topical, and sometimes irreverent, columns

- Joe Victor, Vice President of Marketing at Allendale, Inc.

- Louise Gartner, founder and owner of Spectrum Commodities, which helps with cash market strategies for producers and providing market info and resources for traders

- Joel Karlin, grain and oil seed analyst

- Leroy Louwagie, President of Professional Marketing Associates, working directly with farmers on marketing strategies and education

- Dave Maher, lots of talk about beef, cattle and pork

- Rich Possan, licensed commodity broker and advisor, and is currently a trader/technical analyst.

Figure 5.11 @griculture On-Line *Agricultural Market Reports.*

APPLIED DERIVATIVES TRADING *MAGAZINE*

http://www.adtrading.com/

Edited by the indomitable Patrick Young, *Applied Derivatives Trading* Magazine is a monthly magazine (electronic magazine) devoted to all aspects of derivatives trading throughout the world. All issues are archived on-line. Each issue includes incisive market analysis and commentary by Patrick Young and other derivatives gurus such as Lawrence McMillan. You also get book and software reviews and much more.

Figure 5.12 Applied Derivatives Trading *Magazine.*

JAKE BERNSTEIN'S FUTURES MARKET COMMENTARY

http://www.trade-futures.com/reports.html

This site provides excellent, *free*, futures market commentary by one of the leading analysts in the field, Jake Bernstein. The flow of rich, quality information is occasionally interrupted by brief, entirely appropriate, commercials for Mr. Bernstein's seminars, newsletters, and recommended brokers. But don't let that stop you. Bernstein's track record is outstanding, his arguments cogent, and his recommendations relied upon by many a successful investor in futures.

Figure 5.13 Jake Bernstein's Futures Market Commentary.

Understanding Stop and Market Orders

When you sell and buy securities, the price you pay for the security may not be that at which the security is currently trading. In other words, by the time your order reaches the floor (or the wires of the electronic over-the-counter market), the price may have moved up or down. In most cases, your orders will be *market orders,* which instruct your broker to buy or sell the stock at the best possible market price. At other times, you may specify a minimum price at which you will buy or sell the security, which create a *limit order.* In other words, if the security falls to a specific price, you may want to "get out" and limit your losses. In this case, your limit order would be a *stop loss order.* Likewise, if the security climbs to a specific price, you may want to "get out" of the security and take your profit.

THE COMMODITY FUTURES TRADING COMMISSION

http://www.cftc.gov/

The Commodity Futures Trading Commission was created by Congress in 1974 as an independent agency entrusted with regulating commodity futures and option markets. Come to this site for a mission statement, official reports, and press releases along with brief bios of the commissioners.

Figure 5.14 *The Commodity Futures Trading Commission.*

FUTURES AND OPTIONS WEEK *MAGAZINE*

http://www.fow.com

Today's derivatives industry is suffering from an acute information overload. *Futures & Options Week* provides busy executives and investors with a concise, accurate, and up-to-date source of the latest news from all markets. The magazine is usually the first to cover stories about new contract launches, personnel movements and changes, regulatory developments, new technology introductions, and exchange volumes. That kind of coverage does not come cheap, however. The annual subscription is $634 per year. But you can get one issue for free, either via mail or via download (approx. 100k). Go for it.

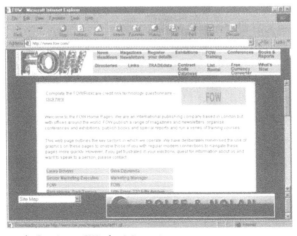

Figure 5.15 Futures and Options Week *Magazine.*

FUTURES *MAGAZINE ON-LINE*

http://www.futuresmag.com

This site is the on-line home of the world's premier magazine by, for, and about those who trade futures contracts.

The site includes the contents page of the current issue of the magazine, along with the full-text of selected articles. You also get the hottest market news, updated daily, from *Futures World News* as well as reports and predictions by leading analysts, the latest on the managed-money segment of the futures industry, and an on-line sourcebook providing hyperlinks to hundreds of futures and options industry professionals. Looking for something on a particular topic? Use the handy tool with which you can search the entire *Futures* Magazine Web site for just the right data with which to make your first, or maybe your second, million. And coming soon: a chat-space called *Futures Talk*, where you will be able to swap advice, tips, and gossip with other investors in futures.

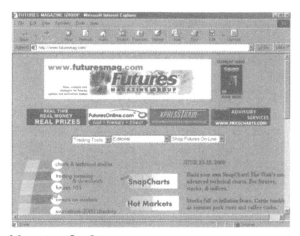

Figure 5.16 Futures *Magazine On-Line.*

GLOSSARY OF FUTURES AND OPTIONS TERMINOLOGY

http://www.cbot.com

This glossary was taken from the Chicago Board of Trade's Commodity Trading Manual which is produced by the Marketing Development Department of the exchange. Find out what Adjusted Futures Price, Arbitrage, and At-the-Money Options is — and that's just under the letter A!

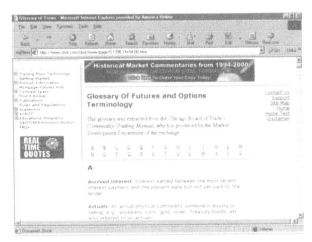

Figure 5.17 Glossary of Futures and Options Terminology.

NEW YORK MERCANTILE EXCHANGE

http://www.nymex.com

The New York Mercantile Exchange is the world's leading physical commodity futures exchange and the preeminent trading forum for energy, precious metals and, in North America, copper. Each day the business community turns to the Exchange where the market's collective assessments of the value of crude oil, gasoline, heating oil, natural gas, propane, gold, silver, platinum, and copper are used as pricing benchmarks. Come to this Web site for detailed information on the exchange along with contract specs as well as charts and data related to energy, financial (index cash & futures), and metal prices.

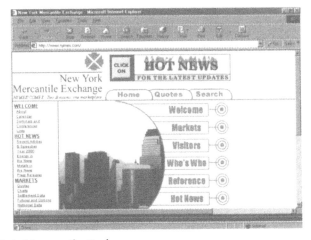

Figure 5.18 New York Mercantile Exchange.

TROUTMAN ON TRADING: FUTURES TRADING SYSTEM REVIEWS

http://www.teleport.com/~troutman

This guy is great! Listen to him: "Understand that I'm not your typical trader, market insider or broker. I don't glorify and follow gurus and their methods. I'm not looking to get rich in fifteen minutes; you can't plan to do that with any certainty. I'm not a scammer who is trying to sell what he wants you to think is a Holy Grail for traders. I'm not looking for the Ultimate Technical Indicator. I will not scream about how easy it is to make a billion dollars. I also won't laugh in your face and tell you that you are guaranteed to lose if you trade. You are perfectly welcome to read my opinions (everything here is my opinion), laugh (or flame me), and go on to somewhere else. I won't mind a bit. But I suspect that there are a number of people that will find that what I say rings true for them."

Who would not/could not believe a guy like that?

Troutman reviews trading systems, books, services, and more. He gives you his opinion. He gives you his informed, savvy, hip and useful opinion and nothing else. But Troutman's opinion is more than worth having.

What you will *not* find here includes: guaranteed ways to make money fast, stock market info, a totally comprehensive library of resources that every trader and would-be trader will find absolutely useful in every way, advice on which way any of the markets are going to go, advertising for other people's products and services, what Troutman calls "multi-level marketing garbage," or anything at all for sale.

If you are a derivatives trader with just one chance to access one Internet resource in your lifetime, make this the one.

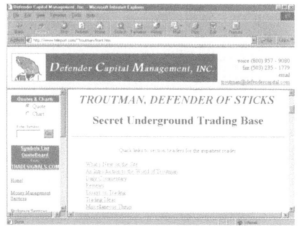

Figure 5.19 Troutman on Trading: Futures Trading System Reviews.

> ## Government Backed Insurance for Investors
>
> When you deposit money within a bank, your money is normally insured by the FDIC (the Federal Depository Insurance Corporation). The FDIC insures your deposits against the potential bankruptcy of your bank. In a similar way, when you work with a brokerage company, your investments are insured (up to $100,000 for cash and $500,000 for investments) by the SIPC (Securities Investors Protection Corporation). The SIPC is a government agency that insures your investments against the bankruptcy of your brokerage firm. Note, however, the SIPC insurance does not cover your investments for losses due to the decreased value of your securities. It provides you with bankruptcy protection only.

ROBERT'S ON-LINE OPTION PRICER

http://www.intrepid.com/~robertl/option-pricer1.html

The option pricer is available in either a non-Java, HotJava, or Java version. Many of the same flavors are also available for other applications, by the way, including a derivatives pricer, a commissions pricer, an option strategy visualizer, a portfolio pricer, a quote sheet, a straight spreadsheet, stock volatility charts, and a tax pricer. Check it out.

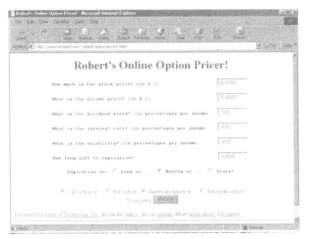

Figure 5.20 Robert's On-Line Option Pricer.

VALUATION MODELS FOR OPTIONS AND FUTURES VALUATIONS

http://www.clem.mscd.edu/~mayest/formulae/frmlindex.htm

This site contains a great collection of valuation models including the Black-Scholes European call option valuation model and the Black-Scholes European put option valuation model. The site also provides models for put-call parity for European options with no cash flows, single-period binomial option pricing for call option valuation, single-period binomial option pricing for put option valuation, and a cost-of-carry model for pricing futures contracts. Links to additional formula pages gives you basic time value formulae, basic security valuation formulae, basic statistical formulae, portfolio formulae, capital market theory models, and bond analysis formulae.

Figure 5.21 *Valuation Models for Options and Futures Valuations.*

AMERICAN FUTURES GROUPS

http://www.blacktek.com/afg

AGF was founded in 1984 as an international oil brokerage firm, now expanded into futures trading. This site offers trade recommendations, reviews, and consultation services.

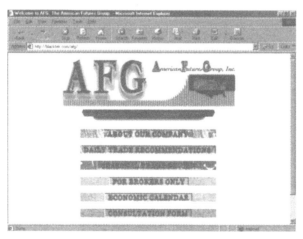

Figure 5.22 *American Futures Group.*

GIBBONS BURKE'S HOT LINKS FOR TRADERS

http://www.io.com/gibbonsb/wahoo/brokers.html

Gibbons Burke is Database Content and Quality Manager for Logical Information Machines, Inc., in Austin, Texas. The firm publishes a historical financial database and technical trading and research software. Burke is also the author of "The Computerized Trader," an absolutely *indispensable* monthly column that runs in *Futures* Magazine. At this efficient, elegantly designed Web site, Mr. Burke provides you with all the most vital links of interest to investors in commodities futures and other derivatives.

Burke provides links to hundreds of sites, including every futures exchange in the world, stock and options exchanges across the US and around the world, 23 futures brokers, ten firms concerned with managed futures, a large list of on-line financial news resources, extensive market data sources yielding free intra-day and end-of-day stock and commodities quotes, usenet newsgroups, extensive sources for financial shareware and freeware, and more than thirty on-line sources for newsletters and market commentary.

You'll even find some great esoterica here. Esoterica? Yes. Like the home page for Professor William F. Sharpe, Nobel Prize-winning creator of the famous Sharpe Ratio for investment analysis and an originator of the Capital Asset Pricing Model.

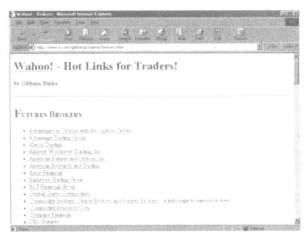

Figure 5.23 Gibbons Burke's Hot Links for Traders.

CLUB 3000: GREAT FUTURES CHAT

http://www.wsdinc.com/pgs_www.w4039.shtml

Club 3000 is a network of commodity traders founded in 1981 and has been in continuous operation ever since. Members discuss all aspects of commodity trading, including but not limited to trading systems and their performance. The club has more than 1,000 members on five continents. The discussion is always completely objective. That is because *Club 3000* has no commercial ties, and, thus, no conflicts of interest. "We have always been, and continue to be, completely independent of any vendors in the industry," writes Webmaster Bo Thunman. *Club 3000* does not sell trading systems or manage money, nor does it have any other connection with any commercial organization in the futures field. So, I know what you are asking. Where did the name come from? *Club 3000*. Just what does that mean? I'll let Bo answer: "For some unexplained reason, most commercial trading systems sell for $3000. Most members of *Club 3000* have written a check for that amount to a system vendor at least once. The search for a perfect system goes on..." And on and on.

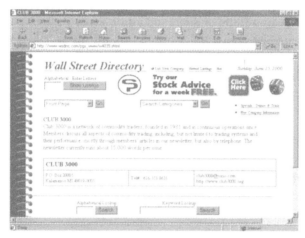

Figure 5.24 Club 3000: Great Futures Chat.

LINKS TO FUTURES GROUPS

http://www.soc.hawaii.edu/future/dator/links.html

This site offers an extensive directory of futures sites.

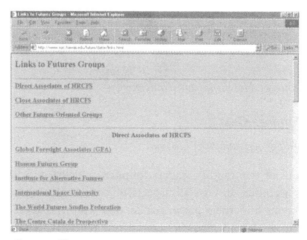

Figure 5.25 Links to Futures Groups.

YOUNG & RUBICAM INC. – BRAND FUTURES GROUP

http://www.yr.com/companies/brandfutures

Y&R's trend-tracking unit serves as a knowledge company. They create products and services that spur thinking on issues, trends, and events that are having some affect on consumer markets worldwide.

Figure 5.26 The Brand Futures Group.

FUTURESWEB

http://www.futuresweb.com

This site is a futures and options portal with quotes, news, charts, links, books and software. You can get daily research, top futures moves, and today's filings. Listen to the S&P 500 trading pit LIVE!

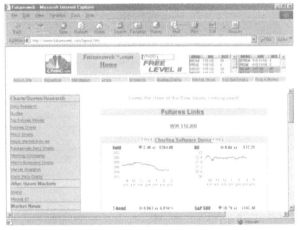

Figure 5.27 Futuresweb.

IPO.COM

http://www.ipo.com

This site provides information surrounding early stage investment opportunities. Get the latest IPO news, IPO event log, calendars, and what's new today in venture capital information, including a "Featured VC Firm." IPO.com shows the most recent filings and pricing, and you can view prospectuses of IPO companies. Get free newsletters from *The Standard.*

Figure 5.28 IPO.COM.

ALERT – IPO!

http://www.ostman.com

This site provides an automated notification system for initial public offerings. You can get hot IPOs, after market reports, the latest filings and pricings, postponements and withdrawals. Subscribe for $34.95 a year.

Figure 5.29 Alert – IPO! Web site.

ALARON TRADING: COMMODITIES TRADING ADVISORS

http://www.alaron.com

OPTIONS EDUCATION

http://www.cboe.com/education

NEW YORK BOARD OF TRADE

http://www.nybot.com

JACK CARL FUTURES: COMMODITIES TRADING ADVISORS

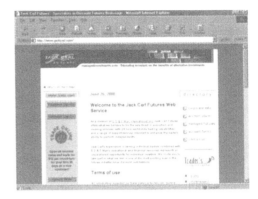

http://www.jackcarl.com

FUTURES EXCHANGE

http://www.cbot.com

COMMODITIES TRADING ADVISORS

http://www.commodity.com

COMMODITY SYSTEMS INC.:
FEE BASED FUTURES INFO SYSTEMS

http://www.csidata.com

DR. ALEXANDER H. ELDER,
FUTURES TRADING GURU

http://www.elder.com

THOMSON'S INVESTORS MARKET

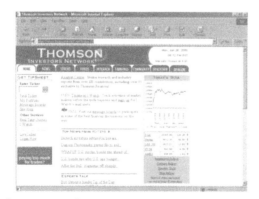

http://www.thomsoninvest.net

SAKURA DELLSHER:
COMMODITIES TRADING ADVISOR

http://www.sdinet.com

END-OF-DAY FUTURES PRICES FROM
RICHARD POTTS

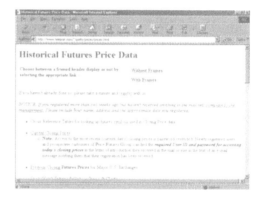

http://www.teleport.com/~rpotts/prices/prices.html

FIMAT FUTURES:
COMMODITIES TRADING ADVISORS

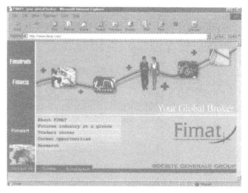

http://www.fimat.com

THE FUTURES MARKET MADE EASY: A TUTORIAL

http://www.midam.com/pit/

DIRECTORY OF FUTURES AND OPTIONS EXCHANGES

http://www.numa.com/ref/index.htm

HARD RED WINTER WHEAT FUTURES

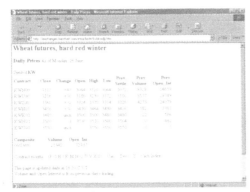

*http://exchanges.barchart.com/
intra/kcbt/kcbtwdp.htm*

GLOSSARY OF DERIVATIVES ACRONYMS

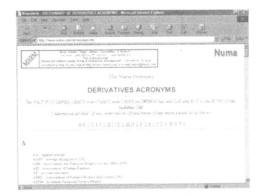

http://www.numa.com/ref/index.htm

OPTIONS STRATEGY GUIDE

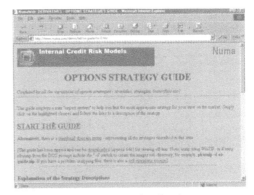

http://www.numa.com/ref/index.htm

TREASURE STATE FUTURES: COMMODITIES TRADING ADVISORS

http://www.montanaweb.com/futures/

HONG KONG FUTURES EXCHANGE

http://www.hkfe.com

HIGH PLAINS JOURNAL

http://www.hpj.com

INTERNATIONAL ADVISORY SERVICES GROUP: COMMODITIES TRADING ADVISORS

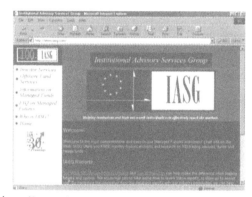

http://www.iasg.com

INTERQUOTE FINANCIAL QUOTE SERVICES: FEE-BASED FUTURES INFO SYSTEM

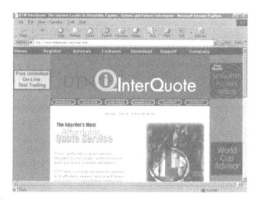

http://www.interquote.com

KANSAS CITY BOARD OF TRADE

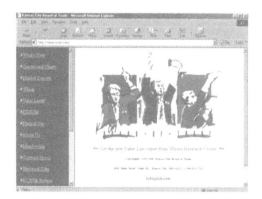

http://www.kcbt.com

THE LIFFE: LONDON COMMODITIES EXCHANGE

http://www.liffe.com

ARGO FUTURES GROUP

http://www.argofutures.com

THE MATIF: PARIS COMMODITIES EXCHANGE

http://www.matif.fr/

THE MEFF: MADRID COMMODITIES EXCHANGE

http://www.meff.es

MINNEAPOLIS GRAIN EXCHANGE

http://www.mgex.com/

MID-AMERICA COMMODITIES EXCHANGE/CHICAGO

http://www.midam.com

MIDSTATES COMMODITIES: COMMODITIES TRADING ADVISORS

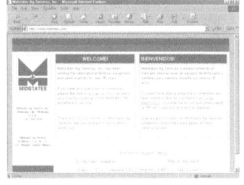

http://www.midstates.com

J.P. MORGAN COMMODITY INDEXES

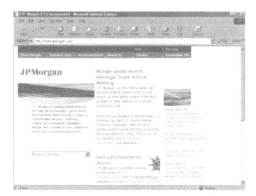

http://www.jpmorgan.com

R.J. O'BRIEN: COMMODITIES TRADING ADVISOR

http://www.askrjo.com

PRUDENTIAL SECURITIES COMMODITIES GROUP

http://www.prusec.com

ESTIMATE VOLUME FOR FUTURES AND OPTIONS

http://www.nybot.com

PROPHET INFORMATION SERVICES: FEE-BASED FUTURES INFORMATION SYSTEM

http://www.prophetdata.com

QUOTECOM: FEE-BASED FUTURES INFORMATION SYSTEM

http://www.quote.com

RAND FINANCIAL SERVICES: COMMODITIES TRADING ADVISORS

http://www.rand-usa.com

SOUTH AFRICAN FUTURES EXCHANGE

http://www.sharenet.co.za

CNNFN COMMODITIES

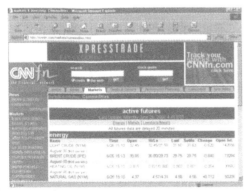

http://cnnfn.com/markets/commodities.html

WAT.CH: SWISS RESOURCES ON DERIVATIVES

http://Finance.Wat.ch

INTERNATIONAL FINANCE & COMMODITIES INSTITUTE

http://Finance.Wat.ch/IFCI/

DISCOUNT FUTURES BROKERAGE

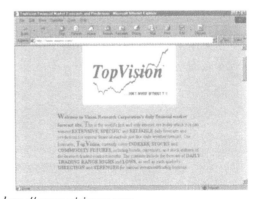

http://www.visionrc.com

INTERNATIONAL FUTURES GROUP

http://www.ifgfutures.com/about.htm

SPRINGBOARD *IPO*

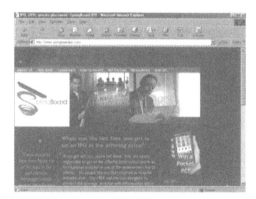

http://www.springboardipo.com

DUN & BRADSTREET CORPORATE PROFILES

http://www.dnbcorp.com/corp/bios/index.cfm

WALL STREET DIRECTORY

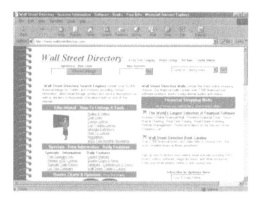

http://www.wallstreetdirectory.com

BARCLAY TRADING GROUP, LTD.

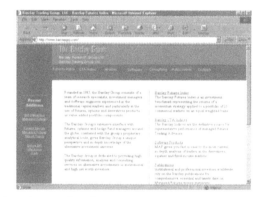

http://www.barclaygrp.com

STEVEN R. MYERS ON FUTURES

http://www.futures-daily.com/news01.htm

FIRST NATIONAL FUTURES GROUP, INC.

http://www.nationalfutures.com

LASALLE FUTURES GROUP, INC.

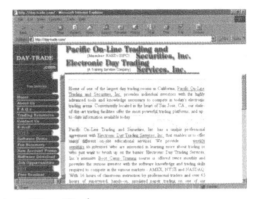

http://Day-Trade.com

ORION FUTURES GROUP

http://www.orionfutures.com

TOKYO GRAIN EXCHANGE

http://www.tge.or.jp/index.html

USDA DAIRY MARKET REPORTS

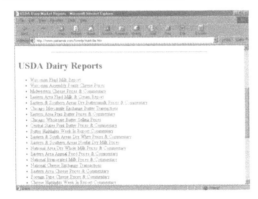

http://www.joefarmer.com/howdy/
markdar.htm

CHAPTER 6

THE ZEN OF BONDS

I'm tired of Love: I'm still more tired of Rhyme. But money gives me pleasure all the time. — **Hilaire Belloc, Fatigue**

SO WHAT IS A BOND?

A secret agent, of course. With a license to kill. But beyond this, a bond is also a fixed-income security that relates to a debt on the part of the bond's issuer (the borrower), and a loan on the part of the bond's owner (*you*, the lender). Most bond agreements stipulate a periodic rate of interest to be paid on the part of the borrower. When you purchase a bond, you are in fact becoming a lender entitled to interest (often payable every six months) and eventual repayment of the principal amount (commonly called the *face value* or *par value*) of the bond you own. But beyond these fundamental similarities, there are many differences among different bond issues that you, the potential purchaser of bonds, need to understand.

WHO ISSUES BONDS?

Governments (federal, state, and local) and corporations issue bonds. Any large, bankable organization that wants to raise money is likely to use bonds. Municipal governments will often issue bonds to raise cash to build bridges, highways, and other such expensive accouterments to the public infrastructure. Corporations will issue bonds to help finance large real estate investments, capital improvements, and acquisition of other firms. The federal government has, on more than once occasion, used bonds to help finance warfare, such as with the famous Liberty Bonds.

TERMS OF BOND ISSUE

Loan agreements for various bond issues will specify the timetable for the repayment of principal and interest. This schedule may be as short as several months but is far more likely to run for many years, since in financial markets the term *bond* is customarily reserved for long-term debt.

Perhaps you can't tell a book by its cover, but you can tell at least something about a bond by what is printed on its certificate. Here you will find a statement of principal amount, interest payments, and the bond owner's name. Further details about any given bond issue are to be found in a formal agreement (the *indenture agreement*) that must always be completed and filed with a commercial bank before the date bonds are issued. The commercial bank where the agreement is on file serves as a trustee appointed by the issuer to enforce the terms of the indenture described in the agreement.

Why Buy Bonds?

Most investors purchase bonds in order to earn interest income. Since bonds by nature provide a precisely defined interest rate, investors in bonds can count upon a set interest rate for a set period of time without having to worry about fluctuations in market-rate interest.

Other investors go for specific bonds because they believe the market value of the bonds will increase. Thus, they hope to gain income both from interest and from a gain in the bond's "real" market value. (For consideration of exactly what events would conspire to increase the value of a bond, see the section below entitled *What Makes a Bond's Price Go Up and Down?*)

Where to Buy Bonds

Corporate bonds, along with all federal obligations other than savings bonds, are best purchased through the same broker you use for the purchase of stocks. Tax-free municipal bonds are best purchased through firms such as Roosevelt & Cross, which specialize in these unique types of financial instruments. The same goes for international governmental bonds, where such brokerages and international banking institutions as J.P. Morgan lead the pack.

Trading in Bonds

There is no law that says once you purchase a bond you must hang on to it until maturity (until the date, prescribed in the indenture agreement, at which the borrower must repay the principal and retire the bond, or debt). Many investors acquire bonds with no intention of holding the securities until maturity, fully intending to speculate in the short-term with what tend to be long-term obligations.

All bonds (save for US Government Savings Bonds, which will be discussed later) are negotiable financial instruments easily transferable from one investor to another. There is absolutely no limit to how many times a bond can change hands in between the dates of issuance and maturity. And the thriving bond market functions very much like the stock market.

THE PRICE OF BONDS

The price at which you sell or buy a bond depends upon several factors: the annual interest payment amounts, maturity length, market-credit conditions and interest rates, and the latest "intelligence" on the bond issuer's financial condition.

You see, bonds can sometimes be "dicey things," and their genuine values are often hard to discern or forecast.

There is no guarantee of repayment of a bond's principal at the end of a bond's term, just as there is no guarantee of future interest payments, should the issuer prove not to be solvent. The state of the issuer's financial health, as well as the rate of interest declared by the bond as compared to rates of interest available at various times in the open market, are both factors that greatly impact the "real" value of a bond.

Thus, a bond's face value and "real" market value are two different things. Two *very* different things. While a bond's "real" market value fluctuates, its face value remains static. A $10,000 note will always have a face value of $10,000, but you may be able to purchase the same certificate on the bond market for $9,000. But look carefully at such sweet deals. Is the issuer heading to bankruptcy court? Is the interest rate of the bond considerably below what you can find via other relatively safe investment vehicles?

ALL BONDS ARE NOT CREATED EQUAL

You see a bond for sale at what appears to be a good price. But how sure are you that scheduled interest and principal will be paid in full and on time? How sure are you that the issuer is good for the debt represented by the bond?

The range of bond-quality types is extensive. US Treasury securities have long been considered the safest bond investment, while some "small-cap" (companies with limited capital) commercial bonds for risky start-up corporations have such a low reputation as to be labeled *junk bonds*. On the other hand, US Treasury securities, backed as they are by the full faith and credit of the United States Government, pay relatively low interest rates compared to the rates offered by high-risk *junk bonds*. The higher the credit "quality" of a bond issue, the lower the interest rate one can expect.

Between the two extremes of the spectrum from US Treasury notes to *junk bonds* lay a number of exciting and lucrative possibilities for bond investment.

THE VARIETIES OF BONDS: READ THE FINE PRINT

A borrower (a bond issuer) is likely to have several different issues of bonds floating out in the market at any given moment. The different bond issues will usually contain different promises for maturities, interest rates and payments, and so on. And this is why the credit quality of the individual bond issue itself is often more important than the credit quality of the issuer.

Picture a new start-up: a high-tech Silicon Valley enterprise that hasn't taken off yet. The partners in the firm long ago exhausted their grandparents' trust funds and their parents' patience. They used to sell minority shares of stock to friends who, at this late date, are barely speaking to them. But the firm's new software product is starting to look very, very good. All they need is a little more money for development. All they need is some capital. But the stock is already sold.

What to do?

Answer: *bonds*. The indenture agreement for their first issue (Series A) pledges all the assets of the firm as collateral against the debt incurred by the bond, and, furthermore, stipulates that this initial bond will have repayment priority over all the firm's other debts and obligations. Their second bond (Series B) is issued a few months later. It comes with no pledge of collateral and with specific language in the indenture agreement stating plainly that this bond issue is subordinated to a previous bond issued by the firm. Series A bonds are relatively secure and probably have a relatively low coupon rate (interest rate—the term *coupon rate* dates back to the days when bonds actually had coupons that bond owners would clip off and take to the bank to redeem their interest) as compared to Series B bonds, which are much more risky.

USING BOND RATINGS

Judging a bond's overall *credit quality* (the quality of the bond along with the stability of the issuer) is a complicated business and not for amateurs. The majority of investors have neither the savvy nor the time to dissect an issuer's cash-flow, income-to-debt ratio, and industry position. Nor do they have the expertise for the companion analysis of intricacies in individual bond issues.

Luckily, someone else is happy to do this analysis for you.

Moody's Investors Service and Standard & Poor's Corporation are privately held firms that make a business of evaluating and publishing the credit quality of bond issues. The rating grades set up by each company vary slightly, though they both consider AAA their highest rating. Each firm groups bonds in ten to twelve quality categories below AAA, and many financial advisers suggest that individual investors restrict their purchases to bonds in the top two or three categories. Bonds rated lower than BBB by Standard & Poor's, and bonds rated below Baa by Moody, are generally considered to be extremely risky and are classified as *junk bonds*.

WHAT MAKES A BOND'S PRICE GO UP AND DOWN?

In a nutshell: Bond values vary inversely with market interest rates. The market value of a bond will increase if the market rate of interest declines after the bond is issued. Conversely, the market value of a bond will decrease if interest rates increase after the bond is issued.

Consider this example. A bond with a 10% coupon rate (interest rate) goes up in value when the market rate of interest goes down to, say, 7% or 8%.

But keep something in mind. Barring fast and vast swings in interest rates of the type we (thankfully) see only rarely, changes in market values for bonds tend to be much smaller than changes in values for common stocks.

Thus bonds, though they certainly may increase in market value, are chiefly vehicles for those of us who seek income from interest while preserving capital.

Inflation: The Bondholder's Boogeyman

The first and foremost risk in bond ownership—assuming we are not talking about junk bond ownership—is that hoary old devil inflation. In fact, inflation is the bondholder's bogeyman, Nosforatu and grim-reaper combined. Inflation is the monster that lurks under the bondholder's financial bed like a nightmare about to spring into reality.

Why?

Think about it. In many ways, a bond is the most static of investments. A fairly stable principal base provides an interest-revenue at a set percentage rate over a prescribed period of time: most often a number of years. Then along comes inflation. Not only is the purchasing-power of the bond-principal eroded, but the market value of the bond goes down as interest rates soar. And the old, pre-inflation interest rate stipulated by the bond does nothing to help the bondholder make up the difference. Inflation soaks up the bondholder's profits, and often some of the bondholder's principal, like a sponge. And with the market-value of the bond plunging, there is no way to get out of the bond profitably. One either sells it for a song or sits around and bleeds cash until the bond's maturity date. Neither option is appealing.

One tool the bondholder can use to protect him- or herself from rising interest rates is the *put option*. The put option prescribed in some (though not very many) indenture agreements allows bondholders to force a bond issuer to redeem a bond prior to scheduled maturity. The put option allows the investor to redeem the bond and then reinvest at a higher coupon rate. Bonds that incorporate the put option are routinely called *put bonds*.

The Call: Boogeyman Number 2

Indenture agreements for many corporate bonds, as well as, many Treasury bonds permit forced surrender of bonds years prior to their scheduled maturity date at the discretion (call) of the bond issuer. The indenture agreements for these securities specify precisely when the instrument may be called and at what price. This price is the *call* price, and it is usually slightly higher than the face value of the bond.

According to the terms of most indenture agreements, there is usually an initial period of years during which holders are inoculated against early retirement of their bonds. However, once this period of time has elapsed, the decision whether or not to call a bond is entirely in the hands of the issuer.

The decision to call a bond almost always goes against the best interests of the bondholders. Obviously, issuers are most tempted to call bonds when market interest rates fall below the bond's coupon rate. But this is exactly the time when bondholders most need and want to hang onto the bonds and their relatively high rate of return.

BONDS VS. STOCKS

Bonds and stocks are both negotiable financial instruments, but there the similarities end. As has previously been discussed, common stock provides you with proportional ownership in a business, a proportional voice in that firm's management, and a proportional claim to profits paid in the form of dividends. There is the potential for great reward with stocks, but also the potential for large losses with elimination of dividends and decline in share values.

Generally, bonds (although not junk bonds) are considered to be a less risky investment than common stock.

Note that most bond indenture agreements call for the payment of the full amount of the bond loan prior to recovery of any cash by a firm's owners (shareholders). As a holder of a company's bonds, you have what is called a "priority claim" to a firm's cash.

Note also that common stocks carry no scheduled maturity dates and no guarantee of dividends. Stockholders can only hope dividends will be declared and can only liquidate their investment by selling their shares to another investor. A bondholder, on the other hand, is guaranteed the interest stipulated in the indenture agreement and has *two* options for liquidation: either selling the bond or holding on to it and waiting for the maturity date and the repayment of principal.

ARE BONDS FOR YOU?

Well, of course, that depends on who you are and what your financial goals are.

But, if you will allow me a broad generalization here, I will say this:

Generally, stocks are a good investment for those who are not yet rich but want to be, whereas bonds are generally a good investment for those who are already rich and want to stay that way.

While stocks offer the prospect of capital *accumulation*, highly-rated bonds offer the prospect of maximized return on capital joined with capital *preservation*.

Thus, bonds (along with other income-generating investments such as long-term certificates of deposit) tend to be favored by investors who, having already accumulated capital, would rather like to keep it and see no great need to unduly risk it in order to achieve a good return.

A HEALTHY BALANCE

You want a balanced diet, and you want a balanced portfolio of investments. In this sense, some degree of bond-ownership is probably for everyone. Having a percentage of your portfolio in bonds offsets the risks that come with other investments, such as common stocks.

What is the proper balance? The proper balance depends on you, who you are, how much money you have, how your money balances against your obligations, where you are in life, and so on.

If you will permit me another broad generalization, I'd say that the percentage of your portfolio you have in bonds and other conservative, income-generating investments should increase as you grow older, approach retirement, and become less able to deal (economically) with short-term dips in equity markets.

Free Trial Newsletters from the Hirsch Organization

The Hirsch Organization publishes three newsletters that detail various aspects of investing:

Ground Floor	examines new technologies
Smart Money	examines market trends and positions
Turov on Timing	examines very short, short, intermediate, and long-term positions

To examine a free sample copy of these newsletters, contact the Hirsch Organization at 1-800-477-3400.

BONDS AND TAXES

Never mind death and taxes, what about bonds and taxes?

Your tax-situation will have a large impact on your consideration of whether or not you should invest in bonds and, if so, to what extent.

If you are in a high-income bracket, you are less likely to benefit very much from the ownership of corporate bonds.

Why?

Consider the situation. If you are already paying a large percentage of your current income in taxes, then an investment that offers additional current income (as opposed to increases in principal value) is less attractive than it might otherwise be.

ON THE OTHER HAND: THE JOY OF TAX-FREE BONDS

Most bonds offered by state and local governments in the United States pay interest that is not subject to federal US tax. (Conversely, bonds issued by the US Treasury and other government agencies pay interest that is not subject to state and local taxes.) Most often state and local municipal bonds have a slightly lower coupon rate than comparable corporate bonds; however, the tax exemption can nevertheless make them appealing for some high-tax bracket investors.

That's right. Tax-free municipals are of special interest to investors in high federal tax brackets. The higher your rate of federal taxation, the more tax-free municipals are likely to make sense for you. The lower your federal tax-rate, the less likely it is that tax-free municipals are the investment vehicle you need.

States and cities issue tax-free municipal bonds to help pay for bridges, prisons, airports, highways, and sewage treatment plants, as well as many other capital improvements. By using bonds, the borrowers can get a lower rate of interest on the debt than they otherwise could by borrowing through other sources. At the same time, factoring in the federal tax exemption, the bondholder in the high federal tax bracket winds up being paid more "real" interest over time than he or she would otherwise be likely to see.

Tax-free municipals are most always issued in multiples of $5,000. Maturities can range greatly: from just a few months to more than thirty years. Zero-coupon municipal bonds are issued at extreme discounts from face value, but pay no interest save for the promise of redemption at face value. Other municipal bonds begin paying interest only a number of years after the date of issue. But the vast majority of tax-free municipals mimic their taxable corporate counterparts in that they are issued at face value with a prescribed coupon rate for semiannual interest payments. Like corporate bonds, the "real" market price of tax-free municipals fluctuates depending on the direction of interest rates and the bond's rating. And like corporate bonds, tax-free municipals may change hands any number of times prior to their maturity dates.

THE DIFFERENT TYPES OF TAX-FREE MUNICIPALS

There are two fundamental types of tax-free municipal bonds, as follows:

General Obligation Bonds (GOs) are guaranteed by the full faith and credit of the state or local government issuing the bonds. The promise of repayment is backed up by the full taxing power of the state or city. But keep in mind, a city or state's taxing power does have one real limit: the limit of the economy in that city or state. Where there is a weak economy, the taxing authority of the municipality may not count for much. Thus, not all GOs are equally credit-worthy. With GOs as with all other bonds, a reference-check using Moody's or S&P's ratings charts is always worth the effort.

Revenue Bonds are tax-free municipals guaranteed only by specific revenues derived by the particular project the bonds are meant to finance. If it is a highway, the debt will mostly likely be paid by tolls collected. If it is a sports stadium, the debt will most often be returned by the rent paid by occupying teams, and so on. No other assets of the governing body issuing the bonds may be attached for payment of the bond interest and principal other than assets generated by the specific project funded by the bond.

Obviously, revenue bonds are, generally, more risky than GOs. But not always. Revenue bonds issued by New York City to finance new port facilities may well be a more stable investment than GOs from some desolate, economic wasteland with a lousy tax base. Your ideal tax-free municipal is, clearly, a very highly rated GO from a boomtown such as New York or Atlanta: one with a rating in Moody's or S&P's top three brackets, and it's even better if it is insured.

Looking for Key Specific Information, Try SIE Newsletters

If you are looking for specific information on bonds, tax-free bonds, or any other aspect of investing (from stocks to options and more), you may want to change to the wide range of newsletters available from Select Information Exchange (SIE). For specifics on the available newsletters, contact SIE at 800-743-9346. Ask them to send you a free miniature copy of their newsletter catalog.

Insured Tax-Free Municipals

Some, though not all, municipal revenue bonds, and a few GOs, are insured. With these bonds, the insurer has received a fee in return for committing to pay interest and principal if the issuer is unable to do so. Insured municipal bonds tend to pay lower interest rates, since they involve less risk than other municipals.

IS ALL THE INTEREST FROM TAX-FREE MUNICIPALS TAX-FREE?

Hold on there, cowboy. Not always. Most of the time, *yes*. But not always.

The interest on a few municipal bonds designed to finance "nonessential" expenditures (as classified by the federal government, such as sports complexes and convention centers) may be subject to either the federal alternative minimum tax (AMT) or straight federal income taxes. Your bond broker is required by law to clearly indicate to you any municipal bonds for which interest will be taxable. On the plus side, these instruments most often pay a higher rate of interest than their nontaxable counterparts.

BUYING BOND PORTFOLIOS "OFF THE SHELF"

Don't feel like doing a lot of bond homework? Rather watch a baseball game or listen to Sting? I don't blame you. In fact, I am right there with you.

Consider using any of a number of bond mutual funds, closed-end bond funds, and unit investment trusts (UITs) who pool investors' contributions to purchase broad portfolios of bonds which in turn are professionally managed to maximize return. The differences between mutual funds and closed-end funds will be discussed in next chapter.

U.S. FEDERAL GOVERNMENT BONDS

US Government Bonds vary in coupon rates and maturity timeframes, but virtually all US Government debt securities are of high-quality and are backed by "the full faith and credit of the US government." That being said, keep in mind that some federal agencies issue bonds (called *agency issues* or *federal agency issues*), which are considered slightly less secure than obligations associated with those old war-horses of investing, US Treasury bills, notes, and bonds.

It is important to remember that the interest paid on all federal bonds is subject to federal taxes but is *not* subject to taxation by state and local government. Thus, federal bonds have high appeal in states such as California and New York, where personal income tax rates are high. The state and local tax advantage is doubly important vis-à-vis federal bonds when we remember that, because of their high credit quality, these bonds tend to carry a coupon rate considerably below that of their more risky corporate counterparts or even most tax-free municipals.

There are four main vehicles for US federal bond debt. These are *US Treasury Bills (T-Bills)*, *US Treasury Notes and Bonds*, *US Savings Bonds*, and *Federal Agency Issues*.

THE SCOOP ON U.S. TREASURY BILLS (T-BILLS)

T-Bills are geared for the most sophisticated institutional investors or private investors with large amounts to invest. They are not something for the little guy to play around with. T-Bills are short-term bonds issued in an initial minimum denomination of $10,000. Additional bills are available in $5,000 denominations once the minimum purchase of $10,000 has been satisfied for any given issue.

Just how short-term are T-Bills? *Very.* Some T-Bills have maturities of thirteen weeks (91 days). Other T-Bills have maturities of twenty-six weeks (182 days). And the longest T-Bill has a maturity of one year.

T-Bills are auctioned at a discount from face value and then redeemed for full face value at their maturity date. Thirteen-week and Twenty Six-Week securities are auctioned each Monday while one-year T-Bills are auctioned only twelve times per year: on the fourth Thursday of each month.

Sold at a discount and redeemable at face value, T-Bills have no prescribed coupon rate and do not pay *regular* interest. The discount at the time of bond purchase replaces the interest payments associated with most other bond debt. In other words, T-Bills are zero-coupon bonds.

Their relatively short maturity windows, combined with the financial strength of their issuer, make T-Bills very secure investment vehicles. Like other such financial instruments, T-Bills are fully negotiable and may change hands any number of times in the brief window of weeks or months before their maturity date. Should you sell a T-bill before its maturity date, you should obviously plan on receiving a price somewhere between the bill's face value and the discounted purchase price.

As has been noted before, the best way to purchase T-Bills, along with other federal and corporate obligations, is simply to go through the same broker you use for stocks. However, should you wish to save on what is often a nominal broker's commission for T-Bill purchase, you can personally buy T-Bills directly from the Treasury. The process, which involves using a non-competitive tender, is somewhat complicated. For complete details you should either visit your nearest Federal Reserve bank or write to the Bureau of the Public Debt, Division of Customer Services, 300 13th Street S.W., Washington, DC 20239-0001. The Bureau of Public Debt also has a Web page referenced in the *Internet Resources* section of this chapter.

U.S. TREASURY NOTES AND BONDS

US Treasury notes and bonds are fundamentally the same thing as T-Bills, except for their time-frames and whether or not they are "callable." Notes mature in from two to ten years, while bonds mature over a minimum of ten years. Treasury notes are not callable. Treasury bonds, however, may often be called five years prior to their scheduled maturities. (What is a *call*? See the discussion earlier in this chapter related to corporate bond call provisions.)

Treasury notes and bonds are issued at face-value throughout the year and carry coupon rates for semiannual interest. Their coupon-rates are routinely lower than corporate bonds, municipals, and even federal agency issues. However, they are so stable an instrument that they represent virtually no risk to principal. Thus, their high rating is not negated by their low interest, which, keep in mind, remains exempt from state and local taxes.

FEDERAL AGENCY ISSUES

Many federal agencies regularly issue bonds to finance a range of projects. There are bonds available from the Student Loan Marketing Association, the Tennessee Valley Authority, the

Government National Mortgage Association, and so on. These bonds come in denominations ranging from just $1,000 up to more than $50,000, and have maturities that range from just one year on up to more than 40 years.

Commonly referred to as either *agency issues* or *federal agency issues*, these bonds are viewed as *slightly* more risky than Treasury instruments. Why? Because agency issues do not formally have the "full faith and credit of the US government" behind them. This is a technicality. Virtually every economic pundit in the business of knowing about these things agrees that the Treasury would most certainly step in to aid a financially-troubled agency, even though there is no formal obligation to do so. Nevertheless, even the slightest air of uncertainty means that agency issues must pay a higher coupon rate than do US Treasury notes and bonds.

The most popular type of agency issue is what's called a *pass-through security*. Pass-through securities are offered by the Government National Mortgage Association (GNMA, commonly referenced as *Ginne Mae*).

In order to raise capital for housing lenders, Ginne Mae gathers insured Veterans Administration (VA) and Federal Housing Administration (FHA) mortgages into portfolio pools and sells shares in these portfolios to investors as separate securities called *Ginnie Mae pass-throughs*. Where does the phrase *pass-through* come in? Ginnie May collects principal and interest payments on the mortgages monthly and (promptly) passes through the cash to holders of the pass-through securities.

This is very high-quality debt. The VA and FHA mortgages are insured. There is absolutely no risk of principal. The only downside to pass-throughs is the threat posed by large principal repayments, which most often occur in clusters. When mortgage rates go down, there is a high probability that holders of current mortgages will refinance with other lenders and, thus, prepay their VA or FHA mortgage debt in a lump sum. This scenario leaves pass-through owners in the uncomfortable position of having all or most of their principal returned to them at a time when other investment vehicles are likely to be offering low, comparatively unattractive interest rates.

SAVINGS BONDS

US Savings bonds are, so far as I am concerned, not very good investment vehicles.

For starters, there is the unwieldy mechanics of them. Unlike other direct obligations of the US Treasury, they are not marketable. In other words, they cannot be exchanged between investors for cash after their initial issue. And Savings Bonds cannot be bought and redeemed through a broker, but instead must be purchased and redeemed through an agent of the US Treasury, usually a bank.

Then there is their lousy return. Series EE bonds have an issue price that is 50% below face value and they pay a variable interest rate: 85% of the rate paid by five-year US Treasury

Bonds. Obviously, this floating interest rate scenario works for you when interest rates rise, and against you when they drop. But on the best day you are still only getting 85% of what an equally-secure Treasury Bond would pay. A certain minimum interest rate, which is prescribed on the day you buy your Savings Bond, kicks in if you hold your bond beyond five years. And this helps somewhat to guard against the threat of lowered interest rates. Furthermore, with Savings Bonds there are no interest payments paid to bondholders throughout the life of the bond. All interest is delivered at the time the bond is redeemed.

Series HH bonds are not much better. These are issued at face value and pay semiannual interest. Series HH bonds cannot be purchased for cash. Series HH bonds may only be obtained in exchange for Series EE bonds. If one exchanges a matured Series EE bond for a Series HH bond, one defers his or her tax liability on interest from the EE issue.

INTERNET RESOURCES FOR BOND INVESTORS

As you surf the World Wide Web, you may encounter sites that discuss bonds: corporate bonds, government bonds, junk bonds, and more. The following site list should help you locate the resources you need.

BONDTRAC

http://www.bondtrac.com

Bondtrac meets the challenge of today's highly competitive business climate by providing comprehensive and reliable information on the municipal, corporate, government, and agency bond markets. Bondtrac consolidates the bond inventories of hundreds of broker/dealers every day to provide thousands of fresh bond offerings to their subscribers.

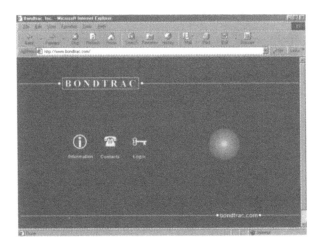

Figure 6.1 Bontrac.

BOND PROFESSOR AT BONDS ONLINE

http://www.bonds-online.com

Got a question about bonds? Just ask the Bond Professor. This is your chance to benefit from Dick Wilson's 35 years of experience in securities research, consulting, and marketing management at investment banking firms, investment advisories, and top-ranked ratings agencies. You will always get a prompt answer. And if your question is a particularly good one, you may well get posted in a place of honor as the "Question of the Week." But before you rattle the professor's cage with an inquiry, check out the FAQ and see if your problem can't be solved there.

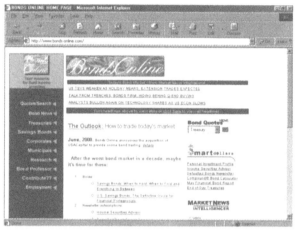

Figure 6.2 Bond Professor at Bonds OnLine.

MANAGED BONDS INFORMATION AT MONEYEXTRA

http://www.moneyworld.co.uk/glossary/gl00159.htm

Managed Bonds are in broad-based funds that aim to spread the risk for the investor by putting money into a variety of different places. Managed bonds tend to be fairly safe, conservative investments overall: no dramatic fast flights to enormous profits, but likewise no crash landings. Come to this informative Web page for more information.

Figure 6.3 Managed Bonds Information.

THE AMERICAN ASSOCIATION OF INDIVIDUAL INVESTORS

http://www.aaii.org

The American Association of Individual Investors is an independent, not-for-profit corporation formed in 1978 to assist individuals in becoming effective managers of their own investments. AAII achieves this aim through publications, nationwide seminars, home-study texts, educational videos, local chapters, and (of course!) a great Web site. Current membership is over 170,000. The primary benefit of membership, however, is the *AAII Journal,* which is published ten times a year. The focus is on providing information and how-to articles that help the individual learn investment fundamentals. The *Journal* does not promote a specific strategy of investment, nor does it recommend particular stocks, nor does it accept advertising. In addition, every March, every member receives a new edition of *The Individual Investor's Guide to Low-Load Mutual Funds*, a reference book providing data on over 800 no-load and – low-load mutual funds. The Guide includes tables of funds categorized by investment objective and ranked by return for various investment periods. An extensive summary of each fund includes performance data and fund descriptions.

Figure 6.4 The American Association of Individual Investors.

NIKKO-BOND PERFORMANCE INDEX (JAPAN)

http://www.nikko.co.jp/SEC/bond/summary.html

The Nikko Securities Co., Ltd., developed the Nikko-Bond Performance Index in 1988. The Nikko-Bond Performance Index is comprised of issues selected with an emphasis on liquidity and reflects, as the proprietors of the Index indicate, "market-capitalization-based-market-momentum." The Nikko-Bond Performance Index is currently being utilized by numerous bond market investors and their fiduciaries (including the Japan Bond Research Institute for its pension index domestic bond valuation) and is also ideal for performance evaluation and bond market analysis needs.

Recently, there have been a large number of changes in the Japanese bond market. The primary market for corporate bonds has been substantially deregulated since the beginning of 1996. And the Nikko-Bond Performance Index criteria has been revised to reflect these changes.

The rate of return for the Nikko-Bond Performance Index is based on value-weighted market capitalization including accrued interest. As a result, the Nikko-Bond Performance Index's cumulative rates of return are most suitable for actual performance evaluation. The inclusion of several sub-indices (sub-indices dealing with issue, term of maturity, and so on) allows the Nikko-Bond Performance Index to provide subscribers with a wide range of required information. These sub-indices are particularly useful for constructing your own custom indices.

Figure 6.5 Nikko-Bond Bond Performance Index (Japan).

NATIONAL ASSOCIATION OF INVESTORS CORPORATION **(NAIC)**

http://www.better-investing.org

The National Association of Investors Corporation (NAIC) is a non-profit organization made up of investment clubs and individual investors. It was founded in 1951 to increase the number of individual investors in common stocks and to provide a program of investment education and information for both experienced and inexperienced investors. At the Web site, you will find complete details on NAIC activities and membership across the country and around the world, links to on-line investment clubs sponsored by NAIC, and more. It is worth noting that the average personal portfolio of NAIC members is over $100,000. The total personal portfolio of all NAIC members combined is over $15.5 billion. And the new money invested by NAIC members through various channels on a monthly basis is over $14 million.

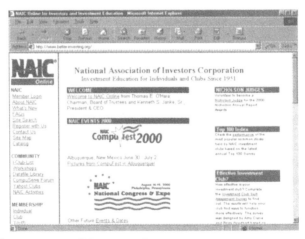

Figure 6.6 National Association of Investors Corporation.

BOND MARKETS ASSOCIATION

http://www.psa.com

The Bond Markets Association (BMA) is the bond market trade association representing securities firms and banks that underwrite, trade, and sell debt securities both domestically and internationally. These debt securities include municipal bonds, US Treasury securities, federal agency securities, mortgage and other asset-backed securities, corporate debt securities, and money market instruments.

The origins of the Bond Markets Association (formerly the Public Securities Association) go back to the founding of the Investment Bankers Association of America (IBAA) in 1912. BMA became a separate organization in 1976.

There are 360 members and associate members of the BMA, along with 21 affiliates. You'll find all the BMA members listed here. Membership in BMA is a sign of integrity in a brokerage. Thus, it is worth a stop here to make sure the brokerage you are considering opening an account with maintains BMA membership.

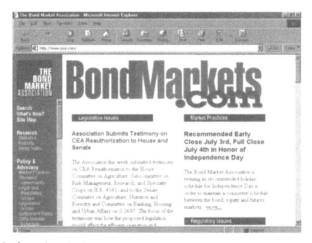

Figure 6.7 Bond Markets Association.

PRUDENTIAL SECURITIES MUNICIPAL BOND INFORMATION

http://www.prusec.com/products_services/muni.htm

This elegantly-designed and well-written Web site includes answers to the questions: What are municipal bonds? Why do municipal bonds make sense as an investment? What is the best method for selecting the bond or bonds that are right for you? And what types of municipal bonds are available? Finally, it also contains one of the most cogent and useful explanations I've found of the often-confusing Alternative Minimum Tax (AMT).

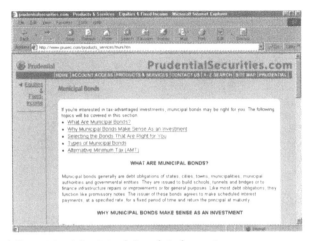

Figure 6.8 Prudential Securities Municipal Bond Information.

ROOSEVELT & CROSS (U.S. TAX-EXEMPT) BOND BROKERAGE

http://www.roosevelt-cross.com

Roosevelt & Cross was founded in 1946 by Archibald B. Roosevelt, the youngest son of President Theodore Roosevelt, and Edwin Cross. Their stated mission was clear and precise: to protect client capital while providing maximum yields. The current incarnation of Roosevelt & Cross evolved from Roosevelt & Son, a hardware and glassware mercantile company founded in the year 1797. Over time, Roosevelt & Son became a banking concern involved with railroad and communication investment, gradually shifting toward the municipal bond market.

Over the years, Roosevelt & Cross has grown from a six-person operation to one with nearly a hundred employees. In addition to a headquarters in New York City, the firm maintains branch offices in Buffalo, Hartford, and Providence.

For those interested in investing in tax-free municipals, Roosevelt & Cross offers diversified tax-exempt bond offerings, competitive bid and ask markets, portfolio management, tax-swapping opportunities, taxable and tax-exempt money market investments, excess SIPCO Insurance covering holdings up to $5 million, and no charge for the payment of principal and interest. They also offer the expertise of a finely-honed municipal research department, unit investment trust expertise, mutual funds, and more.

A particular strength at Roosevelt & Cross is their Over-the-Counter Trading Department. The Roosevelt & Cross OTC Trading Department is an active market maker in 70 New York Stock Exchange and \19C-3-eligible closed-end funds.

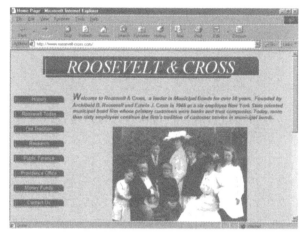

Figure 6.9 Roosevelt & Cross (U.S. Tax-Exempt) Bond Brokerage.

Investment Booklets from Scudder

As you learn about various aspects of investing, you simply can't have too many resources. As it turns out, the investment firm of Scudder, Stevens, & Clark, Inc. also believes that understanding is the key to investing. As such, Scudder has put together several excellent (and easy to read) guides to investing:

Basics in Bond Funds	Explains the ins-and-outs of bonds and how they benefit you.
Investing for College	Explains the costs of college and how to plug your tuition gap.
Investing for Retirement	Explains the retirement plans and tools and the investments you should be making over time.

For more information on these booklets and Scudder services, call 800-225-2470 or check out their Web site at *http://www.aarp.scudder.com* where you can download the Financial Library Guide that gives over 100 different titles of the other guides they offer.

TIPS, INC., FIXED-INCOME ANALYSIS SOFTWARE

http://www.tipsinc.com

Tips is the leading provider of fixed income analytics software development tools. Its SIA/BMA Standard Securities Calculations Software Library is recognized as the "new standard in standard calculations." Tips has a long-standing relationship with the two major trade associations for the securities industry, SIA and BMA. Jointly they have worked on and marketed many products from books to conferences to the newly available SIA/BMA Standard Securities Calculations Software Library.

The SIA/BMA Standard Securities Calculations Software Library is a set of over 800 callable functions, which provide programmatic access to the industry standard calculations you need for fixed income trading operations, finance, research, and portfolio and money management.

The SIA/BMA Bond Analytics Module is a single high-level callable routine for calculating prices, yields, and other analytics on bonds, notes, and discount securities.

The SIA/BMA Mortgage-Backed Analytics Module is a single high-level callable routine for calculating prices, yields, and other analytics on mortgage-backed securities.

And the SIA Standard Securities Calculation Methods Calculator, a Windows-based bond calculator, is available for a free download and a free evaluation.

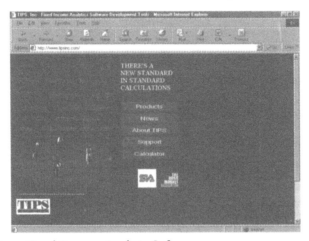

Figure 6.10 *Tips, Inc., Fixed-Income Analysis Software.*

Trial Issue From Success Magazine

Each month, *Success Magazine* is filled with articles on personal finance, running a business, the ins-and-outs of retirement plans, managing people, and more. You'll learn what works and what doesn't, as well as, how successful people accomplish their goals. Check out their Web site at *http://www.SuccessMagazine.com* and get 10 issues for only $14.97.

TAX SWAPS: A TUTORIAL

http://www.moneypages.com/syndicate/bonds/bswap.html

According to this fine tutorial, a tax swap is an investment strategy designed for municipal bond portfolios which allows you to take a loss in your portfolio while at the same time adjusting factors such as credit quality, maturity, and so on, to better meet your current needs and the outlook of the market. With a tax swap you can create a capital loss for tax purposes, maintain or enhance the overall credit quality of your portfolio, and increase current income. Come to this Web tutorial for more information.

Figure 6.11 Tax Swaps: A Tutorial.

YIELD CURVES, INTEREST RATES AND GRAPHS

http://www.stocktrader.com/summary.html

This page gives you the US Treasury Yield Curve (table and graph, approx 41,000 bytes, updated daily), Long Bond Yield History (monthly chart from 1973, updated monthly), Long Term DJIA Chart, Daily DJIA Chart, and the Daily Chicago Board of Trade Treasury Bond Future chart.

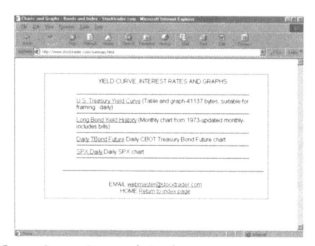

Figure 6.12 Yield Curves, Interest Rates and Graphs.

U.S. SAVINGS BONDS

http://www.publicdebt.treas.gov/sav/sav.htm

This site gives an introduction to savings bonds with a message from the Treasurer of the United States. You can learn about all types of savings bonds and all about purchasing them.

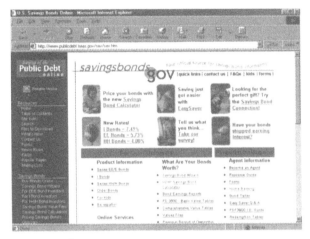

Figure 6.13 U.S. Savings Bonds.

INVESTING IN BONDS

http://www.investinginbonds.com

Here's another down to basics site that provides information about bonds, why to invest in bonds, key bond investment considerations, how to invest, fundamental investment strategies, and a glossary of terms. There is a wealth of information provided by the Bond Market Association.

Figure 6.14 Investing In Bonds.

GLOSSARY OF MUNICIPAL BOND TERMS

http://munidirect.com/glossary.html

This site provides a simple, easy to understand glossary of terms pertaining to municipal bonds.

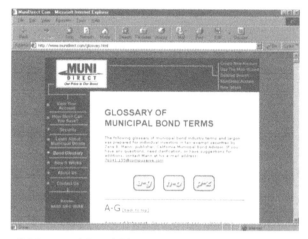

Figure 6.15 Glossary of Municipal Bond Terms.

DAILY REPORT OF MUNICIPAL BOND TRANSACTIONS

BUREAU OF PUBLIC DEBT – U.S. TREASURY

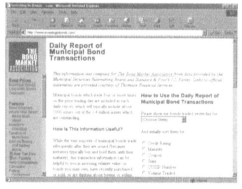

http://www.investinginbonds.com

http://www.ustreas.gov/org/bpdpdacct.htm

CONVERTIBLE BONDS: AN EXPLANATION

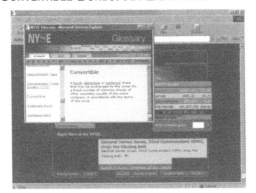

http://www.nyse.com

PLAIN TALK: BOND FUND INVESTING FROM THE VANGUARD GROUP

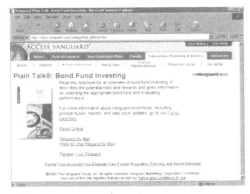

*http://www.vanguard.com/
catalog/lit/catlistPT.html*

FIDELITY BOND FUNDS

http://www.fid-inv.com

DREYFUS BOND FUNDS

http://www.dreyfus.com

FEDERAL RESERVE BOARD

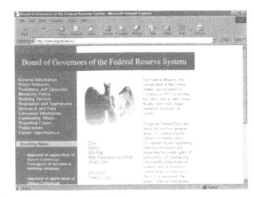

http://www.bog.frb.fed.us

GOVERNMENT BONDS AROUND THE WORLD

*http://www.moneyworld.co.uk/faqs/
bonfaq3.htm*

GOVERNMENT AND CORPORATE BOND INFORMATION: EUROPE

http://www.qualisteam.com/eng/aobleu.html

GOVERNMENT AND CORPORATE BOND INFORMATION: N. AND S. AMERICA

http://www.qualisteam.com/eng/aoblusa.html

HAMMER CAPITAL MANAGEMENT BOND RESEARCH ANALYSIS

http://hcmi.com

LEBENTHAL AND CO. TAX-FREE MUNICIPAL BONDS

http://www.lebenthal.com

JUNK BONDS DEFINED COURTESY OF PRUDENTIAL SECURITIES

http://www.prusec.com/glos_txt.htm#J
troweMutualFundsHome.html

INVESTING IN HIGH-YIELD MUNICIPAL BONDS: A TUTORIAL—T. ROWE PRICE

http://www.troweprice.com/mutual/

JUNK BONDS DEFINED COURTESY OF T. ROWE PRICE

*http://www.troweprice.com/mutual/insights/
junkbond.html*

MOODY'S BOND RATINGS DEFINED

*http://www.moneypages.com/syndicate/bonds/
ratings.html*

J.P. MORGAN WORLDWIDE GOVERNMENT BOND MARKET OUTLINE

http://www.jpmorgan.com

MONEYLINE REAL-TIME BOND QUOTES AND ANALYTICS

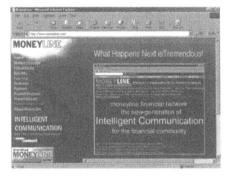

http://www.moneyline.com

MUNICIPAL BONDS: A TUTORIAL FROM MERRILL LYNCH

*http://today.askmerrill.com/education/course/
0,,20106_20129_2_ask0000,00.html*

BLOOMBERG NATIONAL MUNI BOND YIELDS UPDATED DAILY

*http://www.bloomberg.com/markets/
psamuni.html*

COOL TOOLS: BONDS

http://www.cyberinvest.com/cooltools.bonds.html

FREE BOND QUOTES

http://www.quotes4free.com/menu.html

HIGH YIELD BOND FINANCING BY ANDREA HARTILL

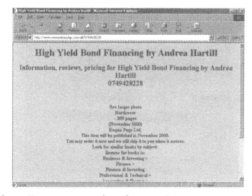

http://www.wwwednesday.com/
all/0749428228

CURRENT FIXED INCOME QUOTES

http://www.investorlinks.com/quotes-e.html

5 TIPS WHEN INVESTING IN BONDS

http://www.dollar4dollar.com/98-0810/
tx0810.htm

THE ONE BOND STRATEGY YOU NEED TO KNOW

http://www.smartmoney.com/si/tools/onebond

GLOBAL BONDS QUOTES INDEX

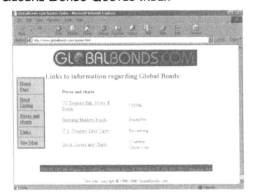

http://www.globalbonds.com/quotes.html

BUREAU OF PUBLIC DEBT

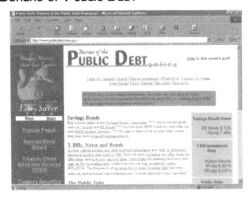

http://www.publicdebt.treas.gov

BOND/FX QUOTES

http://www.briefing.com/tour/bonds/bondquotes

BONDS

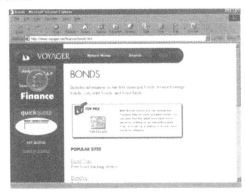

http://www.voyager.net/finance/bonds.html

BOND MARKETS

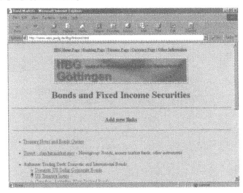

http://www.wiso.gwdg.de/ifbg/finbond.html

BOND RESOURCES

http://www.bondresources.com

BOND AND FIXED INCOME

http://www.rcmfinancial.com/bondsfix.htm

BOND BUYER ON-LINE

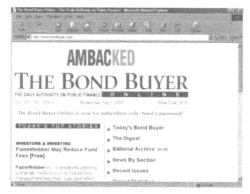

http://www.bondbuyer.com

SELECT SURF BOND SITE

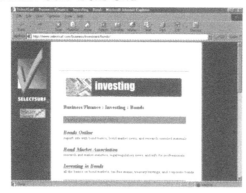

*http://www.selectsurf.com/business/
investment/bonds*

BOND MARKETS

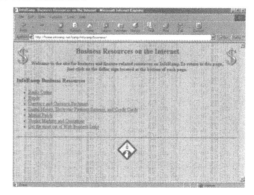

*http://www.inforamp.net/
iramp/inforamp/business*

BOND MARKET RULES (BOOK)

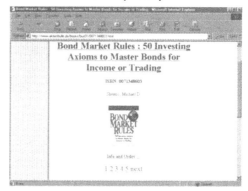

*http://www.aktienbulle.de/books/bus01/
0071348603.html*

BOND LINKS FROM LABPUPPY.COM

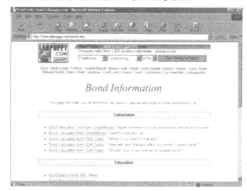

http://www.labpuppy.com/bonds.htm

TRADING: INVESTING IN BOND OPTIONS

http://www.wsdinc.com/products/p7726.shtml

TOP 25 BOND FUNDS

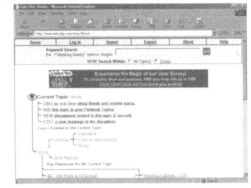

http://www.links2go.com/topic/bonds

WOMEN'S WIRE ON BONDS

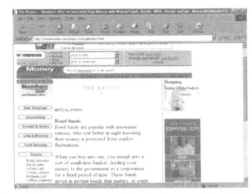

http://womenswire.com/basics/mutualfunds3.html

CHAPTER 7
THE ART OF MUTUAL FUNDS

*Let all the learned say what they can. 'Tis ready money makes the man. — **William Somerville,** **Ready Money,** 1727.*

HOW TO BE A SUCCESSFUL FINANCIAL ILLITERATE

Most investors are financial illiterates. Hard to believe? Well, it is true according to a recent Investor Knowledge Survey released by the non-profit Investor Protection Trust in Arlington, Virginia. In fact, a summary of this survey declared a "national epidemic of financial illiteracy" among investors.

The telephone survey of 1,001 investors conducted by Princeton Research Associates, on behalf of Investor Protection Trust, found that one in five investors were unable to answer seven of eight fundamental investment questions. Two out of three did not have a financial plan. Almost nine out of ten who used brokers or financial planners had never checked their adviser's disciplinary record. Barbara Roper, Investor Protection Director for the Consumer Federation of America, is on record as saying that the survey demonstrates an "appalling lack of basic financial knowledge" and calls into question the ability of most investors to make sound financial decisions. In a similar survey, the majority of mutual-fund investors surveyed by *Money* Magazine and the Vanguard Group could answer only 10 out of 20 basic financial questions correctly.

Unlike other financially illiterate investors, the mutual fund investors surveyed by *Money* Magazine and the Vanguard Group may, at least, have their money in the right place. Because they have chosen the one investment vehicle—the vehicle commonly known as the *mutual fund*—which requires the least amount of personal monitoring and homework. However, even with Mutual Funds, there is some homework you must do. But, as we shall see, Mutual Fund investing by its nature requires significantly less personal knowledge and research than does just about any other form of securities investment.

WHAT IS A MUTUAL FUND?

For those of us who have neither the technical knowledge (nor the time) to track and research individual stocks, nor enough cash with which to broadly diversify our holdings, mutual funds offer a solution. Mutual funds (formally known as *open-end investment trusts*) are vehicles by which we can pool our funds with those of many other investors to buy broadly diversified portfolios of stocks, bonds, and other securities. We also mutually benefit from management of the fund by a team of professional researchers and investment managers supplied by such successful fund stewards as Fidelity, Dreyfus, Janus, Vanguard, and other established, respected, successful mutual fund operators.

There are currently more than 7,000 different mutual funds available to investors, and that is roughly 3.5 times the number of individual stocks listed on the New York Stock Exchange. The many different flavors of mutual funds vary greatly in investment philosophy, in the charges and maintenance fees they levy on shareholders, and in the *track-records* of those who manage the funds. Crucial to your making of an informed (and, therefore, ultimately *profitable*) purchase of mutual fund shares is your understanding of these different aspects with regard to any given mutual fund.

Luckily, you can deduce most of this information from an educated glance at the prospectus each and every mutual fund management company is required by law to make available for every one of its products. But more on these useful documents later.

Understanding Mutual Funds

Mutual funds let you combine your investing dollars with those of other investors to purchase a wide range of stocks or bonds, which becomes the "mutual fund." Each mutual fund is managed by an financial expert, called the fund manager, who is responsible for buying the stocks or bonds that make up the fund. As you will learn, there are a wide variety of funds. Some funds consist of stocks only, some funds only invest in bonds, some funds mix stocks and bonds, while other specialize in "tax free" investments. In short, regardless of your investment goals, you should have little trouble finding a matching fund.

To invest in a fund, you purchase shares—much like you would buy shares of a stock. As you will learn, you can buy mutual fund shares through your broker or directly from the mutual fund company (by phone, fax, or even on-line). If the fund's investments do well, the value of your shares in the fund will increase. As you can guess, different funds will "do better" (see higher profits) than others, based simply on the investments the fund makes. Later, just as you purchased shares in the fund, you can sell your shares. Mutual funds are an excellent investment for just about every investor.

WHAT IS NAV?

Wherever you look for information about a mutual fund—whether it be in a prospectus, an annual report, a Morningstar summary, or your daily newspaper's listings of mutual fund prices—you will find a figure itemized cryptically as *NAV* which stands for *Net Asset Value*.

The Securities and Exchange Commission requires Mutual Funds to declare their net asset value at the close of the market for each day of trading. The fund calculates its NAV, quite simply, by pricing each security in the fund's portfolio and multiplying by shares held, adding any cash-on-hand and accrued earnings, deducting liabilities (such as management fees and charges), and dividing by the number of mutual fund shares outstanding. For example, if the total value of a fund's portfolio after deduction of liabilities is $100 million and there are 10 million shares outstanding, then each share has a NAV of $10.

THE POPULARITY OF MUTUAL FUNDS

Mutual Funds have been popular investment vehicles for more than half a century. But the late-1980s is when they really, quite literally, started to become a household word. Today, nearly 30% of households in the US invest in mutual funds. Compare this to the statistic back in 1980, when less than 6% of all households in the US had mutual-fund investments.

During the 1980s, the investor plunge into mutual funds was spearheaded by people searching for income. During the inflationary days of the early 1980s, many households put cash into money-market mutual funds, which offered attractive interest yields in times of double-digit inflation. In the later 1980s, when inflation and money-market interest rates subsided in tandem, these same investors sought income via bond-oriented mutual funds. According to statistics gathered by the Investment Company Institute (ICI), investment in bond mutual funds increased 18-fold during the decade 1980-1990. At the same time, stock-oriented mutual funds also experienced substantial growth: 10-fold. Additionally, the 1980s saw significant growth in tax-exempt municipal bond funds: from $39.4 billion invested in 1985 to $102 billion in 1989.

According to the ICI, mutual-fund shareholder accounts doubled between 1985 and 1987. Monthly sales in 1985 and 1986 routinely exceeded annual sales for any complete year prior to 1980. This trend in sales has continued over time, despite the famous "crash" of the stock market in October of 1987. Since 1989, investors have routinely put more than $100 billion into mutual funds on an annual basis, and as of 1996 there is more than $2 trillion involved in such investment.

Does any of that smart money belong to you? I certainly hope so.

THE LOW ENTRY PRICE FOR MUTUAL FUND INVESTING

Let's say you've got just $2,500 to invest. By yourself, with just that much cash, you could not buy much diversification in a stock portfolio. And by yourself, with just that much cash, you could not get a full-service stockbroker (offering high-quality research and recommendations) to give you the time of day. But by pooling your small investment capital with the nesteggs of thousands of other small investors, you can not only buy broad diversification but also hire first-rank, top-drawer professional investment management. You can benefit from the same quality of investment research and advice as does a millionaire.

Many, though not all, mutual funds have a basic first-time investment minimum of $2,500, and accept further incremental investments in amounts of $500 or greater. Some companies, among them Dreyfus and Fidelity, offer lower minimum first-time investment thresholds (as low as $1,000) for mutual fund investments associated with an IRA. Of all the *major* providers of mutual fund investment vehicles, the Janus Group is generally acknowledged to have the lowest non-IRA first time investment minimum: $1,000.

YOU DON'T NEED A BROKER

The woods are full of investment advisors/counselors who are anxious to serve as brokers via which you may buy shares in any number of mutual funds. You will pay a sales surcharge for their advice: a sales surcharge you can easily avoid by going to the mutual fund's management and buying shares direct. And by the way, the advice you get from your counselor in exchange for the surcharge may be less than wonderful simply because *any investment advisor's recommendations are confined within the spectrum of mutual fund firms with which that investment advisor/counselor has relationships.* In other words, in exchange for the surcharge, you limit your options as an investor. That's quite a deal.

Browse any issue of the *Wall Street Journal*, or the financial section of *The New York Times*, or any magazine such as *Money* or *Smart Money* or *Your Money*. You will find page after page after page of ads from all the leading mutual-fund management companies with 800 telephone numbers and Web site addresses inviting you to request information on direct sales of their mutual-fund shares. Right now, as I browse an edition of *Smart Money* I find ads from Fidelity, T. Rowe Price, Invesco, The Templeton Group, The Franklin Funds, Janus, The Berger Funds, The Benham Group, Scudder, Vanguard, and literally dozens of other concerns, large and small. All you need do is pick a mutual fund vehicle that sounds like it might be right for you, call or e-mail for the appropriate firm, asking them to send you a prospectus, and then read it (and prospectuses from other similar funds for comparison), before making your investment decision. (Note that a few of the larger mutual fund providers make life very easy by maintaining copies of their prospectuses on Web pages, where you may read them on-line or download them.)

What's that you're asking? Exactly how should you read a prospectus? What key things should you watch for in reports of mutual-fund earnings and charges? Don't worry. All shall be made clear to you. Read on.

THE PROSPECTUS

The prospectus is quite literally a blueprint for the mutual fund into which you are considering buying. First, the prospectus describes the fund's investment philosophy and, in doing so, clearly sets out precisely what the fund managers may and may not do with the money you invest. Managers of a fund that advertises itself as a highly conservative *income* fund may, for example, be prohibited from investing in derivatives and other highly speculative securities. Managers of a fund that advertises its aim as highly-speculative *aggressive growth*, on the other hand, may be specifically empowered, if not compelled, to focus on just such investments. (Indeed, some funds even advertise themselves as *option* funds or *futures* funds.)

Second, the prospectus will give you a brief (in fact too-brief) snapshot of the fund's performance history. This history will often be information on as little as one-year's return-on-investment. Or, it could be information for as many as eight years' performance or more. Brevity in the "Financial Highlights" portion of a prospectus is, for the wise investor, a red flag. Consider the fact that fund managers routinely and quite naturally frame the historical "Financial Highlights" portion of a prospectus to show their funds in the most favorable light possible. For example, if a fund lost value for four years running but in the fifth year finally gained a bit (though not all) of that lost value back, the "Financial Highlights" section of the prospectus for the fund might only remark upon the impressive fifth year return, showing the latest year as profitable and failing to mention that the fund in fact lost value over the course of five years. Obviously, a more detailed presentation of the numbers incorporating several years' performance would leave much less room for obfuscation. *The briefer the history provided in the "Financial Highlights" portion of a prospectus, the more cynical you should be and the more you should count on getting further information on the fund from independent sources.* (More on these shortly.)

And third, the prospectus details the charges ("services fees") it charges its mutual-fund participants. The fund does not bill these charges directly, but rather, the fund takes the charges out of the fund's gross revenue before distribution of returns to investors. These charges—which I will discuss in more detail shortly—can vary greatly from fund to fund and from management company to management company. Thus, the charges can greatly effect your overall return on investment long-term. So be clear on this: It does quite literally pay to read the "Annual Fund Operating Expenses" or "Fee Table" fine-print in a prospectus, and to compare expenses from fund to fund.

Always remember: When it comes to mutual funds, you must comparative shop each fund's investment philosophy, historical performance, and also the fund's fees.

THE ANNUAL REPORT

In addition to the prospectus, it pays to request the latest *Annual Report* of the fund you are considering. (Note: A few major proprietors of mutual funds make their funds' annual reports available on-line. Check the Web sites listed in the *Internet Resources* section of this chapter for details.) The annual report will detail not only the fund's previous year's performance, but also the fund's precise holdings at the time that it closed its books on the previous fiscal year. In other words, it will tell you exactly what stocks and bonds the fund was holding at the time it closed its books, and in what quantities.

Depending on the degree of research you are willing to do, a fund's annual report will help you ascertain the extent to which the fund is living up to the investment philosophy it advertises for itself. For example, is a conservative income fund truly invested mostly in relatively "safe" income-producing stocks as utility issues, or is it in fact also playing around with derivatives and junk bonds and other high-risk issues with which you, assuming you are a conservative investor, would rather not be involved? The annual report will tell you for sure.

BEYOND THE PROSPECTUS AND ANNUAL REPORT: TWO KEY REFERENCES

As valuable as are the prospectus and the annual report for a mutual fund, you also want some independent information. You want information and analysis that comes from a source other than the proprietor of the fund you are considering purchasing.

For this purpose you have two key reference points. The first is the annual *Wiesenberger Investment Companies Service Manual* (commonly known as the *Wiesenberger Manual*). The second is the comprehensive database and ratings service maintained by *Morningstar Mutual Funds*.

The *Wiesenberger Manual* was launched in 1941 and is now published by a firm called Computer Directions Advisers Investment Technologies, Inc. The *Manual* is available on-line for a fee and features a range of detailed statistical information—incorporating expense ratios, sales charges, and inception dates, for some 4,000 mutual funds. Furthermore, the *Manual* provides descriptions of fund investment philosophies and objectives, profiles of fund managers, and 12-year histories for return-on-investment. Conveniently, the *Manual* also includes comparative analyses of the performance of a $10,000 theoretical investment in each fund for periods from 5 to 25 years. This analysis allows you to do side-by-side comparisons for any funds you wish. The Wiesenberger Manual information is available on the Web at *http://www.cda.com/wiesenberger*.

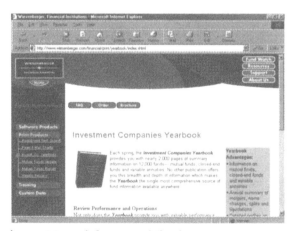

Figure 7.1 The Wiesenberger Manual for mutual funds.

The only resource more useful than the *Wiesenberger Manual* is that provided by *Morningstar Mutual Funds*. First published in 1986, the Morningstar ratings are now available on-line. Morningstar not only rates Mutual Funds by performance-history from best to worst. It also details cumulative return over 13 years as compared to the S&P 500 stock index (for stock mutual funds) and the Lehman Government/Corporate Bond Index (for bond mutual funds). Furthermore, Morningstar provides quarterly rates of return for the past six years. It details sales charges, expense ratios, management fees, and (as a measure of transaction costs) portfolio turnover. And it provides key performance versus risk statistics. Additionally, Morningstar gives you average price-earnings ratios and weightings by industry sector for stock funds. For bond funds it gives you average effective maturity, interest coupon structure, and credit quality. The Morningstar data is available on the Web for a fee. The address for Morningstar's Web site, which is entitled *Morningstar Mutual Funds OnDemand*, is *http://www.investtools.com/cgi-bin/library/msmf.pl*. The information is also available in another format. If you are one of the few still interested in print-media, you may subscribe to the print-edition of the Morningstar reports, which they publish in a spiral binder format. Call 800-735-0700 for details.

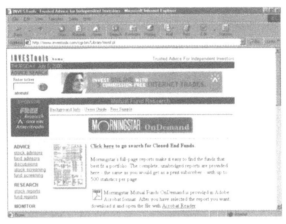

Figure 7.2 The Morningstar Web site.

Morningstar Investor

The *Morningstar Investor* is a monthly newsletter that discusses all aspects of mutual funds, with articles on the latest trends, expert advice, and more. To obtain a free sample of this valuable letter, call *Morningstar* at 800-735-0700. Check out this newsletter. It is filled with key information. Also, ask *Morningstar* to send you a catalog that describes their other products.

Morningstar Principia Pro Software for Mutual Funds

Morningstar promotes Principia Pro as "the industry's premier research and presentation tool" that delivers trustworthy, authoritative, and continuously updated *Morningstar* data on more than 10,000 mutual funds. With Principia Pro you can screen funds by more than 70 categories, including historical performances, manager tenure, *Morningstar* ratings, and more. The software lets you construct and analyze real-world portfolios and track relevant changes in any portfolio. You can also create graphs that compare fund performance, illustrate fund volatility, and access detailed summary reports for each fund, as well as, custom summary reports for specific groups of funds.

The software with a quarterly subscription for four updates will cost you $295. And with a monthly subscription for 12 data updates will run you $495. The minimum system requirements for Principia Pro are a Pentium PC or compatible, 120 MB of free hard-disk space, 16 MB of RAM (32 MB is recommended), CD-ROM drive, VGA monitor, and Windows 95 or 98, or Windows NT 4.0.

The number to call for more information about Principia Pro for Mutual Funds is 800-735-0700 and check out their Web site at *http://www.morningstar.com/Products/clpromf.html.* Check out your local library to see if they subscribe to either the Principia Pro program or the print edition of the *Morningstar* ratings report. If so, you can obviously save yourself some money.

KNOW YOUR FUND'S AGENDA AND RISK THRESHOLD

In Chapter 4, "The Joy of Stocks," we learned about the different types of stocks, such as growth versus income stock. You may remember that growth stocks tend to be more risky investments than income stocks, but that growth stocks also hold the promise of more robust capital appreciation long-term.

The same broad categories apply to stock mutual funds, some of which will label themselves as growth funds, some as income funds, and others as highly speculative aggressive-growth funds. These labels—along with other disclosures that are part of the fund prospectus, annual report, and related literature—are your guides to the types of securities your fund is chartered to participate in.

The same rules of risk versus return apply to mutual funds as apply to individual stocks.

Highly speculative, general aggressive-growth funds will often flirt with IPOs and derivatives (options and futures). These funds hold the promise of very high return over time but come with the short-term risk of dramatic drops in value. Every little downward adjustment of the Dow or the S&P 500 will be *magnified dramatically* in the NAV-change of an aggressive growth fund, whereas, the value of a conservative fund specializing in dividend-producing stocks will be less sensitive to market-shifts, as of course will be a fund specializing in high-grade corporate bonds.

Keep in mind, however, that not all bond funds are safe, conservative investments. Some aggressive, high-return bond funds speculate in "combustible," low-grade, high-coupon rate bonds (junk bonds). The *very* cautious investor will want to keep his or her money in a money-market mutual fund. This type of fund offers a modest return as compared to stock- or bond-related mutual funds but is extremely safe vis-à-vis capital preservation.

Some stock and bond funds, such as growth and income funds, fall into the middle-ground of risk, while small- and mid-cap funds such as *Dreyfus New Leaders* focus mostly on NASDAQ over-the-counter issues.

The range of funds available is staggering. There are a host of specialty funds focusing on a specific industry, country, region, or social agenda. For example, there are funds that specialize in stocks and corporate bonds of the semiconductor industry, of firms based in Ireland or throughout Asia, and of firms committed to do business in a way that is good for the environment. There are option-income funds and precious metal funds. There are even US Treasury bond funds, US Government income funds, Ginnie Mae funds, international-bond funds and, for US investors, tax-free municipal-bond funds. And "diversified" fund options include balanced funds, flexible portfolio funds, and income-mixed funds. Almost any type and flavor of mutual fund is out there. The big question is: *Which among all these mutual-fund possibilities are right for you?*

Understanding Open-End Funds

As you examine mutual funds, you will encounter the terms *open-end fund* and *close-end fund*. In general, an open-end fund has an unlimited number of shares (an open end). A closed-end fund, on the other hand, has a fixed number of shares. In addition, closed-end fund only invests in the stocks and bonds of other companies. In other words, you can think of a closed-end fund as an investment company of which you are purchasing shares of stock. As you will learn, you can purchase (or sell) your shares in an open-end fund either directly through the mutual-fund company or your broker. With a closed-end fund, however, you can only trade your shares through a broker. Lastly, you will find that an open-end fund always trades at its net asset value (NAV), whereas a closed-end fund may trade at a discount or premium.

THE SCOOP ON LOAD MUTUAL FUNDS

Generally speaking, the price of a share of an open-end fund is based on the NAV per share, which the fund recalculates at the close of business every day. However, mutual-fund companies use two very different pricing schemes for open-end mutual funds and you, as an intelligent investor, must make it your business to be aware of the differences between them.

Mutual funds are sold on either a *load* or a *no-load* basis. A *load* is a sales charge imposed by a fund as a fee for executing a transaction for shares with an investor. Front-end loads, as some loads are called, are the most common and are fees charged when you purchase share. There is no additional load charged later, when you redeem your shares by selling them back to the mutual-fund proprietor. A back-end load (less common, but still out there) is a fee that you must pay when you redeem (sell) shares.

Most load fees range from 4% to 8.5% of the cumulative NAV for the shares purchased. For example, if the NAV for a given fund was $10 and you bought 1000 shares, and there was a

8% load, you would pay $10,800 for the $10,000-worth of mutual fund shares. In other words, you would start out in the hole and have to dig yourself out with $800 in earnings *before* you would see any actual profit on your investment.

Note that many load funds have attractive *discount schedules*. The more you invest in a single transaction, the lower the load. A load fund that charges as much as 8.5% in loads for investments of less than $10,000 may well impose a load of just 1% on investments of $1,000,000 or more. All sorts of breakpoints would apply in between these two figures (5% load on investments of $50,000 to $100,000, 3% load on investments of $250,000 to $500,000, and so on).

Some load funds also offer an "accumulation discount" which is not tied to the amount of any single transaction, but instead provides a steadily increasing discount on the standard load commission tied to the degree of your investment in the mutual fund. The more mutual fund shares you hold, the less you will pay in the form of a load when you purchase additional shares.

Other load funds call themselves "low-load" funds and, obviously, charge less hefty loads than their competitors.

THE SCOOP ON NO-LOAD MUTUAL FUNDS

Better yet, simply never pay any load at all. This is what I do.

There are many, many top-flight *no-load* mutual funds managed by major proprietors such as Fidelity and Dreyfus and T. Rowe Price, *which also manage load funds*. These no-load funds are available with absolutely no sales commission charge whatsoever. Thus, when you invest your $10,000 it does not cost you $10,800. It just costs you $10,000, and your first $800 in earnings goes into your profit-column rather than toward recouping commission fees.

There is an "urban legend" on Wall Street that load funds, overall, perform better than no-load funds. But as with most legends, this one is not borne out by hard data. In fact, no-load mutual funds, as a group, routinely outperform load funds as a group. In other words, should you decide to buy into a load fund, the load you pay will buy you . . . *nothing*. What a great investment. Why not just fire-up your grill in the backyard and toss some cash onto it?

Permit me a last point before I leave this topic. Remember earlier in the chapter when I warned you of financial advisers who would be anxious to recommend and then sell you mutual-fund shares? Well, these folks will invariably point you toward load funds. Their commission comes out of the load.

SERVICE FEES

Both load and no-load funds have additional charges, called service fees. Beyond loads, service fees are where mutual-fund proprietors make their money. Service fees are annual fees taken from fund assets to compensate the corporate proprietor of the fund for its management expertise, and to reimburse the fund for distribution and service costs. (These latter expenses are sometimes called 12 b-1 fees, after the SEC ruling that first allowed them.)

Service fees come out of the fund *before* the NAV is calculated. Annually, service fees can be as low as 1.25% to 1.28% of total fund assets, although Morningstar states that the actual average is 1.53%. *Note that the service fees are always stated in the prospectus as a percentage of total fund assets.*

There is no formal cap on service fees. Thus, you want to be sure to read the prospectus carefully to make sure the fees charged by a fund are in line with the competition.

According to a recent article in *Individual Investor* Magazine, one fund group became notorious in 1995 for annoyingly huge fees. This was the Steadman Security Group, which operates a number of funds with about $10 million in assets. Steadman's 1995 fees ran to 11.7%! So you see, it *does* pay to check the prospectus to make sure the fees for your mutual fund are either at or below Morningstar's declared average of 1.53%.

SOMETHING FOR THE KIDS

Mutual funds can be great tools with which you can grow capital for your kids' educations and let your kids learn about the value of saving and investing. For these purposes, just about any mutual fund will do the trick. But there is at least one, which specializes in investment by and for children.

Stein Roe Mutual Funds features the *Young Investor Fund*, which focuses its portfolio on companies children are familiar with, such as McDonalds, Hasbro and Mattel. They also frame their quarterly earnings reports in language kids can understand. Check out the Stein Roe Web site for more details or call 800-403-5437. As with all funds, past returns are no guarantee of future performance.

Learn About Funds Before They Reach the Market

Federal Filings, Inc. is a Dow Jones subsidiary whose primary business is financial news based on information it gleans from SEC filings. Their product, *Mutual Fund Advance*, is a newsletter that provides specifics on new funds before the funds get to the market! To check out a free copy of the *Mutual Fund Advance*, call 202-393-7400. Also, ask them about their Internet services and how you access the newsletter on-line.

CLOSED-END INVESTMENT COMPANIES

Another option, other than the widely popular open-end mutual funds, is a *closed-end investment company*—a corporation that issues a fixed number of shares. Like any other corporation, it can issue corporate bonds and preferred stock to raise capital. But unlike other corporations, what capital it has, it invests solely in the corporate bonds and stock of other corporations.

Investors trade shares of closed-end investment companies (also known as closed-end funds) on the stock market just like the shares of any other public corporation. Some closed-end companies are listed with the Amex and NYSE. Others are traded over-the-counter. Thus, if you want to buy shares in a closed-end investment company, you must do so through your stockbroker.

While the NAV of open-end mutual fund shares is formally calculated and set at the close of each business day, the price of shares in closed-end investment companies ebbs and flows hour by hour in synch with the supply and demand in the marketplace. When the stock price for a closed-end investment company exceeds its NAV, it is said to be selling at a *premium*. When the stock market price of shares in a closed-end investment company is less than the fund's NAV, it is said to be selling at a *discount*.

Free Fund Booklet from Montgomery Asset Management

If you are interested in learning more about mutual funds, call Montgomery Asset Management at 800-572-3863 and ask them to send you their prospectus to the Montgomery Funds. In addition, you might want to check out their Web site at *http://www.montgomeryfunds.com*, where you can ask questions of the experts.

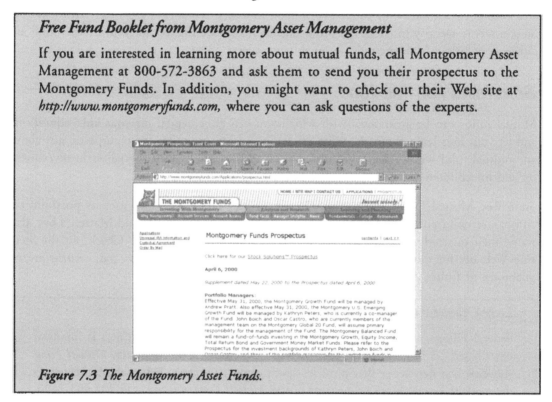

Figure 7.3 The Montgomery Asset Funds.

THE LONG-TERM KEY TO SUCCESS

I've said it before, and I'll say it again before this book is done: the key to all equities investing—whether you invest directly in common stock or via a mutual fund or via a closed-end investment company—is investing for the long term. When speculating in the short-term for a quick windfall, you may win big or you may go down in flames. But if you invest wisely for the long-term, in appropriately researched stocks, bonds, mutual funds, or closed-end investment companies, it is very hard (in fact it is darn near impossible) to lose.

INTERNET RESOURCES FOR MUTUAL FUND INVESTORS

As you surf the World Wide Web, you may encounter sites that discuss all aspects of mutual funds. The following site list should help you locate the resources you need.

CANADIAN MUTUAL FUNDS INFORMATION: THE FUND LIBRARY

http://www.fundlibrary.com/tfl/AboutTFL

The Fund Library is designed to educate and inform investors about Canadian mutual funds. It features the Admax Regent Group of Funds, AGF Management, Altamira Investment Services, Atlas Capital Group, C.I. Mutual Funds, Dynamic Mutual Funds, Elliott & Page, Fidelity Investments Canada, First Canadian Mutual Funds, GT Global Canada, Mackenzie Financial Corporation, Scotia Excelsior Funds, Scudder Canada Investor Services, Talvest Fund Management, TD Green Line Mutual Funds, Templeton Management, Trillium Growth Capital, Trimark Investment Management, and University Avenue Funds. Also check into an e-mail subscription to the Fund Library's *Informed Investor* newsletter.

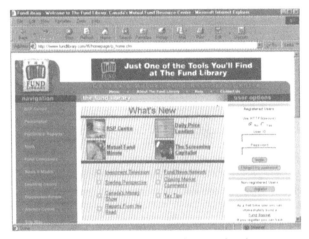

Figure 7.4 Canadian Mutual Funds Information: The Fund Library.

Understanding the Producer Price Index (PPI)

When you measure the success of your investments, you need to take inflation into account. *Inflation* is the general tendency for the price of items to increase over time. Historically, inflation typically increases at a rate of almost 4% a year. In addition to the consumer price index (CPI), one of the measures you should examine is the producer price index (PPI), which is the measure of the rate of inflation at the wholesale level. In other words, the PPI measures changes in the price of raw materials and wholesale goods. The Bureau of Labor Statistics normally reports the producer price index two days before it announces the CPI.

DREYFUS FUNDS: DREYFUS ON-LINE INFORMATION CENTER

http://www.dreyfus.com

In addition to providing general information on investing, the Dreyfus Online Information Center provides listings and descriptions of some of the mutual funds offered by Dreyfus along with the Dreyfus services that make mutual fund investing easy. Here you will also find current economic commentary on the financial markets updated weekly by Dreyfus Chief Economist Richard Hoey, as well as weekly analyses of growth stocks, value stocks, global and international stocks, fixed income securities, municipal bonds, the money market, and small caps.

The site includes a handy investment planning calculator. First, you type in an initial investment amount and a per-month investment for every month thereafter. Then, type in the number of years before you retire and any assumed annual rate of return. The system calculates a retirement fund forecast for you within seconds. Very handy.

Figure 7.5 Dreyfus Funds: Dreyfus On-line Information Center.

COMMERCIAL UNION PRIVILEGE PORTFOLIO: INTERNATIONAL UMBRELLA FUND

http://www.cupp.lu

This is the home page for the Commercial Union Privilege Portfolio, a Luxembourg-registered umbrella fund with 24 sub-funds denominated in 14 major currencies.

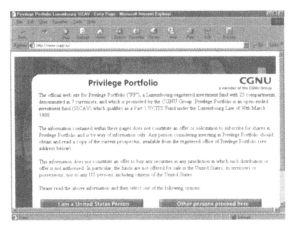

Figure 7.6 Commercial Union Privilege Portfolio: International Umbrella Fund.

EDGAR Mutual Funds Reporting

http://www.wsdinc.com/pgs_www/w7045.shtml

Courtesy of the Wall Street Directory, EDGAR prints mutual funds activity reports based on your choice of four parameters. You can go back LTD (Life to Date) as far as the beginning of the EDGAR Project (1/1/94), or see last week's activity, the last two weeks' activity, or the last month's activity. They actually call it Fast EDGAR. And it is fast.

Figure 7.7 EDGAR Mutual Funds Reporting.

Integra Capital Mutual Funds (Canada)

http://www.integracap.com

Integra Capital is one of Canada's leading pension and private investment management firms with $4.0 billion in assets under management. Come to this Web page to check out *Integra*

Link, a great on-line investment planning guide, as well as Integra's own rich, constantly-updated library of insightful financial market analysis. Come here also for details on the performance of the range of Integra mutual funds.

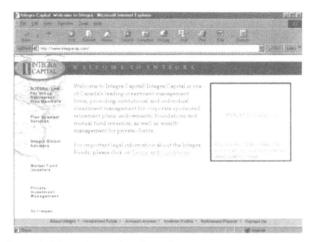

Figure 7.8 *Integra Capital Mutual Funds (Canada).*

THE INTERNET CLOSED-END FUND INVESTOR

http://www.icefi.com/icefi/index.htm

How would you like to buy mutual funds at a discount, often as much as 70 to 80 cents off the dollar? Closed-end funds (CEFs), a close relative of mutual funds, are often available at just such steep discounts, though discounted, closed-end funds are anything but inferior.

Consider:

- The portfolio managers at many CEFs are outstanding, famous investment professionals such as Martin Zweig, John Neff, John Templeton, Mark Mobius, Mario Bagelli, Charles Royce, and others, many of whom run top-tanked mutual funds.

- The funds are run by well-respected financial companies including Fidelity, Morgan Stanley, Oppenheimer, Franklin-Templeton, and Paine Webber.

- CEFs are no slouches when it comes to performance. In the bull market of 1993, for example, no less than 18 of the roughly 150 CEFs delivered eye-popping returns of 100% or more, often handily beating their mutual fund counterparts.

The ability to buy quality funds at attractive discounts has attracted several famous investment figures to CEFs, including Warren Buffet and Benjamin Graham. Nevertheless, CEFs remain largely the realm of just a few savvy individual investors. These investors have recognized that, apart from the traditional benefits of diversification, professional management and economy of scale, CEFs offer the investor control over pricing and timing that mutual funds don't. When judiciously exercised, this control provides the investor with opportunities to often dramatically improve returns, sometimes with reduced risk.

CEFs cater to every style of investor. There are CEFs for growth investors (such as the Jundit Growth Fund), value investors (Royce Value Trust), sector investors (the Global Health Sciences Fund, the First Financial Fund), small-cap investors (the Royce OTC Microcap Fund), global investors (the Clemente Global Growth Fund), international investors (the Europe Fund, the Asia Pacific Fund), single country funds (the India Growth Fund, the Spain Fund), emerging markets funds (the Templeton Emerging Markets Fund, and Morgan Stanley Emerging Markets Fund), gold funds (ASA Ltd.), and so forth. In addition, for traders, CEFs provide exceptional opportunities to capitalize on short-term swings in the discount relative to the long-term historical discounts.

The Internet Closed-End Fund Investor Web site exists to educate investors about CEFs (their peculiarities, investment strategies, risks, rewards, and potential pitfalls). With data provided by CDA/Wiesenberger (the premier supplier of data on closed-end funds, mutual funds, and variable annuities), the Web site now includes detailed information on roughly 500 top-ranked CEFs.

You'll find:

- A hypertext guide to investing in CEFs—Comprising a brief review of the basics of CEFs, their discount/premiums and the factors affecting discount/premiums, major differences between mutual funds and CEFs, the advantages and disadvantages of investing in closed-end funds over mutual funds, and the basics of investing in CEFs.

- Charts—Comprising weekly and daily charts of CEFs specifically tailored for the CEF investor. Apart from the traditional market price and volume, features include weekly net asset value, discount, moving average of the discount, relative discount, +/- 5% relative-discount envelope of market price, ex-dividend dates, and a snapshot of recent data.

- Intra-week NAV estimation—CEFs usually compute their NAV only once a week. For many funds, the analysts of The Internet Closed-End Investor Web site provide an estimate of the NAV during the week. The estimates, and the discount and relative discount based upon this estimates, are also plotted on the charts.

- Relative performance charts—Comprising weekly charts designed to facilitate comparison of the performance and discount of CEFs investing in the same or closely related markets.

- CEF Synopsis—Comprising a synopsis of relevant recent data (price, NAV, discount, long-term discounts and relative discount) for each fund.

- CEF Performance—Comprising a review of the performance of the NAV and market price of each CEF for the last month, last three months, year-to-date, one year, three years, five years, ten years, fifteen years, twenty years, previous two bull markets and previous two bear markets.

- CEF Profiles—Comprising profiles of CEFs that include basic information such as objectives, net assets, shares outstanding, ticker symbol, and more advanced information including portfolio highlights, modern portfolio theory statistics (alpha, beta, R-squared, standard deviation for several periods), and miscellaneous information such as portfolio turnover ratio, expense ratio, and so forth.

- Plus daily overview reports, market sentiment indicators, a public CEF chat forum, and an e-mail daily report service.

Figure 7.9 The Internet Closed-End Fund Investor.

Understanding the Money Supply

If you listen to the financial news, you may hear the terms "money supply," "M1," "M2," and so on. In short, *money supply* defines the amount of cash and liquid investments at the current time, across the country. The Federal Reserve reports on the money supply each Thursday. The M1 money supply defines the amount of coins,

> currency, checking and savings accounts, and travelers checks in circulation. The M2 money supply combines that of M1 with the money market funds and certificates of deposit (CDs). The M3 money supply combines M2 (and hence M1) with large institutional money funds.

MUTUAL FUND EXPERTS' CORNER

http://www.brill.com/expert.html

This great page provides market analysis, opinions, and recommendations from leading mutual fund experts. The information is generally valuable and accurate. But you should also realize that the articles appearing here are sponsored by the financial experts who write them. Nevertheless, it is useful to read Rich Schaffer and Bob Glovsky (the self-styled "Money Experts") on the topic of mutual fund rating/ranking services, Doug Fabian on "safe" investment products that are anything but safe, and Thurman Smith (of *Equity Fund Outlook*) on late-breaking micro-cap opportunities.

Figure 7.10 Mutual Fund Experts' Corner.

MUTUAL FUND INVESTORS RESOURCE CENTER

http://www.fundmaster.com

At this site you can request a free prospectus, account application, or information on any one of over 2,900 popular mutual funds offered by over 75 different financial organizations.

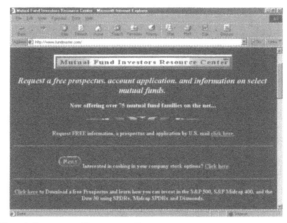

Figure 7.11 Mutual Fund Investors Resource Center.

MUTUAL FUND MARKET MANAGER

http://www.quicken.com/investments/mutualfunds/finder

This free service allows you to search for the top five performing mutual funds over varying periods of time. You define the time parameters.

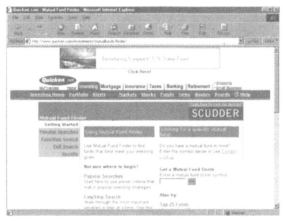

Figure 7.12 Mutual Fund Market Manager.

MUTUAL FUND MANAGER PROFILES

http://www.brill.com/profiles

Access interviews (including audio clips using the *TrueSpeech* player, which you can download here for free) and profiles of many of the leading mutual fund managers at work today. These include:

- Christopher Bonavico, Transamerica Premiere Small Company Fund

- Ronald Baron, Baron Asset Fund, Baron Growth & Income Fund
- Joshua Byrne, Putnam International Voyager Fund
- Donna Calder, SunAmerica Small Company Growth Fund
- Daniel Cantor, Stein Roe Growth & Income Fund
- Sophia Collier, Citizens Index Fund
- Eric Ephron, USAA Aggressive Growth Fund
- Charles Freeman, Vanguard Windsor Fund
- Ken Gregory, Master's Select International Fund
- Irene Hoover, Forward Hoover Small Cap Equity Fund
- Joseph Keating, Kent International Growth Fund
- Kevin Landis, Firsthand Technology Value Fund
- Michael Malouf, Neuberger & Berman Millennium Fund
- Chris McHugh, Turner Midcap Growth Fund
- James Mehling, Mainstay Institutional Multi-Asset Fund
- Charles L. Minter, Comstock Partners Capital Value Fund
- William Nasgovitz, Heartland Value Fund
- Ronald Ognar, Strong Growth 20 Fund
- Guy Pope, Columbia Balanced Fund
- Daniel Rice, State Street Global Resources Fund
- Michael Rome, Lazard Equity Fund
- David Thompson, First Funds Growth & Income Portfolio
- Emerson Tuttle, SSGA Growth & Income Fund
- B. Anthony Weber, Alleghany/Veredus Aggressive Growth Fund
  and many more.

THE MUTUAL FUND NETWORK

http://www.wsdinc.com/pgs_www/w7650.shtml

The Mutual Funds Network gives you an on-line seat on the exchange floor with instant access to on-line prospectuses, fund profiles, performance reports, and account applications. Links include connections to the CGM Funds, the Selected Funds, the Invesco Funds, the Janus Funds, EDGAR Mutual Fund SEC Filings, GNN's mutual fund FAQ and directory of 800 phone numbers, and more.

Figure 7.13 The Mutual Fund Network.

MUTUAL FUND NEWSGROUP

http://www.brill.com/answers.html

Post and read mutual fund questions, answers, and comments at The Answer Desk.

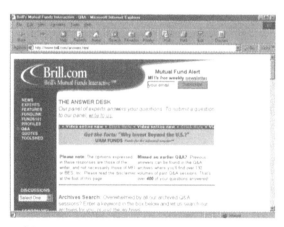

Figure 7.14 Mutual Fund Newsgroup.

MUTUAL FUND RESEARCH PAGE

http://www.litabryna.com/mutualfunds.htm

This site provides great mutual fund research links in education, comparison tools, news and monitoring, women and investing.

Figure 7.15 Mutual Fund Research Page.

T. ROWE PRICE MUTUAL FUNDS

http://www.troweprice.com/mutual/troweMutualFundsHome.html

T. Rowe Price customers (and potential customers) get treated very well at this Web site. Customers and potential customers can customize their own personal Mutual Funds watch-list, which will be updated daily and available to them 24-hours a day, right on-line. These can either be funds they own, or funds they are interested in owning and want to keep an eye on for a time. Here one can also get complete T. Rowe Price Fund profiles, daily prices, and performance information (including yields) along with monthly "Spotlight" features that explain various arcane investment topics in layman's language.

Of course T. Rowe Price is one of the most prestigious and reliable investment services companies around. Founded in 1937 by Thomas Rowe Price, Jr., the Baltimore-based investment management firm is one of the nation's leading providers of no-load mutual funds both for individual investors and corporate retirement programs. In fact, T. Rowe Price and its affiliates manage over $82 billion for four million individual and institutional accounts.

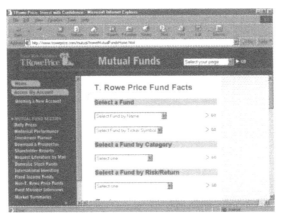

Figure 7.16 T. Rowe Price Mutual Funds.

PRIME TIMES MUTUAL FUND NEWSLETTERS

http://www.theprimetimes.com

Prime Times Mutual Funds Newsletters offers over 100 mutual fund family newsletters covering thousands of mutual funds. Each month this Web page displays a free current edition of a mutual fund family newsletter, complete with charts, recommendations, comments, rankings, etc. That means over a one year period, each visitor is able to view 12 different fund family newsletter editions with information on over 400 different mutual funds. Each week, the "Extra" page provides free updates and analysis on the major markets.

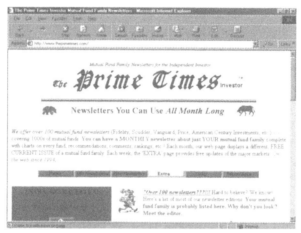

Figure 7.17 *Prime Times Mutual Fund Newsletters.*

STEIN ROE MUTUAL FUNDS

http://www.steinroe.com

The actual name of the company is Stein Roe & Farnham, but the whole world knows it as simply Stein Roe. The firm has been in business since 1932. They launched their first mutual fund in 1949. And today they offer a complete family of 17 no-load equity, bond, and money market mutual funds designed to help meet investors' needs throughout their investing lives.

In addition to details on products and up-to-date market analysis, this site also offers prices/NAVs and fund manager Q & A.

Figure 7.18 Stein Roe Mutual Funds.

THE VANGUARD GROUP

http://www.vanguard.com

The site for the Vanguard Group of mutual funds includes more than just simple hypertext prospectuses for Vanguard products. Here you also get stock market volatility reports, a great tutorial on how to interpret economic reports, a fantastic (continually updated) collection of investment-related articles from various sources, and even a Java-enhanced retirement calculator!

Figure 7.19 The Vanguard Group.

Mutual Fund Center

http://www.mutualfundcenter.com

This site provides free mutual fund reports, FAQs and financial information.

Figure 7.20 Mutual Fund Center.

Charles Schwab's Mutual Fund Marketplace

http://www.schwab-online.com/mutual_funds.htm

This site is a groundbreaking mutual fund supermarket making it easy and economical to invest in mutual funds. Schwab's Mutual Fund OneSource provides more than 1,100 mutual funds and makes them available without loads or transaction fees. Get a seven-day free research pass, and go online with investment professionals to get real-time answers to your financial questions.

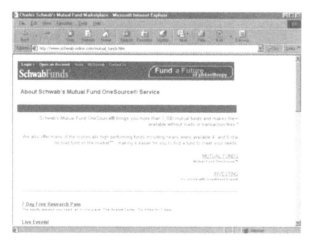

Figure 7.21 Charles Schwab's Mutual Fund Marketplace.

VALUE LINE PUBLISHING

http://www.valueline.com

Value Line offers investment research on stocks, mutual funds, options and convertibles, in addition to a family of no-load mutual funds.

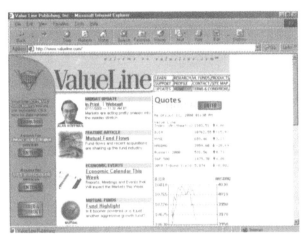

Figure 7.22 Value Line Publishing.

MUTUAL FUND INVESTING ON-LINE RESEARCH TOOLS AND SCREENING

http://www.mutual-fund-investing.com

This is a one-stop site for the best on-line fund screening and investment research tools on the Web.

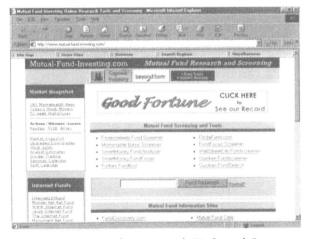

Figure 7.23 Mutual Fund Investing On-line Research Tools and Screening.

Looking for Shareware

If you are looking for shareware software, either investing software or otherwise, there is a great shareware site on the Web from which you can search from Windows-based, DOS-based, or even Mac-based software. To visit this site, connect to *http:// www.shareware.cnet.com.*

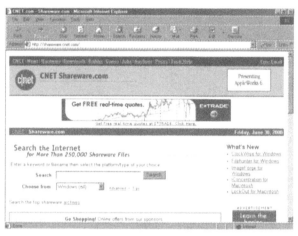

Figure 7.24 The Shareware Web site.

AAL MUTUAL FUNDS

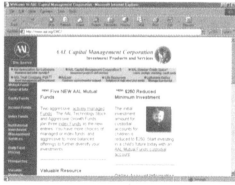

http://www.aal.org/CMC

AMERISTOCK MUTUAL FUND

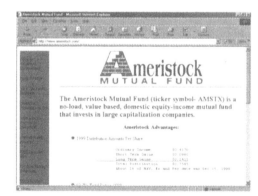

http://www.ameristock.com

TARGET MUTUAL FUNDS FROM PRUDENTIAL SECURITIES

*http://www.prusec.com/investing/
mutualfunds/ivmzz2000.html*

BABSON FUNDS

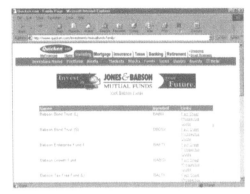

*http://www.quicken.com/investments/
mutualfunds/families*

ECLIPSE MUTUAL FUNDS

*http://www.quicken.com/investments/
mutualfunds/families*

CABOT'S MUTUAL FUND NAVIGATOR

http://www.cabot.net

CALVERT GROUP MUTUAL FUNDS

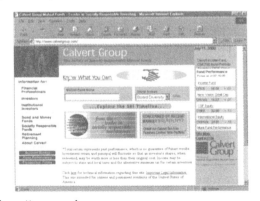

http://www.calvertgroup.com

CITIZENS TRUST MUTUAL FUNDS

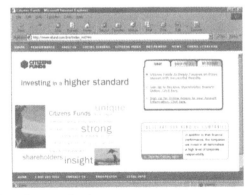

http://www.efund.com

187

LIBERTY MUTUAL FUNDS REPORTS ON-LINE

http://www.libertyfunds.com

FUNDSCAPE: FREE MUTUAL FUNDS ACTIVITIES

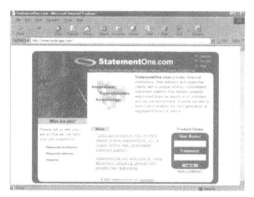

http://www.fundscape.com

FIRST UNION MUTUAL FUNDS

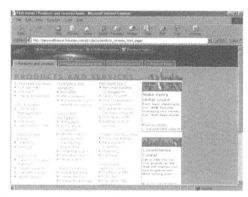

http://www.personalfinance.firstunion.com

GABELLI FUNDS

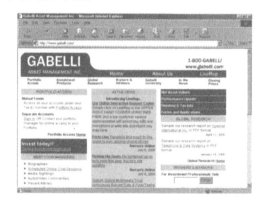

http://www.gabelli.com

KEMPER MUTUAL FUNDS

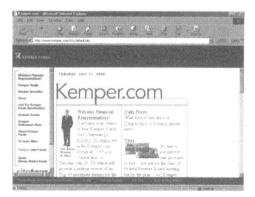

http://www.kemper.com

KIPLINGER'S PERSONAL FINANCE MAGAZINE

http://www.kiplinger.com

MORNINGSTAR FUND SPY

http://www.morningstar.com/news

MUTUAL FUNDS FAQ

http://www.moneypages.com/syndicate/faq/
index.htm

MUTUAL FUNDS MAGAZINE ONLINE

http://www.mfmag.com

BANK OF AMERICA MUTUAL FUNDS

http://www.bankofamerica.com/investments

NORWEST FUNDS

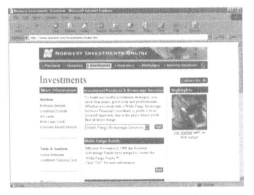

http://www.norwest.com/investments/
index.htm

RESEARCH MAGAZINE ONLINE

http://www.researchmag.com

STOCKMASTER MUTUAL FUND QUOTES

http://www.stockmaster.com

TIAA CREF MUTUAL FUNDS

http://www.tiaa.org/mfs/index.html

INVESTOR PLACE

http://www.investorplace.com

STRONG MUTUAL FUNDS

http://www.strongfunds.com

TRIMARK MUTUAL FUNDS

http://www.trimark.com

INVESTORS ALLEY –
THE MUTUAL FUND CENTER

*http://www.investorsalley.com/funds/
index.shtml*

FREE MUTUAL FUND TIPS

http://www.buysignals.com/mutual-fund.htm

MUTUAL FUND BASICS

*http://www.msfiscallyfit.com/low_impact/
low_impact.html*

MUTUAL FUND TIMING

http://www.mutualfundtiming.com

ASSOCIATION OF MUTUAL FUND INVESTORS

http://www.amfi.com

THE MUTUAL FUND SITE

http://www.mutualfundsite.com

MUTUAL FUND INVESTOR'S CENTER

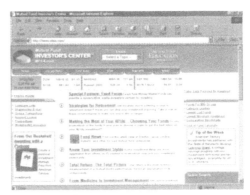

http://www.mfea.com

CAPITALSHARE ONLINE, OFFSHORE, REAL TIME, MUTUAL FUNDS

http://www.capitalshare.com

SMITH BARNEY MUTUAL FUND FAMILY

http://www.smithbarney.com/prod_svc/ mut_fund/2700fund.html

WOMEN'S EQUITY MUTUAL FUND

http://www.womens-equity.com

INVESTMENT FUNDS INSTITUTE OF CANADA (IFIC)

http://www.ific.ca/eng/home/ mutual_fund_ex.asp

FIRST INDIA MUTUAL FUND

http://business.vsnl.com/fiam

FORTRESS MUTUAL FUND, LTD. – CARIBBEAN

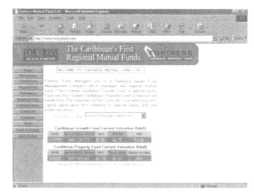

http://www.fortressfund.com

THE MUTUAL FUND CAFÉ

http://www.mfcafe.com

FUNDVISION'S MUTUAL FUNDS DISCUSSION BOARD

http://fundvision.com/wwwboard/
wwwboard.html

PATRIOT MUTUAL FUND

http://www.patriotfund.bc.ca

MUTUAL FUNDS INVESTMENT STRATEGY

http://www.mutualfundstrategy.com

PERSONAL MUTUAL FUND MANAGEMENT

http://www.pmfm.com

SBI MUTUAL FUND

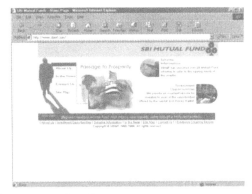

http://www.sbimf.com

FRANKLIN TEMPLETON MUTUAL FUND INVESTMENT COMPANY

http://franklin-templeton.com

UNITED FUNDS, INC.

http://www.ucpb.com/funds.html

IDBI MUTUAL FUND

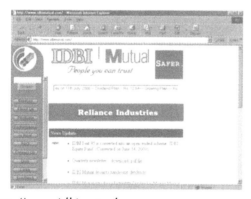

http://www.idbimutual.com

SECURITY AND EXCHANGE COMMISSION (SEC) – MUTUAL FUND COST CALCULATOR

http://www.sec.gov/mfcc/mfcc-int.htm

NUVEEN FUNDS

http://www.nuveen.com

LEGG MASON MUTUAL FUNDS

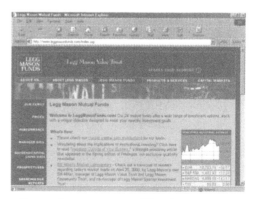

http://www.leggmason.com/Funds

CENTURY MUTUAL FUNDS

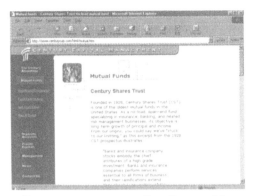

http://www.centurycap.com/html/mutual.htm

HARBOR FUND

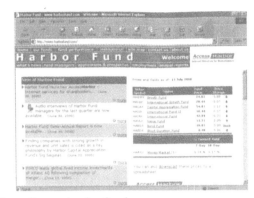

http://www.harborfund.com

MUHLENKAMP MUTUAL FUNDS

http://muhlenkamp.com

RS FUNDS

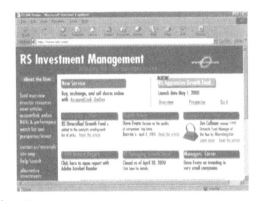

http://www.rsim.com

SAFECO MUTUAL FUNDS

http://www.safecofunds.com

THE ROYCE FUNDS

http://www.roycefunds.com

VAN WAGONER FUNDS

http://www.vanwagoner.com

ZURICH MONEY MARKET FUNDS

http://www.zurichfunds.com

HIGHMARK FUNDS

http://www.highmark-funds.com index.html

HEARTLAND FUNDS

http://www.heartlandfunds.com/individuals/

FORWARD FUNDS

http://www.forwardfunds.com

MFS ONLINE

http://www.mfs.com

CHAPTER 8

INSURANCE FUNDAMENTALS

You can insure everything but domestic tranquility. — *Will Rogers*

Where there is risk, there is the need for insurance. And our world is fraught with risk: the risk of sickness, the risk of death, and the risk of accidents, not to mention the risk of natural disasters and other acts of God.

Thus, insurance is a fundamental aspect of all realistic financial thinking. When planned well, your insurance (in all its various forms) can provide a reasonably watertight life raft to take you across the sea of risk. When not planned well, your insurance (or lack of insurance) can expose you to huge financial losses from which you may never recover.

A Worst-Case Scenario

Sam and Diane have no insurance: no car insurance, no home insurance, no liability insurance, no health insurance. They do, however, have $60,000 equity in their home and another $20,000 in IRAs and other investments.

Then (financial) disaster strikes. Their 16-year old son loses control of the car just as he is arriving home. The car swerves up across the pavement, knocking down and killing a passerby. Then, the car shoots up across the lawn and smashes into the house, which catches fire and burns to the ground with all its contents.

As luck would have it, Sam and Diane get out of the house immediately and are not hurt. They manage to get their son out of the wreck of the automobile, but he has massive injuries.

Sam and Diane have no health insurance to cover their son's medical bills. They have no liability insurance to cover the lawsuit demands of the dead passerby's family. They have no home insurance with which to rebuild and refurbish their home. They have no auto insurance with which to purchase a new vehicle.

Much of the equity they held in their real estate burned with the house. The land is worth only about $10,000. And this combined with the $20,000 in the homeless couple's IRA and other accounts does little to amortize the million dollars they are

---

being sued for by the family of the dead bystander, or the $78,000 in medical bills related to their son's injuries.

They are broke. They are ruined. Fortuitous risk has hit them like an express train, and they weren't prepared for it.

FORTUITOUS RISK

Risk management is the art of protecting your assets to prevent a loss of net worth caused by *fortuitous* acts and events beyond your control.

Fortuitous risks are, in fact, the only risks you can insure against. A fortuitous risk is a risk of the *chance* happening of an event that *may* happen, not one that is certain to happen.

There is a fortuitous risk that a tornado will destroy your house. On the other hand, the risk that you might get drunk, douse your house with kerosene, and light it up is *not* fortuitous. One event would be covered by your home insurance, the other not.

As you shall see in Chapter 9 "What Are You Worth? The Art of Life Insurance," the concept of fortuitous risk even impacts life insurance. Because of the concept of fortuitous risk, life insurance does not, in fact, insure against death, which is inevitable. Instead it insures against the risk of *premature death*, but more on this later.

INSURABLE RISK AND INSURANCE INTEREST

To be insurable, a risk must first be fortuitous as just defined. It must also involve *only* the possibility of financial loss (rather than gain). Investing in junk bonds is risky, but it comes with the potential for profit and, thus, you cannot buy insurance against your junk bond equity going down in value.

Another prerequisite for insurability is something called *insurable interest*. You, as the purchaser of insurance, must have a genuine insurable interest in the thing being insured. In other words, you must have a personal economic stake in the person or thing being insured. For example, you cannot take-out life insurance on a stranger in the hope that he or she will die soon. And you cannot insure your neighbor's house in the hope that the tornado will hit it.

What the concept of *insurable interest* says, in essence, is that you may only insure against fortuitous risks that have the potential to translate to a genuine personal economic loss *for you*.

INSURANCE DEFINED

Insurance is a deal that you strike (and formalize in a contract called a *policy*) between you and an insurance provider (the *insurer* or *underwriter*). The core of your deal is simply this: In return for a fee (a *premium*) paid by you, the insurer agrees to assume various liabilities of your insurable risks and guarantee you protection against their loss.

The underwriter is generally in the business of insurance for profit. By selling as many policies as possible and collecting premiums from as many individuals as possible, the underwriter *spreads risk* over a large number of customers. A minority of these customers will actually suffer losses and file claims. The pool of funds from the broad customer base will service those claims. And the underwriter hopes to take a profit out of what is left.

More on the Business of Underwriting

It is the underwriting company that decides exactly which risks it is willing to insure and which risks it is not willing to insure. The underwriting company also decides how much it will charge to insure various risks.

To derive your premiums, underwriters employ statistical analysts called *actuaries*. It is the job of the actuaries to predict the *probability* that a given loss will occur. After the actuaries derive this probability, the underwriting firm calculates a premium amount which takes into account the numbers of individuals insured, the probability of loss (its estimate of the percentage of those insured who will actually suffer a loss and file a claim), the likely annual payout on claims, and the need for the company to make a profit.

Some elements of risk fluctuate. For example, statistically there are far more car accidents and car thefts in New York City than in Provo, Utah. Thus, the rate someone would pay for car insurance in Utah would be significantly lower than the same person would pay in New York City.

Likewise, actuaries classify various individuals insured according to the probability that they will experience a loss. People with a history of frequent car accidents pay higher car insurance rates than people with clean driving records.

And a 40-year old person who is extremely overweight and smokes cigarettes and washes skyscraper windows for a living will be charged more for life insurance than a 40-year old person who is lean and does not smoke and is employed carving duck decoys.

Understanding the Underwriting Process

An overly simple example of the underwriting process is as follows.

Joe's Insurance Company provides insurance against bowling-ball theft. The average bowling ball costs $50 to replace. Joe's actuaries tell him that there is a 1 in 100 probability that any given bowling ball will be stolen in any given year. Joe has 100 customers to whom he is selling bowling-ball insurance. Given the probability of 1 out of every hundred bowling balls being stolen annually, and the estimated replacement cost per ball of $50, Joe has decided to price the annual premium for his

---

insurance at $4 annually. If no balls are stolen in the course of a year, Joe will have a profit of $400 for the year. If, as the actuaries predict, one ball is stolen, Joe will have a profit of $350 after paying $50 to replace the stolen ball. Should there be a sudden crime-wave of bowling-ball thefts, Joe may *lose* money on his insurance program this year. And he will most certainly, after firing his actuaries, adjust his premiums next year to factor in higher risk.

ANOTHER WAY UNDERWRITERS MAKE MONEY

Along with earning money from premiums, insurance underwriters usually also enjoy revenue from returns on their investments. In good years, when claims are low, underwriters build up cash reserves. An underwriter normally invests his or her accumulated cash in stocks, bonds, mortgages, and other investments. The underwriter then adds the returns from these investments to its profit (or loss) for any given year. In times of heavier than expected claims, the underwriter's investment capital also provides a ready source for needed cash.

THE IMPORTANCE OF INDEMNIFICATION

The third most important insurance concept after fortuitous risk and insurable interest is *indemnification*. This is what an insurance policy offers you: indemnification. Nothing more. Let's go to *Webster's Dictionary*. "To indemnify means to restore lost value or to compensate for damages or loss sustained." In other words, you cannot make a profit through insurance.

If you own a home that will cost $100,000 rebuild and refurbish, it is pointless to insure it for $10 million. Let's say the house and everything in it burns. Because of the concept of indemnification, all you will get in settlement of your $10 million policy will be the $100,000 it actually will cost you to rebuild and refurbish the structure.

Obviously, the purpose behind the concept of indemnification is to keep people from insuring items for more than they are worth and then causing the destruction of the items in order to collect inflated insurance sums.

Moreover, the one area where indemnification is less than useful is in cases of life insurance. How can one define the real value of a human life? Consequently, as we shall see in Chapter 9, which focuses on life insurance, there are few limits on the amount of life insurance one may purchase.

THE DIFFERENT FLAVORS OF FORTUITOUS RISK

In broad strokes, there are three different kinds of risk: personal risks, property risks, and liability risks.

Personal risks include loss of income due to premature death, loss of income due to disability, and loss of financial assets to cover the cost of an illness or injury. These three risks are covered, variously, by *life insurance, disability income insurance,* and *health insurance.*

Property risks include loss or damage to an automobile, loss or damage to a home and/or its contents, and loss or damage to personal property. These risks are covered, variously, by automobile insurance, homeowner's insurance (or renter's insurance), and scheduled personal-property insurance.

Finally, *liability risks* include liability due to home ownership (someone breaks his or her leg in your driveway), liability due to auto ownership and operation (you ram your car into somebody else's, or run somebody over), and liability due to negligence or malpractice related to personal or professional activities. These risks are covered, variously, by homeowner's insurance, automobile insurance, and comprehensive-liability insurance packages, such as malpractice insurance for physicians.

SELECTING AN AGENT

When you select an agent from whom you will buy your insurance, it is important that you realize many agents have specialties. While an agent may be highly competent and informed in one area of insurance, it is highly probable that the same agent will bring less skill to bear when dealing with other another form of insurance. The differences in the various areas of insurance are subtle, yet complex enough that anyone, even an agent, can become lost in the details of clauses and exemptions that define them.

Therefore, many people will use one agent for personal risks (life, health, and disability), another for property risks, and still another for liability risks. Of course it almost goes without saying that the one area where property and liability risks overlap is in auto insurance, which is usually purchased from a property-risk specialist.

Another important thing to remember is that some insurance agents work for a single underwriter, while others—*independent agents*—represent many underwriters. You are best off with an independent agent, who does not owe his or her allegiance to a single company and can therefore give you the broadest range of competitive insurance options from which to choose, as well as, more objective advice concerning the good and bad points of policies offered by various companies.

One good way of getting an indication of an agent's competence is by asking whether he or she holds such professional designations as Chartered Life Underwriter (CLU) or Chartered Property Casualty Underwriter (CPCU). To get these designations, agents must pass vigorous professional examinations. The designations are a sign that your agent truly knows his or her stuff.

SELECTING UNDERWRITERS

In selecting an underwriter, remember several things. First, it is very important that you comparatively shop for rates, because premiums *do* vary greatly from one underwriter to another for what is essentially the same coverage.

Second, it is important to realize that just because an underwriter offers you the best rate on one type of policy, it is by no means a "sure thing" that the same underwriter will give you the lowest rate possible on another type of policy. Comparatively shop for each and every insurance policy you buy.

In addition to cost, it is imperative that you consider the solvency of your potential underwriter. Does Joe's Insurance Company have enough cash on hand to cover all the claims it will have to pay if disaster strikes (50 of the 100 bowling balls it insures are stolen)? After all, if your insurer goes bankrupt, you get *zero*, regardless of what premiums you've paid.

To check your potential underwriter's solvency, check *Best's Insurance Guide*, which is available in most libraries as well as on-line. *Best's* updates its ratings regularly and is your number one source of information on the financial strength of various insurance underwriters. Another source of excellent information along this line is Standard & Poor's Claims Paying Ability Reporting Service, which you can access on-line at *http://www.insure.com/ratings/re-ports/index.cfm,* shown in Figure 8.1.

Figure 8.1 The Standard and Poor's Claims Paying Ability Reporting Service.

More the Best's

By far the cheapest way to access *Best's* invaluable information is to simply go to your local library where you will most likely find the print-edition of *Best's Insurance Guide* in the reference section. Beyond that, however, you may want to consider subscribing

---

to Best's BestLink Services, the home page for which you will find at the Web address *http://www.ambest.com,* shown below in Figure 8.2.

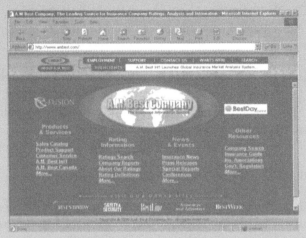

Figure 8.2 A.M. Best Company The Insurance Information Source.

Best's BestLink Services is an on-line network providing complete interactive access to A.M. Best's database of insurance financial data. Elements of the BestLink Services include:

- *A regularly updated on-line database* featuring the majority of the financial and operating data from the annual and quarterly reports of more than 4,000 underwriters, plus value-added indicators such as the exclusive Best's Ratings, all of which you may configure into customized reports by selecting the information you need from a variety of fields.

- *Insurance-related news* from leading newspapers, magazines, and wire services compiled by Best's staff of editors and updated daily. View today's news, news from the last five days, or generate a custom report by searching over four years of industry news and retrieving information by date, topic, company name, key word, or a combination of these criteria.

- Best's Company Reports, containing all the information that appears on a particular company in *Best's Insurance Guide*, is the recognized definitive guide to the insurance industry. You get Best's Ratings, operating comments, company history, key performance ratios, and more for over 4,000 firms. The data is updated daily to make sure only the latest, most accurate information reaches you.

PARTICIPATING POLICIES VS. NONPARTICIPATING POLICIES

Some insurance companies are stock companies. Others are mutual companies.

Stock companies are, as their name implies, owned by their stockholders. As with other such firms, the company either pays out profits to the stockholders as dividends or reinvests the profits back into the company as retained earnings.

Mutual companies (such as Mutual of Omaha, the outfit which brought us the television show *Wild Kingdom* for so many years) do not have stockholders. Instead, they are owned by their policyholders. Mutual companies distribute profits annually to policyholders as policy dividends. Policies such as those sold by mutual companies are called *participating policies*, since they allow policyholders to participate in the profits of the company.

Note that some stock companies may also occasionally sell participating policies.

Obviously, it is *very important* to know whether policies are participating or nonparticipating when comparing costs. This is just as important a factor as maximum coverage amount, deductibles, and so on—because some of the company's profits may be passed along to you.

READING AND UNDERSTANDING INSURANCE CONTRACTS

The piece of paper called an insurance policy is a legal contract between you, the insured, and your underwriter. It is complex. It is boring. It is annoying. *And it is something you must read very carefully before you sign on the dotted line.* Just about every insurance contract features three key sections: the *declarations*, the *insuring agreement*, and the *conditions and exclusions*.

The *declarations section* includes the name of the policy owner (which should bear a remarkable resemblance to your name), a description of the nature of the item or contingency you are insuring, an explanation of the insurance premium (how much your insurance will cost you), and a confirmation of the dates during which the policy will be in force. This latter information usually includes not just dates, but also precise hours of the days when policies commence and end.

The *insuring agreement section* details the obligations of the underwriter under the contract, including the precise risks covered by the contract and the amount of coverage.

Finally, the *conditions and exclusions section* details the precise conditions that must be met before the underwriter is required to pay on a claim. For example, before a claim for stolen property can be made, most policies require that you process a police-report that details the theft. Policies also often require police reports for automobile insurance claims related to auto-thefts or accident-related damage.

To Report or Not to Report, That Is Your Question

All right. So you suffer a loss. An insured loss. Should you report it? The answer seems obvious, but really it isn't. You may want to consider absorbing some small, trivial insured losses yourself.

Why? Well, your "loss experience" as recorded by your underwriter impacts upon the premiums you will pay in the future. For example, if you have a high rate of reporting and making claims on such minor things as paint chips on your car, you will shortly find yourself paying a higher premium than you currently do. And the higher premium rates may well accumulate to far more than what you would you have paid for replacing the chipped-paint yourself.

Of course, you should most definitely make all major claims. You should also promptly report any accident or event to your insurance company that may lead to a liability claim down the road. If you do not report such occurrences to your underwriter within a reasonable time of when they occur, the underwriter may not be liable to "pay-up" later.

Far More to the Story

There is far more to the story of insurance. There are many intricacies associated with the various types of insurance including life insurance, health insurance, and property and liability insurance. And you will examine these forms of insurance in the following three chapters. However, the basic rules and assumptions discussed in this chapter apply equally to *all* insurance, regardless of its nature.

Basic Insurance Resources on the Internet

There are a number of major national and international insurance companies that have a presence on the Internet. Check out insurance resources on the Internet compiled by the staff of Kirstein Business Branch Library at *http://www.bpl.org/www/kbb/websites/insure.htm,* shown below in Figure 8.3.

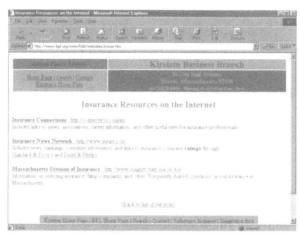

Figure 8.3 Kirstein Business Branch Library Internet Resources.

AETNA LIFE AND CASUALTY

http://www.aetna.com

The Aetna Life Insurance Company home page addresses all aspects of Aetna's life insurance services as well as financial, investment, and health-care coverage services. In addition, the site includes a condensed annual report (hypertext) as well as up-to-date quarterly earnings. Note that Aetna Casualty & Surety Company, a separate entity, merged with Travelers (whose Web site this chapter also features) in the Spring of 1996.

Figure 8.4 Aetna Life and Casualty.

THE AMERICAN INSURANCE ASSOCIATION

http://www.aiadc.org

The American Insurance Association (AIA) has been the leading property/casualty insurance trade association for more than 125 years and represents more than 250 property and casualty insurance companies. The mission of the AIA is to lead the property/casualty industry in the public-policy arena and create a political and regulatory climate that enhances the industry's financial security and global competitiveness.

Figure 8.5 The American Insurance Association.

A.M. BEST COMPANY: BEST'S RATINGS

http://www.ambest.com/rating.html

A.M. Best produces nearly 50 publications and services to meet the need for accurate, authoritative data on every aspect of this complex and ever-changing industry. These services and publications cover insurance company ratings and analysis, information related to loss control/underwriting generally, *Best's Directory of Recommended Insurance Attorneys & Adjusters*, and even great electronic publications such as *Best's Electronic Underwriting Guide* and *BestLine*. At this site, you'll find complete explanations of Best's many ratings categories: what each one means and how each one is calculated and assigned. Here you'll also get the current annual guide to *Best's Ratings* along with a sample company report and a directory of A.M. Best company numbers that you may use in ordering custom reports. Furthermore, the site also includes a database of insurance stock quotes updated daily.

Figure 8.6 A.M. Best Company.

CIGNA CORPORATION

http://www.cigna.com

CIGNA Corporation, with assets of approximately $95.9 billion, is a leading provider of health care, insurance and financial services throughout the United States and the world. They have 45,000 employees, more than 10 million health-insurance customers, 5 million retirement and investment customers, and no less than 23,000 corporate customers. Stop at this informative Web page to find out what they can do for you.

Figure 8.7 CIGNA Corporation.

CNA Insurance Companies

http://www.cna.com

CNA sells personal insurance (individual life, property, and health insurance), business insurance (commercial insurance and excess/umbrella insurance), association insurance for those organizations which wish to offer insurance as a benefit of membership, and more. This page offers details on all CNA products, as well as financial and statistical information on the company, its current stock price, and more.

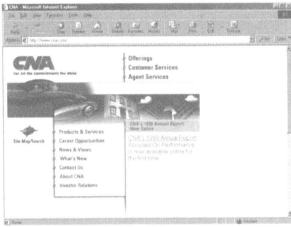

Figure 8.8 CNA Insurance Companies.

CyberApp Worldwide Insurance Network (CWIN)

http://www.cyberapp.com

CyberApp Worldwide Insurance Network (CWIN) serves the insurance needs of the Internet community worldwide. An established focal point for on-line insurance shoppers since 1995, CyberApp has gained wide recognition among insurance buyers and insurance professionals as the singular resource for informing Internet consumers of products and developments in the insurance industry, spawning consumer self-reliance in shopping for insurance coverage on the Internet, and facilitating on-line insurance delivery concepts and agency support services. At this site, you'll find at-a-glance information on insurance coverage and regulatory developments, and insurer listings of products, services, and downloadable applications, and more.

Figure 8.9 CyberApp Worldwide Insurance Network.

THE INSURANCE CLUB

http://www.insuranceclub.co.uk

The Insurance Club is a new Internet service for insurance consumers in the United Kingdom. Be sure, in particular, to check out Cyber Home, the new household insurance policy designed in association with award-winning broker Bervale Mead and underwritten by Independent Insurance Co., Ltd., of the UK's most successful and reliable underwriters. Cyber Home is designed specifically for the modern household. It provides all the protection that a standard household insurance policy offers for buildings and contents, including computers. The folks at Bervale Mead point out that by buying your household insurance through the Internet you can share in the savings offered by transacting business on the information superhighway.

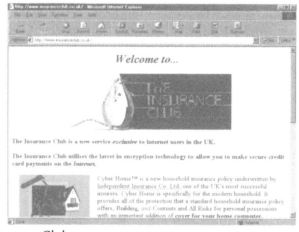

Figure 8.10 The Insurance Club.

INSURANCE INFORMATION EXCHANGE

http://www.iix.com

The Insurance Information Exchange (iiX) is a service created for the insurance industry that provides communication between agents, companies and consumers, and that supplies on-line information on a variety of insurance related topics and services.

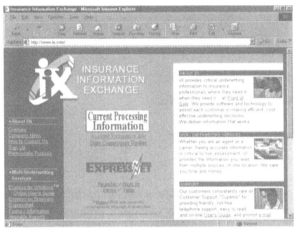

Figure 8.11 *Insurance Information Exchange.*

INSURANCE INFORMATION INSTITUTE *(I.I.I.)* PUBLICATIONS

http://www.iii.org

For more than 30 years the Insurance Information Institute (I.I.I.) has provided definitive, credible insurance information. Today the I.I.I. is recognized as a primary source of information, analysis and referral on property/casualty insurance.

The great, informative hypertext brochures you'll find here address such topics as 12 ways to lower your homeowner's-insurance premiums, how to file an insurance claim, insuring your home business, nine ways to lower your auto insurance costs, and settling insurance claims after a disaster. And there is also an informative, eye-opening report on "Where the Auto Premium Dollar Goes."

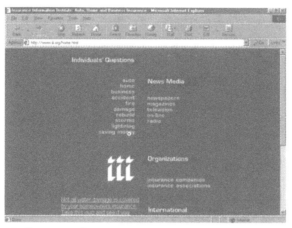

Figure 8.12 *Insurance Information Institute.*

INSURANCEQUOTE SERVICES FOR TERM LIFE

http://www.iquote.com

Arizona-based InsuranceQuote Services operates a free, *independent* computerized data bank which provides prices and details of low-cost term insurance policies. You supply some details about your age, sex, whether you smoke, and the amount of coverage you want. Based on this data, InsuranceQuote compiles from its data bank a detailed description of the five lowest-cost, safest term life insurance policies that fit your request. This is not fly-by-night insurance. InsuranceQuote monitors and reports prices for only the highest-rated, most financially sound life insurance companies. The majority are rated A+ (Superior) by A.M. Best (whose Web site this chapter also features). This site gives you a great, no-pressure way to begin shopping for term life, simply because you can do it all via e-mail. There is no pressure to give your phone number. Submit your request by e-mail and you'll get the information back at you the same way. And promptly.

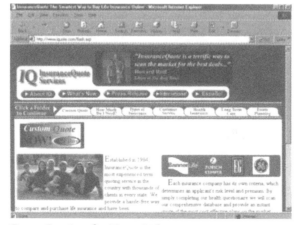

Figure 8.13 *InsuranceQuote Services for Term Life*

INSURANCE NEWS NETWORK: DUFF AND PHELPS/STANDARD & POOR'S REPORTS

http://www.insure.com

At this useful Web site, you can access Duff & Phelps claims paying-ability ratings on hundreds of insurers as well as those from Standard & Poor's. Both sets of ratings are available free and you may view them separately or, in the case of large life/health insurers, in a new combined ratings table. What Standard & Poor's offers here, by the way, are new ratings on more than 1,200 life and health insurers, presented in an easy-to-understand tabular format that includes additional information. The Insurance News Network also presents detailed CPA reports from Standard & Poor's on dozens of major insurers.

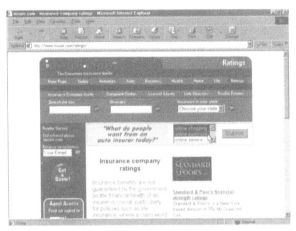

Figure 8.14 *Insurance News Network.*

INSURANCE AND RISK MANAGEMENT (IRM) CENTRAL

http://www.irmcentral.com

This is quite possibly the premier site for doing business or finding information related to insurance and risk management on the Internet. In addition to IRM's own excellent proprietary content, you also have well-organized sets of links to just about all the other insurance- and risk management-related resources on the Net.

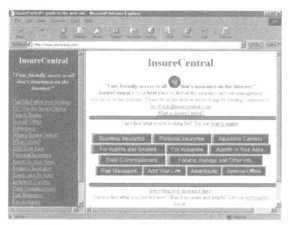

Figure 8.15 *Insurance and Risk Management (IRM) Central.*

INSURANCE YELLOW PAGES

http://connectyou.com/ins/yellow.htm

The Insurance Yellow Pages is a service providing a great searchable database of hundreds of insurance-related Web links. Searching the database will connect you to agencies/brokers, underwriters large and small, claims departments, and hundreds of other resources and contacts.

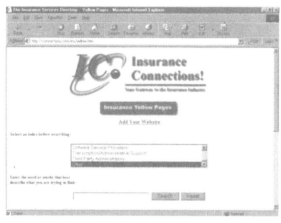

Figure 8.16 *Insurance Yellow Pages.*

INSUREWEB

http://InsureWeb.com

InsureWeb is not so much for consumers as it is for brokers and underwriters. This, in essence, is a bulletin board on the Web where registered agents and brokers can offer risks for placement to registered insurance underwriters, registered insurance wholesalers, and registered carriers.

Figure 8.17 InsureWeb.

METROPOLITAN LIFE

http://www.metlife.com

The origins of the Metropolitan Life Insurance Company go back to 1863, when a group of New York City businessmen raised $100,000 to found the National Union Life & Limb Insurance Company.

The new company insured Civil War sailors and soldiers against disabilities due to wartime wounds, accidents, and sickness. In 1868, after several reorganizations and five difficult years in the field, the company decided to focus on the life insurance business. A new company was chartered to sell "ordinary" life insurance to the middle class. The founders chose the name because they had been most successful in New York City, or the "Metropolitan" district.

This new company also faced difficulties. A severe business depression that began in the early 1870s rapidly put half of the 70 life-insurance companies then operating in New York State out of business. Only very large, well-established ordinary life-insurance companies remained strong. Policy lapses over successive years forced the company to contract, steadily and painfully, until it reached its lowest point in the late 1870s.

In 1879, MetLife president Joseph F. Knapp turned his attention to England, where "industrial" or "workingmen's" insurance programs were widely successful. American companies had not bothered to pursue industrial insurance up to that time because of the expense involved in building and sustaining an agency force to sell policies door to door, and to make the weekly collection of five- or ten-cent premiums.

Importing English agents to train an American agency force, MetLife quickly transferred successful British methods for use in the United States. By 1880, the company was signing up 700 new industrial policies a day. Rapidly increasing volume quickly drove down distribution costs, and the new program proved immediately successful. In fact, by 1909 MetLife became the nation's largest life insurer in terms of insurance in force. In 1991, MetLife became the largest issuer of life insurance in all of North America, with over one trillion dollars of insurance in force.

Figure 8.18 Metropolitan Life.

MUTUAL OF OMAHA

http://www.mutualofomaha.com

The Mutual of Omaha companies provide comprehensive insurance and financial services, managing total assets of more than $10.1 billion with over $80 billion of life insurance in force. Mutual of Omaha maintains a national network of 150 sales offices and a sales staff of more than 3,100 people, providing life insurance to nearly 6.3 million consumers. Oh yeah, and they used to finance Marlin Perkins's *Wild Kingdom*.

Figure 8.19 Mutual of Omaha.

NATIONWIDE INSURANCE

http://www.nationwide.com

Nationwide offers a great variety of policies for individuals, families, businesses, and organizations. These insurance services include auto, fire, homeowners, life, business, and health insurance. Here you'll not only find information on these various policies, but also Nationwide's agency locator (to help you find the Nationwide representative nearest you) and electronic access to Nationwide's Blue Ribbon Claims Service.

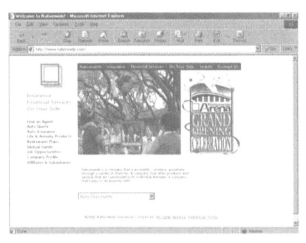

Figure 8.20 Nationwide Insurance.

THE PRUDENTIAL

http://www.prudential.com

Prudential's home page is a little wild and a little weird, but useful. You wouldn't expect the home page of a staid old workhorse of conservative insurance to be wild, would you? But it is. There is a cast of characters, you see: Ellen Pasand, the Tanakas, Luis Herrera, the Paynes, Carol Hearn, the Cooks, and David Springer. Every three weeks, one of these folks faces a life-impacting financial decision. And you have the opportunity to vote on which direction you think they should go in that decision. You hold their financial future in the palm of your hand, as it were, or at least in the click of your mouse. Don't feel like playing? Well, you can also get information on Prudential's various insurance products. They are a substantial outfit, of course. In fact, more than 50 million people all over the world turn to Prudential for their life, health, property and liability insurance.

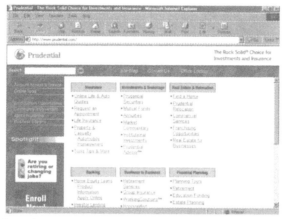

Figure 8.21 The Prudential.

TRAVELERS PROPERTY AND CASUALTY

http://www.travelers.com

Travelers is the leading provider of a broad range of insurance products for commercial markets and a leading provider of homeowners and auto insurance for consumers. Travelers Property & Casualty is a member of Citigroup. The 1998 merger of Citigroup and Travelers Group brought together such brand names as Citibank, Travelers, Salomon Smith Barney, Commercial Credit (now named CitiFinancial), and Primerica under Citigroup's trademark red umbrella. Check out their Web Site and get quotes, find local agents, and learn about personal insurance. Travelers can also provide life insurance, annuities, and business insurance.

Figure 8.22 Travelers Property and Casualty.

YACHTLINE INTERNATIONAL

http://yachtline.com

You thought *buying* your boat was expensive? You thought the mooring fees seemed high? Hah! Just wait till you try to insure it. One is never rich enough to own a boat. Never. But still, like other addicts, we simply must have our fix, whatever the cost. (Also check out the Boat & Yacht Insurance Center, *http://www.trendaw.com/insurance/*).

Figure 8.23 Yachtline International.

Visit Barron's On-Line

For years, investors have turned to Barron's for the latest news on finance and investing. Now, users surfing the Web can turn to Barron's on-line. After you subscribe to their on-line service, you can access financial data and archives of past articles. For more information on Barron's, visit their Web site at *http://www.Barrons.com.*

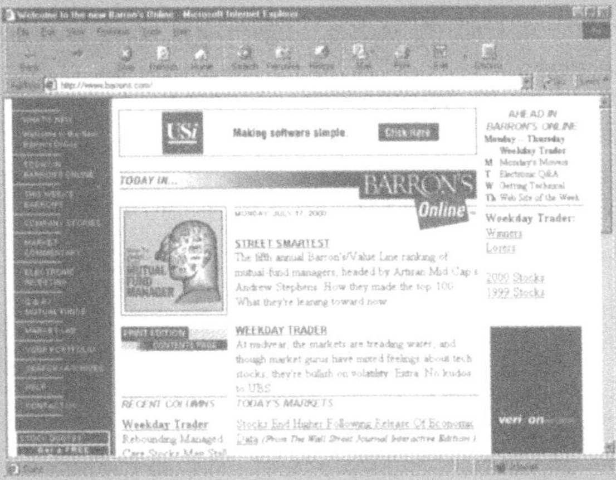

Figure 8.24 Barron's On-Line.

ALLSTATE INSURANCE

http://www.allstate.com

Allstate offers a wide range of insurance products including auto, home, life and business, in addition to, RV, boat, and motor home. This site helps you decide what you need, what you should consider, and coverage options. They also offer discounts and savings. Look for their agent locator and valuable resources and tools.

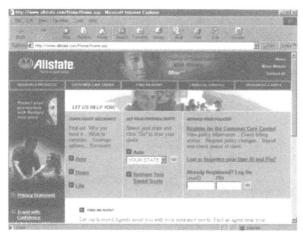

Figure 8.25 *Allstate Insurance.*

WAUSAU INSURANCE

http://www.wausau.com

Wausau operates as an international, multi-line insurer offering a broad range of commercial property/casualty coverage, loss management services, employee benefits and services, and underwriting. They have recently affiliated with Liberty Mutual Group—a Fortune 500 organization and the nation's leading writer of workers compensation. They enjoy an A+ rating from A.M. Best, and nearly one third of their customers have been with them for more than ten years.

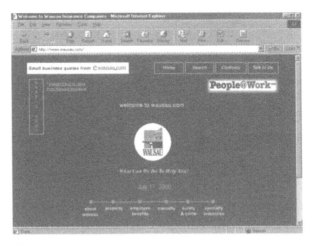

Figure 8.26 Wausau Insurance.

GEICO INSURANCE

http://www.geico.com

GEICO offers a comprehensive number of insurance products that will insure your protection on the road. If you are looking for auto or motorcycle insurance, GEICO will help you determine the best coverages, deductibles, and payment options for you. Visit their Web site and read about their special discount programs for students and educators, as well as, their affiliations with federal and military personnel. Email them regarding information and quotes on homeowners, condominium, renters, boat, and flood insurance.

Figure 8.27 GEICO Insurance.

INSURANCE NETWORKING – INTERNET RESOURCES

http://www.indm.com/resource.htm

This site gives a list of useful and key insurance-related sites on the World Wide Web in order to facilitate information gathering.

Figure 8.28 Insurance Networking – Internet Resources.

INSURANCE NETWORKING- WILLIAM GALLAGHER ASSOCIATES

http://www.wgains.com/links.htm

This site provides the highest quality insurance brokerage and risk management services to technology clients.

Figure 8.29 Insurance Networking- William Gallagher Associates.

THE INSURANCE AND PLANNING RESOURCE CENTER

http://www.LCGroup.com/resource

This site is brought to you by The Lewis-Chester Group. It provides insurance coverage explanations and definitions of insurance terms. Check out "The Complete Glossary of Insurance."

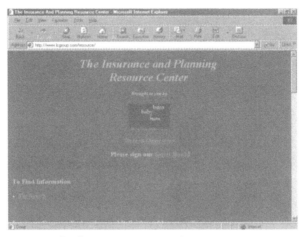

Figure 8.30 The Insurance and Planning Resource Center.

BALDUCCI'S INSURANCE CARTOONS

*http://balducci.math.ucalgary.ca/
icartoon1.html*

FINANCIAL INSTITUTIONS INSURANCE NETWORK

http://www.fiia.org

INSURANCE WORLD

http://www.insworld.com

INSURE.NET

http://www.insure-net.com

STATE FARM INSURANCE

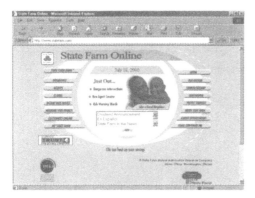

http://www.statefarm.com

NORWEST CORPORATION

http:www.norwest.com

INTERNET PIPELINE: THE INTERNET RESOURCE FOR INSURANCE PROFESSIONALS

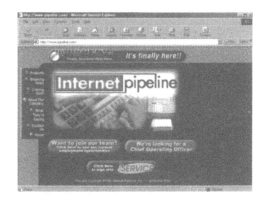

http://www.ipipeline.com

INSURANCE LINKS

http://www.insurance-links.com

LIFE INSURANCE.NET

http://www.lifeinsurance.net/premieragents.htm

PROGRESSIVE CORP.

http://www.auto-insurance.com

COMMERCIAL AND BUSINESS INSURANCE

http://www.broker-insurance.co.uk/index.htm

THE HARTFORD FINANCIAL SERVICES GROUP

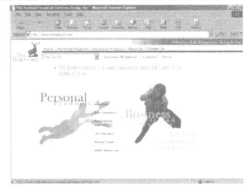

http://www.thehartford.com

Chapter 9

What Are You Worth?
The Art of Life Insurance

If you would insure against death, would you not also insure against daylight? One is as certain as the other. — *Chaucer*

At least one member of virtually every family holds life insurance. Yet, when it comes to life insurance, most families are underinsured. What is the correct method for calculating exactly what the lives of the principal wage-earners of your household are worth? And what is the appropriate sum to pay in order to insure these lives?

Insurance Against the Risk of Premature Death

As explained earlier, life insurance is *not* insurance against the risk of death, per se. Since death is inevitable, it is not a fortuitous risk; therefore, it cannot be insured against. Life insurance is, instead, insurance against the risk of premature death. To be even more precise, the primary purpose of life insurance is to *replace income lost due to premature death*.

It follows, then, that the persons in your household whom you want to insure in this way are the principal wage earners. But also keep in mind that it is sometimes worthwhile to also insure the lives of family members who are not employed outside the home, family members who have primary responsibility for childcare, cooking, cleaning, and so forth. Were this family member to die, and the survivor forced to hire outside help to see to these tasks, the cost would be high.

Who Needs Life Insurance?

Life insurance is essential for anyone on whom others depend for income, for sustenance, for care-giving. My young, swinging bachelor brother needs little or no life insurance. Some would argue that my brother should purchase life insurance now, however, even though he doesn't need it at the moment. They would suggest that his annual-premium payments will be lower if he starts on life insurance now than they would be should he decide to insure himself later. The statement is true enough, but the implication of savings over the long-term is spurious. His premium will be lower, sure. But he will be paying it over the course of a higher number of years and, thus, eradicate any savings.

On the other end of the spectrum, my elderly great aunt, a financially self-sufficient widow, also does not need life insurance. Neither my great aunt nor my brother has dependents. I, on the other hand, have a three-year old daughter, of whom I am the sole support. I absolutely require life insurance. But what flavor? And how much?

THE DIFFERENT FLAVORS OF LIFE INSURANCE

Life insurance is available in several different (and sometimes confusing) flavors. At first glance, there seem to be dozens of different options, combinations, and variations. You will see references to straight term insurance, renewable term, convertible term, decreasing term, whole life, modified whole life, straight life, ordinary life, limited payment life, and permanent insurance, to name just a few. How do all these options differ? What do the labels mean?

Relax. In fact, upon scrutiny, probing beneath the varied toppings, you'll find that there are really only two basic flavors of life insurance from which to choose: *term insurance* and *cash-value insurance*. After you understand the distinction between these two flavors of insurance, you will be a long way down the road to understanding the fundamentals of just about any life-insurance plan that crosses your path.

TERM LIFE INSURANCE

Term life insurance is the most simple of the two forms of life insurance. It is usually also the least expensive.

Under term insurance, the underwriter (the company providing the insurance) simply agrees to pay a stipulated sum (the *face value* of the policy) to the person or persons you name (the *beneficiary* or *beneficiaries*) in case of your death during a specific window of time, which is identified as the *term* of the policy—which as you will learn can vary from one year to many years.

Term insurance builds no cash-value as the policy matures. When a policy expires, it is worthless. However, term insurance has great appeal to the primary life-insurance market: younger, growing families which require large amounts of coverage at a reasonable price. For, as this chapter will show, there is no substitute for term life insurance when it comes to providing the most coverage for the lowest cost.

Term life insurance is available in four different (though often overlapping) varieties called *straight term, renewable term, convertible term*, and *decreasing term*.

Straight term policies provide coverage for a fixed number years—1 year, 5 years, 10 years, 15 years, 20 years, and so on. It is also possible to get policies written to run from whatever age you are now to a certain benchmark age in the future, say, age 65.

Renewable term is term life insurance that you may renew at the end of the term without the necessity of a new medical examination. Of course, each time you renew your premium rates will go up, simply because as your age increases, so too does your probability of death. Many term insurance policies are renewable. Many are also *convertible*.

Convertible term is term life insurance that lets you convert the policy to a cash-value policy (see below for an explanation of cash-value policies) at standard rates, regardless of changes in your health.

Decreasing term is term life insurance that, justifiably, has very broad appeal among families with children and mortgages. These policies feature a fixed premium (that you pay) and a declining face value (that underwriter pays your beneficiaries). Early in the life of the policy (when you need the most insurance), the face value is high. Over time, the policy's face value steadily decreases through the years, until the amount payable upon the insured's death is nothing. The beauty of this type of life insurance is that early in the life of the policy one gets maximum protection for the absolutely lowest premium possible. Many families set up decreasing term policies with face values designed to match the principal on their mortgage loan at any given moment. As the mortgage principal declines, so too does the face value on the household's principal wage-earner. As that debt subsides, so too does the coverage. But the family's coverage always matches their *need*.

CASH VALUE INSURANCE: WHOLE LIFE

Cash-value insurance is also called, variously, *whole life insurance, straight life, ordinary life*, and *permanent insurance*.

Permanent insurance? How so?

Unlike term insurance, whole-life insurance remains in effect throughout your lifetime, since it accumulates a cash-value. The premium you pay on whole life is higher than the cost necessary to insure you. In addition to the premium for coverage, the policy sets aside the additional dollars that you pay. These additional dollars accrue as cash-value in your policy. As the insured, you have the option to borrow the cash value of the policy from your underwriter at an interest rate well below the market rate, while the policy itself remains in force. You may also terminate the policy and receive the current cash-value in a lump sum. Or you may exchange your policy at its current cash value for a new and smaller policy that will begin fully paid.

THE DISADVANTAGES OF WHOLE LIFE

In effect, a whole-life policy represents a forced savings plan. But is this the best way to save? Nope. The interest you will earn on the savings component of a whole-life policy is always well below the rate of return you would earn via other investments over time. And this is a major shortcoming that can cost you, as an investor, a lot of money. Add to this the fact that whole life insurance is much more expensive out-of-pocket over the course of a person's lifetime than is term insurance. All in all, I do not recommend whole-life insurance. Term is a much better deal overall. Nevertheless, here are more details on your whole-life options.

THE VARIETIES OF WHOLE LIFE

There are many variations on the whole-life theme, including *modified whole life, limited payment life, family plan insurance, family income policies, family income riders*, and *family maintenance policies.*

Modified whole life is permanent insurance featuring premium payments that are low in the early years of the policy and higher later on. To hold down costs, modified whole life is actually a combination of term and whole-life insurance. In the early years, when the premiums are low, the insurance is term. Then, over the course of years, it gradually shifts to whole life, and the premiums rise accordingly.

Limited payment life is permanent insurance that requires you to pay premiums only for a fixed term, often 20 years. These policies are sometimes called *twenty pay life* policies. Other limited payment life policies are set up so that your premium payments cease at age 65. Such policies are called *paid up age 65* policies—their premium payments tend to be high compared to other options, simply because you make fewer total payments for the permanent life policy.

Family plan insurance is a mixture of whole-life and term insurance designed to cover an entire family. You might configure such a policy to provide $500,000 in permanent whole-life coverage for the household's principal wage-earner, $200,000 in term life coverage for the homemaker, and $10,000 in term life insurance for each child. For what it is worth, I will tell you that I and most financial advisors see no point in insuring the lives of children other than Macauley Caulkin and other large wage-earners. Should the typical child die, he or she leaves no immediate income-earning potential unfulfilled. And the real, tragic human value of the child's loss can never be measured in dollars.

Family income policies combine decreasing term and whole-life insurance. The decreasing term portion of the insurance package usually runs for 20 years. If the insured dies within the 20-year window, the term portion of the policy pays his or her family a regular income. At the end of the 20 year-window, the regular payments stop and the insured's family is paid, in a lump sum, the face value amount of the whole-life portion of the policy. The *family income rider* policy presents a similar approach, which pays the face value of the whole-life policy at the time of death, rather than at the end of the term policy, while at the same time providing the family with income payments for a fixed number of years.

Finally, the *family maintenance policy* is also a combination of term and whole-life insurance. In this instance, however, the term portion of the policy is level term instead of decreasing term. In other words, it pays income for a fixed number of years after the policyholder's death. If the policy is a 25-year policy calling for 10 years of income payments, the family receives income payments for ten years regardless of when, during the 25-year life of the policy, the insured dies. The insured could die in the 24th year of the policy or the 2nd year of the policy, and ten years of income payments would be the result in either circumstance.

ENDOWMENT POLICIES

Another type of whole-life insurance is the *endowment policy* which, to put it bluntly, *is absolutely the most expensive form of life insurance you can buy*. Sound appealing?

Endowment policies emphasize the savings and income aspects of life insurance. In other words, the policies emphasize the least appealing and least (for the consumer/investor) profitable aspect of life insurance. And since the policies earmark the bulk of premiums for savings, rather than paying for insurance, what you will pay monthly is grossly inflated compared to what you'd pay for similar (and, so far as I am concerned, just as good) term life insurance.

An endowment policy is set for a fixed term. At the end of the term, the underwriter pays you the face value of the policy. If you die before the expiration of the fixed term, the policy pays your beneficiaries the face value. In some cases, instead of paying a lump sum when the policy reaches term, the underwriter pays a monthly amount to the policyholder until the face value and accumulated interest are obliterated.

Stay away from endowment policies. Period.

A LAST WORD TO THE WISE OF WHOLE LIFE

Put your long-term investment dollars in a stock- or bond-mutual fund rather than in inflated premiums for whole-life insurance. Then, insure your principal wage-earner with a nice, affordable term life-insurance policy for an appropriate number of years. Do this and you will end up with much more cash in hand at the end of the road than you would otherwise.

GROUP INSURANCE: THE WAY TO GO

There may be safety in numbers, but there is also economy and convenience. Your employer may have a group life-insurance option that you should look at very seriously.

When underwriters negotiate insurance contracts with large employers, or with professional associations or other large organizations, they compete with each other for exclusive contracts and adjust their prices accordingly. You will always find the best prices for all forms of life insurance under a group-insurance umbrella. If you work for a firm, look into the options they have available. If you are self-employed, see what various professional organizations in your field have to offer. (As an independent writer I, for example, get all my insurance, life and otherwise, through an affiliate of the Authors Guild of America—at group rates.)

Note: If your employer pays for your life insurance, your policy's face value will be subject to income tax. Likewise, if your employer pays for part of your life-insurance premium, an equivalent part of your policy's face value will be subject to income tax.

CREDIT LIFE INSURANCE: STAY AWAY

Credit life insurance is extremely costly insurance sold as part of a debt contract, such as an auto loan. The rationale of a credit life-insurance policy is that if the borrower dies before the debt is paid, the life insurance will cover the balance of principal on the loan.

Don't do it. Consumer protection laws prohibit lenders from requiring a borrower to buy credit life-insurance as a condition for receiving a loan. Also, if you'd like to insure for the same contingency, you can pick up term life insurance that will do the same job at a much lower cost than the equivalent amount of credit life insurance.

HOW MUCH SHOULD A PRIMARY WAGE EARNER BE INSURED FOR?

Calculating your insurance needs is very much the art of calculating your overall professional worth over time and then balancing this figure, realistically, against your family's likely financial *needs* (as opposed to *desires*) over time.

Say you are 40 years old with two small children. Say you make between $80,000 and $90,000 a year and every indication is that you will make this amount or more in coming years. Say that your annual household overhead for mortgage payments, heat, food, clothing and other essentials is $36,000, and that you've got 20 years left on your mortgage. OK, all that being said, now how much insurance would you like to have in the event that you drop dead tomorrow?

To match what you would probably have made professionally in the next 20 years, your family would need $2,000,000. But is $2,000,000 really necessary? Whether it is or not is, of course, a lifestyle choice. How "high on the hog" do you want your survivor's to live in the (keyword) *unlikely* event that you are prematurely gone? Can your survivors get along on $50,000 a year for the next 20 years? Then, all the coverage you need is $1,000,000. This will, obviously, cost you half as much in premiums as would a $2,000,000 policy.

Consider other issues besides lifestyle. Do your children have endowments of trust from grandparents that will cover all or part of their education costs? Does your spouse have a nest egg of stocks and bonds? All such factors, along with your age and the age of your dependents, impact how much coverage makes sense. The main thing is to provide for all contingencies, and to do so at a cost that leaves you some money in hand while you are alive!

Use This Worksheet to Calculate How Much Life Insurance You Need

1. Calculate the income you'll need to replace:

Enter your family's current annual expenses for:

Food $_____

Clothing $_____

Mortgage/Rent $_____

Utilities $_____

Home Maintenance/Taxes (though not mortgage payments) $_____

Insurance (life, property, liability) $_____

Car Expense & Insurance $_____

Child Care $_____

Education $_____

Medical & Dental $_____

= Total Annual Family Cost of Living $_____

Now multiply this by the portion of current expenses your family will actually need after your death. Will there be one less car for the household to support? One less life insurance policy to pay? Would your family likely relocate to another state, with a lower average cost of living, to be nearer to next-of-kin? Take all such things into consideration and then estimate the percentage at which you should discount your family's current annual cost of living, and then do so.

Total Current Annual Expense (from above) $_____

x discount _____%

= Total Actual Annual Family
Cost of Living after your demise: $_____

2. Calculate your family's income after your death:

Enter:

Your spouse's income after taxes & expenses $_____

Estimated Social Security Benefits payable $_____ *

Periodic payment such as pension annuities, that
survivors cannot take as a lump sum (after taxes) $_____

Other income (trust funds, etc.) $ _____

= After Tax Income Available Annually after yr. death $ _____

* Note that annual Social Security Survivor's Benefits are calculated as follows:

worker's age	family profile	annual earnings	annual earnings at death
		$30,000 or more	$60,00 or more
35 & up	spouse, 1 child	$19,000	$25,800
	spouse, 2 children	$22,100	$30,100
	spouse at age 60	$9,000	$12,300
45 & up	spouse, 1 child	$19,000	$25,000
	spouse, 2 children	$22,100	$29,100
	spouse at age 60	$9,000	$11,900
55 & up	spouse, 1 child	$18,900	$23,400
	spouse, 2 children	$22,100	$27,200
	spouse at age 60	$9,000	$11,100

3. Calculate annual supplement required after your death:

Total Actual Annual Family Cost of Living
after your demise: $ _____

minus After-Tax Income
Available Annually after your death: $ _____

= **Annual Supplement Required after your death** $ _____

4. Calculate TOTAL annual supplement required after your death:

For how many years will the supplement be necessary? How long till your kids are grown and gone out of the house, able to support themselves? How long until your spouse comes into likely inheritances from your and your spouse's parents? How long till your children meet the age requirements for moneys held in trust for them? Consider all these possible factors, plus any others that apply to you, and decide realistically for how many years your life insurance must be relied upon to supplement the income of the household you leave behind.

Annual Supplement Required after your death $_____

x total number of years required   _____

= TOTAL Annual Supplement Required after your death $_____

5. Calculate lump sum "capital" requirements:

Add together any lump sums your survivors will need such as funds to cover:

Funeral/Estate Administration $_____

Federal and state estate taxes $_____

Home-Mortgage balance $_____

Other Debts $_____

College Tuition(s) $_____

= Total lump sum requirements $_____

6. Calculate your total life insurance required:

TOTAL Annual Supplement Required after your death $_____

Plus Total lump sum requirements $_____

= Total Life Insurance Required $_____

UNDERSTANDING STANDARD LIFE INSURANCE POLICY PROVISIONS

A number of standard provisions show up in the terms of just about every life insurance policy. These embrace *additional benefits, non-forfeiture rights, settlement options,* and other arcane policy features, which it is important for you to understand.

BENEFITS

First of all, let us consider *additional benefits*. These benefits are sold with most basic life insurance policies and are attached to the policy agreement in the form of a *rider* (a subsequent agreement that "rides along" with your policy). One common rider benefit is the *waiver of premium benefit,* which states that if illness or injury prevents you from working, the underwriter will pay your premiums for you in the event of your total disability. Another common benefit is the *accidental death benefit* (also known as a *double indemnity clause*.) What this says is that if you have died as the result of an accident, you get twice the face value of the life insurance policy. Each of these additional benefits comes "á la carte." You pay for them in the form of increased premiums. The *waiver of premium benefit* is obviously worthwhile. But what of the double indemnity clause? Have you done your insurance planning correctly? If so, then will your survivors really *need* twice as much money if you die in a car crash than they will if you die of a heart attack? I don't think so.

Non-Forfeiture Rights

Non-forfeiture rights are four specifically enunciated rights and values in an insurance policy that you cannot lose under any circumstances, even if the policy lapses. By their nature, term life-insurance policies do not involve non-forfeiture rights. These rights instead come into play with regard to whole life policies.

The first non-forfeiture right is your *reinstatement right*, which gives you a window of time after the lapse of a policy during which you may reinstate the policy by paying the past-due premiums with interest.

The second non-forfeiture right is your *surrender right*, which entitles you to cash in your lapsed whole-life policy for its current cash-value. Of course, the policy need not necessarily be lapsed in order for you to collect your cash-value settlement. You can cash in your whole-life policy at any time, expired or not, simply by surrendering it to your underwriter.

The third non-forfeiture right is your policy's *extended term value*, which allows you to use the cash value of a lapsed whole-life policy to purchase a fully paid-up term insurance policy with the same face value for a limited number of years.

Finally, the last important non-forfeiture right is your *policy's reduced paid-up value*. This is the amount of permanent, whole-life insurance the cash value of your lapsed whole-life policy will buy without your having to pay an additional premium.

Settlement Options

OK. So now you are dead. And your survivors have five basic settlement options as stipulated in the contract for your life insurance. You could have dictated the settlement process when you bought the insurance years ago. But instead you decided to leave it to your beneficiary to choose the means of settlement most auspicious *at the time of settlement*.

The first of your beneficiary's five options is a straightforward *lump sum settlement*. This allows your beneficiary to take the entire face value of your life-insurance policy in one large check, minus any outstanding loans you may have taken against the policy.

Or, your beneficiary may choose an *income for life option*, which will pay a lifetime monthly income to him or her. The amount of the monthly payment will depend, of course, on two things. The first is the amount of your insurance. The second is your beneficiary's age. I should tell you that there is a roulette aspect to the *income for life option* that I do not like. Let me explain. In connection with this option, all policies offer a minimum guaranteed payment period (often ten years). Should your beneficiary die before the stipulated minimum payment period is up, a lump sum payment will be made to your beneficiary's beneficiary. However, after the minimum guaranteed payment period, all bets are off. Your beneficiary will keep getting his or her payments until he or she dies. But after your beneficiary passes, there is no residual value in the insurance policy and your underwriter has no further obligation to pay anyone anything.

Less risky than the *income for life option* is *the income for a specified period option*. This option provides your beneficiary with a regular monthly payment drawing on both principal (the face value of your policy) and interest *over a specific period of time* at the end of which it is forecasted that the principal will be completely liquidated.

Similarly, the *income of a specified amount option* provides for monthly payment of a chosen, arbitrary amount for as long as principal and interest last, but does not have a prescribed date at which it will end. And the *interest only* option is an election to leave the face value of the policy with the underwriter, who will make regular interest payments to the beneficiary. Of all these options, the *lump-sum option* is almost always the best. The other scenarios factor in underwriter's interest rates, which are inevitably much lower than what the same principal could earn in the hands of an experienced, reliable financial advisor. In short, your survivors should take the lump sum payment and invest it wisely.

ADDITIONAL POLICY FEATURES

There are just a few more common life-insurance policy clauses you need to understand. Just a few. I promise. And I will keep this brief.

The *incontestability clause* states that after the policy has been in force for a given number of years (usually two), the underwriter loses the right to challenge any statement made by you in your application (and thus deny payment of a claim).

The *suicide clause* often (though not always) states that if you die by your own hand within two years of buying a policy, the underwriter will not be liable to pay the face value of the policy, but instead will simply return to your beneficiary the premiums paid to date. After two years, the underwriter will often pay the face value in full to your beneficiary after your death by your own hand. (But I certainly hope you won't resort to this!)

The *automatic premium loan clause* included in many policies allows the underwriter to borrow against the cash value of your insurance to pay itself delinquent premiums, thus leaving the policy and its coverage in force.

And the *dividend option clause* allows you four choices in how to deal with whole-life dividends: taking them as cash, putting them toward premiums, leaving them with the underwriter in an interest-generating account (don't do it), or putting them towards the purchase of more insurance.

INTERNET RESOURCES FOR PURCHASERS OF LIFE INSURANCE

As you surf the World Wide Web, you may encounter sites that discuss life-insurance policies, annuities, and other related issues. The following site list should help you locate the resources you need.

AccuQuote

http://www.accuquote.com

AccuQuote makes it possible for you to quickly compare the prices and features of over 800 top-rated life insurance products. Use AccuQuote's automated quote system to do price shopping and save 30% to 60% off the cost of your life insurance. AccuQuote maintains a comprehensive computer database, which includes current rate and feature information for over 800 different life insurance products offered by several hundred different underwriters.

Figure 9.1 *AccuQuote.*

Acordia: Impaired Risk and Hard-to-Place Individual Life Policies

http://www.acordia.com

In the area of life insurance, Acordia has built a national reputation as a provider of life insurance for impaired risk and hard-to-place individuals. Acordia provides products from a number of major life carriers that include accidental death and dismemberment policies, annuities, group and individual life products, pension-related products and services, senior life insurance, and universal and term life.

Figure 9.2 Acordia: Impaired Risk and Hard-to Place Individual Life Policies.

BUDGETLIFE: INEXPENSIVE TERM LIFE INSURANCE

http://www.budgetlife.com

This is one place on the Web where you can really find excellent rates for term life insurance. The list is extensive for preferred and standard term life insurance for both males and females. The folks at BudgetLife (a division of CompuLife) provide this data as a public service. They do not sell insurance, and they are not affiliated with or advertising for any life insurance company.

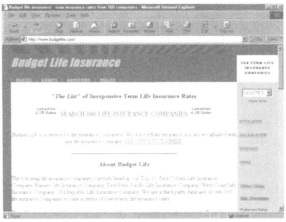

Figure 9.3 BudgetLife: Inexpensive Term Life Insurance.

LIFE INSURANCE QUOTATIONS (CANADA)

http://www.cadvision.com/Home_Pages/accounts/mylesr.life.htm

Canadian citizens can fill out the form and get in return, via e-mail, an array of quotes along with specific term life-insurance policies. Just provide your date of birth and a few health/lifestyle details, along with the length of coverage you are looking for, and you are all set. As a bonus, there is a great downloadable shareware program, which can assist you in determining the amount of insurance you require.

Figure 9.4 Life Insurance Quotations (Canada).

LifeNet

http://www.lifenet.com

On this page you'll find a great interactive calculator to help you figure your life insurance needs. Then you'll also get details on purchasing a range of low-cost life insurance policies.

Figure 9.5 LifeNet.

LIFEQUOTE INSURANCE

http://www.lifequote.com

LifeQuote bills itself as a service that can save you up to 50% or more on term life insurance premiums. The site includes a useful hypertext Consumer's Guide to Life Insurance as well as solid information about annuities. Of course, you can also get quotations on both term life insurance and annuities. As the folks at LifeQuote point out, no *one* company has *the* best life insurance product for *every* age, amount, or situation. Your personal needs are unique. Therefore LifeQuote constantly reviews new products and rates from the top rated insurance companies in America. They always provide a broad selection of competitive plans from different companies. If you need help, LifeQuote provides, at no charge, an expert product consultant who is available to answer any questions. LifeQuote sells most, but not all, of the insurance product it quotes. Some insurance companies only sell their product through full time company career agents. LifeQuote is an independent brokerage. They do not work for, nor are they a part of, any particular insurance company. In the event that the best product for you is not available through LifeQuote, they will still quote it and provide you with information on how to contact the insurance company directly.

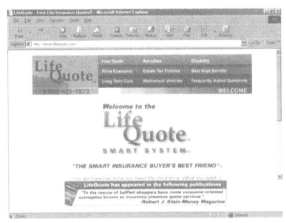

Figure 9.6 LifeQuote Insurance.

QUICKQUOTE LIFE INSURANCE QUOTES

http://www.quickquote.com

QuickQuote is an electronic, interactive quoting and comparison service for on-line users interested in obtaining the best rates available for term life insurance or fixed annuities. QuickQuote gives you free, instant, on-line comparisons of quotes from the nation's top carriers of term life insurance and annuities. After you answer a few questions about your age, lifestyle, and amount and length of desired coverage, QuickQuote displays real-time comparisons from a database of more than 1,500 term life and annuity plans. QuickQuote can save you thousands of dollars, and countless hours and days in getting the information you need to make the right decision. And you can even apply for a policy right on-line! As an independent insurance agency, QuickQuote is licensed in most states and has been appointed by more than 35 major underwriters to represent their insurance products. (By the way, in order to be represented in QuickQuote's database a carrier must have at least an "*A*" rating from the A.M. Best Rating Service. Annuities must carry at least an "*A+*" rating.)

Figure 9.7 QuickQuote Life Insurance Quotes.

NERD WORLD INSURANCE LINKS

http://www.nerdworld.com/users/dstein/nw183.html

The Nerd World Internet Subject Index is a category tree to help find Internet Resources. Nerd World includes many links to World Wide Web resources, USENET resources, and FTP resources. And Nerd World's insurance-related resources number in the hundreds.

Figure 9.8 Nerd World Insurance Links.

QUOTESMITH: LIFE INSURANCE QUOTES

http://www.quotesmith.com

Use Quotesmith to instantly check the rates and coverage of some 130+ leading term life companies and instantly apply for insurance from the company of your choice on-line without having to deal with any insurance salespeople. The service is paid for by the companies listed in the Quotesmith database. Just type in your birth date, state of residence, sex, whether or not you use tobacco, coverage amount desired, and the initial rate guarantee time desired. Then hit "Submit," and within a few seconds you'll have a report.

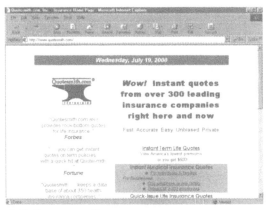

Figure 9.9 Quotesmith: Life Insurance Quotes.

HOW TO BUY LIFE INSURANCE

http://www.nylaarp.com/financialplanning.htm

The AARP/New York Life site sells life insurance, offers a comprehensive guide to buying life insurance and a good consumer page geared toward senior citizens. It also discusses the three biggest threats to your nest egg.

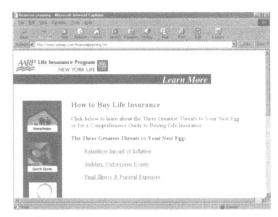

Figure 9.10 How To Buy Life Insurance.

LIFE INSURANCE BUYERS GUIDE

http://www.insbuyer.com/lifeinsurance.htm

This is a commercial site that sells quotes and contacts. They provide a page that explains the differences between three basic kinds of life insurance: term, endowment, and whole life. The site provides insurance news, ratings, and a glossary of terms.

Figure 9.11 Life Insurance Buyers Guide.

LIFE INSURANCE RESOURCE CENTRE

http://www.planned-insurance.com

Life Insurance Resource Centre is an international directory of life insurance brokers, life insurance links and resources. It also offers free listings for independent brokers.

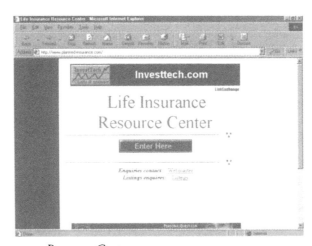

Figure 9.12 Life Insurance Resource Centre.

EZ TERM LIFE INSURANCE

http://www.ez-term-life-insurance.com

At this site you will find online term life insurance quotes, FAQ, definitions, insurance needs calculator, and online application request. EZ's powerful research engine will do the "search and rate comparison" work for you.

Figure 9.13 EZ Term Life Insurance.

CANADIAN LIFE INSURANCE

http://termlife.win.net

Canadian Life Insurance uses the compulife quotation system to give term life insurance cost estimates. The site offers a list of top insurance companies in Canada and an insurance calculator. You can request an agent contact online.

Figure 9.14 Canadian Life Insurance.

BENEFICIAL LIFE INSURANCE COMPANY

http://www.beneficiallife.com

Beneficial Life offers an array of life insurance and other financial products and services, including whole life, universal life, term life, annuities, long-term care and disability insurance. With $1.86 billion in assets and $23.4 billion insurance in force, as of March 1999, Beneficial Life is one of the nation's strongest and most stable life insurance companies. They have received A.M. Best's "A" rating and Standard & Poor's "Aq" (highest quantitative rating).

Figure 9.15 Beneficial Life Insurance Company.

TERM LIFE INSURANCE

http://www.term-lifeins.com

At this site you will find information about whole life, universal life, variable life, term life, and permanent life insurance. They also offer term life quotes online.

Figure 9.16 Term Life Insurance.

LIFE INSURANCE ANALYSIS CENTER – KEY PARTNERS

http://www.underwriter.com

This is an information site sponsored by an insurance company. It has an introduction to life insurance, how to determine current needs, and quotes from this particular insurance agency.

Figure 9.17 Life Insurance Analysis Center.

ABOUT TERM LIFE INSURANCE

http://www.abouttermlifeinsurance.com

This site provides you with the lowest online quotes for term life insurance from top-rated carriers. It includes an insurance calculator, FAQ and glossary. About Term takes you through the insurance process from start to finish saving you time and money.

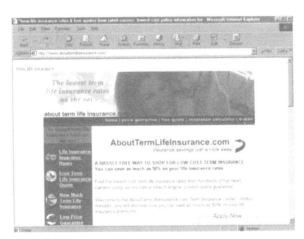

Figure 9.18 About Term Life Insurance.

GENERAL AMERICA LIFE INSURANCE COMPANY

http://www.genam.com

GROUP LIFE INSURANCE HOME PAGE

http://www.risk-managers.com

HOW MUCH LIFE INSURANCE DO YOU NEED?

http://www.insure.com/life/coverage.html

INSTANT QUOTE NETWORK

http://www.iqn.com

KANSAS CITY LIFE INSURANCE COMPANY

http://www.kclife.com

LIFE INSURANCE: WHO NEEDS IT?

http://www.tiaa-cref.org/life1.html

LIFE INSURANCE BROKERS

http://www.heffpete.com

MINNESOTA MUTUAL LIFE INSURANCE CO.

http://www.minnesotamutual.com

TERM LIFE INSURANCE SHOPPING NETWORK

http://www.primenet.com/~rayb

SAVE MONEY ON $1 MILLION+ TERM LIFE INSURANCE POLICIES

http://www.matrixdirect.com

TERM QUEST: TERM LIFE INSURANCE QUOTES

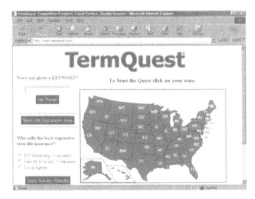

http://www.termquest.com

LIFE INSURANCE BASICS

http://www.insure.com/life/basics.html

SPLIT DOLLAR LIFE INSURANCE

http://www.tne.com/kansascity/products/spli.htm

123 TERM LIFE INSURANCE QUOTES

http://www.123lifequotes.com

AMERICAN INDUSTRIES
LIFE INSURANCE COMPANY

http://www.ailico.com

AMERICAN LIFE INSURANCE

http://www.a-life-insurance.net/references.html

LONDON LIFE INSURANCE COMPANY

http://www.kkl-biz.com/londoninsurance

PAN-AMERICAN LIFE INSURANCE COMPANY

http://www.palic.com

WEST COAST LIFE INSURANCE COMPANY

http://www.westcoastlife.com

JAPANESE LIFE INSURANCE COMPANY

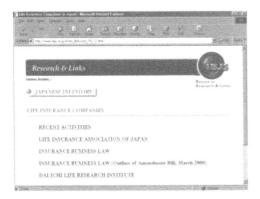

http://www.ibjs.co.jp/e/res_links/
res_19_12.html

NMAA LIFE INSURANCE NEEDS
ANALYSIS WORKSHEET

http://www.navymutual.com/lina

LIFE INSURANCE FOR SMOKERS

http://www.smokerinsurance.com

AFFORDABLE LIFE INSURANCE COMPANY

http://www.affordableterm.com

LIFE INSURANCE.NET –
INSURANCE EDUCATION CENTER

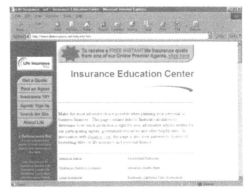

http://www.lifeinsurance.net/edu-info.htm

UNIVERSAL LIFE INSURANCE

http://www.ulinsurance.com

SAMSUNG LIFE INSURANCE

http://www.samsunglife.com

COLONIAL LIFE INSURANCE COMPANY

http://www.clico.com

MISSION LIFE INSURANCE COMPANY OF AMERICA

http://www.missionlife.com

FREE LIFE QUOTE INSURANCE SERVICES

http://www.freelifequote.com

WHAT YOU SHOULD KNOW ABOUT BUYING LIFE INSURANCE

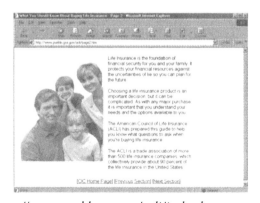

http://www.pueblo.gsa.gov/acli/index.htm

CHAPTER 10
CALCULATING RISK:
THE ECONOMICS OF HEALTH AND
DISABILITY INSURANCE

If you have your health, you have everything. — Anonymous

As a nation, we spend hundreds of billions of dollars a year on health care. Pundits look mournfully at rising health care costs and say, quite simply, that we cannot afford to get sick anymore. There is even a dark joke about a tragic Catch-22: when the sight of one's health-care bill gives one a heart attack.

While politicians and ivory-tower theoreticians debate endlessly about what has come to be called "the health-care crisis," it is we, the people, who are left in the trenches to confront and deal-with the problems of rising health-care costs on a day-to-day basis, trying desperately to provide adequate coverage for ourselves, for those we love, and in some cases for those we employ.

THE MOST IMPORTANT FORM OF INSURANCE YOU WILL EVER BUY

Your health and disability insurance are the most important forms of insurance for you to own. Consider the facts. Should you die without any life insurance, your dependents will probably find some way to get by through the help of relatives, through employment, through governmental benefits. If your uninsured property is destroyed, you can probably replace it eventually, provided you are healthy and continue to work. But an extended, uninsured illness followed by an extended, uninsured period of disability might well deal a fatal financial blow. The potentials in this scenario include bankruptcy and homelessness.

YOUR HEALTH INSURANCE OPTIONS

You have a number of options when it comes to health insurance. Among these are *traditional health insurance, health maintenance organizations (HMOs)*, and *medical savings accounts (MSAs)*.

Traditional health insurance gives the ultimate customer (the patient) freedom and, probably, satisfaction because he or she is free to choose the health-care provider. It also can be more expensive than other health insurance coverage options such as HMOs. With traditional health insurance, customers can choose virtually any doctor or hospital, with little or no restraint on the part of the insurer. In addition to monthly premiums, this coverage usually involves a deductible as well as a set amount of co-payments before the policy's full, 100% coverage kicks in. And unlike coverage issued through HMOs and managed-care organizations, traditional insurance will often have a precisely enunciated cap on coverage: perhaps a half a million, perhaps a million. (I will have more to say on appropriate health-insurance caps later.)

Health Maintenance Organizations (HMOs) are actually prepaid medical care plans. There is one monthly, semi-annual or annual fee, and thereafter virtually all your medical expenses are underwritten, although some HMOs do call for small, token co-payments. Some HMOs own their own clinics and hospitals, and employ their own full-time medical staffs. Others, as is more common, have contractual relationships with physicians, hospitals and other caregivers. These are formally called *Individual Practice Associations (IPAs)*.

The problem I have with HMOs is that while your physician examines and diagnoses and treats you, he or she is actually not working for you. Instead, your doctor is working for the HMO—the employer whom your physician must ultimately make happy in order to keep his or her contract. And the HMO is not necessarily happy when you are alive and well. The HMO is happy when you are inexpensive to treat. I'll have more to say on the pluses and minuses of HMOs a bit later.

Medical Savings Accounts, when combined with high-deductible (sometimes called "catastrophic") traditional health insurance, generally offer the most affordable combination of coverage. At the same time, this combination of coverage provides the same high degree of patient control to be had with more expensive, low-deductible traditional health insurance. The formula is simple. You take out a high-deductible health-insurance policy at a low premium rate. Then, you stash away the cash you save in a savings account—a Medical Savings Account. These funds, in turn, compound and grow. Should you later experience a catastrophic sickness or injury, you use the funds to cover your high deductible. At the same time, should you never experience such an injury or illness, you have the cash on hand.

MAKING CHOICES: ABSORBING RISK

As with any other form of insurance, you can bring down your monthly-premium expense for traditional health insurance by taking on some of the risk yourself.

For example, you can purposely take a policy for your family that does not include the costs associated with maternity expenses, pre-natal care, neonatal care and obstetrics (if you are finished having your babies). You can also take out a health policy that features extensive coverage for sickness resulting from illnesses and accidents, but at the same time has a relatively high deductible. The high deductible helps keep my premiums down, and the money you would normally pay in higher premiums for a low-deductible, you can tuck away in a medical savings account, which I will discuss in detail later in this chapter.

These are examples of how you can bring down our monthly premiums. You will have to make such choices in order to make your coverage match your needs, obligations, and lifestyle. Still, there are certain fundamentals that are non-negotiable, that everyone absolutely must have in their health insurance coverage, but that many health insurance policies *do not feature to the extent they should.*

WHAT YOU NEED TO COVER

With most HMO contracts, *everything* is covered—at least ostensibly. If your physician sends you for an expensive test that reveals an expensive-to-treat but nevertheless curable disease in its early stages, then your treatment will be covered. (That is, *if* you are sent for the test despite the fact that your physician's agreement with your HMO awards him or her more money when fewer of his or her patients are sent for expensive tests.)

With traditional medical coverage, various coverage items come à la carte. And there are certain specific coverage items you will, depending upon your circumstances, want to make sure you order from the menu.

For starters, you need full coverage (after deductibles and co-pays) for *basic hospital services* such as a semiprivate room, board, emergency-room costs, nurses, medicines, x-rays, and lab tests.

You need coverage for *the full cost of surgery* (including anesthesia and outpatient surgery). Note that some policies (actually, more and more policies) state that they will pay only a specific amount for each surgical procedure. It is incumbent upon you to make sure your health-care providers (your surgeon, your anesthetist, and so on) will accept as payment-in-full the amounts your insurer prescribes.

You need *ongoing coverage for children*. This means you want a family policy that will cover your children until age 19, or up to 23 or 25 should they be full-time students. Also, you want coverage for children who are your dependents who live outside your household, such as kids who live with a former spouse. And you want to make sure the coverage extends, if need be, to foster children and step children.

If you are planning to start a family or expand your family, you want to make sure your policy provides *complete coverage for infants from the moment they are born.* You'd think this would be a given, but nothing is a given these days. Nothing. You'd be surprised at how many health insurance policies exclude neonatal ailments. And this is an exclusion you cannot afford.

Furthermore, you need your health insurance to cover *at least part of the expenses* for convalescing in a nursing home after a serious illness, part of the cost of prescription drugs, part of the bill for home health care ordered by your physician, and part of the treatment expense for mental problems and drug and alcohol abuse.

And finally, you probably want *full dental coverage* as part of your health insurance plan. This is quite common these days, although inessential. Should your health insurance budget begin to feel tight, dental coverage (which is routinely quite expensive) should be the first thing to go. You can live without it. You can't, however, live without major medical insurance.

IMPORTANT POLICY CLAUSES TO WATCH OUT FOR

When looking through a health-insurance policy, be sure you read the fine print concerning *deductibles, coinsurance, waiting periods, policy exclusions, renewability*, and *preexisting conditions*.

Almost every health insurance policy has a *deductible clause* which will state that you are to pay a given amount of your own medical expenses each year before the insurance coverage "kicks in." As has been noted before: the higher the deductible, the lower the cost of your insurance. The most liberal deductible clauses allow you to accumulate the deductible over the course of a year for all family members covered by the policy. Rather than demanding that each member of a family of six reach the deductible of $1,000 before his or her insurance will kick in, a liberal policy (the type you'd ideally like to have) might stipulate a family deductible cap of $3,000, after which insurance coverage for everyone in the family would kick in for the year.

Your *coinsurance agreement* is a common feature of just about every major-medical contract and is very important for you to understand. *Make sure that you have a policy which **does not have** an open-ended coinsurance arrangement.* If, for example, your coinsurance agreement calls for you to pay 20% of all medical expenses covered by the policy, with the insurer picking up 80%, you are still leaving yourself open to astonishingly huge personal expenditures. Your tab on a half a million dollar medical bill would be $100,000! Thus, make sure your policy has a *cap* on the coinsurance. For example, you might set it up so that you pay 20% (or even 30% or 50%) of the first two or three thousand in medical expenses, and thereafter your insurer picks up *everything*. That way, you have real coverage for truly major medical expenses.

Make a point of being aware of the *waiting period* language in your insurance contract and what it means. The waiting period language stipulates various periods of time which must elapse before the policy will cover a specified illness or disability. This language is designed to protect the insurer from situations where people might delay needed medical treatment until they can purchase insurance. For example, nearly all health insurance policies stipulate a 9- or 10-month waiting period before childbirth expenses are covered. The waiting period language in your policy also relates to language on preexisting conditions, which are discussed below.

Be sure to study *policy exclusions* as enunciated in your insurance contract. Most policies exclude elective cosmetic surgery. You may want to elect to have your policy exclude maternity costs. Some policies also exclude mental illness. The most common policy exclusion you want to avoid, however, is any exclusion that would leave you uninsured or under-insured when traveling abroad. Make sure you have full health-insurance coverage under the terms of your policy anytime and anyplace. (Sickness while traveling is, by the way, a major problem when you are enrolled in an HMO. See the section below entitled *Some Things To Remember About HMOs* for details.)

Pay special attention to the *renewability* language in your policy. Some health-insurance contracts give the underwriter the right to cancel your policy at their discretion—which is obviously something you want to avoid. Otherwise your insurer has the right to drop you the moment you get sick and start filing claims!

You must also be aware of the language governing *preexisting conditions*. A preexisting condition is, of course, a medical problem diagnosed, treated (or otherwise *obvious*) before you bought your current health insurance. Various health-insurance policies have different waiting periods associated with various preexisting medical conditions. Many corporate-group policies have waiting periods of just three months. Individual plans, or small group plans, might require waiting periods of up to one year for preexisting conditions. Obviously, the shorter the waiting period for preexisting conditions, the better.

THE EXTENT OF YOUR COVERAGE

A traditional health-insurance policy that tops out at $250,000 for an individual or a family is simply inadequate—this is not enough coverage. Not in these days of miraculous, but nevertheless expensive, cures such as heart and kidney transplants. You need more coverage than just a quarter-of-a-million dollars. And the fact is that a policy for half a million or one million dollars does not cost much more than a $250,000 policy. Why? Because so few hospital or doctor bills ever actually go that high. But, if your case winds up being one of the few, you will be glad to have the coverage.

SOME THINGS TO REMEMBER ABOUT HMOS

First thing to remember about HMOs: In an HMO, your doctor is one-part doctor and two-parts gatekeeper and cost-controller. Your doctor decides whether you see a specialist or enter a hospital. And your doctor's remuneration from the HMO goes up the more he or she keeps your total medical costs down. Your doctor is in complete control. And—guess what!—*you are not in control.* In fact, you are nowhere near controlling anything, not with a doctor who gets paid an annual bonus based on how much money he or she saves. And keep in mind that this bonus is often an important aspect of profitability for the physician, since the physician receives only a fixed sum per HMO patient annually, no matter how much time or energy the physician devotes to any given patient.

Second thing to remember about HMOs: The Spartans would have loved HMOs. Your HMO doctor is inspired, through a variety of ingenious financial inducements, to practice the most abstemious type of medicine possible. If a visit to a specialist can be dispensed with, it will be. If a diagnostic exam might *possibly* be done without, it will be done without. Never mind that it might reveal the early stages of a disease that is curable in its early stages, such as many cancers.

Third thing to remember about HMOs: Many HMOs have pools of money that they set aside annually to service lab test and other special treatments for HMO customers. At the end of the fiscal year, the doctors in the HMO get a bonus based on the amount of money remaining in the pool.

Fourth thing to remember about HMOs: Most HMOs only cover emergency services out-of-town. If you travel extensively, or maintain seasonal residences in more than one region of the country, an HMO will prove problematical for you over time.

For the past six years, people enrolled in HMOs have almost doubled from 42 million in 1993 to 80 million in 1998. A recent study suggested that in terms of care, 1999 was the best year in the history of managed care, but they still have room for improvement. An attempt is being made in Congress to create a "Patient's Bill of Rights" mandating access to specialists and an independent grievance process.

SmartMoney recently published a list of the top ten things doctors won't tell you about their HMOs. Among the list was that if you become too much of a financial drain, they have ways of making you walk, and if your doctor treats you too aggressively, he/she could get kicked out. The drugs a doctor might prescribe may not be the best for you, but it is what your HMO offers.

If you are considering an HMO, ask your doctor what he/she thinks of the plan you are considering, and visit some Web sites run by state agencies or business groups that rank HMOs on number of complaints and ease of getting care. In New York, visit the New York State Health Accountability Foundation at *http://rkhost.com/nyshaf.org/main.html.* In California, try The Preeminent Large Business Health Coalition at *http://www.pbgh.org.* And in Texas, try the Office of Public Insurance Counsel at *http://www.opic.state.tx.us.*

THE COMMON SENSE OF MEDICAL SAVINGS ACCOUNTS (MSAS)

Consider this scenario. Realizing that the most valuable and necessary health coverage a person should have is for catastrophic diseases, you shrewdly decide to purchase a health-insurance policy with a high deductible and relatively low premium. Say a $500 deductible policy may cost $4,000. But a $3,000 deductible policy may cost just $1,200.

Since you shrewdly decided to go for the high-deductible policy, and you annually place the $2,800 you've saved by not taking the low deductible policy into a savings account (a Medical Savings Account). You start with nearly enough money in the account to cover your deductible, should the need arise. Within two years, factoring interest, you'd have more than $6,000 stashed away. In five years you could have well over $14,000 in your account, *and the interest paid to you would likely offset your medical insurance premium.*

258

NOT JUST FOR INDIVIDUALS

Many businesses are beginning to offer MSA options to their employees. Instead of buying low-dollar-deductible policies, employers are purchasing high-deductible catastrophic policies and giving employees tax-free money in medical IRAs to spend to spend on routine care, or else inviting employees themselves to establish MSAs with pre-tax dollars. This gives employees the incentive, and responsibility, to make choices and control their own health-care costs. Among the major national firms experimenting (successfully) with MSAs, you will find such names as Dominion Resources, the Forbes Magazine Group, and Quaker Oats.

Compare MSAs with HMOs

Contrast MSAs to the managed care structure offered by HMOs. HMOs represent a bottom-down world view, where the patient is the lowest organism in the food-chain of health-care dollars. The patient is subservient to the command-and-control monolith of that profit engine which is the HMO. On the other hand, MSAs represent a bottom-up world view, where the patients should come first and *do come first*. In the MSA philosophy, the system exists to serve the patient, rather than the other way around.

The managed care/HMO philosophy suggests that medicine is too complex for patients to understand. It propounds the view that patients are too stupid to grasp the complex economics of health care, and that providers can and should play "Big Brother" to their "customers," allocating resources only as the provider sees fit, and limiting consumer choice in order to achieve maximum cost savings (maximum profits for the HMO or Managed Care Organization.)

On the other hand, the MSA philosophy suggests that patients should have choice, responsibility, and economic participation in all aspects of their care. Needs should be determined by individuals, not by a "system."

Where Managed Care Organizations and HMOs smack of paternalism, MSAs have the scent of economic liberty, fee-for-service "free-market" accountability, and individual choice. In the MSA formulation, there are no gatekeepers.

TYPES OF HEALTH INSURANCE TO AVOID

There are a number of specific varieties of health insurance that are "sucker-bait." These include *one-disease insurance, accident insurance, health insurance you see advertised on television or via mail-order, most student policies offered through colleges or prep-schools, indemnity policies,* and (perhaps most notoriously) *double coverage.*

With *one-disease insurance,* you need coverage for every major health risk. Every single one. And once you have it, any other coverage for a specific disease or health-event is redundant and a waste of money.

Accident insurance is insurance which pays specific medical expenses resulting from an accident, rather expenses resulting from illness. Once again, this is redundant coverage with your standard health insurance, which should cover health expenses resulting from either accidents or illnesses. In fact, accident insurance is often *doubly* redundant, because when you have an accident resulting in medical expenses, it often involves not only your own health underwriter but also the liability insurance held by owners of the property where the accident happened, or owners of vehicles involved in the accident, and so on.

Health insurance policies advertised on television at what appear to be fabulously low premiums and promoted by celebrities, usually have a long, long, long waiting period before they cover any preexisting conditions—far longer than the waiting periods required by underwriters who do not have expensive celebrities to compensate and TV ad budgets to maintain.

Unsolicited mail-order promotions routinely "hawk" health-insurance policies that you should stay away from. Once again, we are talking about extremely long waiting periods for the coverage of preexisting conditions. Once again, we are talking about attractively cheap insurance that becomes much less attractive when you check the fine print. "Cheap" insurance can turn out to be very expensive insurance if it turns out you are actually paying a premium for little or no real coverage.

Many colleges and prep schools offer *student-health insurance*. Odds are your student is already covered under the terms of your family health insurance coverage until he or she reaches the age of 18 or for as long as he or she stays in school. Check your policy.

Most *indemnity policies* are "rip-offs" in that they offer relatively low daily payments for every day you are in the hospital. What is the real value of a policy that offers you an indemnity payment of $50 for every day you are in the hospital, when the average daily rate for hospitals is over $500? *If* you go for an indemnity policy, make sure it pays a very high daily rate for hospital stays, something that approximates the rates actually charged by hospitals in your region.

Double policies include some policies of which we've already spoken: one-disease insurance, indemnity policies, and so on. With regard to these insurance policies, keep in mind that your insurance agent has the same wants and needs as you: a nice home, a good car, and a secure future for his or her family. But when it comes to double policies, your insurance agent's wants, needs and best interests are at variance with yours. The insurance agent who tells you to take out "extra" insurance to "fill the gap" left by your standard health insurance policy is, more likely, trying to simply fill the gap in his or her personal financial spreadsheet. Don't do it. You've got your own kids to put through college.

THE OFTEN-IGNORED COUSIN OF HEALTH INSURANCE: DISABILITY INSURANCE

Paying medical bills is just one of the financial problems you'll confront when sick. What of lost wages? Should you be disabled by an accident or illness, your normal income could quite well be disrupted for months, for years, or even for life. To replace that cash-flow you must look to *Social Security, Workers' Compensation plans*, and most importantly, your own *personal disability insurance.*

Social Security provides *some* (generally inadequate) disability coverage. Under Social Security guide-lines, you are considered disabled if you have a severe medical condition which prevents you from working and is expected to do so for at least 12 months. Your Social Security payments begin in the sixth full month of your disability and continue for as long as you continue to be disabled. Note that the Social Security definition of disability is stringent. It demands that your medical condition be one that renders you unable to work at *any* profession. A ballet dancer, for example, with a pin in his or her hip for a year, would be unable to work in his or her profession during that time but certainly would be able to work at other jobs. Therefore, the dancer would not qualify for Social Security disability coverage. Note also that the monthly amount Social Security would pay you for your disability varies according to how much money you personally have paid into the Social Security system through the years. Call your local Social Security office to find out where you stand. But keep one thing in mind. *If you would classify yourself as middle-class or upper-middle-class, the odds are incredibly high that your Social Security coverage will not be enough to cover your needs.*

Workers' compensation plans are state-sponsored programs providing benefits to employees disabled by illnesses or injuries incurred on the job. Details of these plans vary greatly from state-to-state. One thing, however, does not vary. Should you be eligible for Social Security disability benefits, the government will deduct any "redundant" benefits from your Social Security payment.

The dismal combination of the moth-eaten Social Security and workers' comp "safety-nets" is in itself a terrific argument for buying and holding *personal-disability insurance.*

In purchasing personal-disability insurance, you want to make sure that you have enough coverage to cover your entire cost-of-living for the entire time you are disabled, whether that be for a few months or for years. Generally speaking, you want enough cash to keep from defaulting on outstanding debts (such as your mortgage!) while at the same time being able to cover your day-to-day living expenses for utilities, groceries, and so on. You want to sup-port and continue your current lifestyle, if possible. Therefore you ideally want disability coverage which will replace your current income dollar for dollar.

INTERNET RESOURCES RELATED TO HEALTH AND DISABILITY INSURANCE

As you surf the World Wide Web, you may encounter sites that discuss health insurance, disability insurance, HMOs, PPOs, and more. The following site list should help you locate the resources you need.

AMERICAN COLLEGE OF SURGEONS: INFORMATION ON PATIENT CHOICE AND MANAGED CARE

http://www.facs.org/public_info/patient_choice/Ychoicew.htm

This useful page, maintained by the American College of Surgeons, gives good information on what exactly managed care is (as opposed to traditional health insurance coverage), and how it impacts both patient choice and physicians' ability to serve patients. This is a very useful document to read *before* you decide which type of medical coverage to subscribe to.

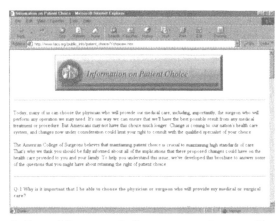

Figure 10.1 American College of Surgeons: Information on Patient Choice and Managed Care.

INTERNATIONAL TRAVEL HEALTH INSURANCE

http://www.abilnet.com/health

Here are three guaranteed issue international health insurance plans for individuals traveling to or from the USA. This is the type of coverage to have when you catch a cold in Katmandu, start to cough in Calcutta, or break a leg in Libya.

Figure 10.2 International Travel Health Insurance.

BETTER BUSINESS BUREAU INFORMATION ON HEALTH INSURANCE

http://www.bosbbb.org/lit/0015.htm

This extensive on-line tutorial discusses just about everything. What is health insurance? What does health insurance do for you? How does health insurance work? Who provides health insurance? What are the basic types of health insurance? What special coverages are generally available, and what is an appropriate premium? Where does Medicaid fit in to the picture? What are Health Maintenance Organizations? How much coverage do you need? What is the deal on limitations and exclusions? And what is the story on renewability? The on-line tutorial addresses all these questions, and more, in detail.

Figure 10.3 Better Business Bureau Information on Health Insurance.

NATIONAL HEALTH PLANS

http://www.nationalhmo.com

National Health Plans, a division of Tenet Corporation, has plans to cover individuals, families, seniors, and both large and small businesses. Come here for information on all their health insurance products.

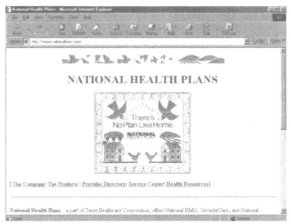

Figure 10.4 *National Health Plans.*

NATIONAL ORGANIZATION OF HEALTH UNDERWRITERS

http://www.nahu.org

This organization is comprised of more than 12,000 health insurance industry professionals representing more than one hundred million insured Americans.

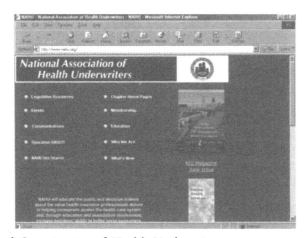

Figure 10.5 *National Organization of Health Underwriters.*

NATIONAL ORGANIZATION OF PHYSICIANS WHO CARE

http://www.pwc.org

Physicians Who Care is a nonprofit organization devoted to protecting the traditional doctor-patient relationship and ensuring quality health care. Formed in 1985 in San Antonio, Texas, the organization now has members in every state, most of them doctors in private practice.

Physicians Who Care believes the responsibility for medical care belongs first and foremost to physicians and patients. They affirm the right of the physician, as the provider of care, to diagnose, prescribe, test and treat patients without undue outside interference (from HMO bureaucrats!) They also affirm the right of the patient, as the person most affected, to choose his or her own physician and help determine the type of treatment received (without interference from any knucklehead HMO bureaucrats!). I like these guys a whole lot.

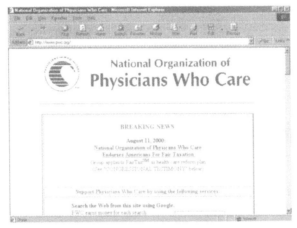

Figure 10.6 National Organization of Physicians Who Care.

AMERICAN ASSOCIATION OF HEALTH PLANS

http://www.aahp.org

The American Association of Health Plans is a national trade association representing more than 1,000 health maintenance organizations for more than 140 million Americans. AAHP embraces a *Philosophy of Care* that emphasizes active partnerships between patients and their physicians, as well as a *Code of Ethics* to communicate facts about how health plans work for the benefit of patients, to make clear they are listening to concerns and provide a mechanism for member plans to demonstrate their commitment to high standards of accountability.

Figure 10.7 American Association of Health Plans.

WELLNESS WEB AA HEALTH INSURANCE CENTER

http://www.wellweb.com/insurance/health_insurance_index.htm

This site provides information about choosing and using health plans and a list of agencies and organizations. When Choosing a plan, know your choices, where to get health plans, what plan benefits are offered, what's most important to you in a plan, how to compare health plans, and then how to utilize the care.

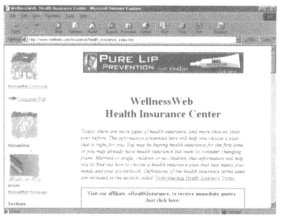

Figure 10.8 Wellness Web AA Health Insurance Center.

FIND INFORMATION ABOUT HOME CARE

http://www.healing-webofcare.com

Web of Care is a community of home caregivers with health information, support services, and products for medical care in the home. They have a resource database you can search by state and area code and a glossary where you will find definitions of more than 40,000 medical terms.

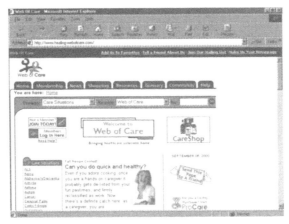

Figure 10.9 Find Information About Home Care.

SINGLE PAYER FACTS

http://www.pnhp.org/fctsht.html

According to this site, all Americans would receive comprehensive medical benefits under single payer. Coverage would include all medically necessary services, including rehabilitative, long-term and home care, mental health care, prescription drugs and medical supplies. The program would also include preventative and public health measures.

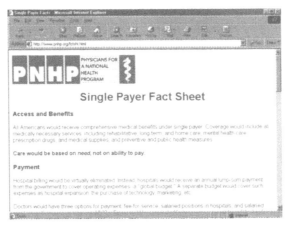

Figure 10.10 Single Payer Facts.

ALMANAC OF POLICY ISSUES: HMOS AND MANAGED CARE

http://www.policyalmanac.org/health/hmos.htm

This site gives links and background information on HMOs and public policy affecting managed care. It provides directories, news, U.S. government issues, organizations, and articles.

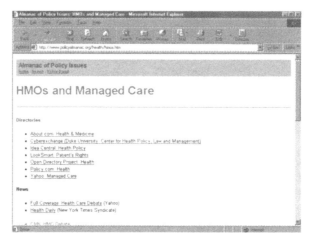

Figure 10.11 Almanac of Policy Issues: HMOs and Managed Care.

HEALTH INSURANCE RESOURCE CENTER

http://www.aswe.org/healthinsurance

Are you confused by the maze of health insurance options? Are you baffled by all the words and terms you hear? Are you afraid that because you are an individual or self-employed, and not part of a group or large company, you cannot get good affordable rates? Are you wondering if you are paying too much for your health insurance, or how you would even know if this were the case? Are you concerned about not being able to afford quality health insurance in the future? Or are you "uninsurable" because of a medical condition?

If the answer to any of these questions is *yes*, then check out the Health Insurance Resource Center for individuals, the self-employed and small businesses. This comprehensive and well-designed site most likely houses the solution to your problem.

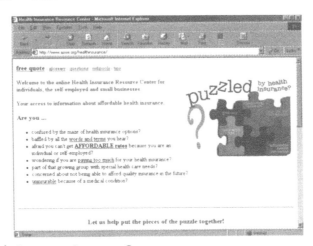

Figure 10.12 Health Insurance Resource Center.

FINANCIAL RESOURCES FOR THE SERIOUSLY ILL

http://www.efmoody.com/estate/viatical.html

The topic, boys and girls, is *viatical settlement*. A viatical settlement allows a person living with any life threatening illness such as cancer, AIDs, Alzheimer's Disease, ALS, cardiovascular diseases, etc., to sell their existing life insurance policy in exchange for a lump sum cash settlement ranging up to 90% of the policy's face value. Many people who are living on limited income while at the same time confronting high medical expenses have used viatical settlements to ease their financial burdens.

This site gives a list of a few viatical companies with varying prices.

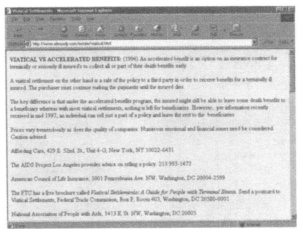

Figure 10.13 Financial Resources for the Seriously Ill.

ALL ABOUT HEALTH INSURANCE

http://www.e-analytics.com/fp21.htm

CITIZENS TOOLBOX: HEALTH INSURANCE REFORM

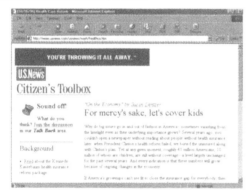

http://www.agtnet.com/USNEWS/ wash/healthca.htm

MEDICAL SAVINGS ACCOUNTS: THE (PERSUASIVE) ARGUMENT FOR

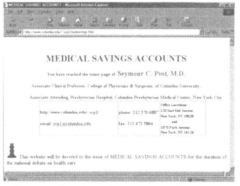

http://www.columbia.edu/~scp2/medsavings.html

BLUE CROSS/BLUE SHIELD FEDERAL EMPLOYEE PROGRAM

http://www.fepblue.org

HEALTH AND HEALTH INSURANCE STUFF ON YAHOO

http://www.yahoo.com/health

NERD WORLD: HEALTH INSURANCE LINKS

http://www.nerdworld.com/nw1654.html

RESTORING THE SANCTITY OF THE PATIENT-PHYSICIAN RELATIONSHIP

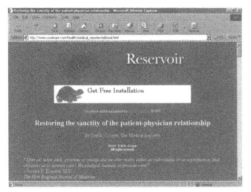

http://www.coolware.com/health/
medical_reporter/editorial.html

HOW TO PICK A HEALTH PLAN

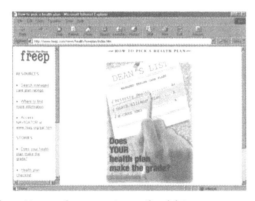

http://www.freep.com/news/health/
howplan/index.htm

AN APPROACH TO NATIONAL HEALTH CARE

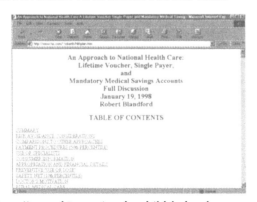

http://www.his.com/~robertb/hlthplan.htm

SOCIAL SECURITY DISABILITY INFORMATION

http://www.ssa.gov

CHECKUP ON HEALTH INSURANCE CHOICES

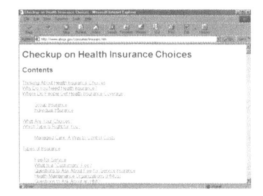

http://www.ahcpr.gov/consumer/insuranc.htm

AN HMO: HEALTHALLIES.COM

http://www.healthallies.com

HMO HEALTH INSURANCE PLAN – 50 STATES!

http://www.pgafinancial.com

THE HMO PAGE

http://www.hmopage.org

HEALTH INSURANCE ASSOCIATION OF AMERICA

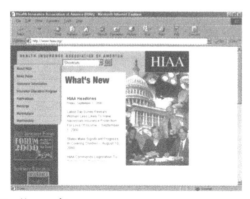

http://www.hiaa.org

COALITION FOR QUALITY PATIENT CARE

http://cqpc.org/menus/index.cfm

ALLIANCE OF COMMUNITY HEALTH PLANS

http://www.hmogroup.com

HOW MEDICAL SAVINGS ACCOUNTS WORK

http://www.medsavings.com

FINDING OUT MORE ABOUT MSAs

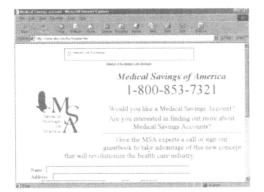

http://ww.dmi.com/kic/msamer.htm

GOVERNMENT APPROVED MSA

http://www.sbba.com/medsavgs.htm

GUIDELINES FOR MSAs

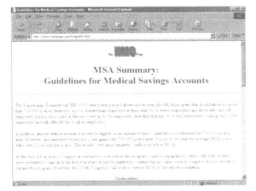

http://www.hmopage.org/msaguide.html

NAVIGATING THE HEALTH CARE SYSTEM

http://www.eqp.org

HEALTH INSURANCE QUOTES

http://www.ahealthinsurancequotes.com

INSURANCE QUOTES—DISABILITY

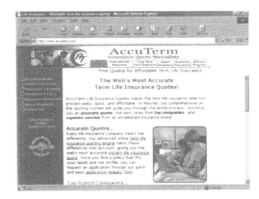

http://www.accuterm.com

DISABILITY INSURANCE RESOURCE CENTER

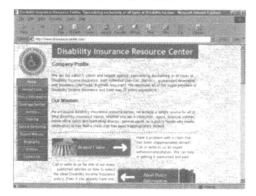

http://www.di-resource-center.com

THE DISABILITY BENEFITS INFORMATION PAGE

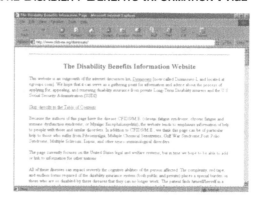

http://www.cfids-me.org/disinissues

CHAPTER 11

THE GROUND WE STAND ON:
PROPERTY AND LIABILITY INSURANCE

Secure the ground you stand on, for it is the foundation of the fortune. — **Ben Franklin**

Property and liability insurance are bound to be essential elements of your overall insurance plan. This will be the case whether you rent or own your apartment or home, or whether you lease or own your car.

HOMEOWNER'S INSURANCE: YOU GET WHAT YOU PAY FOR

There are various standard classes of homeowner's insurance just as (if you will allow me my favorite metaphor) there are various standard classes of sailboats. A little sunfish sailboat of a policy, designed for shallow waters in protected inlets, is the *Basic Form (HO-1) Policy*. Like a sunfish, this policy is cheap compared to other options, and it has its limitations. The *Basic Form* insures you for just a few contingencies. These include:

- Damage to your home from fire or lightning

- Loss of property removed from premises endangered by fire or other perils

- Damage from windstorms or hail

- Damage from explosions

- Damage from riot or other forms of "civil commotion"

- Damage from aircraft *(crash! boom!)*, vehicles *(crash! boom!)*, smoke, and vandalism

- Losses due to theft

- Breakage of windows

A more substantial, and more expensive, vessel of homeowner's insurance is the *Broad Form (HO-2) Policy*. This policy covers everything that a *Basic Form Policy* does, but also includes coverage for damage from falling objects (other than airplanes, which are covered under *HO-1*), damage from the weight of ice, snow and sleet on your roof, and the threat of collapsing of roofs and walls generally. Additionally, it covers "sudden and accidental" tearing asunder, cracking, burning, or bulging of a steam or hot water heating system, or of appliances for heating water. It covers accidental discharge, leakage or overflow of water or steam from plumbing, heating or air-conditioning systems, or a domestic appliance (such as a washing machine or dishwasher). It also covers damage caused by the freezing of plumbing systems and domestic appliances. And, it covers "sudden and accidental injury" from artificially-generated electrical currents anywhere on the premises.

The broadest, most expensive, and most substantial homeowner's insurance vessel is a big old gaff-rigger called the *Comprehensive Form (HO-5) Policy*. This coverage insures you against virtually everything save for damage caused by flooding, earthquake, war, and (gulp!) nuclear radiation. (The latter might seem like a remote possibility. But I'd urge you to ask the residents of Three Mile Island just how remote that possibility actually is.) With all those exclusions, one wonders why the *Comprehensive Form* is often commonly called an *All-Risks Policy*. Nevertheless, don't be surprised to hear it referred to as just that.

I must point out with regret that your boat will not be among your possessions covered by your homeowner's policy. Your boat requires separate paperwork and a separate premium. Often it even requires a separate underwriter. Sorry.

QUESTIONS TO ASK ABOUT HOME INSURANCE POLICIES

Does your policy cover garages, sheds, the pool, fences and other detached structures? Does your policy include coverage for the contents of your house to the tune of at least 50% of your policy's face value? Does your policy cover items lost while you are away from home as well as items lost from your safety deposit box? Does your policy cover living expenses should you have to move out of your house while it is being repaired? Will your policy recompense you for lost rent due to fire or other insured damage? Will your policy cover the cost of removing debris from your property after an insured event? The answer to all these questions should be *yes*. If not, get another policy.

REGARDING FLOODS AND EARTHQUAKES

If your community has met federal flood-prevention guidelines, you can insure yourself against flood damage to your property with such firms as Orion Specialty (formally known as Unison, located in Charleston, SC, ground zero for 1989's Hurricane Hugo!), which act as partners with the National Flood Insurance Program (NFIP) through the *Write Your Own* (WYO) Flood Insurance Program. Orion Specialty is located, conveniently enough, on the Web at *http://www.osflood.com,* shown below in Figure 11.1. If your community has not met federal flood-prevention guidelines, you will not be able to get flood insurance from Unison or any other firm.

Figure 11.1 Information about flood insurance.

If you live on the San Andreas fault, or on some other earthquake-prone portion of the map, you may want to consider buying earthquake insurance. Depending on where you live and what your house is like, these policies can be very expensive and often have high deductibles. In California, for example, the *minimum* deductible is 10%. On a $500,000 home, you'd have to sustain more than $50,000 in damage before you'd collect a dime. Obviously, anyone who lives anywhere near a place where there might actually *be* an earthquake (anyone who might naturally *want* earthquake insurance) is going to pay through the nose for it. But that person will pay less if he or she owns a wood-frame house, which is likely to sway with a quake and, thus, not be knocked down, and which is cheaper than other structures to rebuild should it be knocked down. My advice? Move to Rhode Island. The earthquake insurance is cheap here. But then again, you won't be needing it.

HOW MUCH COVERAGE DO YOU NEED?

Many people make the mistake of assuming that "enough homeowner's insurance" is an amount that equals the resale value of one's home. Wrong, wrong, wrong. That's not enough at all. The resale value of your house is almost always less than the actual cost to rebuild it, not to mention the cost of all the furniture and clothing and other goods you've lost.

Insure your home *and possessions* for 100% (or *at least* 80%) of their estimated *replacement* cost.

And keep in mind that estimated replacement costs are not static. They are continually going up. Consider paying a little extra every month for inflation protection, which raises the face value of your policy by a fixed percentage every three months *or* by a floating-rate pegged to the annual average increase in construction costs for your region.

IDEALLY, GO FOR THE GOLD

If you can afford it, consider purchasing a very expensive but worry-free *Guaranteed Replacement Cost* policy. Under this policy, the underwriter agrees to pay to repair (or rebuild if necessary) your home entirely, just as it was, down to the smallest bit of detail. Better yet, your insurer agrees to do this even if the cost exceeds the policy's face value! But this is unlikely. You see, you must insure for 100% of the expected reconstruction cost. Every year, both the face value (and your premium) will be adjusted for inflation. Further adjustments will be made if you improve your home in any way. And through it all, you pay a very high premium. But, if disaster strikes, there is *nothing* that is left uncovered. You get your house back, just as it was.

> ### Renter's Insurance
>
> If you are a renter or an owner of a cooperative apartment or condominium, you need *Form Four (or HO-4) Insurance*. This covers approximately 18 risks to your personal property, similar to the *Broad Form* for homeowner's. Somewhat more expansive, *HO-6 Insurance* covers personal property as well as structural damage associated with alterations in apartments made by condo and coop owners.

HOMEOWNER'S AND RENTER'S LIABILITY INSURANCE

All homeowner's and renters policies include what has come to be called *banana-peel* liability coverage. You know, this is coverage for when somebody (invariably a stranger) slips on a banana-peel in your driveway and sues you over it—not just for medical costs, but also for pain, suffering and yes, stress.

Briefly, you are covered for injuries on your premises. You and your family (including pets!) are also covered. If your son runs into an old lady with his skate-board three blocks from home, you're covered. If your dog bites the mailman either at your house or up the block, you're covered.

Even your inanimate objects are covered, for those rare moments when they animate. Example: A dying tree on your front lawn finally gives way, cracks, and crashes down on your neighbor's Mercedes. Relax. You're covered!

Most basic policies include at least $100,000 of liability coverage. Consider upping it. $300,000 is the number that makes me feel safe. If I had a swimming pool—which I did in New York—I'd want half a million worth of coverage at least. (There are *all sorts* of banana-peels associated with swimming pools.) Be sure to go for all the liability coverage you realistically need, *but study how you can do so most effectively*. Instead of simply adding liability coverage to your homeowner's policy, it might pay better to purchase some umbrella coverage (detailed later in this chapter).

> ### *Homeowner's Insurance and Your Home Business*
>
> If you run a business from your own home, your homeowner's insurance may not cover any property used for your business, such your computer, copy machine, and fax. Homeowner's insurance is not business insurance. If you plan to work from your home, talk with your insurance agent and make sure you are covered. In most cases, you may need to purchase supplemental coverage to protect your business property.

PROFESSIONAL LIABILITY INSURANCE

Your homeowner's liability provisions won't cover you for damages related to any business you run out of your house. For this coverage, you must get additional policies written by organizations, which specialize in professional liability insurance. These same firms also write malpractice liability insurance for physicians, accountants, lawyers, engineers and other professionals. To find a list of professional liability insurance carriers for each state, check out *http://www.abanet.org/legalservices/pl/home.html,* shown below in Figure 11.2, from the American Bar Association.

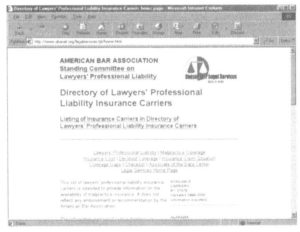

Figure 11.2 Information on professional liability insurance.

AUTO INSURANCE: THE BIG PICTURE

Time change: When the first automobile insurance policy was written in 1887, the overriding (no pun intended) concern was what the horseless carriage might do to the horses it ran into (literally) on the road. Today we have far higher speeds to contend with. We have no horses but plenty of cars to run into. We are looking at over 30 million car accidents each year, over 5 million injuries, and over 50,000 deaths. Someone is killed in a traffic accident in the United States *every ten minutes.*

The speed limits on our highways are going up, not down. The number of accidents we have annually is going up, not down. At the same time, the value of vehicles, limbs, and lives, from a cash-settlement point-of-view, is going up, not down. And the costs to repair our increasingly complex cars is going up, not down. Thus, we should not be surprised that the cost of adequate overall automobile insurance coverage is going—*yes, you guessed it!*—up, not down.

SAFETY PAYS

From an auto-insurance underwriter's point-of-view, you are your driving record. Nothing else defines you. Nothing else about you is important. Not how nice you are. Not how you treat your parents. Not the high regard with which you are held in your community. Not the award the Kiwanis gave you last year for outstanding public service.

You can be a winner of the Pulitzer Prize, a friend of Presidents, and a great benefactor of charities, but your auto-insurance underwriter will still look at you with great suspicion if you have a long history of car accidents, whether large or small. A paroled felon, about your same age with a clean driving record, will be more welcome in your underwriter's office than you are. And he or she will pay a lower rate than you for the same insurance as you, on the same make and model car in the same town.

If your driving record contains a lot of accidents and/or speed and traffic light citations, you are a lousy risk. If you have been driving for years without an impact and without a citation, you are an excellent risk. The better risk you are, the lower your automobile insurance will be. So, my first and most important advice is *drive safely*. You can't afford not to.

OTHER FACTORS THAT INFLUENCE THE PRICE OF CAR INSURANCE

Many of the other factors that influence the price of car insurance are, unfortunately, out of your hands. These are demographic factors over which you have no control. On average, younger drivers have substantially more accidents than older drivers. Men have more accidents than women. Unmarried people have more accidents than married people. And people in cities have more accidents (and experience more car thefts) than people in rural areas.

Beyond demographics, another factor influencing the price of your insurance is what car you drive. Sports cars tend to be involved in more accidents than sedans. They also tend to be stolen more often. Red cars tend to be stolen more often than cars of any other color. Cars with high book-values are more expensive to insure than cars with relatively low book-values, both because these cars are more expensive to replace and because they are more likely to be stolen. Thus, a '00 Mercedes sedan will be far more costly to insure than the "equivalent" '00 Nissan sedan. (And *the* most expensive car to insure in the United States at the moment would be a red '00 Mercedes 500SL driven in New York City or Los Angeles by an unmarried 18-year old male with a history of accidents.)

COLLISION INSURANCE AND THE LAW OF DIMINISHING RETURNS

Yet another large element in the price of your auto insurance is whether or not collision coverage is a part of your policy. The older your car, the less likely it is that collision insurance makes sense for you.

Under collision insurance protection, your underwriter is committed to do one of two things. Your underwriter is committed to cover, after an appropriate deductible has been reached, all costs to repair your car after damage from a crash. *Or,* in lieu of that, your underwriter has the option to simply reimburse you the book-value of the car after a crash. Which option will your underwriter go with? The one that is least expensive, of course.

Should your insurer decide to simply reimburse the book-value amount, your insurer would "total" the car and send you a check. What *you need,* of course, is not a check but rather your car back in good working order. But what you'll get is what the insurer chooses to give you.

Early in the life of your automobile it is quite likely that the estimated cost of repairs after a collision will be less than the book-value of your automobile. However, as your car ages and its book-value decreases, it becomes likely that in the event of a collision your insurer will simply send you a small check for whatever piddling amount is prescribed as your car's book-value and be done with it.

This is when having collision insurance does not and cannot pay. Generally, when your car is three to four years old, you should run the numbers, factoring in your additional premium for collision coverage along with the appraised book-value of your automobile and analyze whether or not collision insurance is any longer worthwhile.

One useful on-line resource for researching automobile book-values is the electronic version of the famous *Kelley Blue Book,* which you'll find at *http://www.kbb.com,* shown below in Figure 11.3. Note that you can invariably find the print edition of the *Blue Book* in the reference section of your local public library. It is also likely that your auto mechanic will have a copy.

Figure 11.3 The Kelly Blue Book On-Line.

FAULT VS. NO-FAULT

The states of the Union are broken up many different ways. Some are North and some are South. Some are East and some are West. Some are rich and some are relatively poor. Some have great sports franchises and some do not. Some have wonderful ocean beaches and others, instead, have awe-inspiring mountains. Perhaps most importantly, some have *Fault* auto insurance laws and some have *No-Fault* laws.

If you live in a *Fault* state, your financial fate after an accident is somewhat more up-in-the-air than it would be in a *No-Fault* state. In a *Fault* state, if you are hurt in an auto accident and the other driver is at fault, you would collect from the other fellow's insurance company, not your own. (The person at *fault*, and his/her insurer, are the responsible parties in this instance. Get it?) Oddly enough, if *you* are not at fault (if you are completely innocent and have done nothing wrong), your own insurer is obligated to pay you *nothing*. So pray that the driver who caused the accident is either well-insured or rich. Should *you* be at fault in the accident, your underwriter is generally obligated to pay to reimburse damages, medical and otherwise, of the party or parties you injured. But your insurer is *not* required to pay *you* anything at all. And you still might get sued by the injured parties if you do not have enough insurance coverage to salve their wounds, financial and otherwise.

In a *No-Fault* state, your insurance covers your own health and car-repair costs while the other driver's insurance covers his or her damages. Everyone collects. It does not matter who was at fault. Of course, you still might sue the other driver for pain-and-suffering, or for substantial damages above and beyond what your own insurer will pick up. In such an instance, *Fault* rules apply even in a *No-Fault* state. The responsible party must pay the piper, or at least defend against paying the piper. If you have *No-Fault* insurance and you get into an accident in a *Fault* state, the *Fault* laws will apply, up to a point. If you are at fault, your insurance will pick up the tab for the other guy or gal and the tab for you. If you are not a fault, your insurance won't pay the other guy or gal a dime and will make-up any shortfall in damages to you that are not covered by the other person's insurance.

DETAILS ON THE DIFFERENT TYPES OF AUTO COVERAGE

There are many different types of coverage related to auto insurance. Some of this coverage is absolutely essential. Others are, quite frankly, a waste of money. In addition to *collision insurance*, these types of coverage include *liability for bodily injury, liability for property damage, medical-payments auto insurance, personal injury insurance, comprehensive insurance, uninsured* and *underinsured motorist insurance, umbrella insurance*, and *towing/rental car reimbursement insurance*. Let's run through them one by one. Which do you need? And which can you afford to skip?

Liability for Bodily Injury insurance is absolutely necessary no matter who you are, what you drive, or in which state you live. This protects you (or a family member driving your car) if you're sued after injuring someone in an accident, whether that someone be a passenger in your own car, a pedestrian, or the driver/passenger of another vehicle. Usually this coverage also extends to a friend who is driving your car with permission, or a family member who is driving a third party's car with permission. How much of this insurance do you need? A good rule of thumb is that you want to get just enough *Liability for Bodily Injury* insurance to protect your assets. It is unlikely you'd ever be sued for more than you are worth, since it would otherwise be impossible for you to pay on the suit. Therefore, try to match your net worth when purchasing this coverage. That way you can be sued for "all you've got," lose, and still keep "all you've got."

Regarding *Liability for Property Damage* insurance, you may want some of this protection but you do not want (or need) a lot of it. Be forewarned that underwriters will be delighted to let you pay huge premiums for gobs of this coverage which you are never likely to use. Why have a million dollars worth of *Liability for Property Damage* coverage when the price tag to replace a brand new Mercedes is only around $75,000? Sure you *might* run your car off the road and crash into a priceless Rodin sculpture depicting some nubile naked form. But how often does this type of thing *really* happen? Myself, I've only done it once. OK, twice. But there are lots of Rodins in my neighborhood, and I'm easily distracted.

Medical Payments Auto Insurance is not often needed, especially in *Fault* states. What this provides is coverage for medical (and, if you are unlucky enough, funeral) expenses regardless of who is at fault in an accident, and whether or not the accident involves *your car in motion*. (In other words, it would cover someone whose hand was crushed in a slammed door of your parked car. Ouch!) This insurance also covers your family if they are hurt while riding in someone else's vehicle, or as a pedestrian. The problem with this insurance is that it is largely redundant with the health insurance you supposedly already have for you and yours. *Medical-payment insurance* nearly always covers *only those expenses not covered by other health insurance*. Thus the payout is routinely small. Generally, the premium amount you'd pay for *Medical Payment Auto Insurance* would be better spent beefing up your standard medical policy.

Personal Injury Protection (PIP) is required in *No-Fault* states. This covers you and your family. It pays your medical bills *up to the limit of coverage*. It replaces your lost wages *up to the limit of coverage*. It usually covers all your funeral expenses (whoopee!) assuming you don't want to be interred in a manner that emulates King Tut. And some *PIP* will even cover replacement services, such as a housekeeper to replace a homemaker who is laid up. But how much *PIP* do you actually need? Depending on the laws in your state, you could need just a little, or as much as $50,000 worth of coverage. In endeavoring to lower the cost of your PIP, analyze the extent to which your auto-related medical bills and lost wages can, under the laws of your state, be covered by your primary health and disability insurance. Then, just plan PIP to pick up the slack.

Comprehensive Insurance is almost always a good idea. It would be more accurately named if it were called *random insurance*. This is insurance against random events, random annoyances, random disaster. A flood comes. Your car gets clean for the first time in two years. But it also gets destroyed. Relax. Your clean car, floating downriver to New Orleans, is covered by your *Comprehensive Insurance*. The same coverage would address the damage from your Dalmatian chewing the upholstery. It also covers the headlight broken by the random stone. And it covers vandals taking your car handles (or worse, your entire car). *Comprehensive Insurance* usually also covers windshields, although separate windshield insurance may be available

283

from your underwriter. In case of theft of a car that is never returned or is returned in an unusable/unsalvageable condition, *Comprehensive Insurance* pays you the *fair market value* for your car, which is something more than the book-value.

Uninsured and Underinsured Motorist Insurance is not really necessary to have if your own life, health, and disability insurance is first-rate, comprehensive, and likely to meet any expenses you wind up with from a crash with an uninsured, underinsured, and/or anonymous driver. It is also not really necessary in states where there are strong, generous *No-Fault* laws, such as Michigan. If, however, your personal health and disability coverage is minimal and the state you're in has relatively ungenerous *No-Fault* provisions, *Uninsured and Underinsured Motorist Insurance* might be worth having. This coverage pays your medical and disability expenses (and in some states, even your auto repairs) resulting from your being hit by an uninsured or underinsured driver who's at fault, or a hit-and-run driver.

If you're reasonably well-off (say, worth half a million dollars or more) consider *Umbrella Insurance*. No, this isn't insurance for your umbrella. This isn't something Mary Poppins would buy. She's not worth half a mil. *Umbrella Insurance* provides umbrella coverage of liability judgments that exceed the value of your auto and homeowner's policies. You usually have to maintain a minimum basic liability policy valued at $300,000, after which your umbrella insurance would kick in. This is the kind of coverage you want to have when the guy you had a fender bender with, after learning you have a lot more cash than him, suddenly comes down with whiplash and many other vague ailments. If you drive someone else's kids to school, ball games, or other activities, make sure you have an umbrella policy.

Finally, when it comes to *Towing And Service/Rental Car Reimbursement Insurance*, if it makes you feel better, you should go for it. The policy is usually cheap. However, if you belong to the AAA or some other auto club, keep in mind that they already provide you with free towing so this aspect of your coverage may well be redundant.

AUTO INSURANCE COVERAGE WHEN YOU RENT A CAR

There are very few times when you need to purchase the auto insurance the rent-a-car company makes available. It is always too expensive. I was visiting a distant city recently and a major national rent-a-car company offered me comprehensive liability and collision coverage for "just $15 a day." That's a premium rate of $5,475 annually! I don't know about you, but I don't buy insurance for that amount, although I might consider buying a car for that amount.

Many times, the standard auto-insurance coverage you have on your family car(s) will extend to you or your spouse when you drive a rental car. Check with your agent.

Barring that, you can often get very good insurance coverage automatically on your rental by simply using your American Express, MasterCard, or VISA to pay for your rental. All of these cards offer very good, very reasonable, automatic car-rental insurance options that you should look into. But first, check with your insurance agent to make sure that even this reasonable amount of coverage won't be redundant with the coverage you already have.

If you are renting a car for business travel, check with your employer to learn your company's policy on a rental-car insurance. Some companies may want you to take out the additional coverage. Others, may want you to assume the risk yourself (on your own insurance). The best alternative may simply be to charge your rental on a company credit card. In this way, you and company are covered.

THE AUTO INSURANCE I RECOMMEND...

Do not—I repeat, *do not, do not, do not*—buy *any* auto insurance from the lender who finances your auto loan, or from any underwriter or agent he or she recommends. Also do not buy insurance from an agent associated with the dealer who sold you your car, or any agent that dealer recommends. All such insurance will be more expensive than necessary because your lender or auto-dealer will be in for a slice of the insurance premium pie.

Here's how you shop for car insurance. Get quotes from the two large organizations generally considered to be among the least expensive providers of automobile insurance. These are GEICO and State Farm. (Both of these organizations have Web sites enumerated in the Internet Resources section of this chapter as well as elsewhere in the book.) Armed with quotes from these low-cost providers, go to an *independent* insurance agent and ask him or her to beat the State Farm and GEICO prices. Often they will be able to do so. If not, simply go with either GEICO or State Farm, both of which are highly regarded, financially sound organizations.

FINDING LOCAL INDEPENDENT INSURANCE AGENTS ON THE WEB

Of course, you need a local independent insurance agent for your homeowner's and automobile policies. But at the same time, you want to let your fingers do the walking across your computer keyboard and the Internet. As luck would have it, scores of independent insurance agents and agencies now maintain Web sites. The best place to find them is at one large Web site where their links are broken out by specialty and by city, state, and region. I am referring to the highly useful Web site entitled *The AAA National Directory of Insurance Agents*. The Web address is *http://www.dirs.com/insure*, shown below in Figure 11.4. Go for it.

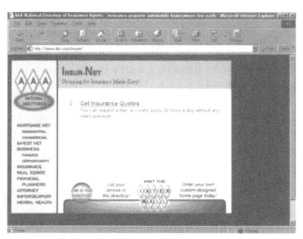

Figure 11.4 The AAA National Directory of Insurance Agents.

INTERNET RESOURCES FOR PURCHASERS OF HOMEOWNERS, RENTERS, LIABILITY, AND AUTOMOBILE INSURANCE

ANTIQUE AND CLASSIC CAR INSURANCE

http://www.hagerty.com/auto

Hagerty Classic Automobile Insurance is the fastest growing insurer of classic and collectible automobiles in the United States. Hagerty's program is based upon the simple principle that owners of such vehicles take considerable pride and care in maintaining and using their appreciating investments. As a collector of classic cars himself, our friend Hagerty has a sincere interest in preserving these valuable pieces of motor vehicle history. To do so, he has designed what is by far the best insurance policy on the market, and backed it with an "*A*" rated, financially secure underwriter and customer service focused on the special needs of classic car enthusiasts. This is comprehensive Agreed Value, Full Replacement Cost coverage at very affordable rates.

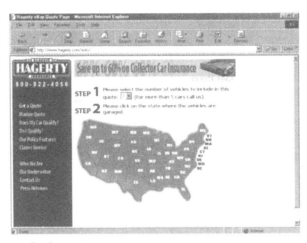

Figure 11.5 Antique *and Classic Car Insurance.*

AUTO LIABILITY INFORMATION

http://www.risk-managers.com

At this site, National Risk Managers provide detailed information on personal automobile policies (PAPs) intended to cover the auto insurance needs of the average individual or family. Typically, the PAP covers losses that occur when the insured is liable for bodily injury to others or damage to the property of others caused by an auto accident. Coverage applies to the insured and the spouse, and usually also to other members of the household. Coverage for damage to your own auto is optional. Come to this informative Web page for more details.

Figure 11.6 Auto Liability Information.

BETTER BUSINESS BUREAU HOMEOWNERS INSURANCE TIPS

http://ww.bosbbb.org/lit/0072/htm

You can also rely on the Better Business Bureau to provide information with which you wind up with the best-designed, most affordable homeowner's insurance package to meet your needs.

Figure 11.7 Better Business Bureau Homeowners Insurance Tips.

BETTER BUSINESS BUREAU AUTO INSURANCE TIPS

http://www.bbb.org/library/autoins.asp

Access this free hypertext tutorial from the Better Business Bureau showcasing key things to know about auto insurance in your state, seven steps to choosing your coverage, seven steps to selecting your insurer, ten questions to ask your agent, ten ways to save money, and do's and don'ts immediately after an accident.

What are the questions you should ask your agent? Here they are:

1. Under what conditions can the cost of my insurance be increased or the policy canceled?

2. How do I contact the company to make my claim? Will I be speaking to an agent in my area or to a central office?

3. What is the average length of time before a claim adjuster contacts the insured once a claim is reported? How soon can one expect all parties to be paid? Do you know how your firm compares with others with regard to promptness in claims handling?

4. What are the requirements with respect to qualified repair shops and pre-inspections? Is there a good choice of shops within a reasonable distance of my home?

5. If pre-inspections are required, how quickly can they be done?

6. Exactly what information does the company require when an accident occurs? May I have a copy of the company's accident form to keep on hand?

7. Exactly what expenses are covered as part of the policy? What about expenses incurred as the result of an accident such as child care costs, lost wages, or rental car costs?

8. What discounts might I qualify for in the categories of lifestyle, multiple policies, car model, and safety features? May I have a list of the discounts that the company offers in my state?

9. What are the deductibles on my policy? How would choosing higher/lower deductibles affect the cost of premiums?

10. Does the collision coverage have a clause allowing me to reject a claim settlement I feel is unsatisfactory?

Figure 11.8 Better Business Bureau Auto Insurance Tips.

DIGITAL FLOOD INSURANCE RATE MAPS

http://users.aol.com/hazardsnfp/Q3.html

Here you will find digital versions of National Flood Insurance Program (NFIP) Flood Insurance Rate Maps (FIRM), which go under the acronym Q3. This is a baseline digital product available that contains information on approximately 900 counties and independent cities. Included in the Q3 files are FIRM 1% and 0.2% flood hazard boundaries, political boundaries, and FIRM panel neatlines. Q3 data is available in three vector data formats: USGS-DLG3 (or SDTS), MapInfo.TAB, and ArcInfo.E00. Q3 file sizes of course vary, but in many cases are less than one megabyte per county, although Dade County, FL, is almost 8 megs. To use the Q3 data you will need a geographic information system or desktop mapping system with several base cartographic data themes, such as transportation and hydrology.

Note: If you are interested in this data, you should also make a point of accessing the FEMA Map Service Center Web Page located at *http://www.aspensys.com/femamap/femmahome.html*.

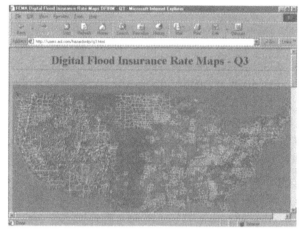

Figure 11.9 *Digital Flood Insurance Rate Map.*

HOMEOWNER'S NEWS FROM MINNESOTA MUTUAL

http://www.minnmutual.com

Get the latest mortgage rates, along with trends and news of interest to homeowners. Check out the mini-dictionary of mortgage terms. View *Money Talks*, a consumer mortgage magazine, and daily mortgage news.

Figure 11.10 *Homeowner's News from Minnesota Mutual.*

GEICO

http://www.geico.com

This is the outfit I use for my car insurance. I use them because they offered me the best insurance coverage I could find at the most reasonable price. And that, I think, sums it up.

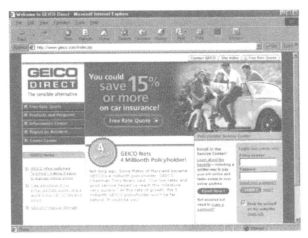

Figure 11.11 GEICO.

DPIC: PROFESSIONAL LIABILITY INSURANCE

http://www.dpic.com

DPIC Companies is a trade group of companies serving the United States and Canada that develops and markets innovative professional liability insurance programs. DPIC's exclusive and independent agency force and separate business divisions are dedicated to meeting the unique insurance, loss prevention, and risk management needs of:

- Architects
- Environmental Consultants
- Accountants

- Engineers
- Construction Project Owners
- Lawyers

The insurance programs offered include up to $10 million standard policy limit, split limits options, multi-year policy options, cost-of-defense options, team coverage and partnered team coverage, education credits, limitation of liability credits, peer-review re-imbursements, loss-prevention seminars, mediation support, retirement coverage, and temporary-staff coverage.

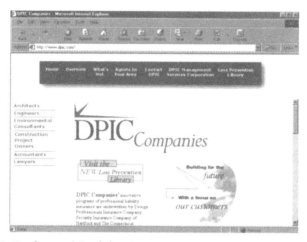

Figure 11.12 DPIC: Professional Liability Insurance.

KELLEY BLUE BOOK—AUTO "BOOK" VALUES

http://www.kbb.com

"What's the Blue Book value of my car?" Across the United States, people have been asking this question since 1926, when the first *Kelley Blue Book Used Car Guide* was published. Today, the Kelley Blue Book remains the nation's leading provider of automotive pricing and value information for new and used cars, trucks, and vans. Come to this excellent Web site for: *History of the Kelley Blue Book* – A fun look back at the auto industry from the perspective of the Kelleys. *New Car Pricing* – The most timely and accurate prices on new cars, trucks, and vans. You get the very latest dealer invoice prices, manufacturer's suggested retail prices, all factory and port installed options prices, standard equipment prices, and more. *Used Car Values* – Don't pay too much (or ask too little) for a used car, truck, or van. Use Kelley's online resources to interactively determine values for used vehicles based on your region of the country, the car's mileage, equipment, and condition. Specify the parameters and then download the results to your computer.

Figure 11.13 Kelley Blue Book – Auto "Book" Values.

PROFESSIONAL LIABILITY INSURANCE FOR ATTORNEYS

http://www.plisinc.com

Insurance for the folks we all love to hate. It is a thankless job, but nevertheless Professional Liability Insurance Services (PLIS) has been an exclusive provider of lawyers' professional liability insurance since 1983. PLIS provides primary and excess insurance programs to law firms across the United States, and is a tribunalized Lloyd's of London broker holding general non-marine binding authority. Lloyds is famous for insuring *anything*. Even lawyers.

EXCESS LIABILITY INSURANCE (AUTO)

Figure 11.14 Professional Liability Insurance for Attorneys.

http://www.sullivan-sullivan.com/excess.html

AAA National Directory of Insurance Agents

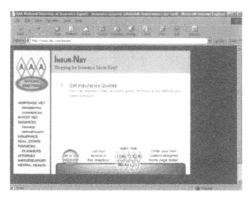

http://www.dirs.com/insure

Automobile Insurance Software

http://www.afsinfosys.com

Homeowners Financial Toolbox

http://www.minnmutual.com

FEMA Flood Insurance Information

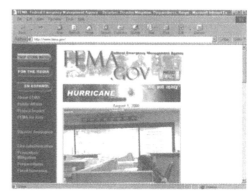

http://www.fema.gov

Homeowners Financial information

http://199.182.58.42/dictionary.html

ITT Hartford – Homeowners Insurance

http://webmaster.itthartford.com/AARPins/home.html

INSURANCE SHOPPING NETWORK

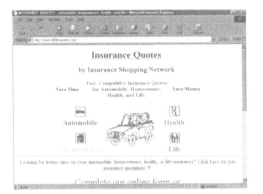

http://www.800insureme.com

NATIONWIDE HOMEOWNERS INSURANCE

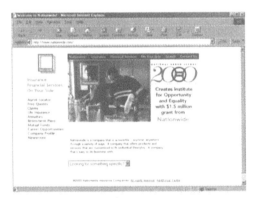

http://www.nationwide.com

OPINIONS, FINDINGS AND DECISIONS ON 2000 AUTO INSURANCE RATES

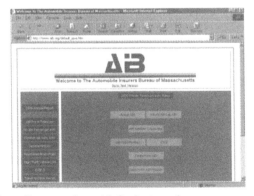

http://www.aib.org/default_java.htm

INSURANCE STORE ONLINE HOMEOWNERS QUOTE

http://www.drbinsurance.com/homeform.html

ONLINE HOMEOWNERS INSURANCE QUOTES

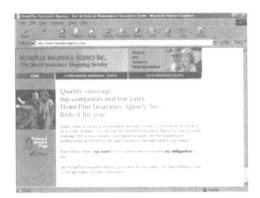

http://www.homeplusagency.com

STATE FARM INSURANCE

http://www.statefarm.com

INSURANCE SHOPPING MALL

http://www.bestinsurancebuy.com

THE INSURANCE SHOP ON THE NET

http://www.theshopnet.com

CURRENT INSURANCE NEWS

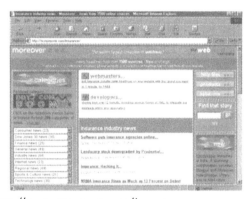

http://www.moreover.com/insurance

INTERNATIONAL INSURANCE NEWS HEADLINES

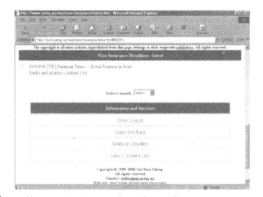

http://www.jaring.my/wqi/news/insurance

INSURANCE RESOURCES

http://www.resinets.com/search4/insure.htm

HOMEOWNERS INSURANCE QUOTE

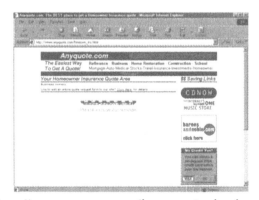

http://www.anyquote.com/hmeown_ins.html

FINANCENTER.COM – COMPARE, CALCULATE, LEARN

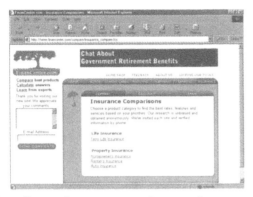

http://www.financenter.com/compare/
insurance_compare.fcs

GE FINANCIAL NETWORK INSURANCE CENTER

http://www.gefn.com/insurance

MONITOR LIABILITY MANAGERS, INC.

http://www.monitorgroup.com

EDUCATIONAL PROGRAMS

http://www.aicpcu.org

FARMERS INSURANCE

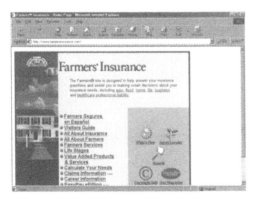

http://www.farmersinsurance.com

EMPLOYMENT PRACTICES LIABILITY INSURANCE

http://www.epli.com

PROFESSIONAL LIABILITY INSURANCE DIRECTORY

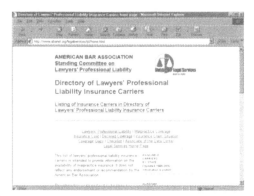

http://www.abanet.org/legalservices/pl/home.html

FLOOD INSURANCE RESOURCES

http://www.cps.cncoffice.com/CPSFlood.htm

FLOOD ALERT HOME PAGE

http://www.floodalert.fema.gov

FLOOD INSURANCE

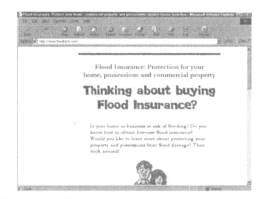

http://www.floodfacts.com

CHAPTER 12

UNDERSTANDING THE DIFFERENT
KINDS OF DEBT

The deceit is not in the money lender, but in the money. — **Charles Dickens**

Debt is schizophrenic. It dwells on both sides of what Luke Skywalker called "the Force." It is a blessing and a curse. It is a valuable tool with which you can leverage your future to great heights. It is at the same time a dark pit into which many descend, never to emerge, with their futures swallowed by compound interest. Debt can save you. It can also corrupt you. In short, it is a two-edged sword. Like "the Force," debt varies greatly in its positive and negative abilities depending on who wields it.

But we *must* wield debt. In that we have no choice. It is virtually impossible to live without at least *some* debt. What types and amounts of debt we take on, and how we manage this debt, are extremely important elements in our overall financial picture. Well-managed debt can improve our lives dramatically. Poorly managed debt can—and probably *will*—destroy us.

GOOD HABITS IN ALL THINGS

Self-control and self-regulation are good habits to develop as they relate to every element of one's life. But they are especially good and necessary habits to cultivate when it comes to debt. As you shall see in the following chapters, it is painfully easy these days to get over one's head in debt.

Debt temptation is everywhere. Credit is fast and easy. To my mind, it is too fast and too easy. A day hardly goes by that I don't receive junk mail from some credit-card vendor assuring me that I've been pre-approved for some massive credit line (with equally massive interest rates). A day hardly goes by that I don't hear a dealer in electronics, furniture, or automobiles advertise easy credit with "no payments for up to 12 months." And a day hardly goes by that I do not read or hear advertisements from second-mortgage financiers urging homeowners to come and get easy cash, "even if you've been turned down by other lenders."

Nothing personal lenders, but keep your quick cash to yourself. Don't do me any favors. If I had ever been turned down by another lender, I hope I'd take it as a sign to slow down on my borrowing rather than a sign to go to another lender who, by implication, cares a bit less than the first fellow about whether or not I wind up losing my house.

POSITIVE DEBT VS. NEGATIVE DEBT

On the bright side of "the Force" lives positive debt. On the dark side abides negative debt. In broad strokes, positive debt is debt, that enables you to build wealth. Positive debt is the mortgage that lets you purchase and build equity in the house of your dreams. Positive debt is a wisely-used business credit line that lets you finance (and thus *grow*) the business of your dreams. Positive debt is also an education loan that enables you or yours to accumulate the wealth that is knowledge. (My [extensive] student loans, which took me many years to pay off, financed the best investment I've ever made.) Furthermore, positive debt is any *necessary* debt: an auto loan for the car you need to drive to work or a consumer loan for large household essentials, such as refrigerators and washing machines.

Negative debt, in broad strokes, is any form of unnecessary debt. The quintessential tool of negative debt is, of course, the credit card and its attached credit line. We all have VISA or MasterCard or Discover cards in our wallet. The credit lines associated with these cards can work for you or against you. Your credit line will work *against you* when you use it to finance a plethora of *nonessential luxury items* and then make minimum payments for years thereafter at an 18% or 19% rate of interest, eventually paying more than twice as much as the item's purchase price!

On the other hand, your credit line will work *for you* if you use it to buy a desperately needed $3,000 computer—a productivity tool with which you will learn and grow and become more productive—and then budget yourself to pay off the entire amount of the purchase within the window of just a few months.

Here is an example of what I am talking about. Say you purchase a big-screen TV priced at $4,000 (that's not including the beer, pretzels and couch). If you pay cash for the TV, you pay $4,000 for it. If you purchase the TV with a credit card on which you have an 18% APR, and you pay the TV set off with minimum payments made over the course of approximately 40 months, your total cost for the television will be a whopping $5,348.34. That's right. You will pay $1,348.34 in [non-deductible] interest. And your minimum monthly payment on the $4,000 credit card debt will be around $133.71. (*Tip:* You can probably *rent* a big-screen TV for less than $133.71 a month. *Caprice?*)

The credit card, like Luke's sword of a Jedi, does the bidding of its master. It is up to you how to apply the magic in that little piece of plastic. Always go for positive debt, never negative debt. Always stay on the light side of "the Force."

A Macroeconomic Aside

I do not intend to unduly politicize this book; however, there is one thing I should point out. In this, and the several following chapters, I'll explain fundamental common-sense rules and guidelines concerning the management of personal debt. These same rules and guidelines, on a grander scale, apply to large organizations, including governments and most particularly the United States Government.

As bad as unrestrained, long-term deficit spending is for a personal budget, it is far worse for a government. It is important to understand that if the US Government were an individual with the debt-ratio (the ratio of debt to income) it now carries, Uncle Sam would most certainly, at the very least, be on "credit-watch" with virtually all of his lenders, would not be an acceptable risk for more credit, and would most likely be headed to bankruptcy court in the near future.

But governments cannot get bankruptcy protection. And unless the US gets a firm grip on deficit spending and the expansion of the national debt, your children and my children will face a bleak financial future *regardless of how well you and I work and invest and plan to get our individual financial houses in order.*

For more information on the federal budget deficit, why it is so huge, and how to fix it, go to the Web site maintained by the bipartisan Concord Coalition at *http:// www.concordcoalition.org,* shown below in Figure 12.1. This organization was founded by Democrat Paul Tsongas and Republican Warren Rudman and is dedicated to eradicating the federal deficit through appropriate legislation.

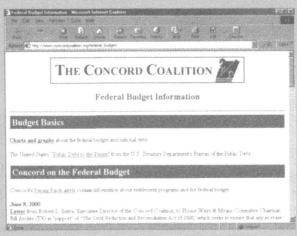

Figure 12.1 Information on the federal budget deficit.

MORE TO THE STORY

As shall be shown in the following chapters, there is far more to the story of debt than what I've just outlined. But there is no more important thing to say about debt than what has been said here:

Control your debt. Don't let it control you. Let debt be a financial tool, not an adversary.

DOWNLOAD DEBT ANALYZER FOR WINDOWS, FREE!

Debt Analyzer for Windows is an extraordinary software tool for studying where you stand vis-à-vis your various debts and their impact on your total financial picture. This shareware is yours to download for a free 21-day trial.

Debt Analyzer for Windows empowers you to work with up to 50 debts at a time to create loan elimination schedules, formulate "what-if" scenarios for loan expansions, consolidations, refinances, and more. The software also lets you instantly-generate interest-savings graphs for "what-if" scenarios, and convert your loan worksheets into international currencies at current exchange rates. To download the software go to *http://www.debtanalyzer.com,* shown below in Figure 12.2.

Figure 12.2 Download the Debt Analyzer for Windows.

ARE YOU ALREADY IN OVER YOUR HEAD?

Want to know how to tell? There are warning signs. Do you regularly maintain credit card balances near or at your various pre-set spending limits? Do you do this for every line of credit you possess? Do you sometimes "juggle debt" in order to make minimum payments? By this I mean, do you sometimes write checks on one credit line to service the minimum payment of another credit line, and vice versa? Does it seem as though you are incapable of getting out from under this mountain of unsecured debt? If you answered yes to any one of these questions, you are probably in over your head. You should either seek some help or learn to help yourself.

IF YOU ARE ALREADY IN OVER YOUR HEAD

Is your phone ringing constantly with collection agencies on the other end of the line? Are repo men breaking into your garage? Have you already maxed out all the credit for which you can possibly qualify? Are you hunkered down in a darkened house, surrounded by your trinkets of consumerism, wondering what to do next and whether or not bankruptcy is the only way out?

There are many reputable credit advisors who can help you out of this mess *if you are willing to help yourself.* You'll find the Web addresses for a few of them listed in the Internet Resources section of this chapter. But be forewarned, there are also a number of *disreputable* people out there who will be delighted to take advantage of your situation, making money on your misfortune and leaving you *worse off than you are right now.*

Be wary of anyone with a pitch resembling: "Bad credit? No credit? No problem! We'll guarantee you a low interest loan, but only if you pay a processing fee of $xxx." You will not get the loan. You *will* get ripped off for the processing fee. No reputable lender ever promises a loan without first doing a credit check.

And be wary of anyone offering a certain brand of credit repair that suggests you'll have a "new credit file overnight!" These guys often offer you a fresh start via a new Social Security number, which they say they can provide (for an enormous fee). This is not only illegal; it is impossible. The fee you pay will not only be stolen from you, but you yourself will be guilty of commissioning a felony. The only real credit repair is that offered by legitimate debt counselors who provide ways to help you restructure and repay your debts. Ultimately, the only credit repair that really works is paying off the credit. There is no way around this. Anyone who tells you otherwise is at best a fool and at worst a thief.

...OR BE YOUR OWN DEBT COUNSELOR

You can do it. Self-discipline is involved, and you have not shown discipline in the past. But nevertheless you are capable of taking control.

First Step: Stop charging things. Just stop. If you can't pay cash for something, don't buy it. This is your new rule: at least until you've got a zero balance on your various lines of credit.

Second Step: Consider consolidating all your outstanding unsecured debt by paying it off with the proceeds from a home-equity loan. The interest on the home-equity loan will be deductible and will also be much lower than the interest you are paying your various lines of unsecured credit.

Alternative Second Step: In the absence of real estate equity against which you can borrow, shop around for a credit line carrying the lowest possible APR you can find to which you can transfer the bulk of your current outstanding debt. There is someone out there who will be glad to have you and your inflated balance; and the lower rate will allow you to buy-down your debt on a faster schedule than you could otherwise.

Third Step: Make the highest monthly payments you can possibly afford on your newly consolidated debt. Put every spare dollar you can find into knocking down the outstanding principal. Scrimp and save. Be cheap. Get your videos at the library rather than at Block-buster. Play at the public golf course rather than the pricey private one. Much as I hate to say it, you should also forget the imported beers for a while and go domestic. ECONOMIZE. Live frugally until you can get out of your financial hole you've dug yourself into. (In other words, live the way you can afford to, remembering you are very poor at the moment.)

Fourth Step: If necessary, take an extra job evenings or weekends to gain extra dollars the sum total of which you will dedicate to paying off your credit card debt.

> ### Understanding the Consumer Price Index (CPI)
>
> If you listen to the business news, you may hear such phrases as, "the consumer price index rose slightly this month to 4.5." Each month, the Bureau of Labor Statistics determines the consumer price index—a measure of what we (consumers) pay for housing, food, clothing, transportation, healthcare, entertainment, and other necessities. In short, the consumer price index is our measure of how much "the essentials" are costing. If the consumer price index is rising, things are costing more. Likewise, when the index drops, so do prices.
>
> You should pay attention to movement in the consumer price index. As it turns out, the Social Security Department does—that's how they decide whether or not to raise payments. Likewise, many larger employers base annual pay increases (cost of living adjustments) on the consumer price index.

BASIC INTERNET RESOURCES CONCERNING CREDIT AND DEBT

As you surf the World Wide Web, you may encounter sites that discuss credit issues such the amount of debt you can afford, ways to consolidate your debt, and ways to improve your debt status. The following site list should help you locate the resources you need.

FINANCIAL HELP

http://www.myvesta.org

Myvesta.org (formerly Debt Counselors of America) is an IRS-approved non-profit organization that assists families and individuals with debt, credit, money, and financial questions, problems, or difficulties. If you think your financial situation is hopeless, Myvesta.org says there is a way out. They have a several programs and self-help guides. You can order a credit report and download free publications such as, "How To Read Your Credit Report." Let Myvesta.org Crisis Relief Team help you solve your problems.

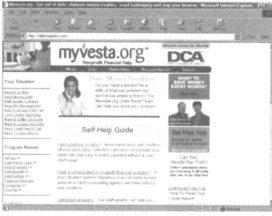

Figure 12.3 Myvesta.org Financial Help.

Family Debt Arbitration and Counseling Services

http://www.center4debtmanagement.com

Family Debt Arbitration and Counseling Services is a federally designated non-profit charitable organization providing debt counseling and debt management services. Note that this site displays best with Netscape, but may be viewed in either graphic or text only mode. The latter runs MUCH faster. Be sure to check out the many available debt counseling services and debt management services available here, as well as the great *Library of Credit and Debt Management* along with the *Shuttle Terminal for Credit and Debt Information*.

Figure 12.4 Family Debt Arbitration and Counseling Services.

Pioneer Credit & Debt Consolidation Services

http://www.pioneercredit.com

Pioneer Credit is a nonprofit agency, located in the Black Hills of South Dakota, dedicated to helping people learn how to manage their money. Through the magic of cyberspace, they can help you, wherever you are, to get out and stay out of debt. "We will contact your creditors and work on your behalf to devise a new acceptable payment plan that you can afford and your creditors can live with," they write. In the end, you'll be making one payment a month on consolidated debt to Pioneer. "We will distribute it, on your behalf, while maintaining a good working relationship with your creditors and answering any of their questions."

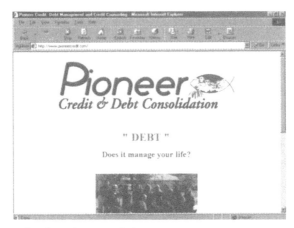

Figure 12.5 Pioneer Credit & Debt Consolidation Services.

PROFESSIONAL BUDGET COUNSELING, INC.

http://www.web-ex.com/creditrepairdebt/creditfix.html

So, you screwed up big-time. You max'd out your credit cards and every other line of credit you can tap. You've got huge bills and no cash. No one loves you. Wait a minute! The folks at Professional Budget Counseling do! So stop those harassing phone calls from bill collectors and reduce your monthly payments on outstanding debt by at least 50%. With Professional Budget Counseling you can get immediate credit relief, consolidate your bills into one monthly payment, and stop paying high interest on credit cards. Check it out.

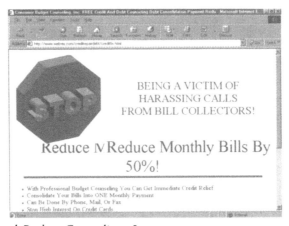

Figure 12.6 Professional Budget Counseling, Inc.

CONFIDENTIAL CREDIT

http://confidentialcredit.com

In these uncertain economic times, it is critical to know what your credit profile is. Now there is a service that lets you verify your complete credit history: Confidential Credit.

There are three national credit bureaus: Equifax, TRW, and Trans Union. And each maintains its own files. The information in these three files can differ substantially. What one credit bureau says about you may not agree with what the others say. Confidential Credit was created to show consumers exactly what all three national credit bureaus say about them. Confidential Credit obtains data from all three of the national credit bureaus and combines it into one easy-to-read report. The report is formatted to give you a line-by-line comparison of what all three bureaus are reporting. Your Confidential Credit report provides the necessary information to spot discrepancies before they cause problems.

Figure 12.7 Confidential Credit.

FREE CREDIT AND DEBT COUNSELING – MONEY MANAGEMENT INTERNATIONAL

http://www.mmintl.org

Do you need debt counseling? MMI offers free professional credit counseling, debt management programs, and consumer education by phone, Internet, fax, and mail. All programs are designed individually to assist consumers with debt repayment. MMI is a national, non-profit agency providing an easy, confidential way to take control of credit. Their phone counselors are available 24 hours a day, 7 days a week by calling 800-762-2271. MMI is also a member of the Better Business Bureau.

Figure 12.8 *Free Credit and Debt Counseling – Money Management International.*

How To Correct Errors

http://www.firstconfederatedmtg.com/errors.htm

Have any of the following been inaccurately placed on your credit report? Late payments? Collection Agency Interventions? Bankruptcy/Chapter 7? Tax Liens? Paid Collections? Someone Else's Info? Charge Offs? Repossessions? Bankruptcy/Chapter 13? Foreclosures?

First Confederated Mortgage has dedicated an entire section of their Web site to understanding credit with a specific page for How To Correct Errors.

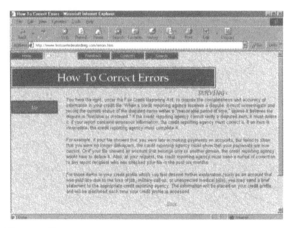

Figure 12.9 *How To Correct Errors.*

BOOKLETS ON CREDIT AND MONEY FROM THE GSA

http://www.gsa.gov/staff/pa/cic/money.htm

NATIONAL ASSOCIATION OF CREDIT UNIONS

http://www.cuna.org

MANAGING PERSONAL CREDIT: A TUTORIAL

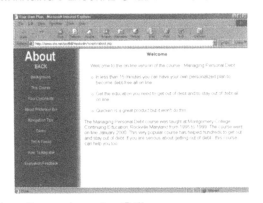

http://www.shs.net/profbill

GET CREDIT REPORT FAST

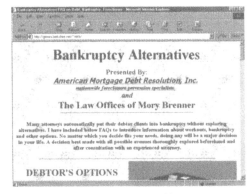

http://www.truecredit.com/index.asp

DEBTOR'S OPTIONS: BANKRUPTCY VS. WORKOUT

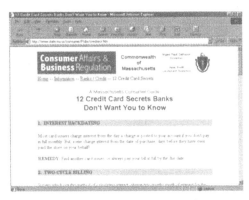

http://gemini.berkshire.net/~mkb/

TWELVE CREDIT CARD SECRETS BANKS DON'T WANT YOU TO KNOW

http://www.state.ma.us/consumer/Pubs/ credsecr.htm

EQUIFAX CONSUMER CREDIT REPORT WITHIN 24 HOURS SECURE ONLINE PROCESSING

http://www.manyhits.com/gate/6/10/shtml

DEBT CONSOLIDATION – FREE QUOTE

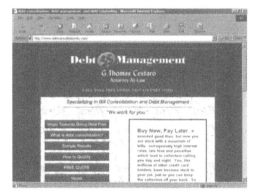

http://www.debtconsolidation4u.com

CREDIT ADVISORS – BE DEBT FREE

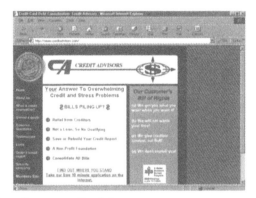

http://www.creditadvisors.com

ESCAPE THE DEBT TRAP AND ELIMINATE DEBT

http://www.thedebttrap.com

ORDER YOUR MERGED 3-IN-1 CREDIT REPORT ONLINE

http://credit-update.hypermart.net

CREDIT PROBLEMS, FREE TIPS

http://www.creditinfocenter.com

CHAPTER 13

GOOD DEBT: MORTGAGE DEBT

My debt is the roof that covers me. — **Jonathan Swift**

Your mortgage loan is your friend. It combines the benefits of tax-deductible interest payments with the opportunity to build equity in one of the best investments going: real estate. The mortgage on your primary or other residences will quite possibly prove to be the best money you have ever borrowed, unless of course you've gone to college on a student loan. In that case, your mortgage might prove to be the second best loan you have ever made. In either case, your mortgage is indisputably *a friend*. And a terrific investment.

BUT HOW MUCH OF A MORTGAGE CAN YOU AFFORD?

Lenders will not be shy to tell you precisely how much mortgage debt you can afford, and what you cannot afford. *Generally*, lenders don't like a scenario where you will be spending anything in excess of 28% of your gross income on housing expenses. Your lender will include under the definition of "housing expenses" your payments of principal, interest, taxes, and insurance. Thus housing expenses are sometimes referred to as *PITI*. Your lender will not include more nebulous, but equally real, numbers in calculating your housing expenses. He or she will not, for example, factor in estimated heating and electricity costs, water costs, maintenance costs, and so on.

The 28% figure is a line, but not a firm one. You can go higher than 28%, sometimes, if— if what? If you put down a large down-payment. If you already spend 28% of your income on housing expenses and have demonstrated that you have no problem in making the payments. If you have a lot of cash on the side, on deposit with your lender, equivalent to a few month's mortgage payments.

If, if, if, if, if. Yes, but how high can you go? The critical mass for a debt/income ratio is usually 36%. No bank is going to want you to have debt in excess of 36% of your gross income. And the 36% max is not just for mortgage debt but for *all your personal debt combined*. The one exception to this rule would be a loan guaranteed by the Veterans Administration, which has a history of allowing debt/income ratios as high as 41%.

THE DIFFERENT TYPES OF MORTGAGES

There are several mortgage vehicles from which you can choose. Some are good for some of the people some of the time. Others are wrong for all of the people all of the time. Among your mortgage options are *adjustable-rate mortgages (ARMs), fixed-rate mortgages, graduated-payment mortgages, renegotiable mortgages, rate-reduction mortgages*, and *balloon mortgages*.

Adjustable rate mortgages (ARMs) feature interest rates that fluctuate every year in tune with the general level of interest rates. If the Federal Reserve (the Fed) raises interest rates, your interest payment goes up. If the Fed lowers rates, your interest payment goes down. One attractive aspect of ARMs is that they often start out two or three percentage points (or *points*) below the market average for interest, albeit with the possibility that the interest percentage rate will rise substantially later. Over the life of a loan, given the cycle of rising and falling interest rates, ARMs *tend* to be less expensive than fixed-rate vehicles, if you can stand the uncertainty.

You see, there is a risk. In times of high inflation, an ARM's interest percentage can sky-rocket. You can minimize this risk by trying to get an ARM with a lifetime interest cap. Then, you will know your precise degree of interest-rate exposure. Note that ARMs are sometimes also called Variable Rate Mortgages (VRMs).

Income Needed to Get a Mortgage Using the 28% Rule

Source of data: National Association of Realtors

			Loan Amount		
Interest %	$50,000	$75,000	$100,000	$150,000	$200,000
8%	$15,724	$23,586	$31,447	$41,171	$62,895
8.5%	$16,477	$24,715	$32,954	$49,430	$65,907
9%	$17,242	$25,863	$34,484	$51,726	$68,968
9.5%	$18,018	$17,028	$36,037	$54,055	$72,074

History of Housing Affordability in the U.S.

Source of data: National Association of Realtors. Data is as of midyear. The average mortgage rate quoted is based on the effective rate of loans closed on existing homes monitored by the Federal Home Loan Bank Board.

Year	Avg. Home Price	Average Mortgage Rate	Monthly Principal/Interest
1982	$67,800	15.38%	$702
1983	$70,300	12.85%	$616
1984	$72,400	12.49%	$618

Year	Avg. Home Price	Average Mortgage Rate	Monthly Principal/Interest
1985	$75,500	11.74%	$609
1986	$80,300	10.25%	$563
1987	$85,600	9.28%	$565
1988	$90,600	9.31%	$591
1989	$93,100	10.11%	$660
1990	$97,500	10.04%	$673
1991	$99,700	9.51%	$671
1992	$100,900	8.48%	$620
1993	$106,100	7.30%	$582
1994	$107,200	8.60%	$658
1995	$109,100	8.00%	$597
1996	$110,600	8.14%	$619

Fixed-rate mortgages, as their name implies, lock you in at a single fixed percentage rate for the life of the loan. I personally find fixed-rate mortgages quite attractive. Should interest rates fall, you can always refinance and, for the price of a few points and closing costs, lock in the lower rate. But should inflation strike and interest rates rise, *your mortgage interest won't.* While the cost of bread and gas and fuel and furniture goes up, the interest on your monthly mortgage will, conveniently, stay right where it is.

Graduated-payment mortgages are available in both adjustable-rate and fixed-rate flavors, and are unappealing either way. I advise you to stay away from them. I don't like them. These vehicles feature very low payments in the early years of the loan, lower than what you'd pay monthly for an equivalent ARM. But there is a catch. A very big catch. And it is called *negative amortization.* In those first years, when your payments are so deceitfully and seductively low, you are not paying enough to cover all the interest that is due. So, even though you make monthly payments, *the principal of your debt grows rather than shrinks*. Those very, very low payments in the early stages of the loan turn out to be extraordinarily expensive over time. Stay away from *graduated-payment mortgages*.

Renegotiable mortgages are what I call "semi-fixed" mortgages. I also call them a bad idea. *Renegotiable mortgages* are ostensibly 20- or 30-year notes. But they can be called in by your bank every two or three years for renegotiation and rewriting at the current interest rate. What is worse, the lender is often, by the terms of most of these loans, *not required* to renew the loan. If your income situation has changed, your lender may very well demand that you settle the loan per the terms of your agreement, thus forcing you to either sell your house or find another mortgage pronto.

In short, *renegotiable mortgages* leave you powerless and you should avoid them.

Rate-reduction mortgages are fixed-rate loans generally timed to 30-years. These loans offer you the option of a one-time rate adjustment within the loan's first few years assuming market rates drop at least 1 1/4 percentage points in that time. There is usually a conversion fee of a few hundred dollars and you may pay a slightly higher (1/8 of a point) interest rate generally over the life of the loan. *But if you are very sure that interest rates are going down soon*, this may be a vehicle to consider. Unlike an ARM, which can go up or down, a *rate-reduction mortgage* can only go down.

Balloon mortgages are practically never a good idea. These vehicles incorporate extremely low, fixed payments for a short period (a few years) early in the life of the loan. Then, at some magic date, *the entire loan falls due*. Usually, the lender has promised to refinance the balloon payment when it comes due. But that "promise" is not a sure thing. You will have to have played by the rules: No payments in your history can have been more than 30 days overdue. The house must be free of liens. And mortgage rates can't have gone up more than 5 percentage points since your first closing. *The only time a balloon mortgage is a good idea is when you are absolutely sure that you are going to sell the house before the balloon payment comes due.*

WHO ARE FANNIE MAE, GINNIE MAE, AND FREDDIE MAC?

Fannie Mae (*http://www.fanniemae.com*), shown below in Figure 13.1, was created in 1938 by the US Congress in a bill called the National Housing Act, which was a response to the massive upheavals in the housing finance system experienced during the Great Depression. President Franklin Delano Roosevelt signed the bill into law. The Federal Housing Authority (FHA) had been established four years earlier to exert a stabilizing influence on the mortgage and residential real estate markets. The FHA mortgage represented a radical concept for its time: a long-term, self-amortizing loan on which principal was repaid gradually over the life of the life of the loan. What a concept!

Fannie Mae was initially created to buy these FHA-insured loans from mortgage lenders so that they, in turn, could make more loans to consumers. This represented the start of the modern secondary mortgage industry. Ten years later, in 1948, Fannie Mae was given authority to purchase loans guaranteed by the Veterans Administration (VA) as well.

In the 1950s, while American housing boomed, the ownership of Fannie Mae changed. In 1954, the corporation became partly owned by private stockholders: Lenders were required to own certain amounts of stock in the corporation before they would be permitted to sell mortgages to Fannie Mae.

The most significant step in Fannie Mae's evolution occurred during the "Great Society" years, in 1968, when Congress divided the original Fannie Mae into two organizations: the current Fannie Mae and the Government National Mortgage Association (GNMA), familiarly known as *Ginnie Mae*. GNMA (*http://www.ginniemae.gov*), shown below in Figure 13.2, remains a government agency within the Department of Housing and Urban Development (HUD), helping to finance government-assisted housing programs. GNMA provides liquidity to the FHA/VA market primarily through its mortgage-backed security guaranty activities. Under this program, lenders originate loans and then package them into pools of FHA-insured and VA-guaranteed mortgages. GNMA guarantees timely payment of both principal and interest to the investor. The lenders issue securities backed by the mortgages and then sell the securities to institutional and other investors.

Figure 13.1 The Fannie Mae Web site.

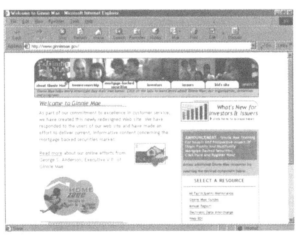

Figure 13.2 The Government National Mortgage Association (Ginnie Mae).

The legislation splitting Fannie Mae from GNMA in 1968 marked the beginning of Fannie Mae's conversion into a privately owned corporation. The newly private Fannie Mae was rechartered by Congress with a mandate to enhance the efficient flow of funds through the secondary market to America's mortgage lenders. Congress also mandated that the corporation operate with private capital on a self-sustaining basis. Its complete transition to private status was accomplished in 1970, after the shareholders paid the US Treasury $216 million for the government's remaining ownership interest.

Closely related to these two organizations is Freddie Mac (*http://www.freddiemac.com*), shown below in Figure 13.3. Created in 1970, Freddie Mac is, like Fannie Mae, a publicly-owned company which, as its Web site explains, is "dedicated to improving the quality of life by making the American dream of decent, accessible housing a reality." Freddie Mac's charter calls for it to make mortgage funds available whenever and wherever qualified Americans need them by linking the worldwide capital markets to the US mortgage markets, to provide a reliable low-cost flow of mortgage capital to the citizens of the United States, and to bring the benefits of the secondary mortgage market to a wide and diverse range of communities across the country. In this way, Freddie Mac sustains a stable mortgage credit system and reduces the mortgage rates paid by homebuyers overall. Over the years, Freddie Mac has helped finance one in six American homes.

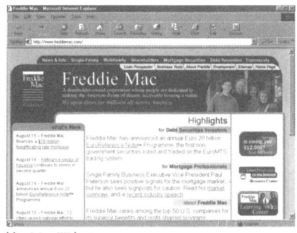

Figure 13.3 *The Freddie Mac Web site.*

HOW TO CHECK THE CALCULATION OF YOUR ADJUSTABLE RATE MORTGAGE PAYMENT

People are human. Stuff happens. Mistakes get made. Your bank is not trying to rob you when it comes time to adjust your ARM. But sometimes it does. Inadvertently. It happens. Sometimes they pick the wrong index percentage to which they key your payments. Sometimes they pick the wrong start date for the new rate. Or sometimes they round the interest percentage up when it should have been rounded down. Be sure you understand exactly when your rate will be adjusted and have a method available to track the index to which your loan is linked. If you can't or don't want to do the research and math yourself, you can have your payment calculations checked by firms which specialize in ARMs. One of the leaders in this field is Loantech, Inc. (*http://www.loantech.com*), shown below in Figure 13.4.

Figure 13.4 Information on ARMs from Loantech, Inc.

HOW TO FIND A MORTGAGE LENDER

Mortgage banks, independent mortgage brokers, and credit unions will generally offer you the best source of a mortgage loan. The next places to check are savings and loans and, as a last resort, commercial banks. Savings and loans and commercial banks tend to have the worst (most expensive) mortgages.

Do your own shopping. Do not allow the real estate agent representing the seller of the house you are buying to "set you up" with a mortgage bank or broker. The agent may well be getting a finder's fee. And the fee will translate as a higher interest rate, or an additional point at closing, for you. There are several organizations that publish weekly surveys of mortgage lenders and rates. Among these is HSH Associates (*http://www.hsh.com*), shown below in Figure 13.5.

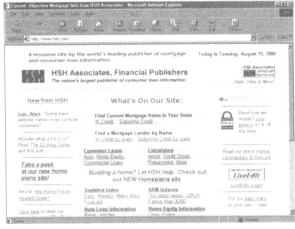

Figure 13.5 A survey of lenders and mortgage rates at HSH Associates.

A POINT ABOUT POINTS

People can't seem to talk about mortgages or loans without someone talking about points. For years, I wanted to know, what is a point? My in-laws live on a point of land that juts boldly but picturesquely into Narragansett Bay. When the University of Nevada Las Vegas (only occasionally these days) wins a basketball game, they do so through the accumulation of points. When I make an argument I try to have a point. When asked directions, I will often point in one direction or another. And were I a writer working in a nondigital age, the point of my pen might have proven a greater weapon than the point of a sword. As it is, in these modern times, I try to make my keyboard a weapon more powerful than more insidious weapons. By now you are not only asking *What is a point?* but also *What is THE point?* Very well.

A point is the equivalent of 1% of the principal of your mortgage loan. For example, if your loan principal is $100,000, one point is $1,000. Your lender sometimes charges points at the time a loan is written (closed). Sometimes you'll pay one point. Sometimes you'll pay as many as three points. Sometimes, with *no-point mortgages*, you'll pay no points. Generally, the more points you pay at the time of closing, the lower the interest rate you pay over the life of the loan.

Principal Amount	1 Point	2 Points	3 Points
$300,000	$3,000	$6,000	$9,000
$200,000	$2,000	$4,000	$6,000
$100,000	$1,000	$2,000	$3,000

Points are negotiable. The larger your loan, the more likely your lender will be willing to lose a point or two if you push the negotiations. Another thing to remember about points is that, for tax purposes, they count as mortgage interest and you can deduct them. The points you pay on your primary residence are fully deductible in the year you paid them. Points you pay on a secondary vacation or investment home, however, must be written off over the life of the loan.

If you expect to own your home for only a few years, pay as little in the way of points as possible and go for a slightly higher interest rate. If you are buying for the long-term, pay as many front-end points as possible in order to "buy-down" your mortgage's starting- or fixed-rate interest percentage.

AVOID LOAN PREPAYMENT PENALTIES

Whether you have a fixed-rate mortgage or an ARM, you want to be sure that you are able to prepay principal as you see fit, whenever you want and in whatever amount you want. Some lenders will charge you a fee (a *fine*, a *penalty*, a *surcharge*, whatever you want to call it) for making prepayments. Such penalties are absurd and unnecessary. The vast majority of reputable lenders offer loans without any prepayment penalties whatsoever. Make sure your lender is one of them. Prepayment penalties are allowed in some form (but not necessarily imposed) in 36 states and the District of Columbia.

Floating Commitment or Lock in?

After you are approved for a mortgage, it may take two or three months before you are able to close. You've still got termite inspections to arrange and other niceties to tend to. What will happen to interest rates in that time? If you think interest rates are headed lower, tell your lender you want a "floating" loan commitment, which says you'll get the interest rate that is current *when you close on your loan*. If you think interest rates are headed higher, be sure to "lock-in" the interest rate available at the time your lender first makes the loan commitment. A floating commitment usually comes free of charge. Your lender may exact a small fee for a lock-in, but it'll be worth it if you are right in your hunch about the direction of interest rates. Check out *Lock or Float? Mortgage Trend Predictions* on the Web, *http://www.mortgage-net.com/trends,* shown below in Figure 13.6.

Figure 13.6 Mortgage trend predictions.

Low-Documentation Loans

Like many self-employed people, I have generally high but also weird and erratic income. I will make a staggeringly high amount of money one fiscal year, then significantly less the next fiscal year, and then more again. These variances are more the result of timing than anything else. Nevertheless, my financial history as revealed by the documentation in my tax returns seems schizophrenic to say the least.

I, like many self-employed people, do not fit the normal profile that most lenders study when deciding who and who not to lend money to. Still, I am completely solvent. In fact, I am more solvent than many people with "day jobs." So mortgage lenders want to lend me money when I ask for it, because that is how they make money and, after all, I am a good risk.

It is for people like me that the low-documentation mortgage loan was invented. Such a mortgage involves a high down payment by me (to the tune of at least 25% to demonstrate that I really and truly am solvent). It involves a cursory check of my income by the lender, which includes looking at recent tax returns (erratic as they may be) and chatting with a few of my key clients (in my case, publishers) to make sure I am really doing work for them. It also includes checking my bank account to make sure I really have some cash on hand. And it involves checking my credit history to make sure I really pay my bills. But there is no problem, as there would normally be, that a 9 to 5 employer does not exist, or that my earnings this year are no guarantee of earnings next year.

In return for all this special handling, I pay about one-half a percentage higher interest rate than I normally would. But I get my mortgage and I proceed with my life.

AVOID CALL PROVISIONS

Never, never, never sign a mortgage contract that includes a *call provision*. Call provisions will occasionally come up when you negotiate a fixed-rate mortgage or an ARM with an interest rate cap. What a *call provision* does is enable the lender to *call* (order you to either repay in full, or refinance) your mortgage at any time. If interest rates go up past your loan's fixed-rate, or past the cap on your ARM, you will be in trouble. Your lender will be sure to call your loan. Count on it. However, many reputable lenders offer mortgages without *call provisions*. You have a choice here. Make sure you avoid *call provisions* in a mortgage.

THE VOODOO OF ESCROW

Your monthly mortgage payment normally includes not only principal and interest, but also moneys that the lender will use to pay your homeowner's insurance and real-estate taxes. Your tax and insurance moneys are maintained in an escrow account, out of which your lender pays bills as they come due. In some states (Rhode Island among them!), your lender is required to pay you interest on your escrow account. In other states your lender is required to pay you *zippo* and will do just that.

The *zippo* interest formulation becomes doubly annoying when you bump into a lender who demands that you keep an exorbitant cushion in your escrow account. Be advised that *by law* this cushion cannot exceed more than two months expected payments of taxes and insurance. Study your escrow statement, find out what's in the account, and if there's too much ask the escrow company for some of your money back.

ABOUT PRIVATE MORTGAGE INSURANCE (PMI)

In the event that you do not have cash on hand for a 20% down payment on your home, some lenders will allow a smaller down-payment, as low as 5% in some cases. With the smaller down-payment loans, however, borrowers are usually required to carry private-mortgage insurance (PMI). PMI involves an initial premium payment of 1% to 5% of your mortgage amount and may require additional monthly fees depending on how your loan and PMI are structured.

Many people who were forced to purchase PMI insurance at loan inception go on maintaining and paying for the PMI through the life of their loan even though they don't have to. The fact is that once you have at least 20% equity in your home, the PMI should go away. Your PMI underwriter will not tell you when it is appropriate for you to cancel. Neither will your bank. So do the job yourself. Keep abreast of your equity position in your home and once you get past 20%, insist that the PMI be removed.

A very goof tutorial related to PMI can be found at *http://www.appraisal-network.com/nopmi.htm,* shown below in Figure 13.7. The solution is to call or write your mortgage service department and request an application to remove it. The site also gives a lengthy list of PMI questions and answers links.

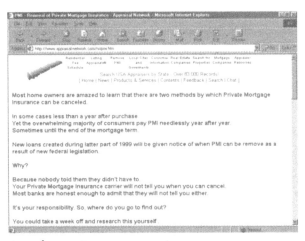

Figure 13.7 Information about private mortgage insurance.

WHEN TO REFINANCE YOUR MORTGAGE

It is generally a good idea to refinance when interest rates fall to a point where you will recoup all of your refinance costs (including qualification fees, points, and closing costs) within two or three years based on the interest savings. Obviously, it does not pay to refinance if you have any thoughts of selling your house within that window of time. Use this rule of thumb:

Generally, interest rates have to fall at least 1 1/2 points before it is even worth beginning to run the numbers to consider a refinance.

If you have an ARM, you also probably have an alternative to a full refinancing. Many ARMs allow you to recast the high and low interest caps on your mortgage to put them in tune with lowered market interest rates. There is generally a fee of several hundred dollars for this recast. However, you avoid closing costs, points, and the annoyance of having to requalify for a whole new mortgage all over again.

So, Is Mortgage Interest Deductible?

Yes. Within limits. All mortgage interest up to a $1 million cap is deductible for the purposes of calculating your federal income taxes. So is all interest associated with home-equity loans up to a $100,000 cap. However, all mortgages closed before October 13, 1987, have an unlimited interest deduction—no cap whatsoever.

I've discussed the deductibility of points earlier in this chapter; therefore, I'll be brief. Points are deductible. Points paid in connection with the purchase of your primary residence are fully deductible in the year in which you pay them. Points you pay in connection with the purchase of a vacation or investment property must be written off over the life of the loan.

Are you building a house? You can't get a mortgage loan on a house that does not stand yet. You have to take out a home-construction loan, secured by the property the house is built on. The interest on the home-construction loan is deductible for two years. As soon as you get the house built, get a permanent mortgage on the house, pay off the home-construction loan, and have your interest be deductible *ad infinitum*.

Prepay Your Mortgage Principal Whenever Possible

It is *always* a good idea to make prepayments on your mortgage whenever you can afford to do so because you can rarely afford not to do so. For every thousand dollars of *principal* you prepay in the first years of a typical 30-year mortgage you could be saving two to three thousand dollars in *interest* over the life of the loan. In general, you can count on saving two to three dollars in interest for every buck in principal prepaid during the early years of your mortgage.

And the mechanics of prepayment, assuming you've been careful to make sure your mortgage does not contain a prepayment penalty, could not be simpler. You simply send your lender a check for a larger amount than the required monthly minimum and attach a note to the check that explicitly states that they should apply your extra payment to principal (rather than, placing the funds in the escrow account).

Prepaying your mortgage principal will shorten the term of your loan. It will not, however, cause a lowering in your minimum monthly payments. Your payments will stay the same. You will just have fewer payments to make at the back-end of your loan.

There is a great mortgage calculator on the Web that can show you, quickly and easily, how to save tens of thousands of dollars over the life of your loan simply by making relatively small extra payments every month. Check it out at *http://www.loanlink.com/calcs.htm,* shown below in Figure 13.8.

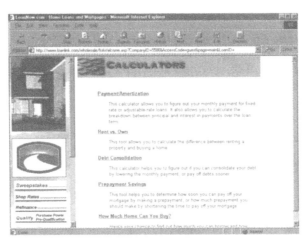

Figure 13.8 A Web-based mortgage calculator.

WHAT THE TRUTH IN LENDING STATEMENT TELLS YOU

Federal law mandates that all mortgage agreements include a formal document titled the *Truth in Lending Statement.* This statement clearly defines the total cost of your mortgage over the life of the loan as defined by the five key elements of your mortgage: the loan amount (principal), the length of the loan, the interest rate, prepaid points, and any associated fees such as application fees and fees for other bank services. The sums associated with each of these elements over the life of the loan are stipulated in the Truth in Lending Statement and then added up within the statement to clearly define what your loan will cost you over the loan's lifetime.

FORECLOSURE IS NOT A FOREGONE CONCLUSION

What happens if you fall behind on your mortgage? Foreclosure, right? I mean, it says so quite clearly right in your mortgage contract: *90 days late on payments and you're out of there! You've only got three strikes, and each lasts for thirty days.* It's inevitable right? Wrong. Your bank certainly has the legal authority to foreclose, but may well find another plan more attractive. Your bank does not want your house. Your bank just wants the money it is owed, with interest. If you can reasonably convince your bank of your ability to pay up on your loan in the future, you will more than likely be able to negotiate a payment plan that will leave you in your home and your bank in the black.

At times a bank will agree to tack on the amount you are in arrears to the back-end of your mortgage. Thus, the bank makes more money in the long run because this extends the length (and therefore your total cost) of the loan. At other times, a bank will agree to go even further, reducing the amount of your monthly payments and thus extending the life of the loan even further, while extending the bank's profits just as much. Conversely, should your fortunes suddenly swell once more, a bank will of course allow you to either make a balloon payment to catch up on the amount you are in arrears, or increase your future monthly payments in order to make up the difference on payments you've previously missed.

INTERNET RESOURCES FOR MORTGAGE SHOPPERS

As you surf the World Wide Web, you may encounter sites that discuss mortgage issues such as the effects of interest rates on your payment, when to prepay principle and how much, the escrow process, and much more. The following site list should help you locate the resources you need.

COMMONLY USED REAL ESTATE TERMS

http://www.sromm.com/forsale/html/terms.htm

What is an *acceleration clause*? An *adjustment interval*? An *assumption*? A *buy-down*? A *cap*? A *Deed-of-Trust*? *Earnest Money*? An *impound*? *Negative amortization*? *PITI*? *Recision*? *Verification of Deposit*? *Wraparound*? Get the scoop on all these arcane phrases and more.

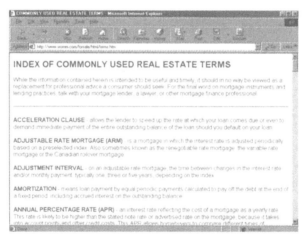

Figure 13.9 Commonly Used Real Estate Terms.

FINANCECENTER MORTGAGE CALCULATORS

http://www.financenter.com/calculat.htm

Am I better off renting? Should I refinance? For how much can I refinance? How much can I borrow? What will my payments be? How much will my closing costs be? How much should I put down? Should I pay discount points to get a lower interest rate? Should I choose a fixed or an adjustable rate loan? Should I choose a 15-year or 30-year loan?

You'll find robust on-line calculators to help you answer all these questions and more.

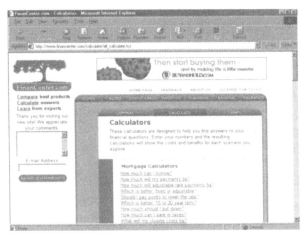

Figure 13.10 Finance Center Mortgage Calculators.

HomeOwners Finance Center

http://www.homeowners.com

"How to House-Hunt on the Web . . . visit the HomeOwners Finance Center . . . where you can compute your mortgage payments, check current rates, and learn about adjustable-rate mortgages and closing costs." So wrote the editors of *Fortune* Magazine in the issue of 13 May 1996. This Magellan 4-Star site is considered by many to be the very best mortgage site on the Web.

The proprietor, HomeOwners Finance, is a California mortgage company writing loans in 43 states. They automate the entire loan-application process. Fill out the form right on-line and you are ready to go. But this is more than just an on-line loan application. Get details on the best-fixed and adjustable rates being offered nationwide. Subscribe to the free *RateWatch* electronic mailing list for regular updates.

Figure 13.11 HomeOwners Finance Center.

HSH ASSOCIATES MORTGAGE SURVEYS

http://www.hsh.com

HSH is quite simply the world's premier publisher of mortgage and consumer loan information. On the Web you can find a lot of places, that offer you some sort of mortgage information. Some are better than others; many are there just to try to sell you a loan. But there's only one *best*, and this is it. HSH has been providing the best information on mortgages and the mortgage market for nearly two decades. And for their trouble they've been rewarded with accolades from publications such as *Money, Kiplinger's Personal Finance Magazine*, and the *Wall Street Journal*. The rates that HSH supplies are not mere advertising. HSH collects them directly from 2,500 to 3,000 lenders in major metropolitan areas from coast to coast *every week*. "We're an objective, independent source of information," they write. "We do not make or broker mortgages." Other mortgage information databases include information that lenders pay to have posted. Not so here. The data in HSH's database is the result of careful, painstaking surveys conducted week-in and week-out over nearly twenty years.

Figure 13.12 HSH Associates Mortgage Surveys.

HUGH CHOU'S MORTGAGE CALCULATOR FOR PAYMENTS AND AMORTIZATIONS

http://www.mortgage-net.com/calculators/hc

This math is wonderful. Type in a few facts and press calculate, and then you can find out wonderful information such as: If you've got an $80,000 30-year mortgage fixed at 8.16% interest, you can shave $74,908.20 in interest (along with 15.83 years of payments) off your loan by simply prepaying $200 in capital every month. Let's see. Where's my checkbook?

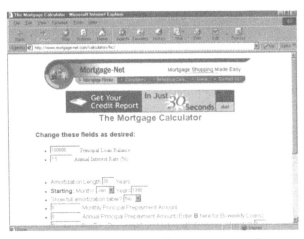

Figure 13.13 Hugh Chou's Mortgage Calculator for Payments and Amortizations.

MORTGAGE SHOPPING MADE EASY

http://www.mortgage-net.com

This terrific site has a lot of very useful features. First of all, there is a fully searchable, nation-wide mortgage-listings database with facilities that let you apply for a mortgage right on-line. You begin by selecting a state. Then you survey a list of mortgage lenders/brokers in your state, along with hotlinks to their proprietary Web sites.

Second, you'll find daily updates on mortgage rate trends, an outstanding collection of links to all the very best on-line mortgage calculators, which enable you to calculate payments, amortizations, the effects of making additional pre-payments or bi-weekly payments, and more. Information on current and historical interest rate indices and a very useful tutorial on mortgage fundamentals ensure that your shopping is made easy.

Figure 13.14 Mortgage Shopping Made Easy.

LOANTECH, INC: SOFTWARE FOR ADJUSTABLE RATE MORTGAGE ANALYSIS

http://www.loantech.com

Loantech currently offers four products that address a wide range of mortgage issues from qualification to least expensive loan comparisons, payment review, and complete loan analysis. These products are available as single products or as a suite. They include:

- *Qualifier*—Software for loan qualification based on income, tax level, and current debt.

- *Rates and Points*—Software that identifies the least expensive loan based on interest rate, points, and estimated stay in home.

- *Arm Indexer*—Software that identifies correct period interest rate based on index used, setback period, and month.

- *Arm Auditor*—Software which performs complete audit/analysis of ARMs using an internal rate database can be updated monthly on-line.

Figure 13.15 Loantech, Inc: Software for Adjustable Rate Mortgage Analysis.

MORTGAGE INSURANCE: HOW IT WORKS

http://www.mgic.com/what_is_mi.htm

What is mortgage insurance? Who is it for? What does mortgage insurance do for borrowers? Who pays for mortgage insurance? What does it cost? Get answers to all these questions and more at this site.

Figure 13.16 Mortgage Insurance: How It Works.

Mortgage Minder Software

http://www.cwts.com

Mortgage Minder is a powerful mortgage acceleration calculator that allows you to see the effect of making extra principal payments. You can download a demo version or purchase Mortgage Minder for $24.95. According to this site, it takes about 23 years to pay off half of a typical 30-year mortgage. Adding an extra $100 a month to your payment could knock ten years off of your mortgage. You can save thousands in interest, build equity three times as fast, all with an unconditional money back guarantee.

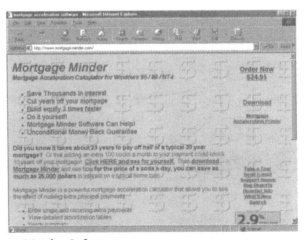

Figure 13.17 Mortgage Minder Software.

AMPAC MORTGAGE COMPANY/CALIFORNIA

http://www.ampacmtg.com

COMMERCIAL LOAN DIRECTORY

http://www.mortgage-net.com/network/usa/
commercial/rz.cgi/com_usa.htm

FITECH SYSTEMS: LOAN SERVICES

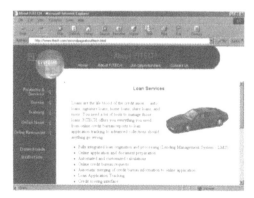

http://www.fitech.com

TOP 10 MISTAKES

http://www.mortgage-net.com/reference/
top10.shtml

INTEREST RATE TRENDS

http://www.mortgage-net.com/trends

DAILY MORTGAGE NEWS REPORTS

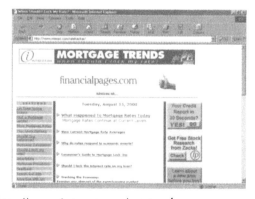

http://www.interest.com/ratetracker

MORTGAGE LENDERS

http://www.mrew.com/mor_list.htm

SOFTWARE DOWNLOADS

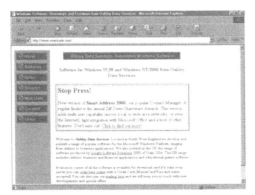

http://www.smartcode.com

MORTGAGE CALCULATORS ONLINE

http://www.financenter.com/homeloan/
AFI/index.htm

MONEYTALKS MORTGAGE MAGAZINE

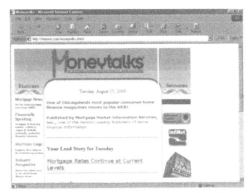

http://www.interest.com/moneytalks.shtml

MORTGAGE MART

http://www.mortgage-mart.com

MORTGAGE RATE COMPARISON, CITY BY CITY

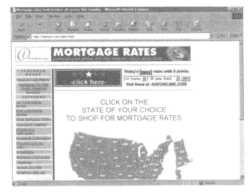

http://interest.com/rates.html

MORTGAGE QUOTES

http://www.mortgagequotes.com

SHOP RATES

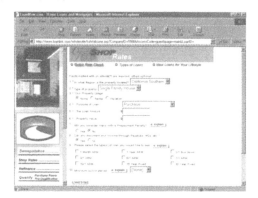

http://www.loanlink.com

THE FUTURE OF MORTGAGES

http://www.mortgagebot.com

PRIVATE MORTGAGE INSURANCE FAQ

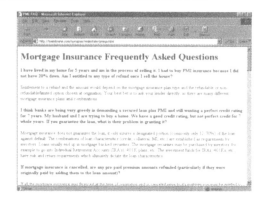

*http://membrane.com/synapse/realestate/
pmiqa.html*

BI-WEEKLY MORTGAGE CALCULATOR SOFTWARE

http://www.southfloridabusiness.com/bmrcalc

CANADIAN MORTGAGE RESOURCES, CALCULATORS, APPLICATIONS, RATES AND TOOLS

http://www.altainfo.com

MORTGAGE INTEREST RATES

http://hfci.1-8.net

MORTGAGE ONLY – HOME LOAN RESOURCES

http://www.mortgageonly.com

MORTGAGE DIRECTORY

http://www.mortgagedirectory.com

ADVANCED MORTGAGE RESOURCES
MORTGAGE GLOSSARY

http://www.mtglender.com/glossary.htm

CALIFORNIA HOME LOANS AND MORTGAGES

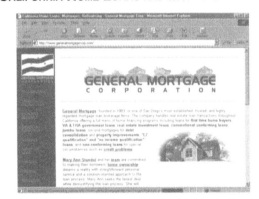

http://generalmortgagecorp.8g.com

FINANCE/INTEREST RATES

http://ired.com/mort

ASK ED ABOUT MORTGAGE FINANCING

http://www.ask-ed.com/calcs.html

MANHATTAN MORTGAGE

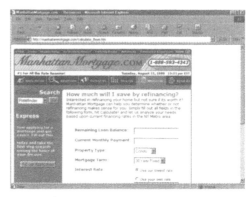

*http://manhattanmortgage.com/
calculator_three.htm*

GET SMART ONLINE MORTGAGE FINDER

http://www.getsmart.com

CURRENT MORTGAGE RATES NATIONWIDE

http://www.compareinterestrates.com

SHOP FOR THE BEST MORTGAGE RATES

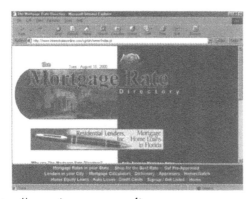

http://www.interestratesonline.com

LOW MORTGAGE RATES

http://www.lowestmortgagerate.com

RATES, INFORMATION, AND CALCULATORS

http://www.amo-mortgage.com

THE ONLINE MORTGAGE SCORECARD

http://www.gomez.com

ELIMINATE PMI FOREVER!

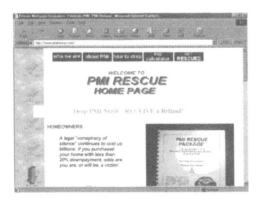

http://www.pmirescue.com

MORTGAGE TERMS

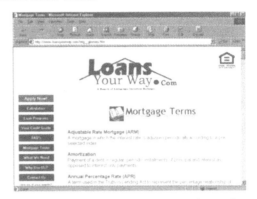

http://www.loansyourway.com/mtg_glossery.htm

MORTGAGE GUIDE AT BEST LOAN DEALS

http://bestloandeals.com

MAKE YOURSELF A HOME WITH PRIVATE MORTGAGE INSURANCE

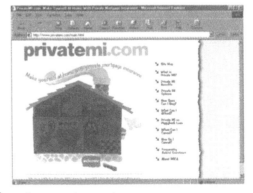

http://www.privatemi.com

PMI – HOW TO STOP IT

http://www.pmibuster.com

NO PMI!

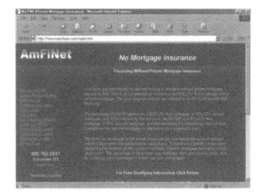

http://www.loanchase.com/nopmi.html

CHAPTER 14

THE RIP-OFF OF REVOLVING CREDIT DEBT

I am forever in your debt. — An old saying

So, you've max'd out your credit card. In fact, you've max'd out your three MasterCards and your one VISA card. It seemed so convenient at the times you made the purchases. You really couldn't afford to pay cash for that grand piano, but you figured you could afford to put a $100 a month toward it if you bought it with your credit card. You really couldn't afford to pay cash for that snowmobile. But you figured you could put $50 a month toward it if . . .

Do Not Go into Debt for Toys

I am a financial puritan. Credit is one of the few topics on which my views are extremely conservative. I think it is foolish to go into debt, any kind of debt, to purchase nonessential items. Did you absolutely have to have the piano and the snowmobile and all the other bobbles, all the other trinkets of consumerism, with which you've surrounded yourself at the expense of max'd out credit cards?

Debt for your mortgage is necessary. And it is relatively cheap compared to high-interest, unsecured, nondeductible credit-card debt. Debt for your automobile and large household essentials like refrigerators and washing machines is also often necessary. And though not deductible, it is still inexpensive compared to (I'll say it again!) *high-interest, unsecured* credit card debt.

You must understand that credit-card debt is the grease on the slippery slope to many people's financial ruin. And you want to avoid the grease. That doesn't mean you want to avoid credit cards themselves, which are useful tools. But you do want to avoid excessive credit card debt: the grease.

CREDIT CARDS VERSUS TRAVEL AND ENTERTAINMENT CARDS— WHAT'S THE DIFFERENCE?

American Express, Carte Blanche and Diners Club are *Travel and Entertainment Cards*. In their bare bones varieties, they do not include credit lines. When you use the generic American Express "Green" card to pay for something, American Express expects you to reimburse them the *full cost* of the item at the time that American Express renders you their monthly bill. American Express is not expecting to have you "carry" the debt over many months with many small payments.

Some *Travel and Entertainment Card* variations include credit lines, such as the American Express' Gold Card, Platinum Card, and Optima Card. I went through a period when I held each of these "prestige cards" in my wallet, paying extra in annual fees for the privilege and getting access to credit lines I never used, because I object to interest rates of 18% to 22%. Now I am back to the simple green card, with the lowest possible American Express annual fee and no credit line. It suits my needs perfectly.

True credit cards are *bankcards* such as MasterCard, VISA, and Discover. These are also called *revolving-credit cards*. As their name implies, revolving-credit bankcards are issued by banks, which are in the business of lending money. The banks not only give you a credit line with the card, but they encourage you to use it as much as possible. If you've got a record of making regular, reliable, but low payments on your credit card bill, and you then max out your credit "limit," expect an enthusiastic letter in the mail announcing that since you are such a wonderful customer the bank is pleased to raise your credit limit by several thousand dollars.

Of course they are. They've found a sucker who is willing to pay an astonishingly high rate of interest for money that should be much cheaper, and who furthermore appears willing to do so forever. The bankers love you. At least they will love you until you maneuver yourself into a position where you can't keep up with your card's minimum payment schedule. Then watch out.

WHY RATES ARE SO HIGH: THE SHAM OF UNSECURED DEBT

One of the main reasons why credit cards carry such high interest rates is that these debts are, at least according to the propaganda, unsecured. Think about it. Your mortgage debt is secured by a lien on your house. Your auto loan is secured by a lien on your car. But there is no lien on the accumulated junk you purchased with your MasterCard: the water skis, the microwave, the ties designed by Jerry Garcia.

Thus, your credit-card debt is, officially at least, unsecured. And banks use this mirage of extenuated risk to explain why they need to maintain excessively high interest rates. According to the banks, your credit card debts are the "junk bonds" of consumer debt. And greater risk demands greater return.

But the bank's analogy is false, because your card is not *really* unsecured and never will be until you are broke and homeless and standing on a street corner begging for spare change.

The bank that issued your card or cards to you has every recourse available to it should you default. The bank can and will come after your assets from every angle in order to redeem the debt. Count on it.

WHY RATES ARE SO HIGH: FOR REAL

The *real* reason interest rates are so high on so many credit cards is that a significant number of people are dumb enough to pay outrageous interest rates in exchange for the privilege of living above their means. In fact, as a society, we are addicted to credit card debt. We put up with high credit-card interest rates just as we tolerate the high costs of liquor, cigarettes, cable-TV, and our other addictions.

WHAT'S THE BEST PERSONAL APPROACH TO CREDIT CARDS?

Despite my ranting about credit-card misuse, it's important that you carry at least one bank credit card. For starters, having a good record of making charges and payments on a bankcard is a vital step in establishing your personal credit history, without which you will not, when the time comes, qualify for "good" debt such as a mortgage. Convenience is another factor. Like the ad says, "some stores and restaurants do not take American Express." If you don't want to carry a lot of cash all the time and don't want to write checks all over town, then you have to have MasterCard or VISA or Discover card.

So by all means, carry and use a bank credit card. But exercise self-control when you are shopping. And then pay off your balance in full every month. And do so religiously. Otherwise you will end up paying two to three times the value on everything you charge. And that becomes extremely expensive.

In short, for every dollar you leave as an unpaid balance on your credit card, you must have a dollar earning more than 18% to 19%—a feat which is sometimes difficult for even top financial managers to sustain.

WHAT'S THE BEST BANK CREDIT CARD TO CARRY?

Assuming you take this book's advice, you want a card that carries no annual fee and that offers a 25-day grace period during which it applies no interest on any charges you have made. Such a grace period is quite important. A few cards charge you interest from the date you make your purchases. Thus, the cards charge you interest even though you pay off your charge card balance in full every month.

One other point about this ideal card: It will usually have a hideously high interest rate attached to it. That's a big part of the reason why there is no annual fee. If you are adhere to the guidelines of paying off your card in full each month, you won't care what the interest rate is because you'll never carry a balance forward on your card and, hence, never be charged interest.

My own MasterCard is a free one ("no annual fee for life!") that I got from AT&T in partnership with some bank. I forget the name of the bank. I also use the AT&T MasterCard as a calling card. An extremely high interest rate is attached to the card. But I don't care. The card has a 25-day grace period, and I pay the bill in full every month.

In effect, I have a totally free MasterCard. I pay no annual fee. I never rack up any interest. And the poor bank does not make a dime on me, though it has the expense of maintaining and servicing my MasterCard account. The bank is willing to continue to do this, I suppose, in the hope that I will someday become a debt junkie.

If you are an unreformed debt junkie, and you are planning to carry a hefty balance on your card, then you want a different card than that described above. You want a MasterCard or VISA or Discover Card with the lowest possible interest-rate you can find—perhaps 12% to 15% instead of 18% to 22%. Plan on paying an annual fee for your card in exchange for a lower interest rate. It'll be a good investment. It won't be as good an investment as paying off your card. But given the path you've chosen, it'll be a good investment.

The Devil in the Details of the 25-Day Grace Period

The 25-day, interest-free grace period offered by many bankcard issuers is a wonderful thing *so long as you pay off your balance every month*, punctually. None of these cards offer any grace period at all for new charges when you are carrying forward a debt from the previous month. If you carry a balance on your credit card, then *forget the grace period on new charges*. It does not apply to you. You will get charged interest on all new charges from the moment you make them.

CALCULATING INTEREST: ADJUSTED BALANCE, AVERAGE DAILY BALANCE, OR PREVIOUS BALANCE?

In shopping for a bankcard, be careful to find out precisely *how* interest is calculated for the card. There are three possible methods. The best deal for consumers is the *adjusted-balance method*, whereby the bank calculates simple interest on the exact amount you owe. Very few cards calculate their interest in this manner.

The next best approach for consumers, and the approach most widely used, is the *average daily-balance method*. This method involves applying interest to the average amount of debt you carry on your card for each day in a given month.

The least attractive approach for consumers, and the most attractive for banks, is the *previous-balance method*. With this method you get hit with interest on the balance you carried at the end of the previous month, even if your current balance is zero.

The moral should be clear: Stay away from any card where your interest will be calculated using the *previous-balance method*.

WEB-BASED BANK CARD INFO FROM *RAM* RESEARCH

RAM Research is an independent banking-research organization that monitors, publishes, and publicizes information pertaining to bank credit cards. RAM Research has several divisions, among them *CardTrak of America, Inc.* (publishers of consumer related bank credit card material including the monthly newsletter *CardTrak*). Since its founding in 1986, the firm has evolved to become the nation's premier source of comparative credit card data for consumers. RAM Research hit the World Wide Web in September 1995, and the address for their highly useful and extremely informative site is *http://www.ramresearch.com*.

Come to RAM Research on the Web for comparative shopping information on literally hundreds of bank credit-card products, with interactive hyperlinks to issuer's Web sites.

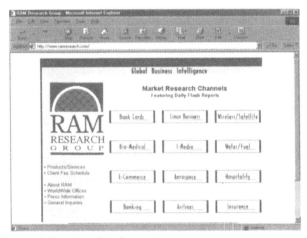

Figure 14.1 RAM Research bankcard information.

TRY NOT TO BE POPULAR

If you carry a lot of debt on your cards, don't have too many cards (no more than three or four), and pay your monthly minimums punctually, then you'll have a cornucopia of bankcard options presented to you with great regularity. The marketers of credit cards will beat a path to your door through your mailbox. They will be falling all over each other with offers to get you to transfer your credit card debt to their card. And they will lure you with slightly lower interest rates on the front end, reduced annual fees, and so on.

You will feel very popular. You will be popular. But you will be popular in the manner anyone else who likes to give away money is popular. And once you run out of money you won't be popular anymore.

THE SCOOP ON SECURED CARDS

If you have a bad credit history (a history of credit abuses, bankruptcies, etc.) the only way you will be able to procure a credit card will be to get a *secured* card. With a secured card, the issuing bank, in effect, has no risk. You deposit money with your bank and your card's credit limit is equal to the moneys your bank account holds. If you don't pay on the card, the bank will seize all or part of your deposit to cover your indebtedness. Meanwhile, you will pay 18% to 22% on your "credit" card balance, while the bank pays you 4% or 5% on your deposit. It is a lousy deal no matter how you look at it. But this is inevitable. A bad credit rating is the most expensive thing in the world.

The Author's Guild MasterCard and Other "Group Support" Cards

Occasionally you will be offered a bank card through your union, or one of the professional organizations you belong to, or your college's alumni association, and so on.

Organizations can go two ways on this type of offer. Your organization can get low or no return on the offering, shopping for the very best deal possible for their members and, thus, offering the credit card as a genuine benefit of membership. *Or* your organization might look for the best deal *for itself*, getting a hefty kickback on the offer and, thus, creating another way for members to support the organization after having already paid dues.

In the latter scenario, the card will be positioned and presented as a great benefit to members. But it won't be, because the organization offering the card will get 0.5% of everything you charge on the card, or perhaps 25 cents per transaction, or maybe simply a finder's fee (or bounty, really) for everyone who signs up. And you will wind up paying more overall to finance your organization's piece of the pie.

My professional organization is the Authors Guild. The Guild recently offered its members a MasterCard on absolutely lousy terms designed, I assume, to make money for the Guild. No thanks. That's the kind of professional fraternity I just don't need. How did I know the card's terms? I took time to read them. It will only take you a few minutes now that you know what to look for.

Charity Credit Cards

Charity credit cards are another matter. There might be an inflated interest rate, but the charity sponsoring the cards gets a small percentage on every purchase you make with the card. If you pay off your monthly balance punctually, you won't care so much about the high percentage rate attached to the card. And your favorite charity will get the benefit of a percentage of your transactions. There is a Wilderness Society MasterCard and VISA Card, a Covenant House MasterCard, and so on. And they all represent painless ways of doing some good so long as you pay off your balance every month, but watch out for those high interest rates.

A FEW MORE IMPORTANT FACTS ABOUT CREDIT CARDS

Fact 1: Department store credit cards are generally less attractive than VISA, MasterCard, or Discover. They have lower credit limits, and they often have higher interest rates. Also, they usually charge interest from the date of purchase. Generally, it is best to use your bankcard for purchases from large retailers such as Macys or Sears or J.C. Penney who offer their own credit cards.

Fact 2: If you are a chronic charger, addicted to high debt, you should probably stay away from American Express, Carte Blanche, and Diners Club. These Travel & Entertainment cards have no spending limit. The guarantor of your bankcard has imposed a preset credit-limit at which you'll be forced to stop buying things; hopefully, before you crash and burn.

Fact 3: Interest rates and annual fees for various MasterCards, VISA Cards, and Discover Cards vary greatly according to who issues them. Each issuing bank sets its own rules. It pays to shop around.

Fact 4: Be prepared to pay a higher interest rate, without a grace period, for *cash advances* on your credit card. Avoid taking cash advances at high interest rates. And avoid cards offered by banks, which insist you take an initial cash advance as a precondition for qualifying for their card.

Fact 5: Lenders ask for a modest payment every month. That's ideally what they'd like to have from you. No more. No less. But be advised that the minimum payment will leave you, as the old saying says, "forever in their debt." Pay the most you possibly can on that debt until it is gone. And once it is gone, make it stay gone.

Fact 6: It is a mistake to have too many credit cards. Too many credit cards can cause you to be turned down for other, more important lines of credit. This is true even if you don't use the credit lines associated with your many credit cards. And it is true even if you have a strong record of paying off every debt promptly.

Fact 7: You may be tempted to think that having many lines of credit, left unused, demonstrates to a potential lender that you have a certain degree of discipline and reliability. But having a lot of unused, unsecured credit available to you actually works against you when go for big loans such as a mortgage. The mortgage bank does not know whether or not you will ever max out all that credit you have on hand. There is nothing to stop you from doing so. And should you suddenly slip the reins of financial discipline and max out those lines of credit, you probably would not have enough cash-flow to service your credit card balances and pay your household expenses. And your potential mortgage banker is not going to want to take the risk. He or she would rather you simply did not have the credit available to you.

AVOID CREDIT CARD REGISTRATION SERVICES

You've seen the solicitations. These services offer to keep a list of all your cards and their issuers. If your wallet or purse are stolen or lost, you make one call to the Credit Card

Registration Service and then the Service calls all your issuers and cancels your cards. For this the Registration Service charges you an annual fee. Skip it. Odds are your cards will never be stolen. Odds are, if they are stolen, you'll be able to manage dialing two or three 800 numbers to cancel the cards yourself. This is not hard.

IF YOUR CARD IS LOST OR STOLEN

Should your credit card (or travel-and-entertainment card) be lost or stolen, be sure to call the card's underwriter immediately and report the missing card. You will generally only be responsible for the first $50 in charges made on the card *after you've reported your loss*. So it is very important to make those calls ASAP. Of course, the numbers you need to call are found on the cards themselves, which you will no longer have. So be sure to write down the relevant telephone numbers, along with your various credit and travel-and-entertainment card numbers, on a sheet of paper that you do not keep in your wallet or purse.

USING YOUR CREDIT CARD OVER THE NET

You should *only* use your credit card on the Net with vendors who offer Netscape or Microsoft Internet Explorer-secured transactions. For this, of course, you need to be using the Netscape browser or Microsoft Internet Explorer. Netscape and Microsoft Internet Explorer feature the industry-standard SSL protocol and RSA encryption for secure communications, server authentication with digital "signatures," and complete message integrity. Thus, Netscape and Microsoft will protect the financial and personal information you exchange with vendors on-line.

In the absence of Netscape or Microsoft Explorer security on *both ends* of an Internet transaction, giving out your credit card information on the Net is akin to leaving your credit-card carbons on a store-counter, or giving out your credit-card information over a conversation on a cell-phone. But the Internet magnifies the risk. While your credit-card carbon is tempting to just one predator lurking near the Macy's cash-register, the digital imprint of your credit-card information in unsecured cyberspace is tempting to millions of predators.

In the absence of Netscape or Microsoft Explorer security, your best bet for transacting purchases over the Net is to set up an account with one of the new breed of "virtual bankers" such as First Virtual (the Web address is *http://fv.com/*). The First Virtual payment system enables safe transactions for Internet users. First Virtual's system is secure, accessible, low-cost, convenient, and can handle both large and small transactions. Check in at the First Virtual Web site to learn how to establish a First Virtual account off-line, and thereby empower yourself with First Virtual "cybercash" to spend—safely and securely—with merchants on the Net.

INTERNET RESOURCES RELATED TO CREDIT CARDS AND T&E CARDS

As you surf the World Wide Web, you may encounter sites that discuss credit issues such as debt-to-income ratios, as well as sites that promote a specific company's credit or travel-and-entertainment cards. The following site list should help you locate the resources you need.

AMERICAN MUSEUM OF NATURAL HISTORY GOLD MASTERCARD/CUSTOM VISA

http://www.webapply.com/amnh

Here's a way to support the (fantastic) American Museum of Natural History in New York, at no extra cost to you. In fact, it may even save you money. There are no annual fees. The interest rate is high after the first year, but if you don't carry a balance, who cares? You may request the AMNH custom-designed Visa alone or in combination with the AMNH Gold MasterCard. The combination account accesses the same credit line. Assuming you don't carry a credit card balance, you come out ahead. And so does the American Museum of Natural History, because the issuing bank makes a contribution to the Museum for every new card issued and every time you use the card(s) to make a purchase. The contributions add up fast. Thousands have chosen to carry these cards to date, and the Museum has received over $2,000,000 in contributions from the program. These are the details: As I said before, there is no annual fee. For the first year you get a 5.9% annual percentage rate on balance transfers and cash advance checks, but you pay a significantly higher rate on new charges not paid in full. Interested? You can apply right on-line.

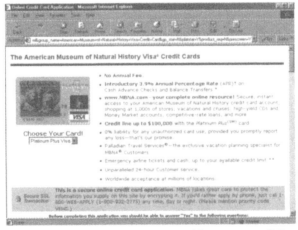

Figure 14.2 American Museum of Natural History Gold MasterCard/Custom Visa.

AMERICAN EXPRESS HOME PAGE

http://www.americanexpress.com

At the American Express home page you can learn all about American Express, its cards, and its cardmember services as well as traveler's checks and other products. Also check out American

Express University, a Web resource for college students allowing them to explore exotic locales on-line, write resumes on-line, and (of course) apply for student cards on-line.

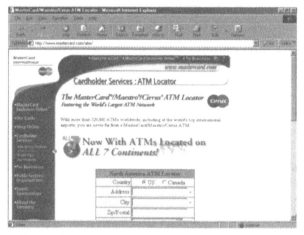

Figure 14.3 American Express Home Page.

MasterCard International ATM Locator

http://www.mastercard.com/atm

Need cash in a strange city? No problem. Using this handy on-line ATM locator you'll find maps and listings for over 200,000 MasterCard/Cirrus ATMs worldwide. Specify the city and street name where you are, and this automated system will direct you to the nearest ATMs. Currently, data is available for Brussels, Chicago, Hong Kong, London, Los Angeles, New York, Singapore, and Sydney. But MasterCard promises to be adding more cities soon, with Paris and Rome coming on-line shortly.

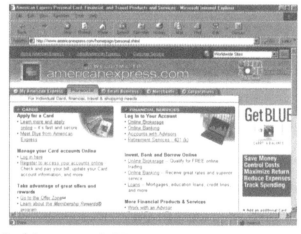

Figure 14.4 MasterCard International ATM Locator.

MASTERCARD PRODUCTS ON THE NET

http://www.mastercard.com/ourcards

The worldwide information source gives you details on MasterCards and which one is right for you. You can even apply right online.

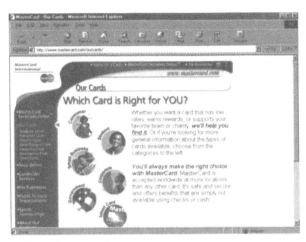

Figure 14.5 MasterCard Products on the Net.

NATURE CONSERVANCY MASTERCARD

http://www.webapply.com/tnc

The Nature Conservancy MasterCard is free and offers all the same bells and whistles as the American Museum of Natural History card described above. For every purchase you make, a contribution is made to the Nature Conservancy. And it does not cost you a dime, so long as you pay that monthly balance in full every month.

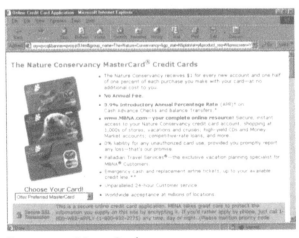

Figure 14.6 Nature Conservancy MasterCard.

Obtaining and Understanding Key Economic Indicators

Admit it. You are vaguely aware of them already: the fabled *Key Economic Indicators*. You may not be sure what they are, but you know that whenever numbers related to one or another of them are announced, there are sometimes wild swings in stock and bond prices. You, like so many other of us financial novices, are not sure why a few esoteric economic measurements can cause such upheaval. But you know when it happens, because all the financial pundits of television come on to discuss and analyze yet another "roller coaster" day for the Dow, a day of volatility fueled by "key economic reports" that showed something different than what these same pundits forecast just 24-hours earlier.

There are hundreds of these reports generated every month, but only about seven or eight that you really have to pay attention to. These are what we called the Key Economic Indicators. The Key Indicators are:

- The Consumer Price Index (calculated the 4th week of every month)

- The Gross National Product Index (calculated around the 20th of every month)

- The Housing Starts Index (calculated between the 17th and 20th of every month)

- The Industrial Production Index (calculated mid-month)

- The Personal Income Index (calculated the third week of every month)

- The Producer Price Index [PPI] (calculated the third Monday of every month)

- The Retail Sales Index (calculated the second week of every month)

- The Unemployment Index (calculated the second Monday of every month)

- The Composite of Leading Indicators for Interest Rate Cycles (calculated usually on the first day of each month and comprising an average of the Manufacturing Capacity Utilization Rate Index, New Housing Starts Index, Construction Contracts Index, Manufacturing Inventory/Sales Ratio Index, and the Composite Index of Lagging Indicators.)

Generally speaking, when any of these indexes save for Unemployment goes up, the stock and bond markets are more likely than not to *go down*. Why is this? Well, good economic news such as higher wages, increased housing starts, increased industrial production, and so on tends to suggest the possibility that the economy might "overheat," as the saying goes, resulting in inflation. If Alan Greenspan and other gurus of the Federal Reserve decide that inflation is threatening, they are more than likely to raise interest rates, which is almost always bad news for stocks and bonds. If, on the other hand, the economic news is bad, with housing starts and employment and prices down, the Fed will at worst leave interest rates where they are or perhaps (hallelujah!) slash interest rates to jump-start the economy. And this would be a very good for stock and bond values.

All of these economic indicators are published as they are available in the *Wall Street Journal*, the *New York Times*, the *Washington Post*, the *Los Angeles Times*, and other major city dailies across the country and around the world. You can also find descriptions of these economic indicators on-line.

LEADING ECONOMIC INDICATORS OF THE INTEREST RATE CYCLE

http://staff.uwsuper.edu/homepage/rbeam/Paris11.htm

Come here for the Composite Index of Leading Indicators, Manufacturing Capacity Utilization Rate, Index of Help Wanted Advertising Nationwide, New Housing Starts, Construction Contracts, Manufacturing Inventory/Sales Ratio Index, and Composite Index of Lagging Indicators.

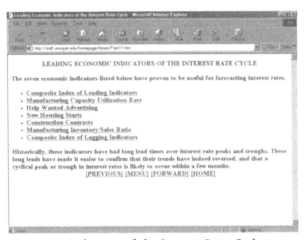

Figure 14.7 Leading Economic Indicators of the Interest Rate Cycle.

CREDIT CARD CATALOG

http://www.creditcardcatalog.com

This site is a complete directory of credit cards you can apply for online. You can check out every Visa, Mastercard, American Express, and Discover card available on the Internet. You can find cards tied to your school or favorite sports team or credit cards that pay YOU back.

Figure 14.8 Credit Card Catalog.

RESOURCE LIST OF BOOKS – CONSUMER CREDIT LAWS

http://www.emich.edu/public/coe/nice/rlcclaws.html

Here is a list of books dealing with consumer credit laws. These books are often available at public libraries. The list includes such titles as *The Ultimate Credit Handbook: How to Double Your Credit* and *Have A Lifetime of Great Credit.*

Figure 14.9 Resource List of Books – Consumer Credit Laws.

AVOID CREDIT CARD FRAUD

http://www.eqmoney.com/rpr.htm

This site provides free information on how to repair your credit after credit card fraud, how to avoid future fraud, how to spot credit card fraud on your credit report and stop fraudulent credit card activities.

Figure 14.10 Avoid Credit Card Fraud.

QUESTION LINKS

http://www.creditcardfreedom.com

This site provides a list of questions that may represent you as a cardholder and helps guide you through the site. It includes card specific questions, credit card debt management and credit card reviews.

Figure 14.11 Question Links.

CREDIT CARD TIPS

http://www.fraud.org/telemarketing/teletips/cardtip.htm

When it comes to credit cards, you need to read the fine print. If you receive an offer for a pre-approved credit card or if they say they can help you get a credit card, get all the details first. Find out what the interest rate will be and how long you will be paying it.

CREDIT CARD TIPS

http://www.fraud.org/telemarketing/teletips/
cardtip.htm

CREDIT CARD DEALS

http://www.creditnet.coom/ccnlstx.html

CREDIT CARD MENU

http://www.gromco.com/cgi-bin/credit

COMPARE CREDIT CARDS CALCULATOR

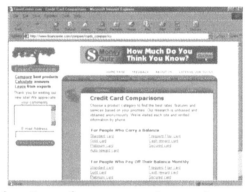

http://www.financenter.com/compare/
cards_compare.fcs

DISCOVER, PRIVATE ISSUE AND BRAVO CARD INFORMATION

http://www.discovercard.com

FINANCECENTER CREDIT CARD DEPARTMENT

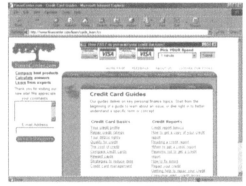

http://www.financenter.com/learn/
cards_learn.fcs

RAM CardTrak Research and Publishing

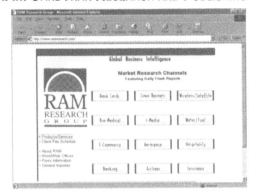

http://www.ramresearch.com

Credit Card Fraud Prevention and Cures

http://www.state.id.us/ag/consumer/tips/
crdtfrd.htm

Consumer Complaints Resources for Credit Cards

http://members.tripod.com/runeholt/
consumer.html

Information for Consumers and Executives

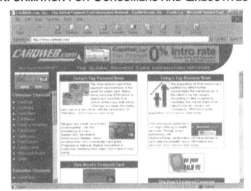

http://www.cardweb.com

Credit Card Comparison

http://www.eyeoncredit.com

Consumer Card Report

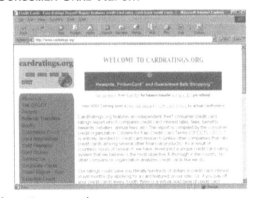

http://www.cardratings.org

CONSUMER GUIDE TO CREDIT

http://www.debtwizards.com

ABCGUIDES CREDIT CARD RATES GUIDE

http://www.abcguides.com/creditcards

CONSUMER CONNECTION

http://strategis.ic.gc.ca/OCA

CREDIT CARD STRATEGIES

http://www.tbwt.com/interaction/cards/html/1.htm

SHOULD I USE MY CREDIT CARD ON THE INTERNET?

http://www.craytech.com/Unlimited/credit.htm

CREDIT RESOURCES

http://www.resinets.com/search4/credit.htm

CHAPTER 15

COLLEGE LOANS AND OTHER SOLUTIONS FOR FINANCING HIGHER EDUCATION

The only college with free tuition is the school of hard knocks. — Scott Nearing

The cost of college is the only thing on the planet that's growing faster than your kids. Based on the average charges for the 1999-2000 school year, the average tuition and fees for one year at an in-state public university is $3,356 and for one year at a private university is $15,380. The annual rise for tuition is steadily increasing at a rate of 5 percent a year. At that rate, in 2006, tuition for an in-state university will be $20,353 a year, and a private university will be $93,276.

Luckily, the World Wide Web is loaded with tools and references to help me, and you, seek out the best college loans available, the shrewdest financing solutions possible, and the range of scholarship options beyond those associated with basketball.

PAY FOR PRESTIGE? FINE. IT WON'T GUARANTEE A GOOD JOB

The broad pronouncement of years gone by, which said that a college degree (*any* college degree) would assure you a better job and higher income, is no longer true. Also untrue is the old popular wisdom which said that a degree, *any* degree, from a prestigious Ivy-League college was inherently better than a degree, any degree, from a non-Ivy college. To be frank, it matters less today where you study than what you study.

Those who work in the publishing business in Manhattan routinely hire Ivy-League English majors fresh out of Harvard and Yale as editorial assistants starting at $18,000 a year—giving them a job and salary they were "damn glad" to get. At the same time, it is common practice to hire junior programmers and systems designers fresh out of the State University of New York or the City University System who start at $35,000 a year. And you would usually have to compete with other employers to get them. This was a few years ago. The programmers from the public colleges had probably paid $20,000 total for their educations. The poets from Harvard and Yale had probably paid $80,000 for their educations. You do the math.

MORE MATH: THE FAST MATH OF FINANCIAL AID

Currently, if you have a household income of $60,000 or more, your hope for financial aid, like mine, is doomed. The amount of financial aid you are likely to be able to get for your kid (barring a full athletic or academic scholarship) is none. If your household income is in the $30,000 to $50,000 range, you'll get some financial aid, but only after you go into "hock" in a big way. If your household income is $25,000 or less, you are about to qualify for a good deal—most of the financial aid on the planet is reserved just for you. I'm not complaining. That's exactly as it should be.

AID BASED ON NEED: WHAT A CONCEPT

All college aid is based on a calculation of *need*. Of course. What could be more logical? But exactly how is *need* calculated? At first it seems quite straightforward. Officially, your *need* is defined by an easy equation that is calculated *annually*. (Yes, you and the financial-aid officers at your son's or daughter's school will get to do this dance *every year*.)

Step 1. Take all your income and assets and add them up: home equity, cash in banks, the value of stocks and bonds you own, mutual funds, and so on. The only items you need not include are funds you have in tax-deferred annuities, life-insurance vestitures, and moneys in retirement plans such as 401(k)s, Keoghs, and IRAs.

Step 2. Subtract the cash you need to live on for a year, plus a small savings allowance. These amounts are not random. You may think you know your cost-of-living, but as usual the Federal Government thinks it knows better. The Feds have denominated your cost-of-living as part of the formal *need-analysis* formula that all financial-aid officers are mandated to use. And guess what? The Feds think you can live on very, very little. The financial-aid officers for your child's college will give you information sheets, which change regularly, telling you exactly how little. And rest assured, the Feds have failed to factor into their calculation your need to go to Chile in August in order to ski.

Step 3. What is left after the subtraction called for in Step 2? Probably plenty. The result of the calculation, which will probably be the bulk of your net worth, is what (from a financial-aid officer's perspective) you officially have "available" to spend for college tuition, room, and board. Lucky you! You suddenly seem rich! You don't need much financial aid at all, do you?

Step 4. Look at the total price of the school your son or daughter dearly desires to go to, on which he or she has mortgaged every hope, and for which you will probably end up mortgaging your house.

Step 5. Subtract the amount derived in Step 3 from the total cost of the school.

Step 6. Subtract whatever amount you hope your son or daughter will pay out of his or her income or savings.

Step 7. The balance, which in most cases is puny, is your financial need. The financial aid officers at your son's or daughter's college will help you with "aid" to fill this gap. But the "aid" they offer very well might be a loan of some sort, including possibly a federally-subsidized or guaranteed student loan. Gee, thanks.

The good news, if you can call it that, is that you'll probably wind up getting a lot more aid for your child's senior year than you did for your child's freshman year. Why? Two reasons. First, you'll probably be a lot poorer. Secondly, if trends continue, the cost of the school will have gone up at least 10% over the course of your child's undergraduate program.

USE THE LOOPHOLES

The less you are worth, the more aid your child will qualify for. There are ways to minimize your worth. There are ways, without lying, to reduce the size of your reported assets:

1. What is your house *really* worth? The college-aid application is not a form on which you maximize your home's potential value. Don't lie, but state the lowest price you would realistically take rather than the highest price you'd like to get.

2. If you are making a major expenditure in the years immediately before your child enrolls in college, such as buying a car, don't take out an auto-loan to finance the car. Instead, borrow against your home. This will reduce your equity, making you look $15,000 or $20,000 or $30,000 poorer on paper, depending on how nice a car you drive. (The poorer you look on paper, the richer you'll look on the road!)

3. Consider taking a course or two yourself. If you enroll in college or graduate school, even part-time, the amount college aid officers will expect you to contribute to your son's or daughter's college war-chest will be reduced considerably.

4. Do you own your own business? There may be opportunities with which you can legitimately restructure your income.

5. Do you have a lot of cash lying around in the bank? Take a chunk of it, as large as possible, and stick it in a tax-deferred annuity. Financial aid officers do not count tax-deferred annuities, IRA/Keogh/401(k) moneys, or vested interest in life-insurance policies when calculating your net worth.

6. If you can do so without taking a big hit in declining stock prices, and if you do not need your stock equity to put toward tuition, do what you can to avoid capital gains during the years your child is in school. Hang onto those long-term stocks a little longer, because your capital gains as income and will affect your financial-aid qualification for the following year.

7. If you are a relatively young parent with the promise of a profitable and long professional life after your kid or kids graduate from college, consider financing college with a home equity loan. First of all, you'll get the best interest rates on loans secured with your house. Second, since a home-equity loan is a mortgage, the interest is deductible— unlike interest on a standard student loan. Third, you'll be knocking down your net worth by reducing the amount of equity you hold in your home (just as with item 2 above). Thus, you'll be setting yourself to qualify for more financial aid next year. (You tricky devil!) But a word of caution: If you are an older parent, hoping to retire with a nest egg not long after your kid or kids get out of school, you may want to think twice about second mortgages. How will you pay back the note? What will you retire on?

FASTWEB: FINANCIAL AID RESEARCH THROUGH THE WEB

The most valuable tool on the Web for those trying to figure out how to finance a child's college education is *fastWeb*, which is located at *http://www.studentservices.com/fastweb*, shown below in Figure 15.1.

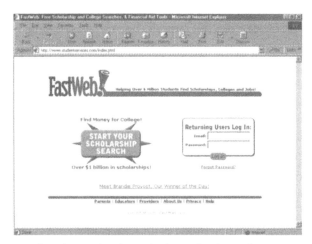

Figure 15.1 The Financial Aid Search Through the Web (fastWeb).

fastWeb stands for *Financial Aid Search Through the Web*. The site provides a free, searchable database of more than 180,000 private-sector scholarships, fellowships, grants, and loans. Previously used for years by college administrators and financial aid officers across the United States, *fastWEB* is now available free to students and their parents via the Web courtesy of the Financial Aid Information Page of Students Services, Inc.

To use *fastWEB*, a student fills out a detailed profile through a series of on-line forms. After the forms are complete, *fastWEB* responds within 15 minutes (via e-mail deposited in the student's personal in-box at the *fastWEB* site) with a list of matching award programs. Each entry in this list includes a deadline for applying, a list of required majors, the amount of the award, a short description, and contact information.

fastWEB has several nice features. As new scholarships are added to the database (as they are at a rate of approximately 1,200 per day!), they are compared with the student's profile and any matching programs are added to the student's mailbox. Students can check this mailbox at their convenience to find out about newly announced programs. Then, students can use *fastWEB* to generate a form letter for requesting applications and further information about the programs, and print this letter directly from their Web browser.

In addition to the free *fastWEB*, Student Services, Inc. also provides several fee-based services, such as the *Money for College Directory*. You'll find information on this and other Student Services programs at the *fastWEB* home page. The best way to learn more about *fastWEB* is to log-on and use it. The second best way, I suppose, is to call the toll-free number that Student Services has set up to answer questions about *fastWEB*. That number is 1-800-fastWEB (1-800-327-8932).

THE TRUTH ABOUT PELL

Claiborne Pell was a senator in Rhode Island for over 30 years. He is one of the last of that great generation of post-World War II senators that included Lyndon Johnson, Barry Goldwater, Hubert Humphrey, John Kennedy, and Lloyd Bentsen. Pell will be remembered for many things, not the least of which is the establishment of the government's Pell Grants. Pell designed these grants to help low-income students. But even if you are not "poor," your child should apply for a Pell Grant (which is done by simply checking a box on your college financial-aid application), whether you think he or she will qualify or not. Why? Because *applying* for a Pell Grant is a prerequisite for other federal programs in which your middle-class child may qualify, such as the federal guaranteed-student-loan program.

COMMERCIAL SCHOLARSHIPS SEARCH SERVICES

Scholarship search services are companies that charge you a fee to compare your profile against a database of scholarship programs and report any matches. In other words, they charge you for services that you can do yourself with *fastWEB*, for free. You will find a large number of scholarship search services listed in the Internet Resources section of this chapter—all of them clearly marked with the word *commercial*. But, before you use any of them, you should use the free search service *fastWEB*. And also, check out the other noncommercial scholarship resources I have listed for the Web. Only if these do not yield adequate results, should you consider hiring a commercial scholarship search service.

It is important that you use extreme caution when you use a commercial scholarship search service, as fraud is rampant. A sign that the service you are dealing with may be "bogus" will be the nature of the guarantee they offer. Some offer guarantees that require you to submit rejection letters from all sources before they will consider a refund of fees. Others offer refunds only in the form of a US Savings Bond. You want a search service that provides you with an unqualified "satisfaction guaranteed or your money back." If you don't get this guarantee, move on to the next option.

THE VARIOUS SCHOLARSHIP DATABASES

Another important thing to remember when you shop for a commercial scholarship search service is that most of these outfits work from the same small cluster of databases. If two scholarship search services use the same database, you will get exactly the same result using the cheaper of the two services. The leading databases are CAS, CASHE, EIS, FAFC, FUNDS and NSRS. Not only is this group a small one, but FAFC is nothing more than a licensed version of the FUNDS database, and the FUNDS database is owned by the same company that compiles the CASHE database. So you can assume a large margin of the databases overlap.

- The CAS database is maintained by College Academic Service (CAS) of Provo, Utah. CAS claims that their database contains more than 300,000 sources of non-federal financial aid.

- The CASHE database is maintained by EdTech, which says the database contains "between 150,000 and 200,000 listings." To me, 50,0000 seems a very wide margin of error. But so be it. That's the level of vagueness EdTech seems to think consumers will be willing to put up with.

- The *EIS database* is maintained by Educational Information Services (EIS) and claims 200,000 listings.

- The *FAFC database* of Sheridan, Indiana, claims 150,000 listings and is a licensed version of the *FUNDS database* from Nebraska.

- The *NSRS database* is maintained by the National Scholarship Research Service (NSRS) and claims 200,000 listings.

SCHOLARSHIP SEARCH SERVICE PRICING

The average fee charged by scholarship search services is $50, although some will charge you as much as $250. If a firm wants to charge you more than $50, move on. Find another vendor. There are plenty of them to choose from. I have not included commercial search services in this chapter's Internet Resources listing which charge more than $50. Wherever I have found a fee considerably below $50, I've been sure to include a mention of that fact in my description of the service.

NO-NEED SCHOLARSHIPS

Is your kid a star? A whiz? The presumptive valedictorian? Are those SAT scores through the roof? Is that high-school GPA something to die for? Or is your kid, while only a moderately bright student, simply the best darned soccer player west of the Mississippi?

Well, here's one more bit of luck for you. It doesn't matter how loaded you are, your kid can most likely go to school for free. Many schools are dying to get their hands on your little Einstein or your little Pele. Forget the Ivy League schools, where Einsteins (if not Peles) are a dime a dozen. At virtually all the other *equally as good* (there, I said it) private colleges in the country you'll find money, big money, waiting for students with precisely defined academic or sports talents. Look into these options using *fastWEB*.

COLLEGE LOANS ON THE WEB

One good place to shop for college loans on the Web is the home page of Livingston & Associates (*http://users.netropolis.net/rogera/college.htm*), shown below in Figure 15.2. Livingston & Associates is a national service company putting borrowers together with lenders under the government's Higher Education Act. Their goal is to make sure that no child wishing to receive a college education will be turned away due to lack of proper funding. Livingston & Associates not only puts students and parents together with the loans needed to attend the college, but does so with a *carefully planned program* that will lead to *manageable levels of debt* after graduation.

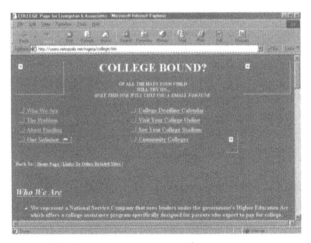

Figure 15.2 Shopping for college loans at Livingston & Associates.

INTERNET RESOURCES RELATED TO COLLEGE LOANS AND SCHOLARSHIPS

As you surf the World Wide Web, you may encounter sites that discuss college loans, scholarships, grants, and other tuition-based topics. The following site list should help you locate the resources you need.

ILLINOIS STUDENT ASSISTANCE COMMISSION SCHOLARSHIP SEARCH

http://www.isac1.org

The nonprofit Illinois Student Assistance Commission (ISAC) runs Higher-EdNet, a scholarship search service that searches the CASHE database (200,000 listings) for a fee of just $10. Their Web page also provides information about grant, scholarship, and loan programs administered by ISAC.

Figure 15.3 *Illinois Student Assistance Commission Scholarship Search.*

INDIANA COLLEGE PLACEMENT AND ASSESSMENT CENTER SCHOLARSHIP SEARCH

http://icpac.indiana.edu

The nonprofit Indiana College Placement and Assessment Center (ICPAC) will conduct a scholarship search using the CASHE database for just $14 and also runs a useful on-line financial aid estimation service, which you can use for just $5.

Figure 15.4 *Indiana College Placement and Assessment Center Scholarship Search.*

MICHIGAN DEPARTMENT OF EDUCATION SCHOLARSHIP SEARCH

http://www.mde.state.mi.us

This nonprofit service uses the MI-CASHE scholarship database, which is a version of the CASHE database specialized for Michigan residents with additional Michigan-specific scholarship sources. The fee for a search is just $15.

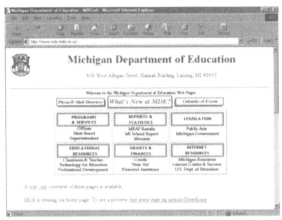

Figure 15.5 Michigan Department of Education Scholarship Search.

Financial Help from MasterCard

Ok, so in Chapter 14 we we're a little rough on the credit-card companies. To help get back on your good side, MasterCard offers guidelines students can follow to improve their chances for obtaining financial aid and steps they should start to perform now to better manage their own finances. Check out this site at *http://www.mastercard.com/college/funds.htm.*

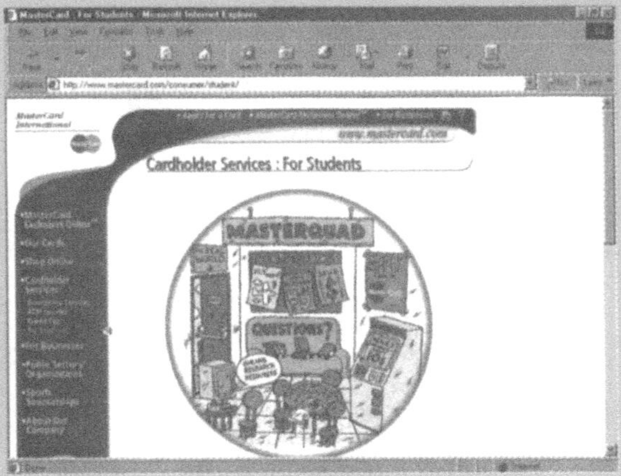

Figure 15.6 MasterCard's suggestions about financial aid.

SALLIE MAE CASHE FREE SCHOLARSHIP SERVICE

http://www.cashe.com

CASHE is a free student financial aid service containing thousands of scholarships, grants, tuition waivers, internships, fellowships, and loans to help finance a college education. CASHE can also assist with the entire financial aid process.

Figure 15.7 Sallie Mae CASHE Free Scholarships Service.

COLLEGE SCHOLARSHIP SEARCH AND FINANCIAL AID INFORMATION

http://www.turbograd.com/scholarship/scholarship_aid.asp

Check out the Scholarship Match at TurboGrad and find the scholarship that is made just for you. TurboGrad has awards totaling over $2 billion.

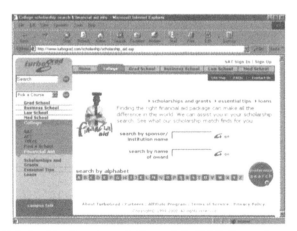

Figure 15.8 College Scholarship Search and Financial Aid Information.

COLLEGE CONNECTION SCHOLARSHIPS

http://www.collegescholarships.com

Here, a new, free college scholarship is posted each month for graduate, undergraduate, vocational/technical, and international college and university students. The site also provides a customized quality search. This free information includes all of the details you need to apply now, including eligibility requirements, deadlines, amount, contact name, address, phone number, and Web site of the scholarship sponsor.

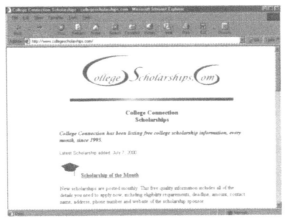

Figure 15.9 College Connection Scholarships.

SPORTS AND ACADEMIC SCHOLARSHIPS

http://www.academic-sports.com

This site provides a sports scholarship search network for men and women, providing the latest search techniques for student athletes. It matches the athlete's report to college profiles and provides a network of prospective recruits for college coaches to choose.

Figure 15.10 Sports and Academic Scholarships.

AMERICAN JOURNALISM REVIEW'S GRANTS, AWARDS AND SCHOLARSHIPS

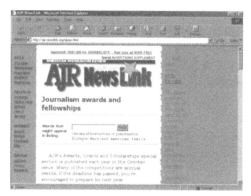

http://ajr.newslink.org/ajraw.html

ART SCHOLARSHIPS AND COMPETITIONS

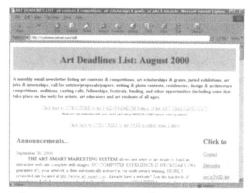

http://custwww.xersei.com/adl

ACADEMIC SCHOLARSHIP SEARCH SERVICES

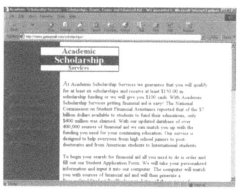

http://www.galaxymall,com/scholarships

LOCI MONEYFINDER

http://www.studentservices.com/loci

SOUTHWEST STUDENT SERVICES CORPORATION SCHOLARSHIP SEARCH

http://www.sssc.com

SCHOLARSHIPS AND FELLOWSHIPS

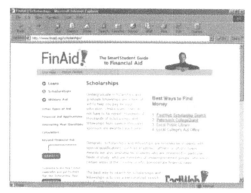

http://www.finaid.org/scholarships

TAJ CONSULTING GROUP SCHOLARSHIP SEARCH (COMMERCIAL)

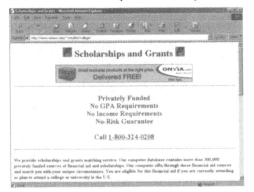

http://www.taj.com/~consltnt/college

UNIVERSITY LINKS: COLLEGE INFORMATION PAGE

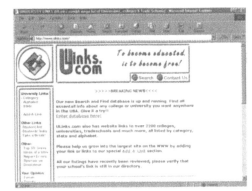

http://www.ULinks.com

SALLIE MAE'S ONLINE SCHOLARSHIP SERVICE

http://scholarships.salliemae.com/context.html

FINANCIAL AID

http://www.du.edu/career/
internetfinancialaid.html

COLLEGIATE SCHOLARSHIP NETWORK

http://www.collegiatescholarship.com/noframes/
about.shtml

ATTENTION STUDENT ATHLETES

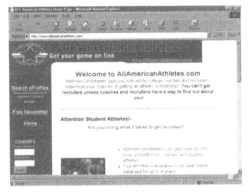

http://www.allamericanathletes.com

SCHOLARSHIP GIVEAWAY

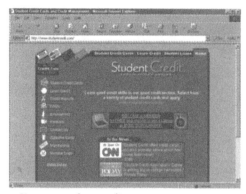

http://www.studentcredit.com

OKLAHOMA STATE UNIVERSITY OFFICE OF SCHOLARSHIPS AND FINANCIAL AID

http://www.okstate.edu/finaid

RICE UNIVERSITY – FINANCIAL AID AND SCHOLARSHIPS

http://www.rice.edu/academic/finaid.html

COLLEGE SCHOLARSHIPS

http://www.of411.com/scholarships.htm

WSU OFFICE OF SCHOLARSHIPS AND FINANCIAL AID

http://www.financialaid.wayne.edu

THE RHODES SCHOLARSHIPS

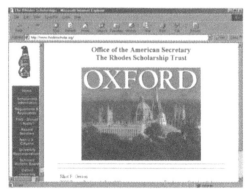

http://www.rhodesscholar.org

IOWA STATE UNIVERSITY – COLLEGE OF EDUCATION – SCHOLARSHIPS

http://www.educ.iastate.edu/scholar

STUDENT AID SCHOLARSHIPS SEARCH SERVICES

http://www.psu.edu/studentaid/html/ search1b1.html

SCHOLARSHIPS FOR ART

http://www.free-4u.com/arts.htm

WEBER STATE UNIVERSITY SCHOLARSHIP OFFICE

http://www.weber.edu/scholarships

FREE ART SCHOLARSHIPS

http://angelfire.lycos.com/cgi-bin/search

THE ART OF WINNING COLLEGE SCHOLARSHIPS

http://www.winscholarships.com

SCHOOL OF ART, DRAMA, & MUSIC – AWARDS & SCHOLARSHIPS

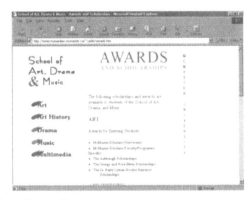

http://www.humanities.mcmaster.ca/~sadm/awards.htm

ART PROGRAM SCHOLARSHIPS

http://www.sulross.edu/~finearts/artsch.html

GRANTS ONLINE

http://studentloan.citibank.com

GRANTS FROM THE U.S. GOVERNMENT

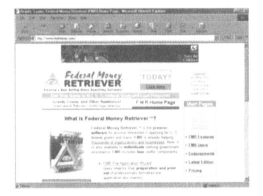

http://www.fedmoney.com

SCHOOL LAW & FUNDING

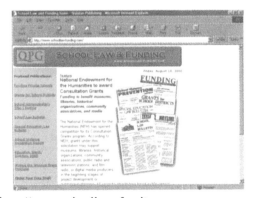

http://www.schoollaw-funding.com

FIND PRIVATE AND PUBLIC GRANT SOURCES

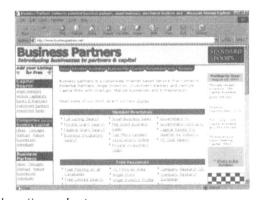

http://www.businesspartners.net

FULBRIGHT SCHOLARSHIPS

http://www.stanford.edu/dept/icenter/orc/scholarships/fbintro.html

WELCOME TO SCHOLARSHIP CONNECTION – BERKELEY

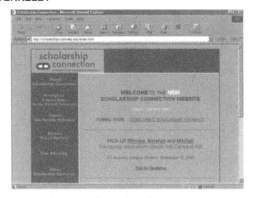

http://scholarships.berkeley.edu

NYU OFFICE OF FINANCIAL AID

http://www.nyu.edu/financial.aid

BYU SCHOLARSHIPS

http://ar.byu.edu/dept_scholarships/scholar.html

ASU SCHOLARSHIPS

http://www.asu.edu/fa/scholarships

UCLA DEPARTMENT OF MUSIC – AWARDS AND SCHOLARSHIPS

http://www.music.ucla.edu/GenInfo/AwardsSchols.html

CHAPTER 16

FINANCING YOUR CAR

You ask what drives my business? Debt drives my business! Debt on four fast wheels! — Henry Ford

THE AMERICAN DREAM

The American dream is a chicken in every pot, a secure home for every family, and a good school for every child. The American dream is a painting by Norman Rockwell come to life. It is peace and prosperity, not to mention liberty and justice and fraternity for all. Oh, and it is one more thing. The American dream is one hot set of wheels in every driveway. Or maybe two. Or even three. All of them have cell-phones and sunroofs. All of them have CD players and BOSE speakers. All of them are bright and shiny and comfortable. All of them are expensive. And very few of them are owned by the people who drive them.

Remember way back in time when people used to actually *own* cars? I mean, a few still do. I still do. But remember when *most people* actually owned their cars? Do you remember the Rambler? It was the Commodore Computer of automobiles—there in a big way one minute, and completely gone the next. People paid cash-down for a brand-new Rambler in 1961 and then drove it into the ground for thirteen years. There were no bells and whistles. No power windows. There was no AC. No sunroof. I don't think the radio even received FM. Yet, I also don't think those Ramblers spent one day in the shop.

But them days is over, Beavis. Like Apple IIs and Commodore 64s, they're never comin' back.

BUY OR LEASE? WHICH IS BETTER?

It depends on your position. Specifically, your *cash* position. If you have enough liquidity to pay cash for a car without borrowing that cash*, then it is always cheaper to buy your car outright than to lease it.* But odds are leasing will be less expensive over time than paying off an auto loan. So if you need to borrow, consider leasing.

Leasing is an attractive option for those who want to drive more car than they can really afford. With auto leasing, you can drive a very classy set of wheels for a small deposit and smaller monthly payments than you would with a loan. Leasing is also attractive to people who simply love having new cars all the time and want to make sure they are in line to get a new car every two to three years.

But if you have cash available, you are much better off paying that cash on a more modest vehicle, purchasing it outright, and keeping it in a condition. You could lease a Mercedes or a Saab or buy a brand new Mazda for cash. You could change the oil every three thousand miles and plan to drive the Mazda for the next ten years with an average daily cost for the physical automobile of $4.10 a day for the life of the vehicle (total car cost $15,000). Compare that to an $11.50 lease cost for the same vehicle on a three-year lease ($12,592 total vehicle cost for the life of the lease) at the end of which you own *nothing*.

How Leasing Works

The leasing formula is fairly straightforward. You usually pay a few month's rent up-front as a deposit on a two or three year lease, and then drive away. You are responsible for insurance, maintenance, and small repairs.

Most leases are *closed-end leases*. This means that your costs are fixed. You have no surprises waiting for you when you return the car at the end of the lease. You simply drive up, hand in your keys, and lease a new car. A few leases are *open-end*. You should avoid these leases, even though the open-end lease will usually have a lower monthly cost as compared to a closed-end lease.

Why avoid the lower monthly payment of the open-end lease? Because, with an open-end arrangement, you may well wind up having to make a large balloon payment at the end of the lease.

Your final cost at the conclusion of an open-end lease depends on the car's resale value (aka: the residual value). In the unlikely event that your leasor can sell the car for more than they expected when you signed the lease, you may get a refund. In the likely event that the car's resell value for less that what the leasor expected, you will have to make up the difference to the leasor between what they got and what they thought they were going to get according to the terms of the lease.

Note that some dealers, in offering highly attractive, low-balled monthly payments, do so by having untutored consumers agree to an artificially high residual value that will most assuredly leave the consumer "in the red" at the end of the lease period. You should avoid such residual-value manipulation unless, of course, you plan on winning the Lottery sometime between now and the end of the lease.

Many closed-end leases give you the option to purchase the car yourself at the end of the lease at a prescribed *acquisition cost*. This may or may not be a good deal, depending on how you've treated the car. If you think you'll want to buy the thing, take care of it.

Lastly, be aware that you may be able to "trade out" of a lease (possibly trading out of a three-year lease after year two, and so on) depending on market conditions. If new cars aren't moving and dealers are hungry, they will be anxious to help you "step up" to a newer car sooner than you would normally. Keep an eye on the new-car market. When sales are slow and dealers are falling over themselves to offer attractive purchase and/or lease arrangements, that is the time to discuss a "trade out."

How Long a Lease and How Many Miles?

The longer your lease, the lower your monthly payments will be. But the longer your lease, the longer you will be stuck driving the same vehicle. And there are early termination penalties—often hefty—built into virtually all lease agreements.

If you realistically think you'll want a car for just two or three years before trading it in, then go for the two or three year lease and do not be seduced by the fact that the five-year lease is $30 or $40 a month cheaper. The same goes for miles. If you realistically think you are going to put more miles on your car than the lease allows, then plan ahead and purchase those miles on the front-end, when they will be cheaper.

Many leases allow you only 15,000 miles a year and then slap you with a surcharge (usually around ten cents per mile) payable at the end of the lease period, when you turn in the car. If you realistically plan on driving 25,000 or 30,000 miles a year over the life of your two or three or five-year lease, then negotiate those miles when you are negotiating the lease. You'll wind up paying less for them, perhaps in the five to seven cents-per-mile range.

The Early Termination You Didn't Count on

If your leased car is stolen or demolished, that's an early termination of your lease. The good news is that your insurance will cover the car's market value. The bad news is that you are still liable for the lease and will have to either continue the lease on the ghost of the car or cancel the lease and pay early termination penalties. Meanwhile, you still need transportation and will have to either buy a replacement vehicle or take out yet another lease. Isn't life wonderful?

Where to Find the Cheapest Leases

Don't go to an auto dealer for a lease. I mean don't go anywhere near an auto dealer or an auto dealership except to check-out the look and feel of the car or cars you are interested in. Then, announce that the car is not for you and leave the dealership promptly. Tell the car salespeople you've decided to stick to your 1968 Volkswagen minibus with the Woodstock stickers on the doors and the peace signs on the windows. Then, talk to an independent leasing company. These outfits are easy to find. And they are your best bet in the same way an independent broker is when you are purchasing any kind of insurance. Independent leasing companies carefully track new-car leases in your region. They are the folks who can (and invariably *will*) get you the best price and terms for a lease on the car you want.

THINKING OF MOVING OUT OF STATE?

Then you may not want to lease. Many lease agreements insist that you pay a hefty monthly surcharge if you move the lease-vehicle out of state. Others insist that you convert your lease to a loan and buy the car. In either case, you are in for costly annoyance. Wait till you get to your new home state, and *then* lease a car.

WHEN YOU BORROW TO PURCHASE A CAR: A FEW TIPS

Tip 1: If the business climate is such that auto dealers are starving for business, they will usually offer great financing options for short-term (often two year) loans, which you might be able to pickup for an interest rate of between 4% and 5%. If so, go with it. But if the business climate is such that car dealers are rolling in dough, they will usually try to rip you off with high interest rates for dealer-financing. In such a climate, do not even think of financing through the dealer. You'll get better rates (and longer terms) from your credit union, savings and loan, or a commercial bank (in that order!)

Tip 2: If your dealer's business is good and his/her financing deal unattractive, get approved for an auto loan with the appropriate outside lending institution *before you agree to purchase the car*. Thus, you'll know exactly how much you can spend. But try not to tell the auto-dealer you already have financing until after you are done haggling over price. He or she may come down in price in the hope that you will finance through the dealership at their high interest rate.

Tip 3: An auto-loan's APR reflects the amount of interest the loan will charge Above Prime Rate. For example, if a dealership is offering 2.9% APR financing, that means the interest rate they'll charge you is the current prime rate *plus* 2.9%.

Tip 4: Shop around. Rates for auto loans, as well as rates for just about every other type of loan you can imagine, vary greatly between different institutions. You can probably shave two or three points off the interest rate for your auto loan *if* you take the time to shop around. To start, check out the rates featured at the Web site: *http://www.banx.com/banx/auto/bq-auto.htm*, which offers a useful, constantly updated survey of auto-loan rates nationwide.

Tip 5: If you are in a position where it makes sense for you to knock down your net worth by cutting the amount of equity you hold in your home, and if you want the interest payments for your car-loan to be tax deductible, consider financing your car with a line of credit on your house: a mortgage. This is also how you will get the lowest interest rate. As a bonus, you eliminate the possibility of being upside down in a loan. Don't know what I'm referring to? See Tip 8.

Tip 6: As I've said in another chapter, don't buy credit life insurance from your lender. You ought to be set up so that you have enough regular life insurance to cover all your family's expenses, including the auto loan, in case of your demise. The credit life insurance your lender offers will be overpriced when compared to the same degree of protection as part of your regular life-insurance package.

Tip 7: Stay away from a variable-rate auto loan. Stick with a fixed-rate. You'll save just a lousy 1% in most cases on the initial rate of a variable-rate auto loan as compared to a fixed-rate. But for that lousy 1% you'll be shouldering the risk that rates in subsequent years will go through the roof. This is not a good deal.

Tip 8: If financing your new car with an auto loan (as opposed to a second mortgage), finance only for as long as you plan to actually *own* your car. There is a temptation to stretch the loan out and thereby reduce the monthly payment. A ten year loan obviously costs less monthly (though more *overall*) than a five year loan. But if you finance for too long, and eventually want to trade in your car before the loan is paid, you may not be able to. Why? Because your car will be *upside down*. This means you are in a situation where you owe more on your car than the car is worth. Don't forget that while you build equity in your car with payments on your auto loan, your car is at the same time depreciating in value, and doing so rapidly. If you have a long-term extended car loan, your car's net value may be zero for quite some time.

Financing Used Cars

The best way to finance a used car is the same as the best way to finance a new car—with cash. But if you can't do that, consider a home equity loan rather than a straight used-car auto loan. Why? Used-car loans have higher interest rates than new-car loans, usually by a couple of percentage points. And mortgage loans are almost always a couple of points lower than even new car loans. Thus, on a loan for a used-car, you can often save about 4 points in interest right out of the chute if you finance with a second mortgage rather than with an official used-car loan.

If a mortgage is not an option, go to a credit union, savings and loan, or commercial bank (again, in that order). Shop around for the best finance rate. Stay with a fixed-rate. And don't even think about financing through the used car dealer. That is *never* a good idea.

Check Out AutoSeek on the World Wide Web

Jay Green's *AutoSeek* Web page bills itself as the "quickest, easiest and most importantly, the most hassle-free way to buy or lease your next car." Using a nation-wide network of dealers, *AutoSeek* is able to negotiate your next new-car purchase quickly and easily. Via the Web, *AutoSeek* will negotiate the best possible purchase or lease deal for the car you tell them you want, and then you can either go with it or not, as you see fit. No commitment. They recommend that you go to a local dealership and test drive the car you want. While there, make note of the options by option code (usually found in the left hand margin of the manufacturer's sticker on the car). Then, you access the *AutoSeek* Web page, give them the details of who you are—the exact make, model, color, and options of the car you want. You'll hear back from them with purchase and lease prices shortly. In the mean time, get some prices for the same vehicle from some other local dealers and see if *AutoSeek* doesn't beat them while at the same offering local delivery. *AutoSeek* also offers financing, and their deals may be just fine, but here too you will want to comparatively shop. The Web address is *http://www.autoseek.com/*, shown in Figure 16.1.

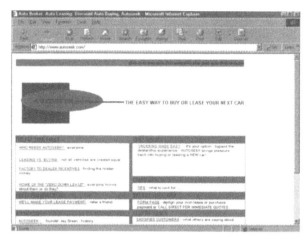

Figure 16.1 Finding a car lease at AutoSeek.

Think of *AutoSeek* as something like a dating service—connecting buyers and sellers. *AutoSeek* will arrange for your purchase and delivery to take place in your current state, eliminating sales-tax considerations that often occur when you purchase a car out of state. *AutoSeek* will never actually possess the vehicle. Instead, *AutoSeek* will work with a local dealer who, in turn, will sell the vehicle to you.

INTERNET RESOURCES FOR CAR BUYERS, THOSE SEEKING AUTO LOANS, AND THOSE WHO WISH TO LEASE

As you surf the World Wide Web, you may encounter sites that discuss cars: new and used cars, antique cars, car financing and leasing, and much more. The following site list should help you locate the resources you need.

FORD MOTOR COMPANY

http://www.ford.com

Learn all about your friends at Ford. Take a virtual tour of showroom boulevard and check out all the latest models. Use the on-line dealer locator to locate the Ford sales establishment nearest you. Get the details on Ford Credit Financial Services, the history of the Ford Motor Company, and even career opportunities with Ford.

For car buffs, the history files on-line here are a treasure-trove filled with vintage images and specifications related to all the classic Ford cars including the Model A, Model T, Thunderbird, and Mustang. What I wouldn't give for a vintage 1965 original edition Mustang.

Figure 16.2 Ford Motor Company.

A CONSUMER'S GUIDE TO CAR LEASING

http://www.leaseguide.com

This is one of the best Web sites I've seen when it comes to explaining leases and how to calculate a good deal. This Web site eliminates the confusion and fear that comes with leasing and shows you how to take on dealers and leasing companies at their own game. They tell you how leasing works, how to negotiate a great deal, payment formulas, the language of leasing, and other helpful tips and tools. This Web site is so clearly written, you'll feel like a leasing pro and wonder why you haven't leased sooner.

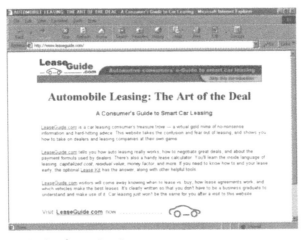

Figure 16.3 A Consumer's Guide to Car Leasing.

AUTOWEB

http://www.autoweb.com

This site should be a companion to LeaseGuide.com shown above. It provides a ton of unbiased research to help you purchase the right car on your own terms. Two important bits of information they offer are the Manufacturer's Suggested Retail Price and the Factory Invoice Price of your desired vehicle. They also have a free lease calculator you can use to determine your lease monthly payments.

Figure 16.4 AutoWeb Web site.

WHERE SMART CAR BUYERS START

http://www.edmunds.com

This site provides Prices & Reviews for new cars, vans, pickups, SUVs, and used cars and trucks. It has a complete buyer's guide, including True Market Value, where you can figure out what price is a good deal before you visit your dealer.

Figure 16.5 Where Smart Car Buyers Start.

CAR BUYING TIPS: AVOID DEALER SCAMS

http://www.carbuyingtips.com

This free consumer advocate site reveals dealer scams, gives negotiating tips, dealer costs, buying and selling used cars, and information on financing and leases.

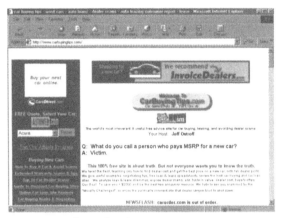

Figure 16.6 Car Buying Tips: Avoid Dealer Scams.

THE INTELLICHOICE CARCENTER

http://www.intellichoice.com

At this site, you can get prices for new and used cars, compare side-by-side, see the lowest cost manufacturer leases, and check the rebates and incentives. They are committed to empowering consumers with the knowledge to make better decisions by showing them what it really costs to purchase and own a new or used vehicle.

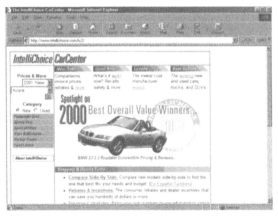

Figure 16.7 The IntelliChoice CarCenter

AUTO LOAN QUOTES NATIONWIDE

http://www.banx.com/banx/auto/bq-auto.htm

CAR LEASE CALCULATOR

http://www.beonthenet.com/cgi-bin/lease.cgi

CAR LINK: USED CAR INDEX

http://www.car-list.com/allidx.html

HONDA

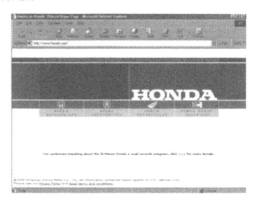

http://www.honda.com

DEALERNET:
THE SOURCE FOR NEW CAR INFORMATION

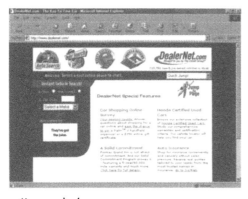

http://www.dealernet.com

SAAB

http://www.saabusa.com/home/index_live.html

WHAT CAR DEALERS DON'T WANT YOU TO KNOW

http://www.carinfo.com

PRICES ON NEW CARS

http://www.invoicedealers.com

HUNT, GATHER, DRIVE

http://www.stoneage.com

CAR BUYER'S GUIDE

http://www.vipps.com/autoguide.htm

ONLINE CAR BUYING

http://www.driveoff.com

CAR BUYING SERVICE

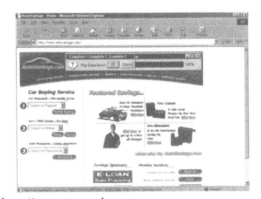

http://www.autoadvantage.com

AMERICAN CAR BUYING SERVICE

http://www.acscorp.com

HOW TO BUY A CAR

http://www.pinn.net/~calvino/lemon_laws.html

FREE CAR LEASING SURVIVAL KIT

http://www.aautofleet.com/
preferred.leasing.html

CONSUMER PROTECTION –
BUYING AND LEASING CARS

http://www.wa.gov/ago/consumer/cars/
home.html

CAR SHOPPING INFORMATION

http://www.duke.edu/~cmg/cars.html

LOAN VS. LEASE

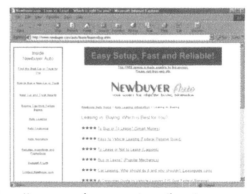

http://www.newbuyer.com/auto/lease/
leasevsbuy.shtm

GET FINANCING

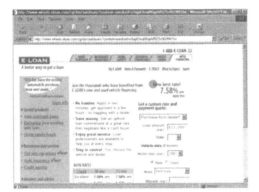

http://www.eloan.com

YOUR CAR, YOUR LOAN, YOUR WAY

http://www.giggo.com

GET A LOAN!

http://www.lendingtree.com

CHAPTER 17

BASICS OF THE U.S. FEDERAL INCOME TAX

In this world nothing can be said to be certain, except for death and taxes. — Ben Franklin

Federal income tax is not the most beloved of American institutions. Some argue it's unconstitutional as did the U.S. Supreme Court in 1895 declaring it was not approportional among the states in conformity with the Constitution. Congress enacted the first income tax law in 1862 to help support the Civil War effort. But it was in 1913 that federal income tax was made a permanent fixture in the U.S. tax system. The 16th Amendment gave Congress the legal authority to tax income and resulted in a revenue stipulating taxes for individuals and corporations. It only took until 1918 for the annual revenue collections to exceed the billion-dollar mark.

FEDERAL INCOME TAX IN BRIEF?

In brief? Are you kidding? The Federal income tax law is one of the most complex, unwieldy documents ever promulgated. The entire document is many times the size of this book. It also changes with great regularity. That's why it is handy to have the whole dynamic thing available on-line at the very useful MIT Web site that is addressed *http://www.tns.lcs.mit.edu/uscode/,* shown below in Figure 17.1.

Obviously, all the rules, provisions, and exemptions cannot be discussed here. But we can catch the highlights. And we can look at the basic formula for how an individual's or household's tax liability is calculated.

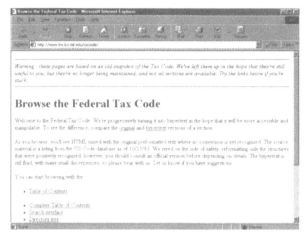

Figure 17.1 The Federal Income Tax Law.

In broad strokes:

Step 1: Start with your *gross income* (including wages, tips, rent, royalties(!), dividends and interest from non-IRA/401k/Keogh investments, and so on).

Step 2: Deduct whatever is allowed from your gross income to arrive at your *adjusted gross income* (AGI). Among the items you might deduct are trade and business expenses (for self-employed hombres), any other expenses associated with generating the income-strains that have culminated as *your gross income*, contributions to tax-deferred retirement plans, alimony, interest penalties on early withdrawals from time savings accounts, and a percentage (it varies every year) of the amount paid by self-employed persons for health insurance. With all these numbers backed out, you've arrived at your *adjusted gross income*.

Step 3: From your adjusted gross income, list your itemized deductions to arrive at your *taxable income*. These deductions include your out-of-pocket medical and dental expenses (if in excess of 7.5% of your adjusted gross income), state and local taxes (though *not* sales taxes), mortgage interest, casualty losses (in excess of $100 for each loss and 10% of your adjusted gross income for all losses), miscellaneous deductions (the value of the clothes you threw in the *Goodwill* hamper, the donation you made to the Sierra Club, and so on), and personal exemptions. With all these sums deducted, you've arrived at your *taxable income*.

YOUR FILING STATUS

The tax-rate the government applies to your taxable income varies, depending upon your filing status. Separate federal income tax rate schedules are in force for different categories of taxpayers. Married individuals filing joint returns have a different schedule than that which is applicable to heads of households, single individuals, married individuals who elect to file separate returns, and so on.

As you fill out your return, it is important that you realize that you may have more than one option in defining your filing status, and that if so you should, of course, go for the status that will treat you most leniently in the amount of taxes owed. For example, some single people may also qualify as heads of household, some married couples will get a bigger bang from filing separate returns rather than filing on a joint return, and so on. If you take the time to run the numbers for the different tax-filing scenarios available to you, the time you invest will pay off.

STOP COMPLAINING—YOU'VE BEEN LIBERATED

If you think taxes are annoyingly high right now, you don't have a good memory or any memory at all of when your grandpa paid taxes in the good ole days.

Prior to the Tax Reform Act of 1986, tax rates ranged from a low of 11% to a high of 50% over 14 progressive tax brackets. Today, broadly speaking, the *most* you are going pay as a percentage of taxable income up to $100,000 is around 29%. And that's if you are a married couple filing separately—the filing status that is treated least leniently from a straight per-centage tax point-of-view. Single people (single-filers) with taxable incomes up to $100,000 will pay a maximum of about 26%. Heads of households with taxable incomes up to $100,000 will pay a max of about 24.5%. Married couples filing jointly, with combined taxable in-comes up to $100,000, will only pay a max of about 23%.

Do those percentages look low? Are you saying, "Wait a minute, my bracket's higher than that! This is bad information."

No, this is not bad information. This is highly accurate information. The most accurate you will find. What I'm quoting above are *actual total marginal tax-rate averages* rather than formal tax-rate brackets. You see, you may be in a 33% tax bracket, but that bracket does not apply to *every dollar* of your income. The 33% rate, for example, kicks in for single-filers with relation to every taxable dollar *over* $49,300. The same single-filer will pay a *lower* rate for every taxable dollar under $49,300, and a lower rate *again* for every taxable dollar under $20,350. Thus the total *marginal rate* for a single filer on $100,000 taxable income winds up at around 26%.

COMBATING BRACKET CREEP

The federal tax law is automatically adjusted annually for the effects of inflation. Items ad-justed include individual tax-bracket schedules, standard deduction amounts, personal ex-emption amounts, and so forth. This indexing is in place to combat what is called *bracket creep*. Bracket creep occurs during an inflationary period when *artificial increases* in income (increases nullified by the effects of inflation) move taxpayers into higher brackets where in reality they don't belong. The indexing of the tax code to the inflation rate makes sure this does not happen.

ALTERNATIVE MINIMUM TAX (AMT)

To keep folks from using too many loopholes, the government has armed itself with a tool called the Alternative Minimum Tax (AMT). The government may at times impose the AMT on individuals, estates and trusts. (Corporations are also subject to a corporate AMT, but this is a *personal* finance book so we'll not be going into that.) AMT only tends to be a factor in the tax calculations of highly affluent people. And that's good, because the affluent are in a position to leave the extremely complex calculation of AMT in the hands of a competent accountant. What the AMT calculation does is minimize the degree to which one can use various tax shelters, exemptions, and other loopholes in the tax code. The AMT code was written to rectify a situation where some wealthy individuals were able, through shrewd planning, to avoid taxes altogether. The AMT is designed to see that everyone who should pays at least a certain minimum in income taxes every year.

Back in the old days, before AMT, the financial-wizard John D. Rockefeller routinely maneuvered himself into situations where he paid little or no tax. Then, later he'd feel guilty about it and make voluntary contributions to the US Treasury. Those days are over.

CAPITAL GAINS AND LOSSES

A *capital gain* is profit from the sale of any capital asset, such as stocks, bonds, preferred stocks, investment real estate, fine art, classic cars, personal residences, and so on. And a *capital loss*, of course, is what happens when you paid more for that Picasso than you were eventually able to sell it for.

Prior to the Tax Reform Act of 1986, long-term capital gains on investments held longer than six months were treated more favorably than short-term capital gains (on investments held less than six months). But now all capital gains are treated equally and are taxed at the same rate as the rest of your income. As an ancillary to that, all capital losses (long- and short-term) are now deductible dollar for dollar up to $3,000.

USE TAX TIMING TO YOUR ADVANTAGE

Pay state and local taxes, deductible on your federal form, strategically. For example, if you've had a good year with high income, try to pay your real estate taxes on your home in December of the current tax year if at all possible, rather than later in the new year. Then, you'll be in a position to deduct those taxes on your federal form sooner rather than later.

CONTACTING THE IRS ONLINE

The IRS has a substantial and impressive on-line presence which they call IRIS (Internal Revenue Information Services). IRIS is a part of FedWorld, a government bulletin board. Here you will find tax forms, instructions, publications, and a rich collection of other IRS information.

IRIS is accessible directly by using your modem to call 703-321-8020. On the Internet, you can telnet to *fedworld.gov* or, for file transfer protocol services, connect to *ftp.fedworld.gov*. If you are using the Web, connect to *http://www.irs.ustreas.gov*, shown below in Figure 17.2.

Figure 17.2 The Internal Revenue Information Service.

FedWorld's help desk offers technical assistance on accessing IRIS (not tax help!) during regular business hours (eastern time) at 703-487-4608.

Note that IRS forms available on-line must be downloaded and printed out on your laser printer. They are not designed to be filled out on-line. You may also request forms and publications via telephone: 1-800-TAX-FORM (1-800-829-3676).

HOW LONG DOES THE IRS INSIST YOU KEEP YOUR RECORDS?

Keep your records of income, deductions, and credits shown on your return, as well as any worksheets you used, until the statute of limitations runs out for that return. Usually, this is three years from the date the return was due or filed, or two years from the date the tax was paid, whichever is later. Also, keep copies of your filed tax returns and any Forms W-2 or 1099 you received as part of your records.

These statutes of limitations are not etched in stone. For example, the feds have up to six years to audit you if you underreport your income by more than 25%. And if the IRS decides to come after you on a straight charge of fraud, or if you haven't bothered to file, there is *no* statute of limitations. None. So behave yourself. Also, find a bigger box and keep your records, just in case.

OOPS! I GOOFED!

OK, so you made a mistake on your return and only realized it after your return was in the mail. You didn't mean to misrepresent your income, but nevertheless you did in some small (or large) way. And now you are sure the marshals will be at your door any minute, ready to cart you away to some federal prison where you'll be forced to play gin rummy all day with junk-bond millionaires and former Clinton aides. But relax. You can amend that return. You can amend it within three years after the date the return was filed, or within two years after the date the tax was paid, whichever is later. Simply use Form 1040X, which you can download from the IRS Web site. But amend the return as soon as possible, before somebody else does it for you.

NOTHING CAN BE SAID TO BE CERTAIN EXCEPT DEATH, TAXES, AND TAXES AFTER DEATH

The IRS does not care whether a citizen is living or dead at the end of the tax year. The IRS only cares whether or not that citizen had income in the tax year. And if so, the IRS wants its cut. A return must be filed by the dead-taxpayer's spouse or personal representative (executor, heir, and so on). If your husband or wife died in a given tax year and you did not immediately remarry in the same tax year, you can file a *joint return* with your dead spouse for that year. A last bit of togetherness—how comforting.

LITTLE THINGS THAT SAY: "PLEASE AUDIT ME"

Less than 1% of tax returns get audited every year. You are most likely to get audited if:

1. You have a job that offers great opportunity for hiding compensation, such as waiting tables, driving a cab, independent contracting, helping high-rollers find their show seats in Las Vegas, and so forth.

2. You use tax shelters that involve inflated assets, deductions exceeding 20% of your principal invested, high promotional fees, and other nebulous costs.

3. Your return involves alimony income or deductions.

4. You claim large charitable contributions that are not within the normal scope of your income level.

5. You make excessive deductions for hard-to-document business expenses, such as those associated with a home office.

6. You claim deductions for what may well be spurious medical expenses, such as the cost of a swimming pool to help provide exercise for a heart patient.

7. You deduct interest paid on a mortgage (or second mortgage) held by someone who is a relative.

A Word About the Flat Tax

Beer is no good when it is flat. A tire is no good when it is flat. So what about a tax? Is a tax any good when it is flat?

Perhaps.

Consider: After decades of being "reformed," the federal tax system is so complex that even the IRS can no longer give accurate advice on it. The IRS sends out *eight-billion pages* of forms and instructions each year. Laid end to end, all these pages would stretch 28 times around the circumference of the earth. Americans spend 5.4 billion man-hours each year calculating their taxes: more man-hours than it takes to build every car, truck and van produced in the United States. To top it all off, the complex tax code creates a *defacto* tax surcharge situation every year in the amount of $232 billion. This is the cost of accountants, copying, and all the miscellaneous expenses of merely filing. This translates to $900 a year drained from the economy for every man, woman and child.

Representative Dick Armey's flat-tax proposal suggests that we replace the complicated tax system with a flat tax so simple Americans can file their taxes on a form the size of a postcard. And, say the plan's proponents, the flat tax is as fair as it is simple. The flat tax proposal repeals special preferences in the tax code and is true to the uniquely American definition of fairness: Everybody should be treated the same.

Proponents also point-out that the flat tax is pro-growth, in that it ends double taxation of savings; thus, promoting investment and job creation. Furthermore, the proposal rewards work by lowering marginal tax rates, and creates a neutral tax system which will liberate individuals to make financial decisions based on common sense economic rather than arcane tax rules.

The details of what we are talking about are these. Armey's proposal repeals today's complicated income tax system and replaces it with a low, simple, single flat tax of 17% on *all* income, whether it be business or personal income.

It couldn't be more simple. Individuals pay 17% of all wages, salaries, and pensions after subtracting prescribed and simple family allowances. Likewise all business income, whatever the source (corporation, sole proprietor, professional, farm, royalties, and rents) is taxed at 17% of the difference, if positive, between revenues and expenses.

But wait. Dick Armey's flat tax proposal gets even better. To help prevent a future Congress from raising taxes in order to reward a special interest, or to prevent a Congress from recomplicating the tax code, the bill contains a provision which requires a 60% supermajority of both the House and the Senate to 1) raise the tax rate, 2) create multiple tax rates, 3) lower the family allowance, or 4) add a loophole.

Maybe your grandpa would have liked it.

INTERNET RESOURCES RELATED TO FEDERAL AND OTHER INCOME TAXES

As you surf the World Wide Web, you may encounter sites that discuss tax laws, tax deductions, tax penalties, and more. The following site list should help you locate the resources you need.

DENNIS SCHMIDT'S TAX AND ACCOUNTING RESOURCES

http://www.taxsites.com

Dennis Schmidt provides literally hundreds of links related to tax forms (federal and state), federal tax law, the IRS, state tax regulation on-line by state, international tax information, associations and policy groups, current tax issues, financial reporting, tax auditing, tax accountants, and more. Schmidt, by the way, is an Associate Professor of Accounting at the University of Northern Iowa. Should you decide you want to thank him for this splendid resource, the e-mail address is *schmidt@uni.edu*.

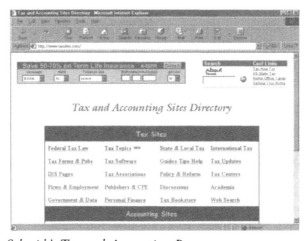

Figure 17.3 Dennis Schmidt's Tax and Accounting Resources.

DOWNLOADABLE TAX FORMS, INSTRUCTIONS AND PUBLICATIONS FROM THE IRS

http://www.irs.ustreas.gov/prod/forms_pubs/

Not only can you download every and any federal tax form, instruction, or publication from this site, you can also search for a particular form by keyword. If you have been procrastinating, you can even file for extensions right on-line.

Figure 17.4 Downloadable Tax Forms, Instructions, and Publications from the IRS.

INTERNATIONAL TAX RESOURCES

http://www.kentis.com/siteseeker/taxintl.html

This page is somewhat less extensive than that discussed above. Nevertheless it has good information for:

- Australia—including a link to the Australian Taxation Office

- Canada—including a link to Revenue Canada

- Italy—including a link to the on-line *Italian Tax Systems Primer* available from the accounting firm of Costanzo & Veronese at its Web site

- The United Kingdom, including links to Inland Revenue, the TAXFAX International Home Page, Professor Doernberg's Tax Law Web Site, and Ernst & Young's Worldwide Executive Tax Guide and Directory.

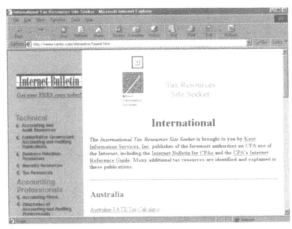

Figure 17.5 International Tax Resources.

TAX DIRECTORY INTERNATIONAL

http://www.cpateam.com/tax-international.htm

This site provides an extensive list of resources with regard to international taxes. Some links include: Foreign Income Tax Sites, Taxes Around the World, International Tax Resources, and KPMG's International Tax Summary Guides by Country.

Figure 17.6 Tax Directory International.

COMPLETE TAX AND INCOME SOFTWARE

http://www.completetax.com

This software is designed to meet your personal income tax needs. The Complete Tax Organizer is free. You can use the software for organizing all of your tax information and to provide a printed copy for your accountant. For $7.50, you can process, print and/or electronically file your federal and state income tax forms. There are just five easy steps.

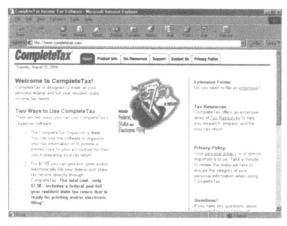

Figure 17.7 Complete Tax and Income Software.

FLAT TAX INFORMATION FROM THE HOUSE OF REPRESENTATIVES

http://www.flattax.com

FLAT TAX HOTLINE

http://www.public-policy.org/~ncpa/pi/taxes/flattax.html

RECENT REGULATIONS FROM THE IRS

http://www.irs.ustreas.gov/prod/forms_pubs/index.html

FORBES FLAT TAX CALCULATOR

http://webreview.com/flattax/

INTERNAL REVENUE SERVICE TAX CODE

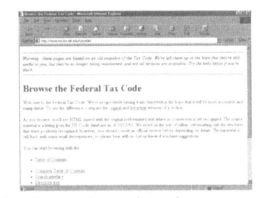

http://www.tns.lcs.mit.edu/uscode

TAX RESOURCES SITE SEEKER

http://www.kentis.com

FREE INCOME TAX INFORMATION

http://www.1-tax-forms.com

TAX QUESTIONS

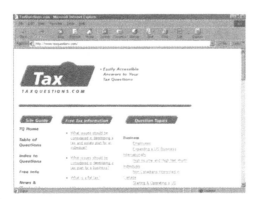

http://www.taxquestions.com

IRS – TAX FAQs

http://www.irs.gov/tax_edu/faq/index.html

COALITION ON HUMAN NEEDS: EARNED INCOME TAX CREDIT

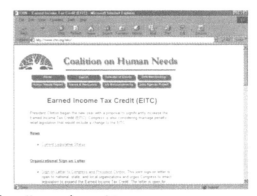

http://www.chn.org/eitc

IRS TAX PROBLEM HELP – FREE CONSULTATIONS

http://www.irstaxes.com

TAX INTERACTIVE: TAXES FOR TEENS

http://www.irs.gov/taxi

TAX RESEARCH SOURCES

http://www.indiana.edu/~stern/research

TIMEVALUE SOFTWARE

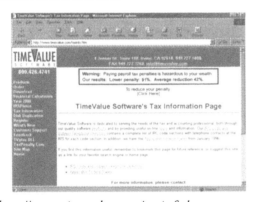

http://www.timevalue.com/taxinfo.htm

A&E TAX SERVICE – TOOLS

http://www.aetaxservice.com/tools.html

TAX TIPS AND TOOLS – ONLINE PREPARATION

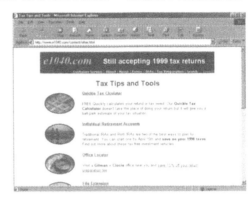

http://www.e1040.com/content/other.html

TAX SEASON SURVIVAL KIT

http://www.freedom.gov/survival

DIRECTORIES AND RESEARCH TOOLS

http://www.taxcast.com/cruiser/tools.htm

TAX HELP CENTER

http://www.wellsfargo.com/per/planner/taxhelp

FREE TAX NEWSLETTER

http://taxmamma.com/AskTaxMama

TAX TIP OF THE DAY

http://infospace.freeshop.com/pg02586.htm

STATE TAX FORMS

http://www.50states.com/tax

TAX NEWS NETWORK

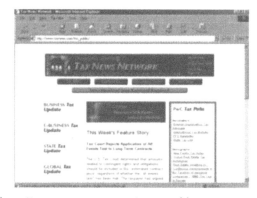

http://www.taxnews.com/tnn_public

CHAPTER 18

TAX-SAVING TECHNIQUES AND THE
ART OF ELECTRONIC FILING

I'm proud to be paying taxes in the United States. The only thing is—I could be just as proud for half the money. — **Arthur Godfrey**

What specific devices can you use to lower your annual income tax? What methods are there available with which you can eliminate, reduce, shift, or postpone income tax? Prior to the Tax Reform Act of 1986, there used to be literally hundreds of little shell games one (at least one with enough assets) could rely on to reduce one's tax. Today, with the playing field leveled, there are fewer gambits for us to use to effectively lower our income tax exposure. But be of good cheer. We still have a few options.

CAPTURE EVERY DEDUCTION

There are many, many potential deductions available to you. Far too many to list here. But you'd be surprised at the extent of them. And you'd be surprised by the number of people who, entitled to these deductions, don't take them.

For example, if you have a chronic illness and you must drive to therapy sessions on a regular basis, the cost of your gas is deductible. If you lent your dead-beat brother-in-law money he hasn't repaid, and you decide to write-off the debt, you can deduct it as a business loss so long as the loan was formalized between you and him with a contract, and so long as the amount is no higher than $3,000. (By the way, your dead-beat brother-in-law will then get taxed on the loan as income. That'll fix 'em!)

Are you self-employed? Then, you can deduct a percentage of the amount you pay for health insurance for yourself, family, and employees. So are out-of-pocket medical expenses that go above 7.5% of your adjusted gross income (AGI).

Did your home get destroyed in a flood? Did your insurance not cover the cost of the entire disaster? You can deduct out-of-pocket itemized casualty losses over $100 that exceed 10% of your AGI.

Here's my favorite. Have you bought a home PC that you will be using more than 50% of the time for business? If you are a sole-proprietor, you can write off the entire expense of the PC in the year you purchased it.

Are you moving from one city to another in order to take a new job? Your expenses for that move are fully deductible so long as you move within a year of taking the job, so long as your new job is at least thirty-five miles farther from your old home than your previous job, and provided you work full-time in the general vicinity of the new location for at least 39 weeks during the 12-month period following the move.

Do you drive around quite a bit to conduct your personal business? You may deduct a mileage expense to visit your broker or financial planner, and to visit investment property you own or investment property you are considering buying. I don't know about you, but I'm considering buying some investment property in the Bahamas.

Are you one of a thousand points of light? Do you do volunteer work at the local hospital or some other worthy, not-for-profit entity from which you receive no compensation whatsoever? You've got a reward coming. Your travel expenses to and from your volunteer-work are fully deductible.

Do you gamble? Believe it or not, gambling losses are deductible. *In a sense.* They are deductible against your gambling winnings in any given year. So keep track of all your good days and bad days and make sure you only pay tax on the *net*. (Which is bound to be a negative number, by the way, although I certainly wish you luck.)

Are you kind-hearted and generous to a fault? You may deduct charitable contributions up to 50% of your AGI in any given year. If you choose to donate more than this percentage, you may do so and still keep it all deductible. Any moneys that go over the 50% cap will simply be carried forward as a deductible in the following tax year.

TAX-EXEMPT BONDS: JUST HOW TAX EXEMPT ARE THEY?

Elsewhere in this book I've talked about state- and city-municipal bonds as good vehicles for collecting reliable, substantial interest that is not taxable on the federal level.

But there is something to remember here—something to watch out for. Only the *interest* you are paid on municipal bonds (the coupon rate x par value) is tax-free. When you buy a tax-free municipal in the open market at a price less than par, that profitable difference (known as the "discount") between your purchase price and the par value is highly taxable. 100%. Following that line of logic, you would think that when a tax-free municipal is purchased at a "premium" (purchase price *above* par value), the negative-discount would be considered a loss for tax purposes. But it isn't. And that does seem quite fair to me. But then, Uncle Sam didn't ask me my opinion.

CREATIVE CHARITY: GETTING THE MOST OF YOUR GENEROSITY

There is a wonderful organization called the Hudson River Sloop *Clearwater*, Inc. *(http://www.clearwater.org)*. *Clearwater* is entirely non-profit. It is a membership organization with many thousands of subscribers. And its main mission is environmental education. To this end, the organization has built and keeps afloat a very expensive boat, probably the most beautiful (and certainly the largest) sloop in the world. The *Clearwater* is a replica of the old Hudson River sloops which dominated river commerce in the 19th century. The sloop is used today as a floating environmental classroom. *Clearwater* visits towns on the Hudson River and takes schoolchildren out on the river where they learn of Hudson history, culture, and ecology.

Figure 18.1 The Hudson River Sloop Clearwater, Inc.

The boat was costly to build. It is even more costly to maintain, staff, and insure. Many hundreds of thousands of dollars are needed every year. Some of the needed money comes from grants. Some comes from *Clearwater* members. Much comes from quarters and dimes and dollars thrust into contribution cans passed at various festivals and concerts. And no small amount comes from wealthy individuals who have chosen to support *Clearwater* on an ongoing basis. Rockefellers, Goulds, Vanderbilts, and other wealthy Hudson River families have made and continue to make substantial gifts to *Clearwater*. And they invariably do so not with cash, but with *appreciated property*, most often stocks.

When one gives a gift of *appreciated property*, one receives as well as gives. What one receives is a tremendous tax advantage.

Say you have 100 shares of stock in xyz company, which you paid $10 apiece for ($1,000). You are a shrewd investor and now, less than a year later, those shares are valued at $25 apiece ($2,500). If you donate the 100 shares to *Clearwater* or some other worthy charity, you can take a charitable tax deduction of $2,500 even though you only paid $1,000 for the stock. Assuming your marginal average tax rate is 28%, the gift will save you $700 in taxes. And thus your total actual cost on the $2,500 gift to your favorite charity will only be $300. The

403

only trick is to make sure the stock you buy in the first place goes up in value. And that, my friend, is another chapter. Specifically, it is Chapter 4.

You can deduct any and all *appreciated gifts* up to 30% of your AGI for any given year. But if you choose to donate more in the way of *appreciated gifts* in any given year, you may do so. The excess deduction will just be carried over to the following fiscal year.

MORE CREATIVE CHARITY: SPLIT GIFTS AND OTHER VARIATIONS

A *split gift* is when you make a gift now of a future interest in property while retaining a present interest in the property.

Huh? What'd she say?

Perhaps an example is in order. Here goes.

One of the most popular *split gift* formulations is the gift of remainder interest in a personal residence. In this scenario, a taxpayer donates real property to a charity, but reserves the right for him- or herself (and spouse) to live in or use the property for their remaining lifetimes. The donor gets a current income tax charitable deduction for the present value of the charity's remainder interest in the depreciated value of the real property. In other words, the donor gets a huge tax write-off. And the donor's heirs *do not* get the house or farm when granny goes to her reward. The charity does.

A whole book could be written about the many creative forms of charitable giving, including charitable gift annuities, conservation easements, gifts of life insurance, partial interest gifts, and several additional *split gift* scenarios including pooled income funds, charitable remainder annuity trusts, and charitable remainder unitrusts. All these options are far too complex and detailed to be gone into at length here. However, I have endeavored to include extensive Internet and Web resources relating to these options in the *Internet Resources* section of this chapter.

REDUCING TAXES BY SHIFTING THE BURDEN TO OTHERS

I am not talking about random others. I am talking about specific others. Most especially, I'm talking about others who are somewhat shorter than you, who live in your house, who drop pizza on your carpet, who argue incessantly between themselves, and who crash your computer's hard drive every other week. I am talking about your kids.

The most obvious way to shift income to others while still keeping it in the family is to put income-producing property in your kids' names by making *outright gifts*. You know what I'm talking about: parents and grandparents giving stock, rental real-estate, mutual fund shares, etc., etc. to their kids and grandkids.

Important Note: In order for the income to be taxed at the kid's rate, which is bound to be the lowest bracket rate, you must give the actual income-generating property itself to the kids, not just the *income* from the property.

Important Note #2: It doesn't pay to do anything like this until your kid is 14. Up until age 14, you and your child are subject to the infamous and much-despised "kiddy tax." Up to age 14, the bulk of your child's net unearned income (after the first thousand or so) is taxed at *your* top marginal federal income tax rate.

But from age 14 up it gets more attractive.

For tax purposes, the receiver of a capital-asset gift (your child or grandchild) is initially taxed as having received only your *income tax basis* in the property received. Thus, if you paid $1,000 for stock that is now worth $5,000, and you give that stock to your son or daughter, your son's or daughter's tax basis on the gift is still just $1,000. Later, if your son or daughter sells the stock for anything over $1,000, he or she will have taxable income in the profit.

And of course, your son or daughter will be taxed on the revenue from the capital assets: the dividends paid by the stock, the rent derived from the real estate, and so on.

For more details on giving gifts to minors please see Chapter 22, "Estate Planning Fundamentals," which relates to planning estates and trusts.

Postponing Income Tax

We all do it every day. It goes by many names: Individual Retirement Account (IRA), SEP-IRA, 401k, Keogh account, and so on.

These are all the standard devices for delaying income taxes. With them, you delay income tax on two fronts. First, you delay income tax on that portion of your annual income that you choose to deposit into your IRA or comparable instrument in the course of a year. And then you defer tax on the revenue generated by that compounding capital. Thus, the bulk of Americans let investment capital "grow hair" for their retirement in a tax-free cocoon where it grows and compounds faster than it would be able to otherwise.

IRAs and comparable accounts (401ks, Keoghs, etc.) embrace the broad range of investment options, from stocks and bonds to mutual funds to money-market accounts. The one area of investment they usually do not embrace is tax-free municipal bonds and mutual funds which specialize in these, because there is less need for tax-free income (and the generally-lower return of tax-free municipals) based on the tax-deferred status the IRA already enjoys.

Smile When You Pay That Bill

When you are done pulling out every possible loophole in the tax law, when you are done whittling your tax down to the last thin dime, just look at the amount you owe Uncle Sam *and smile.* This is not money you are being forced to throw in the trash, or burn on the leaf pile. Your tax dollars go to support the pricey, but worthwhile, fiscal entity that stands behind the Bill of Rights. Your tax dollars go to support the United States of America. No matter what you pay in taxes, this country is a bargain.

CYBER TAX TIP #1: USE FORM 1040PC

Well, what do you think the PC stands for?

A traditional 1040 is a dinosaur of a document, filled with queries, instructions, boxes, blanks, and lines. But these are just cosmetics. All the IRS really needs—and requires by law—are exactly what a 1040PC provides: simple numbers in a three-column format. The 1040PC is not a form. It is a printing format that the IRS can easily process with a scanner. Since processing a 1040PC is more efficient and accurate than processing a traditional 1040, it is generally assumed that refunds are much faster as well. Let's hope so. If you're using personal tax software, you can create a 1040PC with the ease of a few keystrokes. You fill out your return on-screen exactly as if you were going to print out a traditional form 1040. But instead of printing out the traditional 1040, you select the option to print out a 1040PC form. Then, your tax software will output all your 1040 information in the condensed version. Attach your W-2s, 1099s, check (if necessary), then mail (yes, I mean snail-mail, sorry) it all to the IRS and you're done.

CYBER TAX TIP #2: CONSIDER ELECTRONIC FILING

The first experiments in electronic filing in the mid 1980s drew just 25,000 taxpayers. But in 2000 more than 35 million returns arrived electronically in IRS offices. And did you know that the IRS has a goal, by the year 2000, of eliminating paper *entirely*? Yup. They hope to receive 50 million tax returns electronically in the year 2000. Since you are reading this book, odds are good that your return will be one of these.

Electronic filing has many advantages. First of all, less than 1% of electronically generated/transmitted returns contain errors, as compared to 15% of all paper returns. Additionally, electronic returns are verified for receipt (in other words, your tax-return can't get lost in the mail), and on-line filing makes refunds happen quicker. That's right, the IRS has promised that electronic filers will receive their refunds within three weeks of filing. Additionally, for electronic filers, the IRS will even deposit your refund into your bank account by electronic cash transfer, if you'd like them to.

In order to file electronically, you must send the data that is your tax return to an electronic filing center, *not* to the IRS.

Electronic filing centers, such as Universal Tax Systems (UTS) of Rome, Georgia, are independent contractors specifically approved and designated by the IRS to serve as a liaison between the IRS and electronic filers. After receiving both electronic data and supplementary forms from the taxpayer, the electronic filing center checks the documents for accuracy and completeness before submitting the material to the IRS in the IRS's preferred data format. The fee for this, payable to the electronic filing center, is usually about $15.

To find an electronic filing center, look in the documentation that came with the tax software you are using. Many of the leading tax preparation software packages, including TurboTax and Tax Cut, completely automate the process of finding and communicating your tax return to electronic filing centers. These software packages come bundled with communications software with which taxpayers can connect and transmit returns to electronic filing centers quickly and easily. After you transmit your tax return to the filing center, you then forward your supporting documents (W2s, 1099s, etc.) to the filing center via snail-mail. (This aspect of electronic filing is still clunky. Unfortunately, there as yet are no such things as electronic W2s or electronic 1099s, although I'm sure these innovations are coming.)

CYBER TAX TIP #3: CONSIDER FILING VIA AN ONLINE SERVICE

The leading on-line services also provide support for electronic filers, and are in many ways *the most efficient means for electronic filing now available.* America On-line and CompuServe offer options whereby they will take responsibility for transmitting tax returns from subscribers to electronic filing centers for verification and submission. If you use an on-line service to submit your tax return, you do not need to forward your supporting documents to the electronic filing center. You simply send those documents directly to the IRS.

The one very small annoyance associated with filing via an on-line service is that the on-line services tend to dictate which tax-software you may use. As of this writing, America On-line does not want to hear about any tax software other than TurboTax and MacInTax, while CompuServe subscribers may use either of those packages, or TaxCut.

Note that returns filed via an on-line service must be accompanied by a special version of Form 8453 called Form 8453-OL. You can download this form from both America On-line and CompuServe.

Note also that electronic filing, though fast, is not instantaneous. Whether you are filing via an electronic filing center or via an on-line service, allow several days before any deadline. In other words, an electronic return *transmitted* on April 15 is not an electronic return *filed* on April 15. It'll take a few days to get filed with the IRS. And it'll be late.

RECENT RESTRUCTURING OF THE IRS

The IRS Restructuring and Reform Act of 1998 was specifically aimed at reorganizing the IRS. Congress enacted many significant reforms pertaining to the bureaucracy at the audit and collections level. The Act provides new procedural rights and attempts to eliminate abuses. Too long to reprint in this book, here are just a few highlights that may be of interest.

When it came to tax liability, the IRS was always presumed to be correct, but now the burden of proof has shifted with stipulations. In addition, attorney's fees and costs may be awarded when the IRS is not substantially justified in its position. Taxpayers can now bring lawsuits against the IRS for negligence and disregard for the law recovering civil damages up to $100,000. The "life-style" audits of the past, where the IRS asks personal and intrusive questions regarding your spending habits, have been curtailed. The IRS was also required to rewrite Publication 1, which informs taxpayers of their rights under examination and provides information about the examination selection process. The Act also subjects the IRS to the provisions of the Fair Debt Collection Act, which puts a stop to harassing and abusive telephone calls. And lastly, affecting all taxpayers, no matter their liability, checks and money orders are now made payable to the U.S. Treasury and not the Internal Revenue Service. To see a more detailed outline of the IRS Restructuring and Reform Act, visit *http://www.us.kpmg.com/irs_rnr_1998/tax_rite.htm.*

Start with a Good Book

If you have questions regarding your taxes, specific deductions you can take, issues relating to an audit, and so on, you will find a wealth of information not only on the Web but also in within numerous books. To start, the Wall Street Journal's *Guide to Understanding Your Taxes*, published by Lightbulb Press (New York) explains the role of taxes, the purpose of the IRS, your need for tax planning and more (ISBN: 0-671-50235-2). Also, *Kiplinger's Cut Your Taxes*, provides you with a myriad of ways to reduce your taxes (ISBN: 0-8129-2643-9) at 800-727-7015. Or, check out the Kiplinger Web site at *http://www.kiplinger.com.*

INTERNET RESOURCES RELATED TO LIMITING INCOME TAX EXPOSURE

As you surf the World Wide Web, you may encounter sites that discuss tax issues such as "creative" deductions, tax shelters, tax policies such as the flat tax, and even government sites from which you can download specific tax forms. The following site list should help you locate the resources you need.

ERNST & YOUNG ONLINE

http://www.ey.com/us/tax

Ernst & Young is the leading tax practice in the United States, providing tax compliance and consulting services to thousands of individuals and businesses of all sizes. And their Web site is rich with valuable information. Come here for mutual-fund tax-saving strategies, 10 smart tax planning tips, 50 easily-overlooked deductions, the latest tax changes, the current year's tax calendar, and information on *Prosper*, a new financial planning software package that *The New York Times* has called the "most comprehensive yet in terms of personal financial planning." By the way, AOL subscribers should be sure to check-out the complete text of the *Ernst & Young Tax Guide* which is available on-line. Key word: *tax guide*.

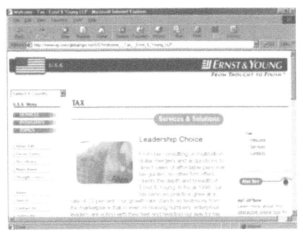

Figure 18.2 *Ernst & Young Online.*

TAX ANALYSTS: QUALITY INFORMATION FOR TAX PROFESSIONALS

http://205.177.50.2/default.htm

This excellent Web resource includes:

- *The Tax Notes Newswire*—Updated daily at 10 AM, noon and 4:30 PM eastern time, features highlights of the latest tax news from the US and around the world.

- *Feature of the Week*—An in-depth news story related to taxes, published Tuesdays.

- *Discussion Groups*—27 moderated groups, covering every aspect of taxation including damage awards taxation, employment taxes, estate and gift taxes, farm and ranch taxes, individual income taxes, international taxation, and more.

- *Tax Snapshots*—Noteworthy facts from the world of tax, published Fridays.

- *Tax Calendar*— A listing of the week's scheduled tax events.

- *Tax Clinic*—A public service providing in-depth tax research and information.

- *Tax Links*—An impressive collection of links to other important tax-oriented Web sites.

The price for this insightful, timely information resource? Absolutely nothing. This Web site comes to you courtesy of Tax Analysts, Inc., a non-profit organization dedicated to providing timely and comprehensive information on taxes and the tax code.

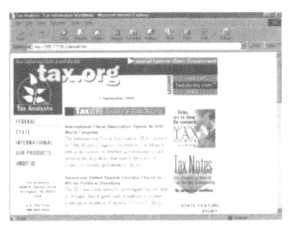

Figure 18.3 Tax Analysts: Quality Information for Tax Professionals.

SOFTWARE AND ONLINE PROGRAMS FROM TURBOTAX

http://www.turbotax.com

This site furnishes software and products to do taxes online. Try a free demonstration and download tax forms.

Figure 18.4 Software and Products from TurboTax

HOW TO MAKE TAX-SAVING GIFTS

http://www.aier.org/tg.html

With the growth of individual wealth, there is a greater demand for information and instruction on how to save taxes through lifetime gifts. This site provides valuable information on how to make tax-saving gifts.

HOW TO MAKE TAX-SAVING GIFTS

http://www.aier.org/tg.html

SECURETAX.COM—ONLINE FILING

http://www.securetax.com

ELECTRONIC TAX FILING ONLINE

http://www.efs.com

PROFESSIONAL TAX PREPARATION SOFTWARE

http://www.wwwebtax.net

H.D. VEST ONLINE

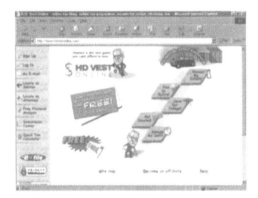

http://www.hdvestonline.com

THE TAX ESTIMATOR

http://www.intuit.com/turbotax/taxcenter/
estimator/start.htm

SOFTWARE FOR MACINTOSH USERS

http://www.macintax.com

MORE FILING ONLINE

http://www.e1040.com

TAX PREP 1: FILE YOUR TAXES ONLINE

http://www.taxprep1.com

FILING ONLINE

http://www.proseries.com/efiling

HOW TO DO YOUR TAXES ONLINE

*http://www.netguide.com/special/primers/
tax/home.html*

ONLINE INCOME TAX PREPARATION CENTER

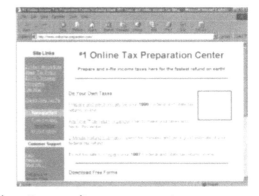

http://www.online-tax-preparation.com

TAX CUT

http://www.taxcut.com

TAX ADVICE FROM THE ARMCHAIR MILLIONAIRE

http://www.armchairmillionaire.com

TAX ADVICE FROM THE TAX PROPHET

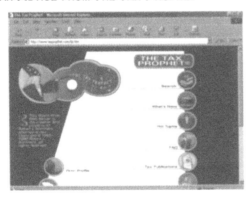

http://www.taxprophet.com

TAX TIPS AND FACTS

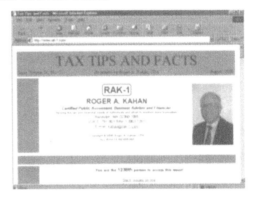

http://www.rak-1.com

ESSENTIAL LINKS TO TAXES

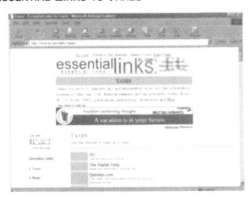

http://www.el.com/elinks/taxes

TAX LOGIC

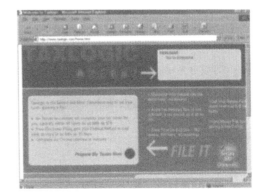

http://www.taxlogic.com

WHY ARE YOU PAYING TOO MUCH INCOME TAX?

http://www.tax-deductions.com

TAXES AND DONATIONS

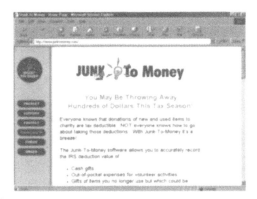

http://www.junktomoney.com

TAX EFFICIENT GIFTS

http://www.cliveowen.co.uk/tax.htm

#1 STRATEGY FOR HOME BUSINESS DEDUCTIONS

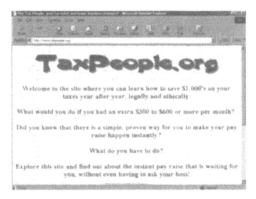

http://www.taxpeople.org

TAX RULES FOR GIFTS

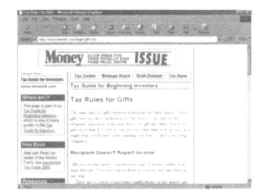

http://www.fairmark.com/begin/gifts.htm

FAMILY CARE FOUNDATION—EXAMPLE OF TAX-SAVING GIFT

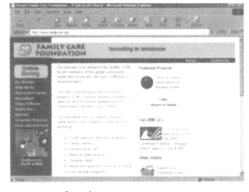

http://www.familycare.org

CHAPTER 19

GIMME SHELTER: THE ART OF
TAX-SHELTERED INVESTMENTS

Gimme, gimme shelter, or else I'm gonna fade away. — **Mick Jagger and Keith Richards**

It is appropriate that Mick Jagger and Keith Richards, longtime tax exiles from Great Britain, are the composers of a song entitled *Gimme Shelter.* Jagger and Richards, along with the other Rolling Stones, have sought the ultimate shelter from British taxation by becoming ex-patriots. No small number of wealthy Americans have done quite the same thing. Many painters and writers, for example, have left the US for the Republic of Ireland, where creative artists are not subject to income tax.

Luckily, for those of us with neither the resources nor the inclination to take things quite so far, there are a few tax-shelter options which demand something less in the way of a lifestyle change.

TAX SHELTERS DEFINED

The term *tax-sheltered investment* is a broad one. Technically, it refers to any investment the return on which is secured against exposure to taxes. Thus, formally speaking, a tax shelter could be anything from tax-deferred buildup of life insurance to the purchase of a tax-free municipal bond.

However, the term *tax shelter* has generally come to be applied to something else entirely. It has come to be applied to a specific class of tax-free investments, such as those associated with the real estate or the oil and gas businesses, and those involving particular tax benefits associated with depreciation, amortization, deferral of taxable income through current income-tax deductions, and special statutory deductions (such as percentage depletion). Another characteristic of tax shelters, as the term is generally applied, is that these investments tend to be financed with borrowed money. The owner of the tax shelter takes a tax deduction for the debt interest, as a business expense.

WHOM TAX SHELTERS ARE NOT FOR

Tax shelters are not for—how can I put this delicately? They are not for those who are not considered affluent. Is that OK to say? Is that politically correct? Or is financially-challenged a better phrase? Very well then, tax shelters are not for the financially-challenged. And they are not for you if you do not have a great deal of money, some of which you can afford to lose.

Initial minimum investments for tax shelters are often in the tens of thousands of dollars. On top of that, tax shelters are often hard investments to get out of in a timely manner. And, they tend to be highly-speculative. In other words, there is a good chance you'll lose every dime you invest.

Another reason why tax shelters tend to be for the well-heeled is that they can be written off only against "unearned" income. In other words, as passive investments themselves, tax shelters can only be used to offset income from other passive activities, such as income from a trust fund. They cannot be used to offset income from wages, salaries, professional fees, and stock portfolios.

LIMITED PARTNERSHIP TAX SHELTERS

Many tax shelters are marketed as limited-partnerships. Limited partnerships provide a measure of financial protection for the investor (the limited partner). While all of the limited-partner's investment capital is indeed at risk, the limited-partner is insulated from claims against the partnership. In other words, the limited partner is not liable for the debts, obligations or repercussions of losses of the partnership beyond the limited partner's original (deductible) contribution to the partnership's war chest.

Limited partnerships also have general partners who, unlike limited partners, *are* responsible for debts and obligations of the partnership, and who maintain management and operating control of the partnership. These general partners are invariably the people who were the promoters/marketers of the tax shelter limited partnership in the first place. And your investment is in their hands.

Thus, it is very important to know exactly who you are dealing with when buying into a tax-sheltered limited partnership. (More on this later.)

ONCE YOU ARE IN, IT IS HARD TO GET OUT

Tax shelters are not only high-risk, they are high-risk for the long-term. If your partnership is building a skyscraper or a luxury hotel, it is going to take a while before there is a profit. If your partnership is exploring for natural gas in Siberia, it is going to take a while before there is a profit. *If* there is a profit. Additionally, it is quite likely that you, as a limited partner, will be prohibited from assigning or selling your interest in the tax shelter without consent of the general partners. And, even if the general partners do give you the nod to sell your interest, who will you sell it to you and how will you calibrate the selling price? There is no stock exchange for shares in tax shelters. Perhaps your Uncle Fred will buy your interest in the partnership, at the price you want, if you ply him with enough martinis first. Happy New Year, Uncle Fred.

WHAT IS AN ABUSIVE TAX SHELTER?

The IRS defines an *abusive tax shelter* as any scheme that involves artificial transactions with little or no basis in economic reality. Generally, the IRS wants you to invest money with the *realistic expectation* of making money back. An abusive tax shelter offers you inflated tax savings based on large write-offs and virtually guaranteed "losses," whereas a legitimate tax shelter exists to reduce taxes fairly while at the same time producing income.

Abusive tax-shelters are often marketed in terms of how much you can write off in relation to how much you invest. This "write-off ratio" is frequently greater than one-to-one. And any such write-off ratio should be your warning to stay clear of what is probably a transaction meant to defraud the United States Government.

One typical abusive tax shelter involved the leasing of master recordings (original recordings by famous music groups) overvalued by promoters at 100 times their actual cost. The prospectus for the shelter promised investors tax write-offs not only in the future, but for prior years. Another abusive tax shelter involved overvalued art works which, when donated to charitable organizations, led to substantial (though completely bogus) write-offs for investors. Many, though not all, abusive tax shelters involve film production, master recordings, lithographs, and rare books and other collectibles.

Generally, you should be wary of any tax shelter that promises tax savings many times the cost of investment. This unrealistic promise is a tell-tale sign of tax-shelter abuse.

THERE ARE LAWS

There are laws designed to halt abusive tax shelters. These include laws requiring sellers of tax shelters to register them with the IRS. The laws also require investors to report the registration numbers of tax shelters using Form 8271 when filing their tax return. Taxpayers found to be involved with abusive tax shelters may incur negligence or fraud penalties in addition to a penalty on any substantial understatement of income. Furthermore, stiff penalties, including jail, are a distinct possibility for any person who directly or indirectly participates in the promotion or sale of an abusive tax shelter.

HOW TO BE A SHREWD INVESTOR IN TAX SHELTERS

There are steps to take to make sure that any tax shelter you invest in is a legitimate, non-abusive entity providing genuine investment promise coupled with fair and *honest* tax protection.

1. Ask for an *independent* tax attorney's *written* opinion as to the tax consequences of the proposed investment.

2. Obtain all relevant information as to the fair market value of the property or partnership being sold as an investment. That is, get an *independent* appraisal by a *reputable third party* in order to ascertain whether the fair market value of the property or partnership is what the promoter says it is.

3. Obtain all brochures, copies of agreements, and prospectuses associated with the investment and discuss these with your own personal financial adviser, *not one associated with the promoter.*

CASE STUDY: A WORST-CASE SCENARIO

Meet Scott the Idiot. We'll just call him Scott, for short. Scott puts $10,000 into an oil and gas drilling venture that advertises a five-to-one tax write-off and promises a $25,000 tax saving for a $10,000 investment. Scott is so blinded by the unrealistic prospect of a $15,000 windfall that he dives in without checking the legality of the tax shelter and without checking the credentials of the shady promoter touting the deal.

In addition to the $10,000 investment (which he borrows), Scott also signs $20,000 in "recourse notes" for the promoter. The promoter fails to drill any wells (what a surprise!) and Scott, on the promoter's advice, duly deducts $25,000 from his income on his tax return. Scott also claims an additional $1,000 credit pursuant to the promoter's transmittal of an IRS statement (Form K-1) to Scott that details how much the promoter thinks can be deducted. Subsequently, the promoter sells Frank's recourse notes to a bank and disappears with the cash.

A red flag goes up. The IRS investigates the tax shelter. The IRS winds up disallowing all deductions associated with the shelter. Scott loses his deductions, gets hit with penalties and interest payable to the IRS, and loses his initial $10,000 cash investment. He still owes that $10,000 to his bank, and he must also pay another bank the full $20,000 loan associated with the recourse notes, plus interest.

QUESTIONS SCOTT THE IDIOT SHOULD HAVE ASKED

1. How long has the promoter of the tax shelter been in business?

2. What kind of record does the promoter have with similar tax-shelter programs?

3. What kind of periodic reports will be provided to investors to document revenue and expenses relating to the investment? Will these reports be audited by an independent certified public accountant?

4. Is the tax shelter registered with the government? Is the promoter licensed as a securities dealer?

5. What is the timeline for *profit* as defined in the business plan for the investment?

6. How much of his or her own money is the promoter putting into the tax shelter? None? That's the wrong answer.

7. What does the prospectus for the investment indicate about the percentage *load* (or profit to the promoter) involved in the price of a share of the partnership? If the load is very high, then it is a sign that you might want to check out other tax shelters. The more money the promoter takes for him- or herself upfront, the less cash there is for the investment agenda of the partnership; thus, profit becomes that much less likely.

ALL ABOUT REAL ESTATE INVESTMENT TRUSTS (REITs)

One very popular tax-shelter is the Real Estate Investment Trust (REIT).

A REIT is very similar in concept to a closed-end investment company as defined in the mutual funds section of this book. It is a corporation organized for investment, but investment in real estate rather than stocks and bonds. Shares of REITs are bought and sold just like stocks and mutual funds. There are 220 REITs listed on stock changes currently, according to the National Association of Real Estate Investment Trusts.

A REIT delivers many advantages for the would-be investor in real estate including centralized management, limited liability for investors, continuity of interests, easy transferability of ownership, and of course, special tax treatment.

In fact, the unique tax status of REITs is most appealing. While public corporations are subject to corporate income tax, REITs (like other investment companies) can avoid, or largely avoid, the corporate income tax by distributing its earning to its shareholders. The distribution is then taxed to the shareholder as ordinary income. In other words, earnings are only taxed *once* from an investment in a REIT. Whereas, they might be taxed twice otherwise were you to set up your own real estate investment corporation, say, and then pay yourself a salary from the corporation. Of course, in the latter scenario, you have absolute control of the management of the corporation, and with a REIT you have no control at all. You abdicate that to the professional management controlling the REIT. (So make sure they have a good track record *before* you invest!)

It is important to note that REITs, like most other stocks, generally do better when interest rates are low. That is when developers build and buyers buy, and that is also when REITs are most profitable. A REIT that has had very good returns during periods of generally low interest rates may not do so well if rates increase. So keep this in mind when looking at a REIT's past performance records and endeavoring to use these to forecast future return. The picture may change.

As attractive as are REITs, there is another real-estate tax shelter that is even better, especially for regular folks. And that is . . .

YOUR HOME MORTGAGE: THE BEST REAL ESTATE TAX SHELTER GOING

That's right. As should be clear now, your home mortgage with fully deductible interest is absolutely the best real-estate tax shelter available to the typical wage earner. You build equity in your home, you deduct all interest, and you *live* in the house. Additionally, your home mortgage is nowhere near as risky as the other shelters itemized above. I don't know about you, but my favorite part of calculating my income tax each year is deducting that huge slice of mortgage interest from my gross income.

WRAPPING IT UP

There are many legitimate tax shelters out there. They come in many forms including labor-sponsored venture-capital funds, real estate, and natural resource flow-through shares. Remember, they are all risky. If you proceed prudently, however, you can limit this risk and make tax shelters work for you rather than against you. As a rule of thumb, remember to consider a tax shelter first as a straight investment, ignoring the tax-savings. Critique the investment first and then, if that looks worthwhile, factor in the tax-savings as icing on the cake. As one financial advisor puts it, "If an investment fails economically, you are probably going to lose money in real dollars, and, consequently, it does not make much sense to go into it for tax reasons." The thing to keep in mind is something Will Rogers used to say:

"It's not the return on my money that I worry about— it's the return of my money."

INTERNET RESOURCES RELATED TO TAX SHELTERS

As you surf the World Wide Web, you may encounter sites that discuss tax shelters and REITs. The following site list should help you locate the resources you need.

LEGAL TAX SHELTERS

http://www.intuit.com/turbotax/taxcenter/perguide/taxshelt.html

Here, courtesy of TurboTax, you will find discussion of such legal tax shelters as those related to shifting income to children by gifts of income-producing property, gift leasebacks, family partnerships, and transfer royalties.

Figure 19.1 Legal Tax Shelters.

TAX SHELTERS DIRECTORY

http://www.venturedirectory.com/taxshelters.htm

This site gives a directory of tax shelters that are completely legal, saving taxpayers a lot of money. Each of the supershelters are presented, explained, and structured in detail to show you how to legally reduce your own taxes to zero. They also provide Canadian tax shelters and offshore trusts. Learn about techniques and strategies that allow you and your family to shield assets from current and possibly future taxation.

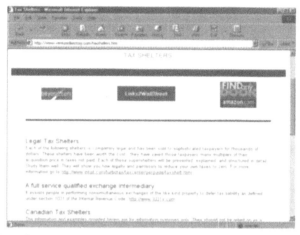

Figure 19.2 Tax Shelters Directory.

DELOITTE & TOUCHE: HEADS UP

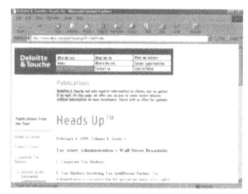

http://www.dttus.com/PUB/HEADSUP/
6-1/tax01f.htm

TAX TALK – SHELTERS

http://www.ios.com/~taxtalk/axhole.html

TAX SHELTER – DERIVIUM

http://www.invest-derivium.com

TAX SHELTERED ANNUITIES

http://www.huttodean.com

TAX SHELTER REPORTS

http://www.taxshelterreport.com

TAX PROTECTED INVESTMENT STRATEGIES

http://www.fielderfinancial.com

WARD CONSULTANCY – TAX SHELTERS

*http://www.wardconsultancy.plc.uk/
docs/tax.htm*

OFFSHORE TAX SHELTERS

http://www.offshore-tax-shelters.com

OFFSHORE TRUSTS, TAX SHELTERS

*http://www.atlantica.co.uk/gateway/
jsneddon.html*

TAX SHELTER

http://www.ppando.com/teletax/tc454.html

SEC. 6111 REGISTRATION OF TAX SHELTERS

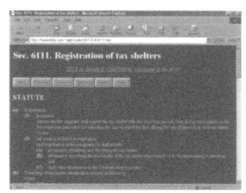

http://teaminfinity.com/~ralph/code/
t26-F-61-B-6111.html

SHAKY SHELTERS

http://www.fm.co.za/97/0314/economy/
shake.htm

CHAPTER 20
RETIREMENT PLANNING USING
EMPLOYMENT-RELATED
INVESTMENT OPTIONS

Live long and prosper. — *Mr. Spock of* Star Trek

We've spent a fair amount of time in this book discussing the financial risks associated with premature death. But there is another risk: the risk of living "too long" and thereby outliving one's cash-reserve. Obviously, the solution is not to die young. The solution is to plan well and carefully, thereby leaving yourself with enough cash on hand to enjoy some fruity drinks on a hot beach for your 120th birthday.

BEWARE OF ROSEANNE

Never believe popular wisdom. Popular wisdom says that if you handle a toad you'll get warts on your hands. You won't. Popular wisdom says Roseanne is humorous. She isn't. Popular wisdom says the best things in life are free. They aren't. And popular wisdom says you'll need less money after you retire than you do now. That's right. Popular wisdom actually says that it is somehow cheaper to be unemployed and elderly than it is to be employed and young.

If you want to live *less well* than you do now after you retire, then popular wisdom will hold true for you. But who wants to do that? Who wants to trade a new Mercedes for a used Pinto? Who wants to trade a fine old house overlooking San Francisco Bay for an aluminum tenement in a Fresno trailer park?

In fact, if anything, your retirement years will probably be *more* expensive than your working years. That is, if you live them well. After all, you'll have a great deal of leisure time. If you plan on being active and enthusiastic about life, if you plan to use your extensive leisure time to its fullest potential, you'll have trips to pay for, greens fees, tennis club dues, and (my personal favorite) mooring fees.

There are less expensive alternatives, of course. You could just sit in front of a TV, in a trailer park somewhere, watching Roseanne.

FORGET THE FEDS

I am only 28 years old, and it would be very foolish of me, with the Social Security and Medicare systems facing shortfalls within the next few years, to count in any way upon receiving even one thin dime from those lumbering bureaucracies once I come "of age" in thirty-five or forty years. What they pay out *now* is not enough to live on and not enough to cover medical expenses. Imagine what the picture will be like in thirty years. I am making plans so as to not have to rely on the Feds. My best advice to you is to do the same.

If you are around my age, do whatever it takes to have two million dollars in cash, not including your equity in your house, free and clear in your hands at age 65. More if you can. Does that sound like a lot of money? It isn't. Assuming a 5% annual rate of inflation, in 25 years $2 million will be worth exactly $592,981.16 in 2000 dollars. In other words, the price of milk will be somewhat higher than it is today. And the cost of medicine? Well, you can imagine.

Your tools for insuring your financial health upon retirement include various employer-provided retirement plans such as 401(k)s, Keoghs and IRAs for the self-employed, and so on.

EMPLOYER-PROVIDED RETIREMENT PLANS: THE BASICS

Assuming you are not self-employed, you will derive a large part of your retirement funding from employer-provided retirement plans. I use the plural because so few of us spend our lives working for a single employer these days. In fact, by the time most Americans retire, they've had an average of four different employers, with the highest number of job changes being associated, generally, with those who have the highest salaries. (In other words, executives tend to change jobs more regularly than steamfitters.)

Employer-provided retirement plans might include qualified pension plans, profit-sharing plans, and savings plans. The term "qualified" means that the plans qualify for special tax treatment. In addition to standard qualified pensions, profit-sharing plans, and savings plans, some firms may also provide simplified employee pensions plans (SEPs), tax-sheltered annuity plans (TSAs, for nonprofit corporations only), qualified stock bonus plans, nonqualified deferred-compensation plans, and supplemental executive retirement plans. These last two items, by the way, may of course be discriminatory. Uncle Sam says it is OK. And that's good because they are, in fact, inherently discriminatory.

DEFINED-BENEFIT PLANS VS. DEFINED-CONTRIBUTION PLANS

Defined-benefit plans and *defined-contribution plans* are the most common employer-provided retirement programs. They may sound similar, but there is a fundamental difference between them. And the *defined-contribution plan* is, to my mind, much more appealing.

A *defined-benefit plan* has a prescribed dollar-amount benefit *etched in stone*, as it were, for what the plan will be worth to the employee upon his/her retirement at some future date. Both the employee's and the employer's contributions to the plan fluctuate with the ebb and flow of interest rates and other market factors, ultimately aiming toward the prescribed dollar-value at the prescribed point in the timeline. Also, there is no real individual element to the *defined-benefit plan*. All contributions go into a communal pot. Employee and employer contributions are most often prescribed by the employer. The employer, or a representative of the employer serving as administrator of the "retirement fund," directs the investments of the fund. All employees, upon retirement, ultimately get their *share* as prescribed by the precise dollar amount etched in stone so many years before.

A *defined-contribution plan*, on the other hand, has no prescribed dollar-amount benefit etched in stone for the date of retirement. It will be worth what it'll be worth depending upon the extent of employee and employer contributions to the pot, and the ebb and flow of investment returns over time. It is also an *individual* program. In the typical *defined-contribution plan*, such as a qualified savings (or *thrift*) plan, the employee directs the investment of his/her capital by choosing from (a usually limited, but sufficient) menu of investment options ranging from company stock to some mutual funds to a money market account. The employee usually has the option to allocate percentages of his/her nest egg to these various investment options. And the employee can further decide what percentage of his/her salary to contribute to the plan, with the company matching the employee contribution up to a certain percentage maximum. Invariably, for both *defined-benefit plans* and *defined-contribution plans*, there is a period of several years during which the employee *vests* in the company contributions to the plan, usually to the tune of about 20% per year with 100% vestiture after five years of service. Which means that if you were to leave the company after the first year, you would receive 20% of the employer's contribution. Likewise, after the second year you would be eligible for 40% and so on. Finally, after the fifth year, you would be "fully vested," meaning you would be eligible for 100% of the employer's contribution.

Traditional pension plans, save for "money-purchase pension plans," are always *defined-benefit plans*. And virtually all the more interesting retirement options, such as profit-sharing plans, savings plans, stock bonus plans, and employee stock ownership plans, are *defined-contribution plans*.

How a Plan Is "Qualified"

Your employer will most likely offer a *qualified* retirement benefits plan, which as I explained before, means the plan has met certain federal guidelines that qualify it for favorable tax treatment. There are four key criteria associated with qualifying:

1. There has to be a legally binding agreement regarding the plan set in writing and communicated to the employees.

2. The plan must be for the exclusive benefit of employees and their beneficiaries.

3. It must be impossible for capital associated with the plan to be diverted from its purpose of generating dividends, which in turn become capital, in the plan. There can be no diversion of plan funds for any other purpose.

4. Finally, as I mentioned earlier, the plan must benefit all employees equally and not favor one class of employees (say, executives) over another (say, assembly-line personnel). The plan must be democratic in its liberality.

THE JOYS (ECONOMICS) OF BEING QUALIFIED

The tax advantages associated with qualified-retirement plans are substantial. There are three key advantages, and they all add up to significant tax-savings over time for employee and employer alike:

1. No moneys in the plan, either moneys contributed by the employer or employee or interest and dividends earned by those moneys, are taxable at all until such time as they are actually distributed to the employee.

2. Lump-sum distributions (such as those doled out when an employee leaves one firm to join another) are accorded favorable tax treatment in that most of these can be rolled over (or directly transferred) into another qualified plan, or deposited in an IRA, without any tax ramifications whatsoever.

3. Most contributions made by the employer are fully deductible by the employer as a business expense.

CODA: THE FAMOUS 401(K)

The majority of qualified defined-contribution plans allow employees to make contributions on a before-tax basis under a Cash Or Deferred Arrangement (CODA, as it is sometimes called). The more popular name is a *401(k) plan*—this name being derived from the Internal Revenue Code (IRC) provision defining CODAs.

With CODAs, participants in a plan authorize their employer to deduct x dollars from their salary on a before-tax basis (up to a certain level). Participants further instruct their employer to contribute that deduction to a qualified-savings plan, profit-sharing plan, stock-bonus plan, or money-purchase pension plan.

In the majority of instances, the 401(k) is a qualified-savings plan and, in such instances, employers also match the employee's contribution (up to a certain level of investment) as a form of profit-sharing. Qualified savings (sometimes known as *thrift*) plans are, in fact, so pervasive as a 401(k) instrument that many people think the only type of 401(k) available is a qualified-savings plan. However, the 401(k) rules can apply to other profit-sharing plans, stock-bonus plans, or money-purchase pension plans just as easily.

Restrictions on Distributions

CODAs are great investment vehicles. The tax sheltering will help your money grow faster than it could in just about any other environment. But remember, *don't plan on seeing that money back in your pocket until you retire.* At least don't expect to get it back in your pocket without paying a hefty penalty. For the most part, dollars invested in a CODA on a pre-tax basis may not be distributed to the employee unless:

- The employee reaches the age of 59½.

- The employee separates from the firm (in which case the money must be rolled over or directly-transferred into another qualified plan, or an IRA, within a relatively short period of time in order to avoid tax penalties).

- The employee dies, in which case his/her beneficiary gets the money in a lump sum.

- A long-term disability (as defined by strict IRS rules) hits the employee.

- There is a case of extreme hardship (as defined by strict IRS rules) involving the employee.

The one way to tap into some of the money in your 401(k) is to arrange for a loan from your account balance, assuming that such loans are allowed under the terms of your particular plan. In this instance, you would in effect borrow money from yourself, from your 401(k) plan account, and pay yourself back in a timely manner with a reasonable rate of interest prescribed by the plan. The money you borrow would not be taxable as a distribution so long as you did not default on the loan from yourself.

Default. Fail to pay yourself back. And you'll get slammed with taxes plus penalties on a premature distribution.

HR-10 or Keogh Plans: For the Self-Employed

The Self-Employed Individuals Tax Retirement Act of 1962, also called HR-10 or the Keogh Act, makes it possible for owner/employees of unincorporated business and other self-employed people (like bookwriters!!) to have qualified-retirement plans. The one main rule to remember here is that parity is necessary. The Internal Revenue Code insists on it. If you are the proprietor of an unincorporated business with full-time employees for whom you provide retirement benefits, your Keogh Plan may not treat you more favorably than your standard-retirement plan treats your employees. As a self-employed author, I have no employees so I can treat myself pretty darned well without having to worry about treating anyone else pretty darned well. It is one of the few perks of my line of business.

TAKING THE MONEY OUT

When you come of age and it becomes time to receive a distribution or distributions from your 401(k) or other qualified plan, it is also time to talk very seriously with a competent financial/tax consultant. You will invariably have a number of options on how to take your money. You might just take a small federally-prescribed minimum payments. You might want a distribution of the entire value of your account in a lump sum. Or you might want to receive the value of your account as a periodic (or annuity) distribution. Which scenario is right for you depends on your financial situation, your health (your life expectancy), whether your plan was contributory or noncontributory (which impacts the tax-treatment of distri-butions), and other key factors.

The tax-code relating to distributions from qualified-retirement plans is complex, to say the least. In order to keep most of your retirement money in your pocket, always talk to a competent financial/tax advisor. *Always.*

INTERNET RESOURCES RELATED TO RETIREMENT PLANNING

As you surf the World Wide Web, you may encounter sites that retirement planning, employer-sponsored retirement plans, and more. The following site list should help you locate the resources you need.

FACTS YOU SHOULD KNOW ABOUT RETIREMENT

http://www.prusec.com/financial_concerns/retr1.htm

Did you know that the first retirement act was established more than 100 years ago? It happened in Germany. And the man who established it was Otto Bon Bismarck. Thus, it was old Otto himself who first set the retirement age at 65. Of course, back then only 2% of the population even lived to age 65! Thanks a lot Otto! That would be something like setting today's retirement age at 95.

Prudential Securities helps you plan for retirement by providing products and strategies, including a wealth calculator so you can compute how much you will have. This page gives 15 smart solutions for better retirement planning.

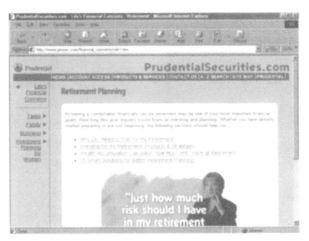

Figure 20.1 *Facts You Should Know About Retirement.*

MPOWER

http://www.401kforum.com

mPower has been online since 1995 giving retirement investment advice. Their service is not about crunching numbers or making general suggestions. They will give you proven research methods to give specific, easy-to-follow advice on buying and selling funds. Their goal is to empower employees to make sound retirement investment decisions,

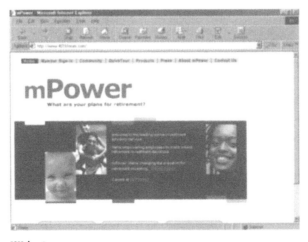

Figure 20.2 *mPower Web site.*

RETIREMENT INVESTMENT OPTIONS

http://www.quicken.com/retirement

MFS 401K INVESTMENT RESOURCES

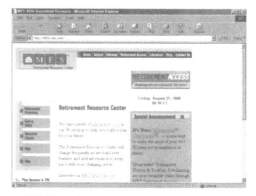

http://401k.mfs.com

401K RETIREMENT PLANNER

http://shrike.depaul.edu/~jjachim

401K RETIREMENT PLANNING SOFTWARE

http://www.webcalcs.com/retplan.html

FINANCIAL ADVISOR FOR RETIREMENT 401K ADVICE AND PLANNING

http://www.guidedchoice.com

401K LINKS – CONSUMER WATCH

http://www.kwtv.com/investigators/401k.htm

401K INVESTMENT ADVICE

http://www.logicinvesting.com/pers_fin/401k.htm

A STEP-BY STEP GUIDE TO RETIREMENT

http://www.planningforretirement.com

SEARCH STEPS – PLAN YOUR RETIREMENT

http://www.searchsteps.com

THE RETIREMENT CENTER

http://www.familyhaven.com/retirement

RETIREMENT TROUBLESHOOTER

http://www.thirdage.com/features/money/retire

401K ADVICE AND INFORMATION

http://quicken.aol.com/retirement/401k

IRA INFORMATION AND TOOLS

http://quicken.aol.com/retirement/IRA

WOMEN'S WIRE ON RETIREMENT

http://www.womenswire.com/basics/
retirement5.html

TIPS FOR THE SELF-EMPLOYED

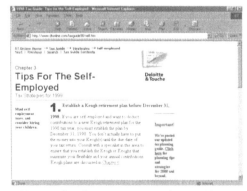

http://www.dtonline.com/taxguide98/self.htm

WORKPLACE SAVINGS: RETIREMENT PLANNING

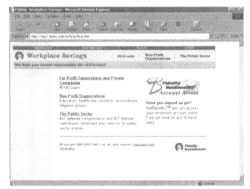

http://wps1.fid-inv.com/tx/fir/rp/fir-rp.htm

RETIREMENT PLANNING: KEOGH PLANS

http://www.e-analytics.com/fp33.htm

RETIREMENT PLANS OF THE SELF-EMPLOYED

http://www.isquare.com/retire.htm

CHAPTER 21

THE ART OF HOME BUYING

A home is an unremarkable thing unless you don't have one. — *Will Rogers*

It is appropriate that we should move from retirement planning directly to a chapter on home ownership. Why? Because home ownership is a fundamental part of sound retirement planning. Retirees who rent all their lives not only wind up with no equity in real estate to factor into their wealth, they also wind up with more rent to pay. Homeowners, on the other hand, have usually paid off their mortgages by the time they retire. Thus, homeowners not only enjoy the stable rock of equity in their home, underpinning their wealth; they also get to live rent-free after they take care of their real-estate taxes, home insurance, and maintenance and utilities.

You and I will never make a fortune on our homes as our parents' or grandparents' generation did. In 1956, a house on Long Island was $12,000. Now that same home is worth $210,000. That means it has gone up in value more than 1600%! Over a 40-year period, 1600% translates to an *annual increase in value* of 40% per year! Of course, the number is somewhat less impressive when you adjust for inflation. But even then it looks good. Assuming an (high) annual 5% rate of inflation, you are still looking at a 1400% increase in *real value* over 40 years. And, while my parents were enjoying the benefit of that investment, they were also writing off mortgage interest *and* living in the house, raising their family.

That kind of return on real estate will never happen again. Never. But still, home ownership is the wise thing to do. Chapter 13, "Good Debt: Mortgage Debt" studies mortgages in detail. This chapter, therefore, focuses on non-mortgage fundamentals associated with the art of finding the right home at the right price without getting ripped-off in the process.

YOU'RE NOT INSOMNIAC, ARE YOU?

I hope not. But if so, you've probably seen late-night infomercials where some guy with a cheap toupe, standing on the deck of beautiful luxury yacht, explains how he made a fortune in real estate with "no money down." You can do it too, if you buy his course on the subject. That'll cost you $500. You may not have to put money down on real estate, but you sure do have to put money down for the course!

The first question that comes to mind is, of course, how can this guy be able to afford such a gorgeous boat but not be able to afford a descent-looking hairpiece? The second question that comes to mind is: Can you really purchase real estate with "no money down" and then turn around and sell it within a few days at a staggeringly high "profit." Furthermore, can you really buy two houses with no cash down, sell the second one for a fat profit within days, and live in the first one for the rest of your life virtually rent-free? Is life really that easy? If so, why does anyone bother working for a living?

Of course life is not that easy. Your first step toward any form of real estate investment should be to keep to yourself the $500 the man with the hairpiece wants to take from you.

WHAT HE'S REALLY SELLING

The guy with the fake hair is actually selling a program that instructs you how to invest in *distressed* real estate. This, he wants you to believe, is an investment you can make without capital. He misses the point of course—or at least he hopes *you* will miss the point—that the idea of investment without capital is an oxymoron. It can't be done. Investment without capital is like singing without a song, speaking without words, swimming without water. Without a song there is no singing. Without words there is no speech. Without water there is no swimming. And without cash there is no investment.

Distressed real estate is bank-owned property. It is property associated with bank foreclosures. The bank does not want the property. But the bank does want cash. And before they give you the property they are invariably going to want you to give them some money, no matter what Mr. "I bought fifteen houses without investing a cent" has to say about it. (By the way, if he's made so much money in real estate, what is he doing peddling his course on TV? Does he really need the cash he charges for the course when he can buy and sell real estate, making a fortune in the process, with no startup cash at all? Think about it.)

How do you really buy bank-owned properties? Usually through a real-estate agency, just like any other property for which you might be shopping. The real-estate agency will be working for the bank and will be striving to get the bank fair market value for the house. The bank, in this most common situation, is just another ordinary seller, and you are just another ordinary buyer. Sorry. They are going to ask for and get whatever the market will tolerate. There is no defacto cut-rate in place for distressed properties.

Beyond this, however, there are special situations. Let's say the foreclosed property is in an area where there is dramatically low demand for real estate. Let's say it is in an area where there are many foreclosed homes, block after block of them, and little or no local economy to support much of anything in the way of home ownership. In that case, you probably can pickup a foreclosed home very cheaply, although not for free.

To find out about these great investments, you don't have to give $500 to the guy with the wig. Just contact your good old friends at the Federal National Mortgage Association (Fannie Mae) at *http://www.fanniemae.com* and ask for the *free* booklet entitled *How to Buy a Foreclosed Home*. Fannie Mae has more than one forclosed home they'd love for you to buy, and they'll make it darned easy for you to do so.

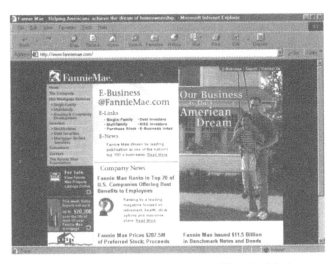

Figure 21.1 The Federal National Mortgage Association (Fannie Mae).

THE FRIENDLY REAL ESTATE AGENT IS NOT YOUR PAL

Whenever you are looking to purchase any property whatsoever, whether it be a private home or an office building, remember one thing. The person touring you through the place, the person with the wide smile who whispers conspiratorially to you that the asking price is ridiculously low, is *not* your friend and is *not* your best source of information.

You are the buyer. The real estate agent works for the seller. The real estate agent's charter from the seller is to get as much cash as possible out of you, the buyer. This basic tenet of the seller/agent relationship is bolstered by the fact that the agent is compensated on a percentage basis. The higher the sales price for the property, the higher the real estate agent's compensation.

So keep your own counsel. Don't blab too much to the real estate agent. Don't confide *anything*. Don't say something like: "We really love this house, we'll do whatever it takes to get it. We'll offer $150,000 right now but, between you and me, we'll be willing to go higher if the seller rejects that offer. We can qualify for enough of a mortgage that we'll be able to go to $165,000 if we have to." In this scenario, there is no way the agent is going to allow the seller to accept the $150,000 offer. There is no "between you and me" with a buyer and a real estate agent. The agent will undoubtedly say to the seller: "Joe Schmuck has offered $150,000 but I know he is willing to pay another $15,000. So I advise you to say the lowest price you'll take will be $165,000." And that's exactly what'll happen. And you'll wind up paying an extra $15,000 for your naivete.

> ### Check Out Books and Videos
>
> If you are shopping for a new home, take time to drive to the library or bookstore and pick up a few books and videos on "Buying and Selling a Home." The few hours you spend reading about the "perils" other homebuyers have experienced may save you time, money, and many headaches later on down the road. You might start with *Kiplinger's Buying and Selling a Home* (ISBN: 0-8129-2780-X) at 800-727-7015.

NO ONE THE REALTOR RECOMMENDS IS YOUR PAL EITHER

Get *your own engineer* to look at the house you are considering purchasing, not the one the realtor recommends. Do your own mortgage shopping. Don't go with the mortgage company or bank the realtor recommends. Investigate the local schools yourself. Talk to the principal and ask to see achievement test scores for the school and school district; this is public information. Don't trust the realtor's knowledgeable reassurance that "the schools around here are excellent." According to realtors across America, the schools everywhere are excellent.

THE GOOD AND THE BAD OF CONDOS AND CO-OPS

As it turns out, the home you buy may not be a house, but rather, it may be a condo or coop. There are several fundamental differences between condominiums and coops. And they all conspire to make condos more appealing as investment vehicles.

In a condo arrangement, you own your individual unit outright. You own the walls, the door, the windows, and the patio. Beyond that, you and your neighbors share (and jointly own) communal areas and services (the lobby, the swimming pool, the pool staff, and the grounds maintenance staff, and so on). The fixed costs of maintaining/staffing the communal aspects of the condo are shared by the condo owners, who make monthly maintenance-fee payments to service these costs. Individuals, of course, also make monthly mortgage payments, including tax-deductible interest, as well as property tax-payments, insurance payments, and so on.

In a co-op arrangement, the picture appears to be the same, but is not. You live in your own unit, but you do not own your own unit. You own a piece of it, just as you own a piece of all your neighbors' units as well. You do not, in fact, own any real estate at all, at least not outright. What you own are shares in a corporation, which in turn owns your entire building.

Since you have not purchased any real estate, the loan you took out to buy your coop is not secured with a lien on property. Thus, it is not a mortgage but rather a personal loan secured with a lien on some shares in a corporation. What's the difference? On a mortgage loan your interest payments are deductible. On a personal loan, they are not. Furthermore, the co-op corporation may have, at the time of the building of the co-op, taken out a mortgage to finance that construction. A portion of your monthly maintenance will go to service this debt, inflating your monthly maintenance above and beyond the cost of maintaining and staffing communal areas. Thus, in addition to having no deductibility for interest, monthly maintenance costs are routinely higher for co-ops than for condos. If you care to look for a silver lining to all this, there is a thin one: that *portion* of a co-op's monthly maintenance that goes to service interest on the corporation's mortgage debt is deductible. Lucky you!

Would you like another reason to hate co-ops? Ok. Here goes. You can't sell your co-op to just anybody. Prospective buyers of your apartment (prospective buyers of your shares in the corporation) usually must be approved by a co-op residents' committee. Not only do you have to find someone with the finances and instinct to buy, you have to find someone with the finances and instinct to buy you out *of whom the co-op committee approves*. Nice. If the co-op board is overly finnicky, you may be sunk. You're so swell to have around, they just might want you as a neighbor forever!

Renting Better Than Buying?

Not often. But every once in a while it does make more sense to rent than to buy. This would be the case, say, if you have a rent-controlled apartment that features an incredibly cheap rent combined with a panoramic view of New York harbor. This would also be the case if you know you are only planning to stay in a given city for a year or two before relocating. It might likewise be shrewd to rent if you see houses going down in value in your region, and you want to let them slip *before* you buy rather than after. But, barring these factors, you will generally be better off buying rather than renting, at least in the long term.

Think You Love It, But Aren't Sure?

You think it might be the house of your dreams. But you are not absolutely sure. You'd like to try out the house, the neighborhood, the local markets, the schools before you make your final decision. Fine! See if the owner of the house you are interested in will consider a *lease with an option to buy*. If the seller is motivated, you just might have a deal.

In a *lease with an option to buy arrangement* you sign a lease agreeing to rent the home for *x* number of months at *x* amount of rent. It is written into the lease that at the end of the lease period you will have the option, though not the obligation, to purchase the house at a pre-scribed price. Your option to buy the house remains in force throughout the duration of the lease. The owner of the house cannot sell the house to anyone else during that period of time.

From a property-value point-of-view, the option can't help but work for you. If the value of the house goes down during the period of your lease, and you wind up thinking that your option price as stated in the lease is too high, simply don't exercise the option to buy and instead negotiate new sales terms. However, if the value of the property goes up during your option period, you can hold the seller to the terms of the option (including the option price) and therefore get a bargain!

The downside of a lease is that your lease payments are not tax deductible, as would be the interest on a mortgage payment.

SELLER FINANCING: GREAT NEWS FOR THE BUYER

Seller financing is rare, but it is also great news for buyers. There are usually few or no closing costs and no points. What's more, there are no formal income requirements, just whatever the seller is willing to put up with.

Keep in mind that by providing financing the seller is not in fact laying out any money. What the seller is doing is simply transferring the property to the buyer with an appropriate percentage lien placed on the property as the seller's surety for payment of the mortgage he/she has "written" by transferring the property.

Your interest payments are still deductible in an owner-financing situation. And the interest must be declared as income by the seller. So make sure you have the seller's social security number. Also make sure you get an annual statement from the seller describing property tax payments, and so on.

All of these details should be stipulated in the formal mortgage agreement executed between buyer and seller (mortgagee and mortgagor). And both your lawyers should review that document completely before either of you signs it.

Do Drive-Bys

"I'll meet you there at 10 AM on Sunday," said the realtor after giving you the address for a home he wanted to show you. You went on Sunday at 10 AM and you fell in love. The house was adorable. The backyard was immaculate. And the street was quiet and uncrowded.

However, good thing you had read this section in *Net Worth* about drive-bys. Good thing it told you to be sure to cruise past your dream house at random hours of the day and night to see what was going on and what the feel of the neighborhood was like.

When you went back to drive past the house on Monday morning, you found the quiet street had turned into a virtual parking lot for the office building three blocks away. People evidently show up about 8:30 AM in the morning, lock their cars, and

---

440

leave them until just after 5:00 PM at which time there is a congested snarl for about 20 minutes while they all try to squeeze their cars out of the little street at once, honking and shouting at one another. In the interim, with cars parked on top of each other up and down both sides of the street, many residents of the block find it tricky to maneuver their cars in and out of their driveways.

When you went back at about 10 PM the same night, you noticed some rough looking kids standing on the corner three doors away from the house you are in love with. They had a radio and they played it loud. A few of them held beers. Some others smoked cigarettes that did not appear to be Marlboros. When you cruised past an hour later they were still there. In fact, there were more of them. And the radio was cranked up even louder than before. No wonder the real estate agent wanted you to see the place at 10 AM on Sunday!

KNOW YOUR MARKET

Be an educated consumer. Make a study of the prices in the neighborhood you are interested in. Make it your business to know more than just the *asking prices* of the houses currently available. Make it your business to know the *actual selling prices* of recently sold homes in the neighborhood—this, again, is public information. In most places, such as my town here in Rhode Island, every property transfer is listed in a weekly newspaper column that shows property addresses, buyers' names, sellers' names, and *the amount* associated with each transfer. Armed with actual recent selling prices for equivalent homes in the neighborhood, you'll be a better-educated home shopper and be better able to make astute, realistic offers on properties.

INTERNET RESOURCES RELATED TO HOME BUYING

As you surf the World Wide Web, you may encounter sites about home buying. The following site list should help you locate the resources you need.

HOME BUYER'S INFORMATION CENTER

http://www.ourfamilyplace.com/homebuyers/index.html

At this site, there are over 100 pages of free information on buying a home, from preparation to mortgages. A complete step-by-step guide helps you find the best home and more!

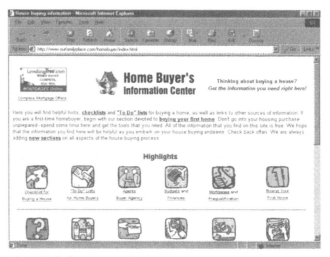

Figure 21.2 Home Buyer's Information Center.

HOME BUYERS FREE RESOURCE CENTER

http://www.fsboadvertisingservice.com

You can buy homes, search their national database, get free email notification of new listings, free school information, homeowners insurance quotes, and apply for a loan—all for FREE!

Figure 21.3 Home Buyers Free Resource Center.

HOME ADVISOR

http://www.homeadvisor.msn.com/default.asp

HUD HOMES FOR SALE – NO DOWN PAYMENT

http://www.snmcmortgage.com

HOME BUYING

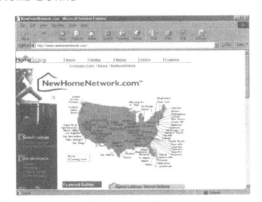

http://www.newhomenetwork.com

HOME BUYING – RELOCATION

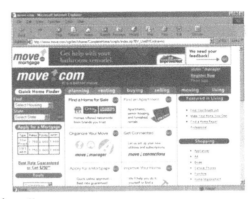

http://www.move.com

HOME LOAN RATES AVAILABLE

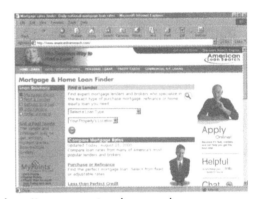

http://www.americanloansearch.com

SMART HOME BUYERS – SECRETS TO BUYING A HOME

http://www.smarthomebuyers.com

FREE LOAN CALCULATOR

http://www.fasthomeloans.com/calculator.html

RELOCATION SERVICES

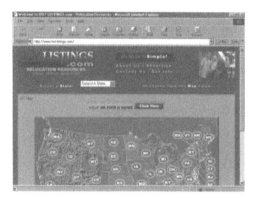

http://www.hot-listings.com

HOME INSPECTIONS

http://www.usinspect.com

MORTGAGE RATE DIRECTORY

http://www.e-interestratesonline.com

NATIONAL MORTGAGE BROKER DIRECTORY

http://www.idealrates.com

BUYING FORECLOSURES

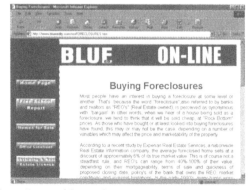

http://www.bluerealty.com/
reoFORECLOSURES.htm

FIND FINANCING FOR YOUR HOME

http://www.mortgage-x.com

INFORM YOURSELF

http://www.informyourself.com

BOISE (IDAHO) REAL ESTATE

http://www.group-one.com

HOMEBUYER'S KIT

http://www.hud.gov/buyhome.html

BEST MORTGAGE RATES, LOW FEES

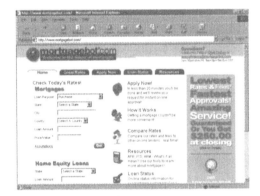

http://www.mortgagebot.com

CALIFORNIA REAL ESTATE HOME PAGE

http://www.californiarealestate.com

CANADA REAL ESTATE

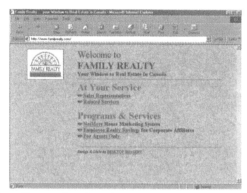

http://www.familyrealty.com

COLORADO REAL ESTATE

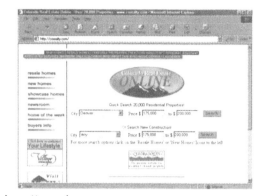

http://corealty.com

DALLAS (TEXAS) REAL ESTATE

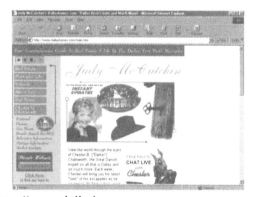

http://www.dallashomes.com

DAYTON (OHIO) REAL ESTATE

http://www.dayton-real-estate.com

FLORIDA INTERNET REAL ESTATE GUIDE

http://www.floridaguide.com

HELPFUL HINTS ON BUYING/SELLING A HOME

http://www.tgx.com/durocher/realst.htm

FRESNO (CALIFORNIA) REAL ESTATE

http://www.guarantee.com

LOS ANGELES (CALIFORNIA) REAL ESTATE

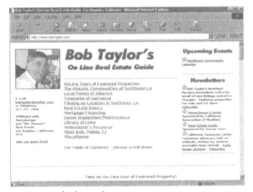

http://www.bob-taylor.com

REAL ESTATE AND HOME RESOURCE CENTER

http://www.homenet.com/barkin.htm

HOMEFAIR REAL ESTATE RESOURCES

http://www.homefair.com

INDIANA REAL ESTATE NETWORK

http://realty.mibor.net

MASSACHUSETTS REAL ESTATE WEB

http://www.bisweb.com

GLOBAL REAL ESTATE

http://www.corcoran.com

MARYLAND/VIRGINIA REAL ESTATE

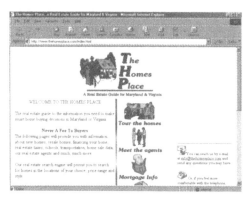

http://www.homefinders.com

NEW ENGLAND REAL ESTATE GUIDE

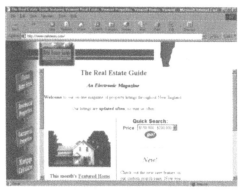

http://www.nehomes.com

MICHIGAN REAL ESTATE

http://michigan-real-estate.com

MONTANA REAL ESTATE

http://montanamax.com

NEW YORK/NEW JERSEY REAL ESTATE

http://nyrealty.com

NEW HAMPSHIRE REAL ESTATE

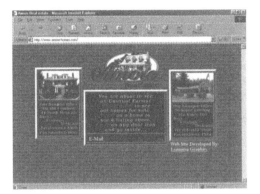

http://www.amore-homes.com

OHIO (CENTRAL OHIO) REAL ESTATE

http://www.buckeyehomes.com

TAMPA (FLORIDA) REAL ESTATE

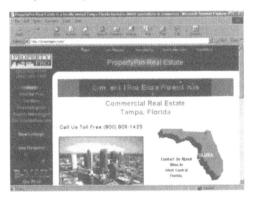

http://propertypro.com

WORLD WIDE REAL ESTATE NETWORK

http://www.america-homes.com

SAN DIEGO HOME BUYING

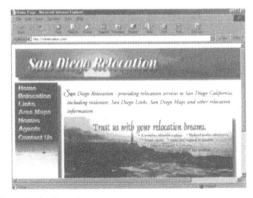

http://sdrelocation.com

SANTA BARBARA REAL ESTATE

http://www.coastalrealty.com

PHOENIX AREA REAL ESTATE

http://www.mazeltovrelocation.com

UTAH REAL ESTATE ONLINE

http://www.osmondrealestate.com

LAS VEGAS REAL ESTATE – FREE VIDEO

http://www.remaxlv.com

WICHITA HOMES

http://www.realtor-shorty.com

MINNESOTA REAL ESTATE

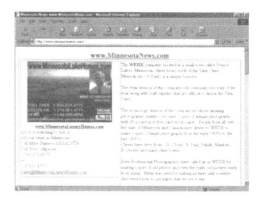

http://www.minnesotanews.com

CHAPTER 22
ESTATE PLANNING
FUNDAMENTALS

Put not your trust in money, but put your money in trust. — *Oliver Wendell Holmes*

I'm not going to die. Not ever. But you are. So you'd better plan in order to make sure that your wealth is transferred as smoothly as possible, and as *entirely* as possible, to your heirs. Tax minimization is the key here, since the maximum estate tax is a whopping 60%! And the good news is that if you plan correctly, you can reduce estate and inheritance taxes substantially. But before we can understand estate planning, we have to define some fundamentals about property and property ownership.

THE DIFFERENT TYPES OF PROPERTY

Estate planning calls for preparing plans for the disbursement of personal property. *Personal property* is, obviously, anything that can be owned by an individual. It is land, a house, and so on. Personal property includes *real property*—it is a car, a boat, furniture, jewelry. Personal property includes *tangible property* —and it is stock certificates, bonds, bank deposits, and life insurance vestitures. Personal property also includes *intangible property*. You can't hold or smell or live in intangible property, but it is there. In my case, intangible property would also include some copyrights.

THE DIFFERENT TYPES OF PROPERTY OWNERSHIP

The way in which property is held impacts greatly on the way it is transferred as part of an estate. There are three main types of property ownership: *outright ownership, joint ownership*, and *community property*.

Outright ownership is, of course, the most straightforward and simple model. This is property held 100% in the name of an individual. This individual can do anything he or she wants with the property: sell it, use it as collateral, give it away, or designate heirs to receive it at the appropriate time. Outright ownership can apply to any form of property at all, anything that can be owned: jewels, cars, houses, computers, sailboats (notice how I keep coming back to sailboats?), and so on.

Joint ownership is, clearly, when two or more persons have ownership rights in a property. Joint ownership applies in cases as simple as joint bank accounts and jointly owned government savings bonds. But more complex varieties of joint ownership include *joint tenancy with right of survivorship (WROS), tenancy in common,* and *tenancy by the entirety.*

In a *joint tenancy WROS* situation, if one of the joint owners dies the deceased's share of the property passes automatically to the surviving owners. One important thing to remember is that rights of survivorship are not transferable. What this means is that if Herman and Gladys own property as joint tenants WROS, and Gladys sells her share in the property to Samantha, then Herman and Samantha will thereafter own the property as *tenants in common.* This means joint tenancy *without* rights of survivorship.

Tenancy by the entirety exists in some states and is applied when property is held jointly by a husband and wife. There are survivorship rights here. And these cannot be terminated except with the consent of both husband and wife. A common mistake is to assume that all the property owned by a husband and wife is automatically held jointly by them. Except in community property states, to be discussed below, this is not the case. Only property specifically titled or received as joint property, shared between husband and wife, is deemed to be so. Thus a husband may own some property outright. And a wife may own other property outright. And neither will necessarily inherit all of the other's property unless careful plans are made. States where community property laws are not in effect are generally called *common law* states.

In *community property* states (such as Arizona, California, Idaho, Louisiana, Nevada, New Mexico, Texas and Washington), husbands and wives can own both *separate property* and *community property.* Although laws vary from state to state, generally *separate property* is a term used to describe (1) property that a husband or wife possessed before their marriage, (2) property each receives as a gift or inheritance, or (3) property purchased with funds held before marriage or received as gift or inheritance. Income derived from *separate property* becomes *community property* in some states, and not in others. *Community property* is property that either spouse acquires (through means other than those enumerated above) during marriage. Each spouse owns a 50% interest in all *community property.* And there generally is no automatic right of survivorship. Each spouse can dispose of his or her share of community property anyway he or she likes, as enunciated in a will.

MOST RIVERS FLOW...

Most rivers flow one way and not the other. And so too does the river of *community property.* *Community property*, acquired in a *community property* state, remains *community property* even if the owners move to a *common law* state. However, property acquired by a couple in a *common law* state does *not* then become *community property* when they move to a *community property* state. Got it?

SO WHAT IS AN ESTATE, ANYWAY?
(AND WHY IS NEVADA THE BEST PLACE TO DIE?)

Simply defined, your *estate* is the whole enchalada. It is everything you are worth. It is all that you leave: all your real property, all your tangible property, all your intangible property. *The works*. But your estate can (and is) looked at in several different ways at several different points in time, and because of this the term *estate,* precisely defined, means different things at different moments and in different circumstances. Sometimes, the term *estate* will be used to refer to your *probate estate*. At other times, it will be used to refer to *your gross estate for federal estate tax purposes*. At another point, it will be used to refer to your *accumulated state death tax value*. And then finally, the term *estate* will be used to describe the "net" estate your heirs finally wind up with.

The *probate estate* relates to the bulk of your assets and contains all property that is to be handled/distributed by the executor or administrator of your estate. This usually includes any property owned *outright* in your own name (but not your share of any joint tenancies), interest in property you hold as a tenant in common, life insurance payable upon your death, and your share of community property.

The *gross estate for federal estate tax purposes* is your worth as defined by tax law and is the amount your estate gets taxed on. Most of estate planning, per se, goes into whittling down the amount of your gross estate for federal estate tax purposes. Your gross estate includes everything and anything in your probate estate. But it also includes more than that. It includes one half of property owned jointly WROS by a husband and wife and all the property owned jointly WROS with others than a spouse.

The *state death tax value* is the value of your taxable estate as appraised by the state in which you reside. From this perspective, Nevada is the best state of the union in which to die. Nevada is the only state that does not have a death tax or an inheritance tax. (By the way: there is a fundamental difference between estate taxes, death taxes, and inheritance taxes. *Estate taxes* and *death taxes* are levied on the right to give or bequeath property, while *inheritance taxes* are levied on the right to receive property. When an estate tax is levied, it is a corpse that is paying the bill. When an inheritance tax is levied it is, in theory, the heir to the corpse who is paying the bill. But this all just rhetoric. The taxes, all the taxes, whatever they are called, all come out of the same piece of pie.)

After all the taxing is done and other costs of dying (debts, claims, etc.) are finished with, you wind up with the *net estate* for your heirs. This is the actual property your heirs wind up with. All of your estate planning should be targeted on making this number as large as possible.

ALL ABOUT INTESTATE

When people leave valid wills behind them, they control, from the grave, the destiny of not only their estate but also their children. Their property goes into the hands of those they designate and is put to any specific purpose they further designate. A will for example, can leave an estate to minor children and, in addition, can designate a guardian for those children and endow that guardian with powers to oversee the estate in the interest of the children until they come of age.

On the other hand, if someone dies intestate without a leaving a will behind, the situation is quite different. In this case, you have abdicated power over both your property and your children. State courts will appoint an administrator to see to your estate. That's right, a civil servant will control the destiny of your property and your children. This is something to be avoided at all costs.

People with property should always execute wills. And people with property and minor children should *really always* execute wills. And do yourself a favor. Don't try to execute it yourself. Don't use some software you can buy for $49.95. Don't pull some boilerplate out of a $6.95 paperback. Hire a ghostwriter with a law degree. Wills are too important to fool around with. You have to make sure your will is *watertight*—and watertight for the specific state in which you live. And that reminds me: If you execute a will in one state and then move to another, (i.e., if you feel like you are getting ready to die and decide to move to Nevada), have a lawyer in your new state look at your will and make sure it covers all the bases vis-à-vis the inheritance laws in your new environment.

USING A TRUST TO MINIMIZE ESTATE TAXES

A *trust* is a formal fiduciary agreement set up by you (variously called the trust *grantor, creator*, or *settlor*). With the trust, you give a person, corporation, or other such organization (designated as the *fiduciary administrator* of the trust) *legal title* to property placed in the trust by you, the *grantor*. And you give that fiduciary administrator *legally binding instructions* to mange the property in the trust for the benefit of whomever you designate as the *beneficiary* or *beneficiaries* of the trust.

Moneys deposited in trusts before your death will not be a part of your probate estate.

There are dozens of different kinds of trusts. For the purposes of minimizing individual estate taxes, the two for you to consider are living (or *inter vivos*, as the lawyers say) trusts and insurance trusts.

Living trusts are personal trusts created by individuals during their lifetime to benefit a beneficiary or group of beneficiaries. *Insurance trusts* are also living trusts, but the property in the trust (the *corpus* of the trust, as the principal of the trust is often called) consists in part or entirely of life insurance policies which turn to into cash upon the grantor's death.

Among living trusts, *revocable trusts* are the most appealing. With a revocable trust, you as grantor can revoke or revise the terms of the trust at will. (So, in a pinch, you can get the principal of the trust back into your pocket should that become necessary.) Less appealing is an *irrevocable trust*, which is (you guessed it!) irrevocable.

You also have two options when it comes to insurance trusts. These may be *funded* or *unfunded*. A funded trust contains life insurance along with other assets, the revenues on the latter being used to pay the premiums on the former. An unfunded trust, on the other hand, contains only life insurance, or is empty and simply named as beneficiary of life insurance. And the life insurance is funded from other sources (most likely by you, with nontrust money).

Minimizing Federal Estate Taxes with the Marital Deduction

Federal estate tax codes—and most state codes with regard to death taxes and inheritance—tend to treat a husband and wife as a single economic unit. On the federal front, there is an unlimited marital deduction for gifts and estate transfers. This enables the transfer of property between spouses during their lifetimes, and upon the death of one, with little or no tax impact.

Property qualifying for the deduction includes outright bequests, property held by spouses as joint tenants WROS, life insurance proceeds payable to a surviving husband or wife, and other funds of the deceased's gross estate.

Are Your Heirs Loaded?

No. I don't mean: *Are they drunk?* What I mean is: Are your kids doing just splendidly? Is Jay an eye-surgeon in Manhattan? And is Veronica a major shareholder in Microsoft? Then think about leaving them a *life interest* in your estate in trust, rather than bequeathing them your property outright. They and the grandkids will thank you for it, because with a life interest they'll all get to keep more of your (and their) money in the end.

Consider: Jay and Veronica already have large estates of their own. *Consider:* By piling even more piles of money onto the piles that Jay and Veronica already have, you'll just be increasing the tax-hit that all those moneys will take when Jay's and Veronica's estates pass to their heirs. Plus, your money gets hit with estate taxes twice. With a *life interest*, Jay and Veronica can enjoy all the benefits of your estate while not having its corpus thrown in with their gross estates. There is still some small exposure to the federal Generation-Skipping Transfer (GST) tax. But this is nowhere near as severe as the standard federal estate tax would be.

Like the Idea of Lifetime Gifts?

Another effective way to reduce the size of your estate for tax purposes is to make gifts to your heirs (or anyone else, perhaps your favorite author) before you die.

The gift tax annual exclusion in the tax code allows you to give up to $10,000 apiece, tax-free, to any number of individuals annually ($20,000 if the donor is married and the donor's spouse consents). Since the maximum total estate tax at the moment is 60%, you could, depending upon your situation, be saving your estate and family $6,000 with every $10,000 you give as a gift.

Where You Should Look Next

In addition to the Web sites presented in this chapter, there are several excellent books and videos that can help you get started with your estate planning. To start, you might turn to the Kiplinger book *12 Steps to a Worry-Free Retirement* or their video *Guide to Estate Planning*. For more information on Kiplinger products, check out their Web site at *http://www.kiplinger.com*.

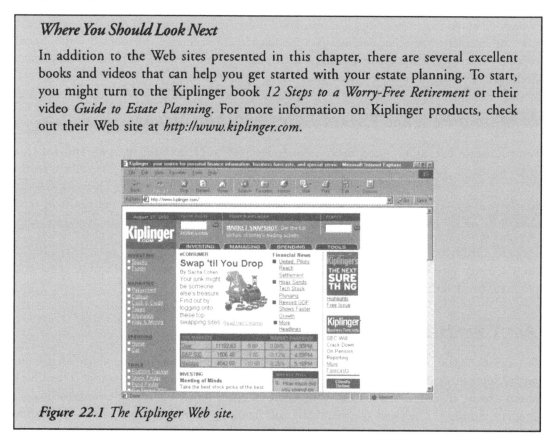

Figure 22.1 The Kiplinger Web site.

INTERNET RESOURCES RELATED TO ESTATE PLANNING

As you surf the World Wide Web, you may encounter sites that discuss estate issues such as taxes, trusts, gifts, and more. The following site list should help you locate the resources you need.

COMPLETE LIST OF U.S. ESTATE PLANNING, TRUST, AND PROBATE ATTORNEYS ON THE WEB

http://www.probateattorneylist.com

This list of all known estate planning and probate attorneys with Web sites is broken down by state and loaded with hyperlinks. There are hundreds of attorneys listed here. The list has been compiled by Mark Welch, himself an estate planning and probate attorney located in Pleasanton, California.

Figure 22.2 Complete List of U.S. Estate Planning, Trust, and Probate Attorneys on the Web

ESTATE PLANNING LINKS

http://www.estateplanninglinks.com

This site contains, hundreds of links related to estate planning: estate, gift, generation-skipping transfer and other taxes, elder law, probate and living trusts, and much more. This is *by far* the most extensive collection of estate planning links to be found *anywhere* on the Internet, even surpassing Mark Welch's impressive collection of links discussed above.

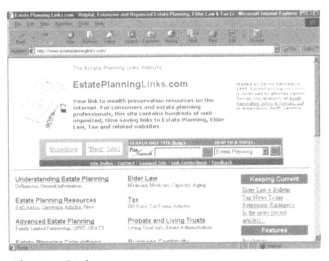

Figure 22.3 Estate Planning Links.

ESTATE PLANNING—SIX IMPORTANT PLANNING POINTS

http://www.lenabarnett.com

This site is provided and written by Lena S. Barnett, a recognized expert and leader in the field of estate planning. Read articles and FAQs to help you in your research.

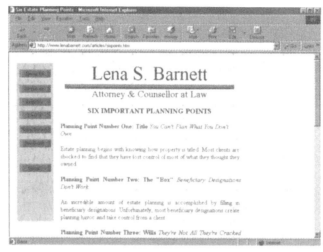

Figure 22.4 Estate Planning—Six Important Planning Points.

GUIDE TO ESTATE PLANNING

http://www.savewealth.com/planning/estate/index.html

This site provides the reasons you should plan your estate, introduction to wills, living trusts, power of attorney, estate taxes, family limited partnerships and funding your estate planning.

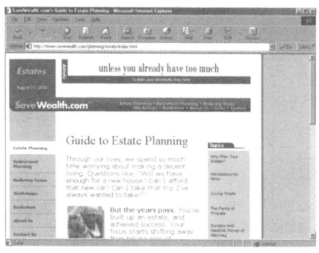

Figure 22.5 Guide to Estate Planning.

ESTATE PLANNING GLOSSARY

http://www.sunlife-usa.com/estate_glossary.html

This site gives a list of definitions to assist you through the estate planning process. You must have Acrobat Reader to view.

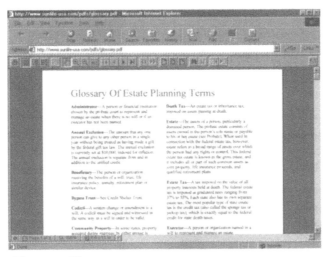

Figure 22.6 Estate Planning Glossary.

ESTATE PLANNING BRIEFS

http://www.nolo.com/estat.html

ESTATE PLANNING BASICS

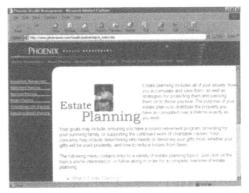

*http://www.phoenixwm.com/wealth/partnership/
e_index.htm*

GENERATION-SKIPPING TRANSFER TAX TUTORIAL

http://www.pmstax.com/estate/gst.html

WEB LAW OFFICE—ESTATE PLANNING FOR CALIFORNIANS

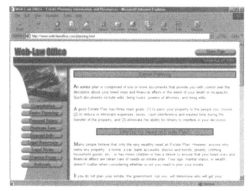

http://www.web-lawoffice.com/planning.html

GEOFORTUNE: THE WEALTH BUILDER SITE

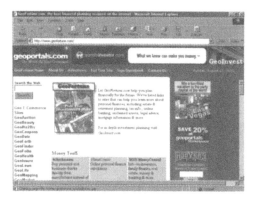

http://www.geofortune.com

QUESTION ABOUT ESTATE PLANNING?

http://www.seniorglobe.com/finances.htm

ULTIMATE SOURCE OF SELF-HELP LEGAL KITS

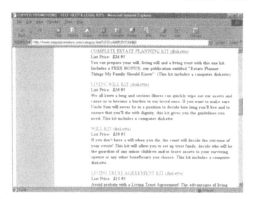

http://www.copperpromotions.com

ESTATE PLANNING ASSOCIATES

http://www.estatesafe.com

FINANCIAL & ESTATE PLANNING CENTER

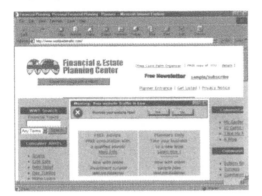

http://www.worldwidetraffic.com

NATIONAL NETWORK OF ESTATE PLANNING ATTORNEYS

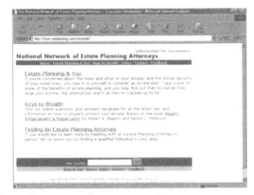

http://www.netplanning.com/consumer

NATIONAL ASSOCIATION OF FINANCIAL & ESTATE PLANNING

http://www.nafep.com

ESTATE PLANNING PAGES

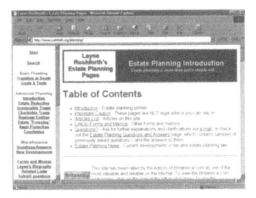

http://www.rushforth.org/planning

CRASH COURSE IN WILLS AND TRUSTS

http://www.mtpalermo.com

ESTATE PLANNING

http://www.estateplanning.com/coleman

Estate Planning Guide

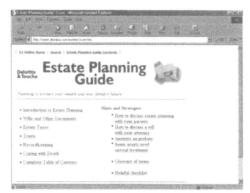

http://www.dtonline.com/estate/cover.htm

Estate Planning Software

http://4estateplanning.4anything.com

Estate Planning Services

http://www.estateplanningservices.com

Estate Planning from Smart Money

http://www.smartmoney.com/ac/estate

American Academy of Estate Planning Attorneys

http://www.aaepa.com

AAEPA Estate Planning Information Center

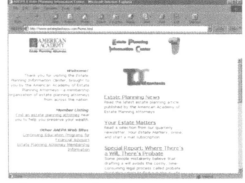

http://www.estateplanforyou.com

ESTATE PLAN ONLINE

http://www.estate-plan-on-line.com

ESTATE AND RETIREMENT PLANNING

http://www.trustsandestates.net

PLANNING YOUR ESTATE—
THE FEDERAL ESTATE TAX

http://ext.msstate.edu/pubs/pub1745.htm

ESTATE PLANNING LEGAL MATERIALS

http://www.ll.georgetown.edu/lr/rs/estate.html

ESTATE PLANNING & LIVING WILLS

http://www.illinoisbar.org/PublicInfo/estate.html

RETIREMENT AND ESTATE PLANNING

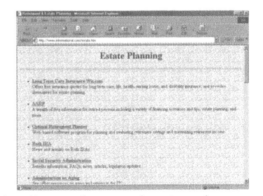

http://www.informational.com/estate.htm

ESTATE PLANNING RESEARCH GUIDE

http://www.law.ukans.edu/library/este_res.htm

INTRODUCTION TO ESTATE PLANNING

http://www.estateweb.com

ESTATE PLANNING

http://www.hannaian.com/finance/page6.htm

ESTATE PLANNING—LIVING AND TRUST PROBATE

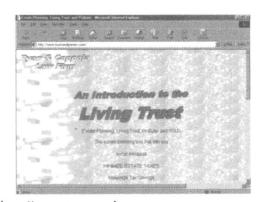

http://www.trustsandpowers.com

ESTATE PLANNING EXPLANATIONS

http://www.chicplan.com/explanations.htm

ESTATE PLANNING

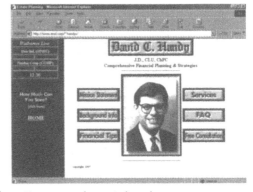

http://www.enol.com/~handys

ESTATE PLANNING SEMINARS

http://www.awtgroup.com/awtgroup/
seminars.htm

ESTATE PLANNING TIPS

http://www.jerryfg.com/tips.htm

ESTATE PLANNING BOOKS

http://www.hazbro.com/booklist.html

ESTATE PLANNING LAW

http://ceb.ucop.edu/catalog/ep.html

IS ESTATE PLANNING MORE THAN HAVING A WILL?

http://www.attypip.com/html/
estate_planning.html

INSTITUTE FOR ESTATE AND FINANCIAL PLANNING

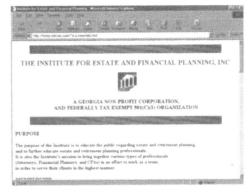

http://www.netcom.com/~m.a.rome/iefp.html

FARM ESTATE PLANNING

http://www.joefarmer.com/farm/0403.htm

27 TIPS TO ESTATE PLANNING

http://www.denmarkinfo.com/estplan.htm

ESTATE PLANNING IS FOR EVERYONE

http://www.wellslaw.com/estateplanning.html

ESTATE PLANNING FOR CHILDREN OF A PRIOR MARRIAGE

http://www.bizmonthly.com/news1999/january/focus/matricciani.html

ESTATE PLANNING AND THE TRUST CENTER

http://www.thetrustcenter.com

CHAPTER 23

EZBANKING @ YOURHOME.COM

Convenience, convenience. My time is precious as money. I would kill for convenience. — George Bernard Shaw

Picture yourself in a comfortable place. OK, now do your banking there.

You use your home PC to play games, write letters, and do your taxes. Now you can use it to do your banking as well. You'll save a lot of time writing checks and traveling to and from the bank. Best of all, you'll do your banking on your own schedule, from the place that's most comfortable for you—your home PC. This is banking you can do with just your socks on.

From the seat before your home PC, you can balance your checkbook, transfer funds, pay bills and do many other banking tasks, whenever it is most convenient for you, just with the click of a mouse.

THE BANK DOWN THE STREET ONLINE

Most banks offer home PC banking these days. If you have an account with a local branch of a bank such as Bank of America or Chase, you can sign up for their online banking. You can view your account information 24-hours a day, seven days a week. Most banks allow you to transfer funds, pay bills online, process service requests, such as reordering checks, requesting check or statement copies, keep track of payments, balances, and interest earned for accounts. You can usually view transactions that have cleared your checking, savings and credit card accounts. You can view these transactions going back two months and, in some cases, for longer than a year.

THE BANK EXCLUSIVELY ONLINE

Now you can go online and open an account without ever having to enter a bank. Web sites such as CompuBank.com offer 24-hour banking exclusively over the Internet or by phone. They offer the same services as your bank. You can set up direct deposit of your checks, bill payment, free ATM card, Visa Check Card, transfer funds from one account to another – all absolutely free! CompuBank, as well as other online banking institutions, is compatible with

Quicken software which helps you maintain complete monthly and annual records. You can reorder checks and take advantage of overdraft protection. Some online banks will even give you $20 just for opening an account, but make sure you check for a minimum balance.

CompuBank, shown below in Figure 23.1, is a member of the FDIC and was rated the #1 bank online by Smart Money. See more online banking institutions in the Internet resource section at the end of the chapter.

Figure 23.1 *CompuBank Online E-Banking Web site.*

WHAT YOU NEED

In most cases all you need now is a browser, namely Microsoft Internet Explorer or Netscape Navigator. How easy is that? Most banks support other software such as Microsoft Money for Windows 95, Microsoft Money 3.0, and Quicken so you can download your account information and maintain your monthly or annual records.

Client-based banking uses money management software and your own computer to access the bank using a modem and a phone line. It is the integration of banking and personal finance. The downfall is that switching banks may require new software and reentry of data. Internet-based is just that. As I said before, all you need is a browser. It's easy to use, portable, and often, cheaper.

COMPLETELY SECURE

All banks online use security measures which are extensive, rigorous, but yet easy to navigate. Most employ strict privacy policies and operate in what is called, a "secure environment." Security measures most likely include limited display of account numbers, access ID and personal passwords, automatic log off if no action is taken after a limited amount of time (15 minutes), and constant monitoring. Authentication insures you are communicating with the correct server and that no other computer is impersonating your bank. Everyone uses encryption, which scrambles transferred data, and data integrity, which verifies that the information you sent was not altered during transfer.

SOMETHING NEW? BILL REPAYMENT

The next step in online banking may change the way consumers can pay their bills. It's called *bill repayment*. The computer prints the bill right on the screen, and customers are alerted that the bill has been issued via email. You can view the bill, manipulate the data for budget purposes, and authorize the bank to send payment. Critics want such options as partial payments and question security and privacy issues. The MSDFC now guarantees that neither banks nor billers can use consumer data for any purpose, and audit trails reassure some consumers. What if your computer breaks down and you can't access your billing statements? If your email is not retrieved after a specified number of days, the biller will send you a paper copy in the mail.

INTERNET RESOURCES RELATED TO ONLINE BANKING

As you surf the Web, you may find sites about online banking. The following site list should help you locate the resources you need.

MYBANK.COM

http://www.mybank.com

This site provides a comprehensive list of banks you will find by state on the World Wide Web. Check out the directories in other countries, as well.

Figure 23.2 MyBank.com Web site.

LEARN MORE ABOUT HOME BANKING

http://www.coastalbancvalley.com/internetbanking/LearnMore.htm

This site answers questions to FAQs about home banking.

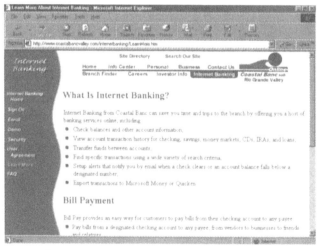

Figure 23.3 Learn More About Home Banking.

ONLINE BANKING: THE BASICS

http://www.bankrate.com/brm/olbstep2.asp

This site explains online banking, the advantages and disadvantages, the varying levels of service, the dial-in and Internet methods of connection, and fees. You can also find out about paying bills online.

Figure 23.4 Online Banking: The Basics.

BANKS ON THE WEB

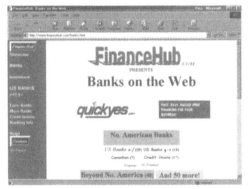

http://www.FinanceHub.com/banks.html

WORLDWIDE GUIDE – BANKING ON THE WEB

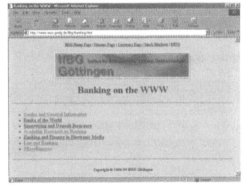

http://www.wiso.gwdg.de/ifbg/banking.html

WANT TO LEARN MORE ABOUT E-BANKING?

http://www.vendors-rep.com

THE COMMUNITY BANKER

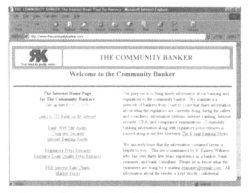

http://www.thecommunitybanker.com

HOME BANKING RESOURCES

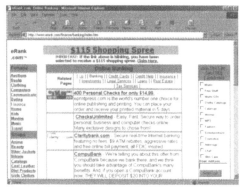

*http://www.eRank.com/finance/banking/
index.htm*

HOME BANK FAQs FROM MONEY ONE

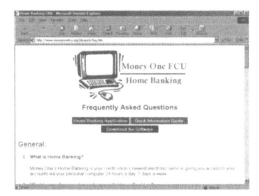

http://www.moneyonefcu.org/pbranch/faq.htm

HOME BANKING RATES

http://www.cheapestrate.com/banking.html

LOW COST HOME BANKING INFORMATION

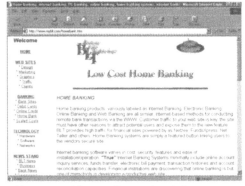

http://www.myblt.com/hoomebank.htm

INTERNET BANKER SCORECARD

http://www.gomez.com/channels/
index.cfm?topcat_id=1

LINKS TO FREE ONLINE BANKING

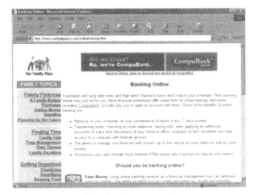

http://www.ourfamilyplace.com/
onlinebanking.html

PRESIDENTIAL ONLINE BANK

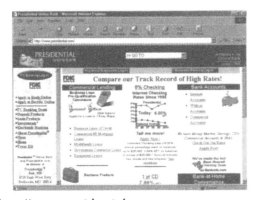

http://www.presidential.com

NETBANK

http://www.netbank.com

METRO BANK ONLINE

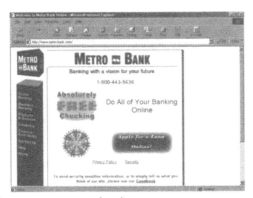

http://www.metro-bank.com

AMERICAN BANK ONLINE

http://www.pcbanker.com

CLARITY BANK

http://www.claritybank.com

ONLINE BANKING REPORT NEWSLETTER

http://www.onlinebankingreport.com

AMERICAN SAVINGS BANK/HAWAII

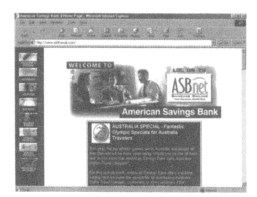

http://www.asbhawaii.com

EVERBANK

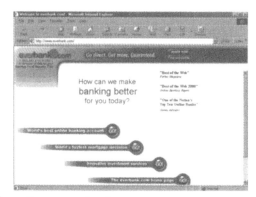

http://www.everbank.com

AMARILLO NATIONAL BANK/TEXAS

http://www.anb.com

BANK ONE/NATIONWIDE

http://www.bankone.com

BANK OF AMERICA/NATIONWIDE

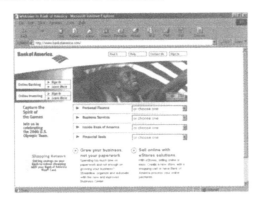

http://www.bankamerica.com

BANK OF ELK RIVER/MINNESOTA

http://www.the-bank-er.com

BANK OF GALVESTON/TEXAS

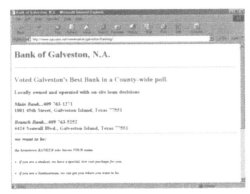

*http://www.intergate.com/wwwmarket/
galveston/banking*

BANK OF PETALUMA/CALIFORNIA

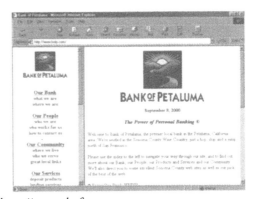

http://www.bofp.com

BANK UNITED/TEXAS

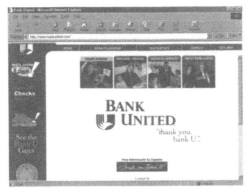

http://www.bankunited.com

BLACK RIVER COUNTRY BANK

http://members.aol.com/BRCBank/index.html

BUSEY BANK/CENTRAL-WESTERN REGION

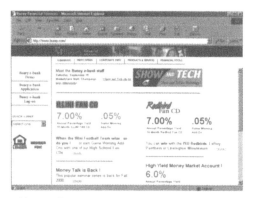

http://www.busey.com

CARLSBAD NATIONAL BANK/NEW MEXICO

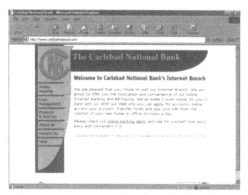

http://www.caverns.com/~cnb/index.html

CENTRAL NATIONAL BANK/TEXAS (WACO!)

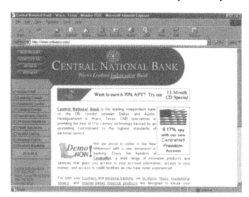

http://www.cnbwaco.com

CALIFORNIA FEDERAL BANK/CALIFORNIA

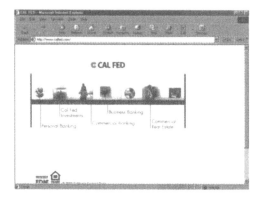

http://www.calfed.com

CENTRAL BANK/BOSTON

http://www.centralbk.com

CENTRAL PACIFIC BANK/CALIFORNIA

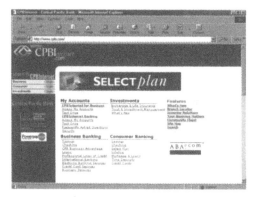

http://www.cpbi.com

CENTURA BANKS/NORTH CAROLINA

http://www.centura.com

CITICORP-CITIBANK/NEW YORK

http://www.citicorp.com

COMPASS BANK/ALABAMA, TEXAS, FLORIDA

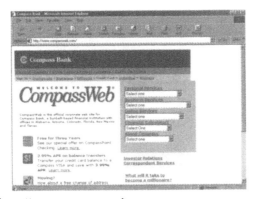

http://www.compassweb.com

CHASE MANHATTAN/NEW YORK

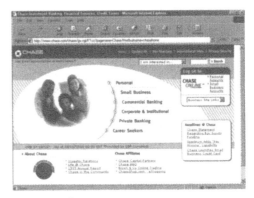

http://www.chase.com

COLORADO CREDIT UNION/ COLORADO AND WYOMING

http://www.colocu.com

COUNTRY CLUB BANK OF KANSAS CITY, MISSOURI

http://www.countryclubbank.com

CREDIT UNION LAND/NATIONWIDE

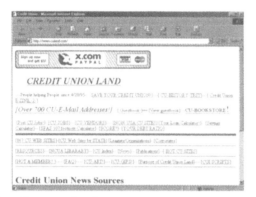

http://www.culand.com

D&N BANK/MICHIGAN

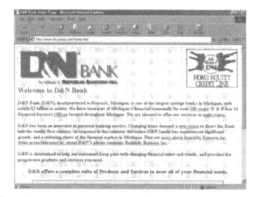

http://www.dn.portup.com/home.html

FEDERAL RESERVE BANK OF MINNEAPOLIS

http://woodrow.mpls.frb.fed.us

ENTERPRISE NATIONAL BANK/FLORIDA

http://www.enterprisebank.com

GREAT WESTERN BANK

http://www.greatwesternbank.com

FEDERAL RESERVE BANK OF ST. LOUIS

http://www.stls.frb.org

First Citizens Bank/Virginia, North Carolina

http://www.firstcitizens.com

First Federal/New York State

http://www.firstfederal.com

National City

http://www.foa.com

First Union Corporation/Nationwide

http://www.firstunion.com

Georgia State Bank

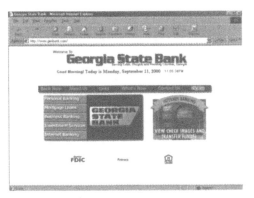

http://www.geobank.com

Grand Bank

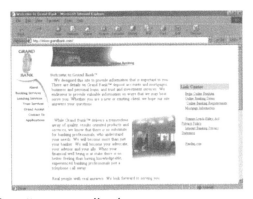

http://www.grandbank.com

HIBERNIA NATIONAL BANK

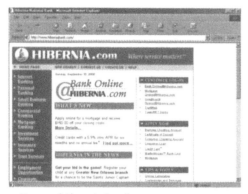

http://www.hiberniabank.com

OLD KENT BANK

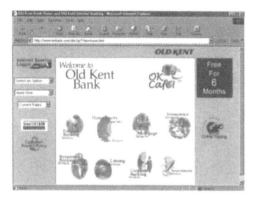

http://www.bny.com/~mnb

OXFORD BANK/MISSISSIPPI
(WILLIAM FAULKNER'S BANK)

http://www.oxbc.com

LA JOLLA BANK/CALIFORNIA

http://www.ljbank.com

NANTUCKET BANK/MASSACHUSETTS

http://www.nantucket.net/banks/nantucket

PATELCO CREDIT UNION/SAN FRANCISCO

http://www.patelco.org

PEOPLE'S BANK/CONNECTICUT

http://www.peoples.com

PEOPLES BANK/TAOS, NEW MEXICO

http://www.taosnet.com/peoples

REPUBLIC BANK & TRUST COMPANY/KENTUCKY

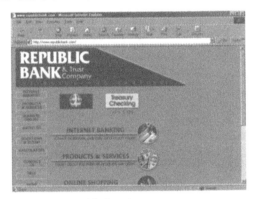

http://www.republicbank.com

DIRECT BANKING

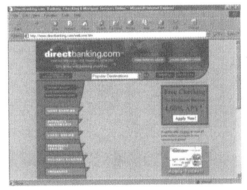

http://www.directbanking.com/welcome.htm

SAVINGS BANK OF ROCKVILLE, MARYLAND

http://www.sbr.com

SECURITY FIRST NETWORK BANK/NATIONWIDE

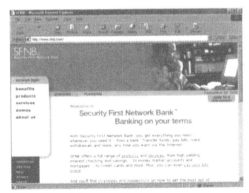

http://www.sfnb.com

TREASURY BANK/WASHINGTON, D.C.

http://www.treasurybank.com

U.S. TRUST OF BOSTON

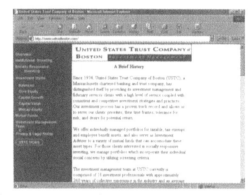

http://www.ustrustboston.com

WELLS FARGO BANK/NATIONWIDE

http://www.wellsfargo.com

UMB BANK/MIDWESTERN UNITED STATES

http://www.umb.com

WEBBANK/NATIONWIDE

http://www.banking.com

WEST SUBURBAN BANK/ILLINOIS

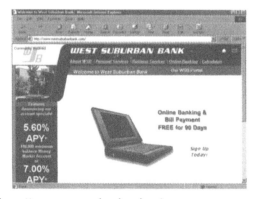

http://www.westsuburbanbank.com

WINONA NATIONAL AND SAVINGS BANK/MINNESOTA

http://wnsb.com

INDEX